FELIX A. SOMMERFELD AND THE MEXICAN FRONT IN THE GREAT WAR

by

HERIBERT VON FEILITZSCH

First published in the United States of America in 2014 by Henselstone Verlag LLC

First Edition

Every effort has been made to locate and contact all
holders of copyright to material reproduced in this book.
For information about permission to reproduce selections from this book,
write to Heribert von Feilitzsch, P.O. Box 201, Amissville, VA 20106.

Library of Congress Control Number 2014912024

Keyword Data

von Feilitzsch, Heribert, 1965-

Felix A. Sommerfeld and the Mexican Front in the Great War / Heribert von Feilitzsch.
p. cm
Includes biographical references and index.

ISBN 978-0-9850317-4-9

1. United States – History – World War I – 1914 to 1917
2. Germany – History – World War I – 1914 to 1917
3. Mexico – History – Revolution, 1910-1920 – Diplomatic History
4. United States – Foreign Relations – Mexico
5. United States – Foreign Relations - Germany
6. Mexico – Foreign Relations – United States
7. Mexico – Foreign Relations - Germany
8. Germany – Foreign Relations – Mexico
9. Germany – Foreign Relations – United States
I.   von Feilitzsch, Heribert. Title.

www.felixsommerfeld.com

Printed in the United States of America

"'Sic transit gloria mundi [Thus passes the glory of the world].' I am very sorry for General Villa. I am convinced that he in his own way wanted to do right. He did not know how [to] do it. But nobody can take away from him the glory which is his and in spite of all vehement accusations against him at this moment, the history of Mexico must and will do him justice and give him his place as one of the ablest soldiers of Mexico."

Felix A. Sommerfeld to General Hugh Lenox Scott on December 23rd 1915, commenting on the defeat of Pancho Villa.[1]

Praise for
Felix A. Sommerfeld
and The Mexican Front in the Great War...

Outstanding. Loved your manuscript. You have a winner. Congratulations!

Louis R. Sadler
Professor Emeritus, New Mexico State University

Thank you so much for sending me "The Mexican Front in the Great War." I found it so fascinating and instructive that I read it twice. You have done a masterful job not only of analyzing Sommerfeld's pivotal role but also of describing the role of lesser fi gures such as Meloy and Krumm-Heller. And all this based on an impressive array of archival sources. Congratulations!

Charles H. Harris III
Professor Emeritus, New Mexico State University

Once again, von Feilitzsch mines mountains of archival documentation, bringing the story of German intrigue in revolutionary Mexico into the sharpest focus yet. After President Madero's death in 1913 and the outbreak of World War I in 1914, provoking conflict on the US-Mexico border became a vital part of Germany's strategy to keep U.S. arms and troops from aiding the Allies. The names of German spies Felix Sommerfeld and Dr. Arnoldo Krumm-Heller, among others, emerge from their shadowy pasts in footnotes and mere asides, as men at once brilliant, dangerous, and far more influential than previously imagined.

C.M. Mayo
Author of *Metaphysical Odyssey into the Mexican Revolution*

For Matthias

TABLE OF CONTENTS

LIST OF PHOTOS AND ILLUSTRATIONS

ACKNOWLEDGMENTS

THERE ARE MANY PEOPLE WHO supported me on this endeavor, certainly my beautiful and understanding family who had to suffer through periods of absolute preoccupation with "my spies." Much gratitude belongs to the late professor Michael C. Meyer of my Alma Mater, the University of Arizona, who set me on the course of this research. Reinhard R. Doerries, the preeminent scholar on the topic of German secret agents and Ambassador Johann Heinrich Count von Bernstorff, gave me his time and kind feedback. Justus D. Doenecke read my early manuscript and gave me lots of valuable suggestions. Thank you! Charles H. Harris III and Louis R. Sadler, two scholars whose work I admire beyond any other historical scholarship, have helped me through my first book and have remained good friends and great supporters of mine. Without their encouragement and example of how to write "good history" I might have given up long ago.

I thank my friends Marc Cugnon and Alaina Love, whose The Passion ProfilerTM instrument opened my mind to a thorough understanding how personalities unveil themselves. Their momentous work made me understand the motivations, interactions with other players, strengths and weaknesses of the characters in this story. My friend and artist, Otto Conner, tirelessly listened to my theories about what really happened. In a conversation with him, I realized how Sommerfeld pulled off the Columbus attack. Rosa King, a novelist, Spanish teacher, and fabulous editor made this manuscript digestible. Thank you so much! Writer, historian, translator and intellectual powerhouse, C. M. Mayo, has been an incredible inspiration not only for writing skills, research, and intellectual curiosity. She also is a great example for how to thrive in today's publishing world.

I will never be able to repay the dedicated educators and intellectuals who sharpened my skills as a historian and businessman throughout college, graduate school, and beyond. Without the brilliant minds of George Brubaker, University of Arizona, John Rossi, Pennsylvania State at Erie, Leonard Dinnerstein, University of Arizona, and Melvin Leffler, University of Virginia, my research would have ended in the many dead ends that I maneuvered out of in the years of writing this book. Equally as important as my training in history was the MBA program I attended at Wake Forest University in Winston-Salem, North Carolina. Special thanks to Professors Bern Beatty and Jack Meredith who worked hard on sharpening my strategic thinking and thorough understanding of the inner workings of corporations. These skills allowed me to trace the various money trails so crucial in understanding the historical events described in this book.

There is a group of people who work tirelessly in the halls of our libraries and archives. Their knowledge of the nooks and crannies of tons of files in the National Archives, Library of Congress, Deutsches Bundesarchiv, and Archivos Municipales Chihuahua provide the keys to successful research. I can never repay the selfless kindness they have shown over the years. I would like to especially mention Michael Hieronymus, curator of special collections at the Benson Library of Latin American Studies in the University of Texas at Austin. His kindness, incredible knowledge, and experience with all kinds of crazy historians who peruse through the materials are unsurpassed. I also want to thank David Kessler of the Bancroft Library at the University of California at Berkeley. The Bancroft Library acquired the papers of Silvestre Terrazas in the 1960s. This collection and many more, such as the Holmdahl Papers and German Diplomatic Papers, contribute to the valuable documentation of the Mexican Revolution. Thank you! In the National Archives in Washington, D.C., I met several of the most dedicated, motivated, and knowledgeable archivists in the world. I owe immeasurable gratitude to Richard Peuser and his staff. They assisted me not only in finding documents I asked about but also with recommending archival materials I was not aware existed. These dedicated archivists have such admirable command over so many collections that they truly have the power to bring history to light. Thank you! In the Bundesarchiv für Militärgeschichte in Freiburg, Achim Koch, Andrea Meier, and Jan Warssischek assisted me with great knowledge and dedication. I am eternally grateful for their courtesy towards an unknown researcher who barged in all the way from overseas with little time and an insatiable appetite for obscure files.

I have been able to find the great grandchildren of Frederico Stallforth online. Believe it or not, video of Frederico Stallforth is available on You Tube, lighting a cigarette, courtesy of Mary Prevo of Hampton Sydney University to whom I owe special gratitude. She allowed a total stranger to spend weeks on end in her upstairs study and sort through her great grandfather's personal papers. We bounced ideas and impressions back and forth. I shared my drafts and opinions on Frederico Stallforth with her. There are many others whose patience, intellect, and support have accompanied my journey. Please forgive me for not mentioning you by name. Thank you.

CAST OF CHARACTERS

Albert, Heinrich Friedrich
German lawyer and Commercial agent for the German government in New York during World War I. German Commercial Attaché 1915 to 1917. Head of the Secret War Council, the German clandestine organization in New York in charge of propaganda, economic war, sabotage, and finance during World War I. German Treasury Secretary and Secretary of reconstruction 1923.

Ángeles, Felipe
Mexican general and revolutionary. Commanded the Military College at Chapultepec under President Madero. Opposed the putschists against Madero in 1913. Joined Carranza in 1913 and became his Secretary of War. Switched sides in 1914 and became Pancho Villa's most important military strategist. Left Mexico in 1915 and was executed when he returned in 1919.

Bernstorff, Count Johann Heinrich
German ambassador to the United States from 1908 to 1917 and to Turkey from 1917 to 1918. After World War I, co-founder of the Democratic Party in Germany (Deutsche Demokratische Partei). Member of the Reichstag 1921 to 1928. Went into exile during Nazi regime.

Bielaski, Alexander Bruce
American lawyer and Chief of the Bureau of Investigations, 1912 to 1919.

Boy-Ed, Karl   German Naval Attaché in New York from 1913 to 1915. Then head of the *Nachrichtenabteilung* N in Berlin 1915 to 1918 (Naval Intelligence).

Bryan, William Jennings   American lawyer and Democratic politician. Ran as a candidate for the U.S. presidency three times. Served as Secretary of State under Wilson between 1913 and 1915. Resigned in 1915 and pursued law practice.

Carranza, Venustiano   Mexican politician from Coahuila. Led the Mexican opposition against Victoriano Huerta. Mexican President from 1915 to 1917.

Cobb, Zach Lamar   Democratic politician and U.S. customs collector in Texas. Also served the intelligence organization of the State Department. Arranged for the arrest of Victoriano Huerta in 1915. Warned his superiors of the approaching Villistas before the raid on Columbus, New Mexico in March 1916.

De La Garza, Lázaro   Mexican businessman, financial agent, and treasurer for Pancho Villa. Organized Villa's supplies from the United States 1914 to 1915. Was accused of stealing by Villa. Lived in exile in Los Angeles until his death.

Dernburg, Bernhard   Imperial Secretary of Colonial Affairs 1907 to 1910. Head of German propaganda in the United States 1914 to 1915. German Finance Minister and Vice Chancellor in 1919. Member of the German parliament 1920 to 1930.

Díaz, Félix   Mexican politician and soldier. Nephew of Porfirio Diaz. Conspirator in the overthrow of Francisco Madero. Aligned with Victoriano Huerta in quest to take power in Mexico in 1915.

Eckardt, Heinrich von   German Minister to Mexico 1914 to 1918. Recipient of the infamous "Zimmermann Telegram" in 1917. In charge of various clandestine mission for German intelligence agencies.

Enrile, Gonzalo   Mexican officer and politician. Supported the Felix Diaz faction. Traveled to Germany to propose an alliance between Mexican opposition factions with Germany.

Garrison, Lindley Miller   Lawyer and Democratic politician. Served as Secretary of War under Woodrow Wilson between 1913 and 1916.

Heynen, Carl   German shipping agent and businessman in Tampico and Veracruz. Headed the HAPAG offices in Mexico before World War I. As a naval intelligence agent he became Heinrich Albert's treasurer in new York between 1915 and 1917. Managed the German owned Bridgeport Projectile Company. Was detained from 1917 to 1919 and returned to Mexico after the war.

Hintze, Paul von   German Admiral. Switched from military to diplomatic career in 1910. German Minister to Mexico from 1911 to 1914. Head of German naval intelligence in China 1914 to 1915. Became German Foreign Minister in 1918.

Holtzendorff, Henning von   German admiral and commander of the German High Seas Fleet 1909 to 1913. Chief of the Imperial Navy from 1915 to 1918. Strong proponent of unrestricted submarine warfare. He received Sommerfeld's proposal to create a war between Mexico and the United States.

Hopkins, Sherburne G.	American lawyer and lobbyist in Washington D.C. Involved in various uprisings and revolutions in Central American and Mexico. Important link between U.S. financial interests, the American and Mexican governments, as well as Mexican exiles and revolutionaries. Worked closely with Felix A. Sommerfeld during 1910 and 1922.
Huerta, Victoriano	Mexican general and usurper of the presidency in 1913. Held responsible for the murder of Francisco Madero. Went into exile in 1914. Attempted a return to power in 1915 but was arrested in Texas.
Krumm-Heller, Arnold	German doctor and occultist. Became Francisco Madero's personal physician and spritual adviser in 1911. Worked for Felix Sommerfeld in the Mexican secret service 1912 to 1913. Joined Carranza faction while serving the German naval intelligence. Became Obregon's chief of artillery. Supported the implementation of the *Plan de San Diego* in 1915 and 1916. Went to Germany in 1916 and served as Mexican military attaché in Berlin until the end of World War I.
López, Pablo	Revolutionary commander under Pancho Villa. Led the troops that massacred American miners at Santa Ysabel and commanded the attack on Columbus, New Mexico in 1916. Was executed in 1917.
Maytorena, José Maria	Mexican politician from Sonora. Governor of Sonora during the Mexican Revolution from 1911 to 1915. Aligned with Pancho Villa 1914 to 1915. Fought Carrancista army during battle of Naco in 1914.

Meloy, Andrew D.   American businessman with financial interest in Mexican railways. Conspired with Franz Rintelen, Felix Sommerfeld and others to end Mexican Revolution. Arrested with Rintelen in England in 1915 but released.

Mondragón, Manuel   Mexican general. Secretary of War under Mexican Dictator Porfirio Diaz. Part of the putsch against Francisco Madero. Aligned with Victoriano Huerta in his quest to regain control of Mexico in 1915.

Obregon, Alvaro   Mexican general and politician from Sonara. Defeated Pancho Villa in 1915. President of Mexico 1920 to 1924.

Olin, Franklin W.   President of the Equitable Powder Company and the Western Cartridge Company in Alton, Illinois. Supplied majority of munitions to Pancho Villa. Received German aid to build factory. Expanded after World War I and purchased Winchester Arms in 1931.

Orozco, Pascual   Mexican businessman and revolutionary chieftain. Led uprising against Francisco Madero in 1912. Joined Victoriano Huerta in 1915. Killed while fleeing from U.S. authorities in 1915.

Papen, Franz von   German Military Attaché in New York from 1914 to 1915. After World War I German politician and member of the Prussian parliament. German Chancellor in 1932.

Pershing, John J. "Blackjack"   American general. Commander of the Punitive Expedition 1916 to 1917. Then commander of the U.S. expeditionary forces in Europe during World War I.

Rintelen, Franz   German naval intelligence agent. Came to the United States in 1915 to incite labor unrest and oversee sabotage operations. Was discovered and arrested in England in the summer of 1915. Convicted and sentenced to penitentiary in 1917, he spent the rest of the war in prison. Wrote two books about his time in the United States. Settled in England in the late 1920s.

Scott, Hugh Lenox   American general. Commander of Fort Bliss, then Army Chief of Staff under Woodrow Wilson 1914 to 1917. Considered a friend by both Felix Sommerfeld and Pancho Villa.

Sommerfeld, Felix A.   German naval intelligence agent under the command first of Minister Paul von Hintze then German Naval Attaché in New York, Karl Boy-Ed. Chief of Staff for President Madero, chief of the Mexican secret service, 1912 to 1913. Chief weapons and munitions buyer for Pancho Villa 1914 to 1915. Villa's diplomatic envoy to the U.S. 1914 to 1915.

Stallforth, Frederico   Mexican-German businessman from Hidalgo del Parral, Mexico. Became a German secret agent in 1913. Worked closely with Felix Sommerfeld, Franz Rintelen, Heinrich Albert, and Andrew Meloy. Had financial responsibilities in the German sabotage campaign in the U.S. between 1915 and 1917. Arrested several times during the World War. After 1919 he became prominent financier in the United States and Germany. Joined the OSS in 1942.

Tauscher, Hans   German agent and representative of Krupp Arms and several other German arms manufacturers in the United States. Married to the famous soprano Madame Johanna Gadski. Worked for Franz von Papen during World War I.

Villa, Francisco "Pancho" Mexican general and revolutionary chieftain. Raised the largest army of the Mexican Revolution. Attacked the United States in 1916. Assassinated in 1923.

Wilhelm II of Prussia German Emperor 1888 to 1918. Presided over the outbreak of World War I. Resigned in 1918 and went into exile to Holland.

Wilson, Thomas Woodrow Democratic politician, educator, and intellectual. President of Princeton University. Governor of New Jersey, 1910 to 1913. U.S. President 1913 to 1921.

PROLOGUE

I N THE EVENING OF JUNE 24th 1918, America's top cop, A. Bruce Bielaski, chief of the Bureau of Investigations, sat back in his chair and pondered the end of a massive investigation. Three days earlier, his agents had arrested Felix A. Sommerfeld. Bielaski himself did not attend the days of intensive debriefing at the Federal Building in downtown Manhattan, mainly because he did not want to insert his personal acquaintance and long standing cooperation with the suspected German agent into the transcripts. B.I. Special Agent Fred H. Haggerson, Captain Roger B. Hull of the U.S. Naval Intelligence Division, and R. W. Sprague, Special Assistant to the Attorney General conducted the questioning. Sommerfeld was the last of a cell of German agents based in New York to be arrested. This group of agents, loosely organized around the German Commercial Attaché Heinrich F. Albert, worked behind the scenes and briefly led a German secret service effort that resulted in unprecedented acts of sabotage and labor unrest in the United States.

The German secret agent Carl Heynen coined the term Secret War Council in 1915 for this first foreign terror cell known to have operated in the United States. The leading members of the Secret War Council included the German officials in New York, Franz von Papen (military attaché), Karl Boy-Ed (naval attaché), Bernhard Dernburg (propaganda chief), Karl Alexander Fuehr (propaganda), and Heinrich Albert as chief (commercial agent and financial controller). Agents such as Franz Rintelen, Felix Sommerfeld, Frederico Stallforth, Walter Scheele, and Franz Wachendorf reported to these clandestine leaders in New York and received funding from them. German spies brought the United States to the brink of war with Mexico on several occasions and had infiltrated the highest levels of the Wilson administration, Wall Street, and industry.

Although hot on the heels of many of the conspirators since the fall of 1914, the German spies proved hard to prosecute. Until the passing of the Espionage Act on June 15th 1917, American law enforcement had few legal tools to stop various foreign agencies from operating on American soil. Laws existed to prosecute criminal acts such as destruction of property, murder, and assault, which covered some acts of sabotage German agents had committed between 1914 and 1916. Along the Mexican border, agents of the Justice Department prosecuted arms smugglers, recruiters, propagandists, revolutionaries, and filibusters of all shades and backgrounds using the Neutrality Act of 1794. However, none of these legal frameworks netted the masterminds of the German espionage ring in the United States.

Bureau of Investigations Chief Bielaski's federal agents, with the help of local law enforcement, other agents of the Justice, War, Interior, Treasury, and State Departments, even Mexican, British, Czech, and various other foreign agents, filed over one hundred thousand pages of reports detailing the activities of presumed German spies and agitators between 1914 and 1918.

Heinrich Albert, the German commercial agent and spymaster of the Secret War Council, found himself in a compromising situation at 3:30 pm on July 24th 1915, when American Secret Service Agent Frank Burke snatched the German's briefcase. Most of the contents, papers detailing German secret operations in the U.S., appeared a few days later in the New York World. Public outrage mixed with ridicule over the unbelievable carelessness of the German spymaster. Following the lost briefcase episode, German agent Franz Rintelen, who had organized labor unrest, fire bombings of ships, and sabotage of American munitions factories, sailed into a trap set for him in England. There, Franz Wachendorf, alias Horst von der Goltz, another German agent, was already cooling his heels in solitary confinement. Also that same year, American authorities detained and charged notorious agents Werner Horn and Robert Fay for their sabotage acts. Dr. Walter Scheele, a chemist and bomb maker for the German cell in New York, fled to Cuba in 1915, but left his co-conspirators and lots of evidence behind.

As a result of the multiple arrests and trials, the German Military Attaché in the United States Franz von Papen and his colleague, Naval Attaché Karl Boy-Ed, received their passports and had to return to Germany in December of 1915. Wachendorf, Fay, and the group around Dr. Scheele had implicated von Papen as the mastermind behind their missions. The American government had also found out that von Papen's colleague, Naval Attaché Karl Boy-Ed, had financed the Rintelen mission in the spring and summer of 1915.

Given these arrests in 1915 and the expulsion of the two attachés, the Bureau of Investigations felt that it had succeeded in breaking the back of German secret activities. American newspapers celebrated the "stupidity" of German agents. First-page spreads appeared in all major newspapers in 1915 on the ignorance and arrogance of the likes of Franz von Papen who wrote to his wife in a letter captured by British authorities about these "idiotic Yankees." The American public fretted over stories of failed bombings that led to the arrests of Horn, Wachendorf, and Fay, and the most ridiculous of all, Albert's briefcase. To this day, historians contend that German agents acted "clumsily," had little or no training in clandestine operations, and, as a result, were quickly rounded up and tried.[2] However, Bielaski's men and other U.S. intelligence agencies had to realize by the spring and summer of 1916 that the German agents were alive and well. Not only did the sabotage campaign in the United States continue unabatedly, but the Mexican-American border suddenly blew up in March of 1916.

Since the days of Porfirio Díaz, the German government had maintained well-placed clandestine assets high up in the Mexican ruling elites and in the revolutionary leadership. On March 9th 1916, Francisco "Pancho" Villa attacked the American town of Columbus, New Mexico. Federal agents could not prove it, but also suspected German involvement in the incident. This book outlines the chain of events by which one of the most intricate and brilliant German clandestine operations forced the hand of the American government to intervene in Mexico. While all but one division of the U.S. army busied itself with securing the Mexican border and pursuing Pancho Villa in the summer and fall of 1916, the masterminds of German intrigue freely plotted their next moves.

The German war strategy towards North America had two goals: Weakening the British blockade through unrestricted submarine warfare and disrupting the Entente supply lines in the United States. German agents pursued this latter goal through sabotage, incitement of labor strikes, propaganda, and through cornering the markets of critical supplies. German war planners took into consideration that these acts of war against the United States could precipitate her entry into the war on the side of the Allies. German strategy, therefore, sought to blunt the impact of a likely U.S. declaration of war by fomenting troubles along the Mexican-American border. While tying up the then badly equipped American army on the American continent, the U.S. government could be forced to consume weapons and ammunition that otherwise would be sold to the Entente. Especially due to the on-going revolutions in Mexico, the southern border was wide open for intrigue. German money not only supported the conservative forces of the deposed elite under President Díaz, but anyone else with the potential to create problems for the U.S.

The Bureau of Investigations, Treasury's Secret Service, Army and Navy Intelligence, and the State Department's Intelligence Service all clearly identified the top leadership cadre of the German Intelligence organization in 1914 and early 1915. Correctly, they traced command and control to the two German attachés, von Papen and Boy-Ed, as well as commercial agent Albert. Bielaski and his colleagues also correctly identified the more blatant violators of U.S. law, such as Rintelen, Wachendorf, Horn, Scheele, and Fay. What they missed were the second-tier leaders the German attachés had cultivated under the eyes of their U.S. intelligence shadows. This group of men actually executed the largest foreign intrigue ever mounted on American soil. While American media celebrated American counter-espionage achievements in the fall of 1915 and ridiculed the "clumsy" German agents, a few men skillfully executed the German war strategy against the U.S.

By the summer of 1916, these agents had succeeded in opening a strategic window in which the U.S. had briefly lost the power to intervene in the European war. This window of opportunity for Germany to resume unrestricted submarine warfare and possibly bring England to her knees closed as a result of power struggles within the German government. The chance of bringing to bear the full weight of German weaponry on the Entente powers had disappeared by the spring of 1917, when the German government finally did declare unrestricted submarine warfare. As expected, the United States declared war on the Central Powers. The U.S. military had created a semblance of order along the Mexican border in the spring of 1917, and was ready for a decisive intervention in Europe. The rift between the German foreign office and the military leadership, as well as the indecision of the German Emperor Wilhelm II and his chancellor von Bethmann-Hollweg, not the "clumsiness" of German agents, caused the failure of Germany's U.S. war strategy.

One of the most elusive of these German agents who executed the German strategy in the U.S. and Mexico was Felix A. Sommerfeld. Bielaski personally knew him since around 1911. However, even after extensive investigation and interrogations, the B.I. Chief never quite realized how much influence his prisoner wielded in the German war strategy. Felix Sommerfeld, a German-Jewish naval intelligence agent who worked for the German government in Mexico before the war, was an expert on all things revolutionary. A German army veteran of the Boxer Rebellion and a reservist, he had served as the head of Mexico's secret service under President Madero from 1911 to 1913. His exploits in that time are legendary. With the help of American lawyer and lobbyist Sherburne G. Hopkins, Sommerfeld created the largest foreign secret service organization on American soil in U.S. history.

He procured most of the arms and ammunitions first for Venustiano Carranza and then for Pancho Villa between 1913 and 1916. Sommerfeld became Villa's unofficial diplomatic envoy in the United States. Under orders from the German admiralty he manipulated Pancho Villa into attacking the United States at Columbus, New Mexico, in March of 1916. Living lavishly at the Hotel Astor in New York from 1914 to 1918 he was well known both to the general public and American officials who liked him and sought his help. Sommerfeld had contacts high into the American government. President Wilson's Army Chief of Staff Hugh Lenox Scott was his friend. Secretary of War Lindley M. Garrison would have tea with him when Sommerfeld passed through the U.S. capital. Senators William Alden Smith and Albert Bacon Fall would invite him to the Select Committee on Mexican Affairs to testify. Any industrialist who wanted to do business in Northern Mexico was well advised to call on him. Unbeknownst to American officials, Sommerfeld also was a German agent since at least 1908. Before the Great War, he acted as the liaison to the Mexican government for the German ambassador in Mexico, Admiral Paul von Hintze, and provided him with valuable intelligence on both Mexico and the United States. When the war started, he knew which foreign power bought how many shells and guns at which factory. In the fall of 1914, the German government decided to corner the U.S. arms and ammunition market. The German Military Attaché von Papen and Naval Attaché Boy-Ed, both attached to the German embassy in Washington D.C., could not think of anyone more effective and with better connections to sell off the weapons and ammunition to Mexico.

Felix Sommerfeld and a handful of second tier German agents in New York maintained the critical links between the Imperial Foreign Office, the German General Staff, and German covert agents in the United States and Mexico between late 1915 and early 1918. Under their auspices and under the radar of all intelligence services and law enforcement officials, as well as all major scholars on the topic, the war strategy of the German General Staff came to fruition in 1916. The extensive debriefings of these agents with Justice Department officials in 1918 are now public. This book correlates Sommerfeld's statements with private and public collections. Declassified and available to historians for years have been the Justice Department and FBI files on Mexico and Germany from 1908 to 1922, the Mixed Claims Commission files, files of U.S. Naval and Military Intelligence, and extensive collections contained in the U.S. National Archives under the title, "Captured German Documents." Also available are the personal papers of Pancho Villa's financial agent Lázaro de la Garza, of Villa's main strategist and Governor of Chihuahua, Silvestre Terrazas, of Commercial Attaché and spymaster Heinrich F. Albert, of General Hugh Lenox Scott, of President Woodrow Wilson and his cabinet members, and of soldier-of-fortune Emil Holmdahl. Never seen before are the personal papers of Frederico Stallforth. This book resulted from the minute correlation of American, Mexican, and German archival sources. Only sporadically available and scattered among multiple collections are the German Secret Service files, most of which were destroyed by fire in 1945. Felix Sommerfeld's personal papers have yet to be discovered.

Many great books have been written on the larger picture of German-Mexican-American diplomatic history, the Mexican Revolution, and the First World War. With very few exceptions these works deal with the question of what happened. This book focuses the lenses of history on the questions of who and how, the prerequisite for answering more precisely the question of what. This focus on the mechanics of the German war strategy in North America led to a fascinating character who deserves a place in history. Although certainly not the only player in this vast war effort, Felix Sommerfeld kept the German spy operation in business after their superiors and co-conspirators had been exposed, eliminated, expelled, arrested, or had simply fled.

CHAPTER 1:
A MAN WITH PEDIGREE

BY AUGUST 1914, WHEN THE German government made him choose between his idealistic love of revolutionary Mexico and the cause of his fatherland, Felix A. Sommerfeld had paid his dues. Like so many expatriate Germans, as well as first and second generation German-Americans that the Kaiser had summoned to the flag, Sommerfeld was conflicted. Until the World War shattered the largely harmonious relations between Germany and the United States, the German naval intelligence agent had successfully juggled various diplomatic, economic, and financial challenges between his Mexican employers, the German Empire, and the U.S. government.

Felix Armand Sommerfeld stood five feet, eight inches tall, had broad shoulders, was barrel chested, with protruding muscles, dark brown hair with some curls, "short neck, [and] heavy eyebrows."[3] Over the years, the muscular contours of his body had softened and given way to some fat around the waist. Sommerfeld was highly intelligent with hints of a daring and sometimes reckless nature. Throughout his career as a soldier, prospector, revolutionary, businessman, and spy, he was a fearless daredevil, but also someone who, according to a German saying, 'one could steal horses with.' Sommerfeld did not respect limitations, either internal or external. "In the golden lexicon of youth," he once wrote in Frederico Stallforth's guest book, "there is no such a word as 'fail'."[4] The end justified the means, which led him as a teenager to "borrow" money for a fare from New York back to Germany after he had deserted the U.S. army. In later life, he vacillated between bullying and polite diplomacy.[5]

The key to Felix Sommerfeld's success was the confluence of interest between Germany that required his spy work and the U.S. that appreciated his often selfless efforts in maintaining productive relations with the various Mexican revolutionary factions. American businessmen counted on Sommerfeld's help. The State and War Departments approached Sommerfeld first when citizens had run into trouble. Even when the famous writer, Ambrose Bierce, disappeared on the battlefields of northern Mexico in 1913, it was Sommerfeld who the U.S. government asked first for help. The growing divergence of political, financial, and economic interests between the German Empire and the United States after August 1914 forced Sommerfeld to throw in his lot with one side or the other. True to character, a division of loyalty was inconceivable. He chose Germany. Given his longstanding relationships with people high in the American government, Wall Street, and industry, Sommerfeld became a tremendously effective asset for the German government. His reputation and personal contacts allowed him to remain under deep cover throughout the First World War and beyond.

This most fascinating, complex, and enigmatic personality was born on May 28th 1879.[6] Felix had two sisters and three brothers.[7] The family lived in Borkendorf, a little village six miles or half-an-hour away by coach from Schneidemühl, in the eastern province of Posen close to the Polish border.[8] The Sommerfeld family operated the Borkendorfer Mühle, a grain mill and warehouse. Despite the ups and downs of the economy of the latter 19th century, Sommerfeld grew up in a wealthy Jewish household. By the time he graduated from high school his two older brothers, Julius and Hermann, had already decided to seek their fortunes in the United States. Sommerfeld followed in his brothers' footsteps, both of whom had become American citizens by the early 1900s. He came to the U.S. still a teenager in 1898. His third brother Siegfried, four years his senior, remained in line to take over the family business.

The Spanish-American War swept Sommerfeld into the U.S. army from which he deserted within months. He claimed his father had taken ill and needed him. More likely, he had been looking for action and could not envision months of military training and idle time in rural Kentucky. Lacking the funds to pay for his fare back to Germany, Sommerfeld stole $275 from his brother's landlord, paid for the steamer to Antwerp and came home. Why he stole that much is unknown. The ticket to Germany cost less than $50. He possibly had to bribe someone to issue a passport to him since he was listed as a deserter. Felix's relationship with his oldest brother was injured after the 1898 trip. It is likely that Hermann had a hard time forgiving his brother for "borrowing" $275 from his landlord, a good portion of the man's annual income. As will be discussed later in the book, the affair would come to haunt him almost twenty years later. Two years after he returned to Germany, the German mobilization to quell China's "Boxer Rebellion" struck the young adventurer's fancy. He volunteered for a one-year service as a horse messenger. The now degreed mining engineer returned to the United States in 1902. This time, he joined the hordes of adventurers who thought they could make quick riches in the booming mining industry of the western United States and northern Mexico. In 1908, Sommerfeld finally settled in Chihuahua, Mexico. He claimed to friends and acquaintances that he was engaged in mining and journalism. In reality, he used these covers to collect intelligence for the German government on the evolving opposition to the aging dictator of Mexico, Porfirio Díaz.

The Mexican Revolution started in earnest in the spring of 1911, when presidential contender turned revolutionary leader Francisco Madero swept the Mexican dictator from power. Sommerfeld had observed the development of the Madero revolution under cover as an Associated Press stringer for the German government. Weekly reports from the battlefields of Northern Mexico kept his handlers, German Consul of Chihuahua, Otto Kueck, and German Commercial Attaché in Mexico City, Peter Bruchhausen, abreast of developments. His friends and acquaintances noticed in amazement that Sommerfeld managed to become one of Francisco Madero's closest confidantes as the revolution progressed.

Porfirio Díaz vacated the presidential chair of Mexico in the end of May 1911, and chose exile over the likely fate of his forebears that clung to power for too long. Madero installed Francisco León De La Barra as the provisional president until democratic elections could be held later in 1911. However, below the surface of the successful ouster of the Mexican dictator, not all was well. Conspiracies hedged by members of the old regime and cracks in the hitherto united revolutionary coalition surfaced almost immediately after the fall of Díaz. Identifying the enemies of the new state and countermanding their efforts to topple the new regime fell to Francisco Madero's brother, Gustavo. Sommerfeld, who had been in charge of Francisco Madero's security, now worked under the auspices of Gustavo and an influential American lawyer and lobbyist, Sherburne G. Hopkins. As Francisco Madero sealed his ascendency to power with winning a free and democratic election in the fall of 1911, Sommerfeld became the head of the Mexican Secret Service. He subsequently organized and commanded the largest foreign secret service operation ever mounted on U.S. soil. In his capacity as Mexican Secret Service chief, the German agent also worked closely with the American military, divisions within the Justice Department, as well as the State Department. Sommerfeld became the only foreigner in the innermost circle of the new revolutionary government. His friends admired him, while his enemies learned to fear his unscrupulous use of power.

The first serious challenge to Madero's government was a direct result of the elections. General Bernardo Reyes was a popular politician who had challenged Porfirio Díaz as a presidential contender in 1910. He returned from exile in Europe to try his luck as a presidential candidate for a second time against Francisco Madero. The political campaign faltered in the face of overwhelming popular support for Madero. Reyes withdrew his candidacy in a huff and left Mexico in protest. Then he launched a military challenge to the Mexican government from San Antonio, Texas. He gathered at his side disillusioned members of the old regime as well as politicians who had fought with but now opposed Madero. Sommerfeld went to the border and, in cooperation with the American Justice Department, subverted Reyes's plans for an insurgency. A warrant for the general's arrest resulted in his becoming a fugitive and fleeing to Mexico. There, Mexican authorities arrested him. He was tried and sentenced to prison.

The defeat of Bernardo Reyes laid the groundwork for further cooperation between the Mexican Secret Service and the American government. Through the connections of Sherburne Hopkins in Washington D.C., Sommerfeld established an effective organization along the Mexican-American border with Mexican and American agents cooperating closely against any attempt of arms smuggling, armed incursions into Mexico, and violations of American laws by Mexican revolutionaries.

The biggest challenge to Madero's presidency came in the spring of 1912, when Pascual Orozco, a disillusioned general in Madero's revolutionary forces, declared himself in rebellion. While

Reyes's uprising fizzled through a lack of popular appeal, money, and organization, Orozco executed a highly effective challenge to the Mexican government. Within weeks of declaring himself in revolt, the popular former mule driver and entrepreneur occupied most of the state of Chihuahua with its customs houses along the border. Financed by the erstwhile largest landholder in Mexico, Luis Terrazas, the Orozco rebellion threatened to engulf most of the vital northern states of Mexico. However, Sommerfeld's organization along the Mexican-American border and the irregular forces of Pancho Villa, who entered the fray against Orozco, managed to starve the supply lines of the rebels and deal them painful defeats on the battlefield. By the summer of 1912, Orozco had been declawed. Sommerfeld had proven to be a formidable organizer, strategist, leader, and diplomat.

While the German agent defended the Madero presidency, he also worked behind the scenes in shaping German foreign policy towards the revolutionary government. German Minister Paul von Hintze used Sommerfeld as his informal channel of communication between Madero and himself. Sommerfeld provided detailed intelligence from the most inner circles of the new government and, in return, the German government came to accept and work with the Madero administration. After several German citizens had been murdered in a textile factory, Madero's administration made a special effort to find and try the murderers. In the end, the Mexican government paid compensation for the murders to Germany, while American, British, and French governments never received any remuneration for crimes committed against their citizens. It was Sommerfeld's work behind the scenes that gave von Hintze the extra edge. The German agent also brokered arms deals between the German and Mexican governments. Through these deals, Sommerfeld made important contacts to the munitions industry in the United States and Germany. These contacts laid the groundwork for much of his work during the coming world war.

In February 1913, Sommerfeld's commander-in-chief Francisco I. Madero, Mexico's Vice-President José Maria Pino Suarez, and Gustavo Madero, the president's brother, who also was Sommerfeld's direct superior, all perished in the violent coup d'état known as the *Decena Trágica*, the Ten Tragic Days. Hunted by death squads of the usurper general, Victoriano Huerta, Sommerfeld found refuge in the German legation in Mexico City. Barely escaping the wrath of the new regime, German Minister Paul von Hintze accompanied his charge out of the country into safety. In the immediate aftermath Sommerfeld's friend, Sherburne Hopkins, sent him back to Mexico to join the Constitutionalist army under Venustiano Carranza that had quickly sprung up in opposition to the Huerta coup. Sommerfeld proceeded to organize the U.S. supply lines of this Mexican rebellion. At this historical juncture, the financial and political interests of the United States coincided largely with those of the Mexican opposition that sought to defeat Huerta. As a result, Sommerfeld found himself in a crucial position brokering events between the American government, American business interests, and the Mexican rebel chiefs Carranza, Villa, Obregón, Maytorena, Zapata, and several others.

In the spring of 1914, an ever-increasing rift developed between the two most powerful rebel chiefs Venustiano Carranza and Pancho Villa. By then, Villa commanded the largest army in the Mexican Revolution, the famed *División Del Norte*. Faced with the uncomfortable decision, Hopkins, as a representative of large financial interests in New York, as well as Sommerfeld, switched allegiances and sided with Pancho Villa in the early summer of 1914. Sommerfeld became Villa's chief arms buyer as well as his de-facto ambassador in the United States. After political enemies ransacked Sherburne Hopkins's offices in May 1914, they proffered compromising papers to New York's newspapers in the end of June. The Washington lawyer appeared to have peddled influence and funding between Mexican revolutionary factions and oil tycoon, Henry Clay Pierce, the Wall Street financier Charles R. Flint, President Wilson's special envoy to Mexico John Lind, as well as Secretary of State William Jennings Bryan. Politicians, revolutionaries, and business leaders scurried for cover as more details of the corruption within Wilson's cabinet and Mexican revolutionaries appeared on the front pages of the *New York Herald* and other major dailies. As Sherburne Hopkins's career teetered on the edge of collapse in the face of the national exposé of his dealings, Sommerfeld, as well, found himself in the public eye; however, not in a negative light.[9] The German agent had managed to stay clear of the scandal. He now became the go-to person for the media and the American government, just as Pancho Villa became the most powerful force in the Mexican Revolution.

However, the outbreak of World War I caused American and German interests in Mexico to diverge for the first time since Sommerfeld had mingled in Mexican affairs. As the largest oil-producing country in the world and, at the same time, engulfed in a violent revolution that threatened to spill across the U.S. – Mexican border at any time, Mexico was of strategic importance to the nations facing off in the Great War. No other intelligence agent in the Northern hemisphere was better suited to implement German clandestine missions in Mexico than Felix Sommerfeld. Likely acting on instructions of the German admiralty, Sommerfeld settled permanently in New York in August 1914 and reported to Naval Attaché Karl Boy-Ed.

CHAPTER 2:
SOMMERFELD, VILLA, AND FRANKLIN W. OLIN

GERMAN NAVAL INTELLIGENCE AGENT FELIX A. Sommerfeld was busy managing the affairs of the Mexican revolutionary Pancho Villa in the Hotel Astor on New York's bustling Times Square. As a guest in the plush hotel, renting one of the finest suites with its own bath, the German had acquired a celebrity status. Always dressed impeccably and displaying perfect manners, Sommerfeld projected an aura of untamed power underneath the fine fabric of his suit. His intelligent but cold, steel blue eyes focused intensely on the people with whom he conversed. He commanded respect. Those who shared in his business ventures knew intuitively that to cross this man would have dire consequences. Sommerfeld's carefully groomed image as a wealthy and successful businessman could not conceal the raw energy of the revolutionary that also defined him. Every morning, he checked out a horse at the Central Park stables and rode for an hour.[10]

Horseback riding was one of Sommerfeld's passions. He was an excellent horseman with experience in the German cavalry as a soldier in the Boxer Rebellion, in the desert Southwest, where he had worked as a prospector, spy, and journalist, as well as in downtown New York, where the wealthiest of New York's Who-is-Who took their morning rides in Central Park. In his statement to American authorities in 1918 he admitted that, on occasion, he met another passionate horseman and German cavalry officer who made his rounds through Central Park in the early morning hours of the New York summers: German Military Attaché Franz von Papen.[11] Since the two disliked each other thoroughly, a tip of the hat might have been the only observable communication between them.[12]

Many times in the months after he settled in New York, journalists loitered in the lavishly decorated reception hall of the Astor

Hotel hoping to catch Sommerfeld for a comment as he was check-ing for messages and telegrams at the front desk. Although most of Sommerfeld's telegrams were coded, the receptionists knew from the newspapers that their wealthy guest worked for Pancho Villa, the famed Mexican revolutionary whose exploits excited the movie goers of the day. Sommerfeld had stayed at the Astor on previous occasions but on August 13th 1914, two weeks after the Great War had broken out, he rented a three-room suite to become his wartime residence. The Hotel Astor was owned and operated by William C. Muschenheim, a German immigrant who had risen from obscurity to become a New York success story. With the backing of the prominent German-Amer-ican Waldorf-Astor family, Muschenheim had built and expanded this landmark establishment on Times Square between 1904 and 1910. A higher-end room cost between $4 and $5 per night. How much Felix Sommerfeld paid exactly for his suite is unknown, but $20 per day ($420 in today's value) would be a safe guess. This was quite an upgrade in living arrangements for the man who had boarded in the Sheldon Hotel in downtown El Paso for $1.50 per night for the previ-ous twelve months.

Ostensibly, Sommerfeld had done well for himself. While he had claimed in interviews and to anyone who would listen that he had not received a salary from Madero, his new job with Villa was extremely lucrative.[13] Newspapers reported in July 1914, that Villa had ceded Sommerfeld the monopoly of dynamite importation to north-ern Mexico. According to the papers, the concession paid up to $3,000 per week.[14] Sommerfeld, who seemed incensed over the publication of his income, wrote to his friend and Army Chief-of-Staff Hugh Lenox Scott on the day of the newspaper story,

> 7/6 1914
> General H. L. Scott
> Washington DC
>
> My dear General,
>
> I suppose you saw the story in this mornings [sic] N.Y. Herald, supposed to come from El Paso, Texas, in which it says that I have the biggest concession, the

[illegible] dynamite concession, which pays me about $2000 a week. I do not care what the *N.Y. Herald* says nor what some of its readers might say, but I do not like to appear in the eyes of my friends as a man, who solely for the purpose of supporting the revolution, has been and is still serving it to the best ability.

In January some Mexican from Philadelphia asked General Villa for the dynamite concession that is the sole privilege of importing dynamite into Chihuahua through the port of Juarez. This concession has always been in the hands of the dynamite factory in [illegible] Durango, belonging to Limantour and other Científicos and some Frenchmen. Instead of giving this privilege to the man from Chihuahua, General Villa gave it to me, I think some of my friends told Villa, to show me some appreciation for services rendered to him and the cause. I never asked for it. [Underlined in the original] The import duty on dynamite under the constituted government, that is under Porfirio Díaz and Madero, was 24 ½ cts mex per kilo and as duties are paid in 4.5 gold at present, about 12 cts gold I got the duty down to 6 cts gold per kilo that is about 1 ¼ cts per lb. From these 6 cents gold I pay about 3 ¾ cts to the federal government, state government and the municipality of Juarez. Since January about 7 cars of dynamite were passed to Juarez paying me after deduction of all other expenses $1900 net.

These 7 cars were passed during March and beginning of April since then not a single car of dynamite has been passed across to Juarez and since that time I have not received a single cent for duties on dynamite.

In the first place since I have the socalled [sic] concession, the mining men pay less for dynamite than they paid before, when conditions were normal, as the dynamite trust sold them the dynamite for a much higher price as nobody could import dynamite on account of the prohibitive duty. In the second place

I did not ask General Villa for the concession and in the third place I have never received from President Madero nor from Carranza or Villa any salary nor any other gratification for my services and never asked for anything. At the same time I can not [sic] see anything extraordinary nor illegal in accepting a privilege which under the constitutional government is perfectly legal and justified.

I do not have to defend myself against such attacks, but I thought I owe this explanation to you as you have always been so exceedingly kind to me. . .

With kindest regards,

Very sincerely and gratefully

F. A. Sommerfeld[15]

The story obviously hit a nerve with the German agent. Apparently, the letter to Scott did not suffice. The next day, Sommerfeld notified Lázaro De La Garza, Villa's chief financial officer, that he would be available at the Hotel Shoreham in Washington D.C. He likely conferred with Sherburne Hopkins about the scandal involving his friend, but his main concern was the War Department. Sommerfeld was working hard on cultivating a close relationship with Secretary of War Lindley M. Garrison.[16] Before the revelations of Hopkins's dealings in Mexico on behalf of American high finance, the Washington lawyer and lobbyist had been Villa's main channel of communication to President Wilson's cabinet. Since Hopkins had been discredited, the Wilson administration was keeping its distance. While Hopkins's troubles seriously affected Villa's access to the U.S. government, Carranza had secured the powerful lawyer and former judge, Charles A. Douglas, as his lobbyist a few months before. Douglas was a close friend of Secretary of State Bryan.[17] The only remaining direct channel of communication between the Villa faction and the American president in the summer of 1914 was Sommerfeld. The last thing Sommerfeld and his backers in New York and Mexico needed was the risk of a second scandal. While the Hopkins scandal involved influence peddling on behalf of Henry Clay Pierce and Charles Flint, the revelation of Sommerfeld receiving large amounts of cash from Pancho Villa was certain to raise eyebrows. The German had established ties with Hopkins as well as access to the highest echelons of the U.S. government. For what would Villa pay him if not the kind of access the Hopkins's papers had revealed? This constellation explains why Sommerfeld went into a serious damage control mode as soon as the first article on his income appeared in the press.

His worry over appearing to be a war profiteer to members of the American government did not prevent him from taking a suite at the Astor in August nor cause him to undertake anything to dispel the image of being a successful and wealthy businessman. Even if his dynamite concession continued to pay "only" $950 ($20,000 in today's value) per month, as he tried to convince General Scott, he failed to mention his other sources of revenue. His main income consisted of sales commissions on arms and ammunition that he sourced for the *División Del Norte*. According to the financial records of Lázaro De La Garza, Villa's main financial agent in the U.S., Sommerfeld received a commission of $2 per case of 1,000 cartridges (approximately five percent).[18] His actual sales, which were shipped and paid in the first half of 1914, are listed in the books of the *División Del Norte* as $377,800.[19] This translates to a commission of slightly more than $7,556, or about $1,250 per month. However, in June 1914 alone, 150 railroad cars of munitions valued at $500,000 were impounded at the border. These seem to have been shipments arranged by Sommerfeld, as well.[20] At $35 per case of 7mm Mauser ammunition, the commissions on those cars would have been $28,570.[21] The basis for paying sales commissions is the amount of value shipped, not the value of contracts entered into. Using delivery contracts as the basis for income is one of the basic mistakes journalists made when calculating Sommerfeld's and other agents's commissions. Historians have fallen into the same trap. Some contracts ended up never being shipped, which meant no commissions.[22] The Bureau of Investigations reported that in August 1914, 1.7 million cartridges passed from Flint and Company (Sommerfeld's supplier) to Villa through the Port of Galveston, Texas, alone. Commissions on that amounted to $3,500.[23] Altogether, Sommerfeld's income in the summer of 1914 added to somewhere between $2,200 per month ($46,200 in today's value) and over $5,000 per month ($105,000 in today's value). By any standard, this was a sizeable paycheck indeed.

As the end of the Huerta presidency approached in July 1914, efforts to manage the Mexican situation went into overdrive. With the support of Argentina, Brazil, and Chile the Wilson administration had organized a peace conference at Niagara, Canada. Ostensibly, the United States wanted to hammer out a settlement that ended the American occupation of Veracruz. However, reading between the lines of the proposals, one could infer that Woodrow Wilson had the ambition of influencing the takeover of Mexico by the Constitutionalists and their *jefe*, Venustiano Carranza. The First Chief, as Carranza had self-titled his position, saw through the U.S. president's strategy and refused to participate publicly in the Niagara conferences. As a great disappointment to all who had participated, the summit that Carranza had boycotted fizzled in the end of June without a meaningful result. On the verge of decisive victory over the Huerta government, the Mexican revolutionaries had no interest in engaging the Huerta government diplomatically.

Pancho Villa, as well, had no public representation at the meeting since he served nominally as a military commander under Carranza and had no foreign policy responsibilities. However, informally both Carranza through his representatives in New York and Washington, as well as Villa through Hopkins and Sommerfeld, clandestinely jockeyed for favor with the Wilson administration. Sommerfeld became the public face of Villa in the United States with the Niagara conferences ending on June 24th 1914 and Hopkins engulfed in the scandal that erupted from his stolen papers. Pancho Villa enjoyed large public support as a result of his brilliantly organized publicity campaign in the U.S., as well as his spectacular military successes. In his obstinate, yet strategically correct, rebuttal of President Wilson's efforts at Niagara, Carranza not only had irked the American government but had attained the image of an anti-American, stubborn, and aloof leader in the public eye. Showing his aptitude in focused public relations and propaganda, Sommerfeld kept Villa's positive image alive in the headlines, as well as in crucial circles of the American government.

Immediately after the end of the Niagara conference, news of an impending split between Pancho Villa and Carranza resurfaced. The disagreements between the two revolutionaries had been in the news off and on for months. However, at this crucial juncture, with the Huerta government in its last throws of existence, infighting between the revolutionary factions would have had devastating consequences. Huerta could use the split to his ends. The U.S. government, which had supported the rebels, would be faced with throwing its weight to one side or the other. Most importantly, other factions currently on the sidelines could enter the fold. The Wilson administration was worried and rightfully so. During this complicated international situation, Felix Sommerfeld evolved into a reliable source of information for the American government and a calming influence on the diplomatic stage. As he had done in February 1914, Sommerfeld now publicly denied reports of Villa's disloyalty vis-à-vis the First Chief.

A new controversy, this one largely concocted by Hopkins and Sommerfeld, erupted simultaneously in the middle of June, when Felipe Ángeles's name floated through press reports as a possible presidential contender for Mexico. Ángeles, a conservative former officer of the federal army, had faithfully supported President Madero. However, Carranza, Obregón, Zapata, and other revolutionary leaders considered Ángeles a remnant of Dictator Porfirio Díaz's oppressive military machine. To Pancho Villa, Hopkins, and Sommerfeld, Ángeles had solid revolutionary credentials and possessed the potential to bridge the gap between the forces that were tearing Mexico apart, the Catholic Church, the military, land owners, business, labor, and the peasantry. The trial balloon failed miserably. All corners of Mexico reverberated with outrage over an Ángeles candidacy. On the 21st of June, Sommerfeld denied the rumors in Villa's name.[24] On June 28th, the Carranza secretary Alfredo Breceda publicly attacked Sommerfeld and Ángeles in a press conference in Washington and included State Department official George Carothers, as well as Secretary of State Bryan in the tirade. Again, Sommerfeld crowned the headlines with carefully weighed comments on the first pages of national dailies.[25] Smugly, he not only defended Villa and Ángeles, but also endeared himself to the American secretary of state as a levelheaded negotiator. "As far as the attack on me is concerned, I do not want to dignify it by defending myself against his [Breceda's] accusations. My conduct at all times has been the same, open and above board, and will invariably stand the acid test. But I will protest against the malicious attack on Gen. Angeles."[26]

Carranza representatives arrived in Washington D.C. on July 2nd, to negotiate the terms under which Huerta would leave Mexico. However, in the typical Carranza manner, the delegates had "verbal instructions... but no power to negotiate."[27] Meanwhile, in Mexico, Carranza and Villa representatives met in Torreón to settle their leaders' differences. At the very least, the two chieftains would vow to cooperate until the Constitutionalists had taken Mexico City. Sommerfeld kept the American press apprised of the summit in Torreón. The New York Times reported on July 3rd, "Felix Sommerfeld, personal agent of Gen. Villa in the United States, today received a dispatch from Villa stating that three mediators had arrived at Torreón in an endeavor to adjust the Villa-Carranza differences, and that the prospects for a settlement of the trouble are encouraging."[28] The dispatch mentioned on the 3rd of July in the paper had already reached the desk of Secretary of War Lindley M. Garrison the day before:

Dear Sir:

Enclosed find copy of telegram I received at this moment.

Respectfully yours,

F. A. Sommerfeld[29]

The telegram originated from Lázaro De La Garza who stated Villa's condition for "... a satisfactory understanding ... I am sure that if they [Carranza's faction] give the Division of the North its corresponding place everything will be alright."[30] However, Villa's powerful army never received its corresponding place in Carranza's designs for Mexico. The conference at Torreón lasted until July 8th, one week before Huerta's demise as president. On July 9th 1914, Villa showed an agreement to the U.S. special envoy, George C. Carothers. The agreement was a sort of armistice in which the commander of the División Del Norte submitted to Carranza's authority for the time being.[31] "No member of the rebel armies or provisional official would seek permanent office. Carranza would remain the 'First Chief' and Villa would retain command of the Division of the North... Villa would report to

Carranza for 'rectifications and ratifications.' Carranza would provide Villa with coal and munitions and give him freedom of action in his area of domain... A Villista would remain in charge of the railroads in the north..."[32]

The two leaders also agreed upon personnel questions for the new Constitutionalist government. Carranza ceded access to supplies for Villa, and Villa ceded most of the control of the national railroads, only retaining a loyal manager of his own in the north.[33] The imminent split had been averted, but the military might of the *División Del Norte* precipitated the ultimate showdown a few months later. Villa's forces had smashed the defenses of Zacatecas in the last days of June and destroyed Huerta's largest army of over twelve thousand men. At the same time, Álvaro Obregón's army defeated the federals on the west coast of Mexico and steam-rolled towards the capital. Emiliano Zapata's forces, meanwhile, raided the suburbs of the capital. The situation became hopeless for Huerta. He resigned on the 15th of July, retreated to Puerto México from where he left the country on July 20th 1914. The German cruiser *Dresden* took Huerta, his wife and four daughters, as well as the Secretary of War Blanquet and his wife to Jamaica. The exiled president transferred to London from there.[34] A few months later, Huerta settled in Spain. There, he contemplated his next moves. Huerta's designs on Mexico had not come to an end. He resurfaced in New York less than a year later.

Villa did not enter Mexico City at the head of his powerful army. That honor fell upon Constitutionalist General Álvaro Obregón who took control of the capital on August 15th. Huerta had left the capital to the interim president, Francisco Carvajal. After less than a month in the presidential chair, Carvajal fled Mexico before the advancing Constitutionalists arrived. An estimated twenty-five thousand federal troops fled the capital or surrendered to the revolutionary army. The governor of the federal district, Eduardo Iturbide, received the thankless task of handing power over the city to General Obregón. Iturbide, a descendent of the first emperor of Mexico, had earned the ire of both Emiliano Zapata and Pancho Villa because of his cruelty as police chief of the capital. Zapata, in particular, vowed to kill the governor if he ever had the chance because Iturbide had fought off the Zapatista advance until Obregón's forces arrived at the outskirts of the capital. This daring move earned the Mexican nobleman eternal gratitude from the foreign colony in Mexico City who had feared looting, rape, and destruction should Zapata's peasant army have taken the city first. For the time being, Obregón, who represented the Carranza government, left Iturbide unmolested, especially since the powerful foreign lobby protected him. First Chief Venustiano Carranza made his triumphal entry into the city on August 20th 1914, flanked by his staff and celebrated by an enthusiastic crowd of 300,000 citizens.[35] In the meantime, Villa went into high gear to consolidate his power in the northern parts of Mexico, hoarding supplies and reserves for the eventual showdown with Carranza.

The light cruiser SMS Dresden passing through the Kiel Canal in Germany [36]

Sherburne Hopkins operated in the background in the United States, while Sommerfeld managed General Villa's interests vis-à-vis the American public and the Wilson administration. Winning American hearts and minds had been a primary goal ever since the public relations disaster in February resulting from the apparent murder of William S. Benton. Villa tried to cover up the fact that the British rancher was murdered in the revolutionary's immediate surroundings, maybe even at his own hand.[37] Sommerfeld's efforts with the American and British governments on behalf of Villa prevented an escalation of the scandal. He also interceded with Villa and others on behalf of

American and British mining interests. While Sommerfeld emphasized his "unselfish" efforts to help American businesses, keeping the mines operating raised his take on the dynamite imports.

Sommerfeld also engaged in matters of international diplomacy. On June 23rd 1914, the Villistas captured the British vice-consul of Zacatecas, George S. Douglas, and charged him with working for the federals.[38] According to "Interim Governor [of] Zacatecas, Lieutenant Colonel Manuel Carlos Dela [sic] Vega... The British subject G. S. Douglas was taken prisoner when this place fell in[to] our hands and is accused of having installed and handled the powerful searchlight which the enemy had on the La Bufa hill and which, during the first attack on this city, caused great damage to us."[39] The British consul in Durango seemed to have validated the accusation as accurate.[40] Constitutionalist General Natera, who had ordered Douglas to be arrested, likely mustered all available self-discipline not to have Douglas summarily executed. His troops had been decimated in the initial attack on Zacatecas, which caused Villa to sweep in and save the day. A huge embarrassment for Carranza! Luckily for the prisoner, Villa had thus taken control of the city, which probably saved Douglas's life. Sommerfeld saw the arrest of Douglas as an opportunity to prove Villa's cooperative nature to the American government. Releasing the prisoner did not require any big sacrifice from Villa who had no beef with the consul.[41] On June 30th, Sommerfeld contacted Villa through Lázaro De La Garza on behalf of Douglas.[42] The effort paid off. On July 6th, the customs collector of El Paso, Zach Lamar Cobb, reported to the Department of State that Douglas had been released after all charges were dropped.[43] Secretary Bryan informed the British Charge d'Affairs two days later. The quick release of the British captive made Sommerfeld look highly effective to the American authorities.

Secretary Bryan also appeared on top of the Mexican situation to the British government. The secretary of state who had cleansed his organization from republican holdovers of the Taft administration lacked seasoned diplomats in Mexico and, indeed, anywhere else. The lack of experienced personnel threatened to make the Wilson administration look weak in foreign policy matters. It is against this background that efforts from people outside the diplomatic chain of command, such as Felix Sommerfeld, received such appreciation.

Just as the Douglas situation was unfolding, the German government asked Secretary Bryan to represent its citizens in the parts of Mexico that came under Constitutionalist control. Secretary Bryan had to admit to the German Charge d'Affairs Haniel von Haimhausen that Carranza refused permission for U.S. officials to intervene on behalf of other nationalities. As a result, the British had to appoint a vice-consul of their own in El Paso who dealt directly with Carranza's foreign secretary, Isidro Fabela. William Jennings Bryan suggested to the German government to do the same, a humiliating admission of his lack of influence and power.[44] Enter Felix Sommerfeld, who skillfully manipulated the strained diplomatic situation. Rather than mediating between the British government and Mexican revolutionaries, Sommerfeld opened channels between the U.S. State Department and Villa, thus brokering the release of Douglas and making it appear as an apparent diplomatic success for the American government. Cementing the reputation of being a reliable partner for the U.S. government, Sommerfeld's clear goal was for a potential Villa administration to be the only viable candidate for diplomatic recognition.

Sommerfeld's diplomatic prowess also showed in regards to an American soldier-of-fortune who found himself in hot water in Sonora. On July 8th 1914, Sonora's military governor, José Maria Maytorena, arrested Emil Holmdahl on suspicion of being a spy. Holmdahl was indeed a spy. He had worked for Sommerfeld's secret service organization in 1912 and 1913.[45] According to Holmdahl's personal papers, he switched allegiances in the spring of 1914, left the services of Pancho Villa (and Sommerfeld), and joined Félix Díaz as "Chief Military Advisor."[46] The truth was that Holmdahl served under Carrancista general, Benjamin Hill. Hill had the task of checking Maytorena's attempt to establish militarily control over the state of Sonora. With the backing of Pancho Villa, Maytorena fought a proxy war against Venustiano Carranza. Complementing the effort, but unbeknownst to Maytorena, Sommerfeld sent Holmdahl into the Hill camp to spy on the Carrancistas. Within two days of his arrest, Sommerfeld cleared things up with Maytorena and succeeded in having Holmdahl released. Clearly, Holmdahl could not have been a Carrancista or a Díaz supporter as he had claimed. As a traitor, Sommerfeld would have left him to rot in Maytorena's prisons or worse. More importantly for Sommerfeld, again without telling the American government all the details of Holmdahl's work or illuminating the back story, he appeared to be quite the statesman. He wrote to Secretary of War Garrison, "Holmdahl will be released at once ... " and asked Garrison to contact General Scott for him with the news.[47]

As was the case with helping American mining companies, Sommerfeld endeared himself to the U.S. government by helping his associates at the same time. By the summer of 1914, and with Sherburne Hopkins having disappeared from the public eye, Sommerfeld had grown into the role of a trusted adviser and important diplomatic channel to Mexico for the U.S. government. Secretary of War Garrison and Secretary of State Bryan frequently called upon him for help, which he would render without obvious remuneration. Of course, General Scott and Secretaries Garrison and Bryan provided the mechanism for Sommerfeld's larger scheme of gaining access to the highest echelons of the U.S. government. He not only understood but was also in a position to influence U.S. foreign policy, as well as military strategy from within.

As the crisis in Europe deteriorated into a full-blown world war, arms and munitions procurement in the United States changed overnight. Starting on August 1st 1914, Mexico moved from the front pages of U.S. dailies to the back burner of the American public conscience. Armed with suitcases of cash, multi-million dollar loans, and revenue from war bond sales, Russian, French, and British agents swarmed the relatively small munitions industry of the United States. Contracts with Entente agents quickly swallowed up capacities in the country and drove the market price for ammunition sky-high. In addition to the U.S. arms manufacturers, the German arms trading agency of Hans Tauscher in New York had been one of Sommerfeld's main sources for German Mauser rifles and 7 mm ammunition. As the British blockade tightened, Tauscher's supplies dried up. As a result, Sommerfeld only lost his German arms merchant and other U.S. supplier who rather supplied the Entente powers than him. Even his main supplier throughout the Mexican Revolution, the merchant house Charles Flint and Co. in New York, preferred to engage in large and highly lucrative contracts with the Entente rather than supplying Sommerfeld for his clients in Mexico.[48]

The United States arms and munitions industry in 1914 was tiny in comparison with the huge companies of continental Europe, where the likes of Krupp, Rheinmetall, Deutsche Waffen - und Munitionsfabrik, Skoda, Steyr, Hotchkiss, Vickers, Brandt, Schneider, and St. Chamond supplied the vast armies of their respective countries. While central Europe had engaged in a prolonged arms race in the years prior to 1914, American manufacturers produced mostly hunting and sporting guns, and mainly supplied the domestic mining industry with explosives. The only other major power with an underdeveloped arms and munitions industry was England. Supposedly, Great Britain did not have a single domestic munitions factory when the war broke out in August of 1914.[49] In the first nine months of the European war, the U.S. exported only $7 million worth of firearms, $9.6 million worth of cartridges, and $5.4 million worth of high explosives to the Entente powers.[50] Comparatively, even before the war in 1913, Germany spent over $500 million on defense.[51]

Felix Sommerfeld had established himself firmly in the diplomatic realm of Mexico and the United States. His main purpose of supplying the Constitutionalist forces and Pancho Villa's army, in particular, with arms and ammunition brought the German agent into the center of what would be the most important preoccupations of the German government: Infiltrate, manipulate, and, ultimately, sabotage the American munitions industry. The German strategists initially sought to divert American munitions production away from Entente buyers and steer it to neutral countries, Mexico being the most obvious choice. Sommerfeld and the German agent, Hans Tauscher, were the absolute experts when it came to understanding and having powerful contacts within the American munitions industry.

The largest manufacturer of gunpowder and the only manufacturer of trinitrotoluene (TNT) in the United States was E.I. DuPont de Nemours and Company. TNT (Trinitrotoluene) "... is obtained by the nitration of toluene, contained in the crude benzene distilled from coal tar and washed out from coal gas."[52] In 1912, anti-trust lawsuits had forced DuPont to split its explosives division into the Atlas Powder Company, which made ammonium nitrate, and the Hercules Powder Company, the main TNT manufacturer in the country.

DuPont also founded the Aetna Explosives Company for the production of smokeless powder in 1913. A German chemist had invented smokeless powder in 1842. It consisted of thirty percent nitroglycerine, sixty-five percent nitrocellulose (also called gun cotton), and five percent mineral jelly. While saltpeter-based black powder emitted a strong cloud of residue, smokeless powder burned clean. Aetna also manufactured TNT. However, it was the virtual monopoly on smokeless powder that made the U.S. manufacturer so strategically important. Several smaller companies produced various high explosives, all based on picric acid (trinitrophenol). Picric acid was the base for most high explosives. It was manufactured from coal tar through a complicated fractional distillation process.[53]

The manufacturing processes for high explosives posed significant hazards. Only two companies in the United States managed to produce significant amounts of picric acid and TNT in the World War, Aetna and Semet-Solvay. TNT should not be confused with dynamite, a nitroglycerin with sixty percent more energy density. Because of the blasting power of dynamite, the large North American mining industry preferred this explosive to all else. What became critical intelligence for the German war planners was the fact that the entire explosives production in the United States was based on a handful of critical base materials, made by only a handful of producers. If one bought up critical supplies of toluene and picric acid, no one in the United States could produce high explosives.

The Equitable Powder Manufacturing Company, headquartered in the Midwest town of East Alton, Illinois, supplied powder and dynamite to the coalfields of Ohio, Indiana, and Illinois since the early 1890s. The founder and president of Equitable Powder was an enterprising engineer and a successful baseball player from Vermont with a degree from Cornell University. Franklin Walter Olin proved to possess an uncanny ability to see the potential for profitable expansion of his business. In 1898, he founded the Western Cartridge Company, also in East Alton, where he produced small arms ammunition and shotgun shells. Because of his unique location in the Midwest and not in Connecticut or California, where most of his competitors had settled, Olin could ship cheaply and safely down the Mississippi river to New Orleans. He quickly became an important supplier of dynamite for the mining industry in Mexico.

Although there is no historical record to document Olin's initial acquaintance with Felix Sommerfeld, it probably occurred around the time when the German agent first held the dynamite concession from Pancho Villa. Sommerfeld seemed particularly impressed with

Olin and his two older sons Franklin Jr. and John. He pushed the enterprising engineer to invest in the production of 7mm Mauser type cartridges.[54] Unlike the other large cartridge manufacturers in the United States, Winchester, Remington-Union Metallic, and United States Cartridge, Western Cartridge initially did not have a significant share of the munitions market. However, after the 1908 recession left a gaping hole in the U.S. capacity to supply the Mexican revolutionaries, the industry consolidated.

Sommerfeld, in particular, bore the brunt of the tightening munitions supplies, exacerbated by the refusal of all U.S. manufacturers, save for Remington, to produce German caliber 7mm ammunition. However, he was also one of the most high-powered arms buyers in the United States at the time. On July 27th 1914, just a few days before the World War started, Sommerfeld detailed the volume of munitions he had shipped during the previous month. He wrote to Villa's financial agent, Lázaro De La Garza, in a telegram, "…up to July Flint have [sic] shipped to Gral [sic] Villa 5 million 300 thousand cartridges 7 mm and 650 thousand 30/40 and will ship 2 million 700 thousand of 7 mm more and 3 million of 30-40 and 4000 rifles 30-40. Shelton Payne [of El Paso] have received 1000 rifles and 1000 rifles are in Galveston…."[55] The accounts of the División Del Norte dated July 28th showed $117,800 ($2.5 million in today's value) paid directly to Sommerfeld and $260,000 ($5.5 million in today's value) to Flint.[56] The German agent had acquired huge purchasing power.

The situation changed dramatically once the World War started. Sommerfeld's German supply line via Hans Tauscher fell apart because of the English sea blockade. Entente buying agents swarmed the market buying up all they could for their respective countries. Prices for munitions rose sky-high since the production capacity in the U.S. lagged far behind demand. Somehow, the German agent had to find a way to source Mauser caliber cartridges in the United States. His control over Villa's purchasing contracts gave him unique power to steer contracts to a new manufacturer, the fledgling East Alton concern of Franklin Olin. It made economic sense, and as a result, the Western Cartridge Company started to produce small amounts of 7mm Mauser cartridges in 1913.[57] Production expanded in 1914 but was hampered by the scarcity of brass cups. Thus, at the onset of the war, Franklin Olin and Felix Sommerfeld became business partners. Sommerfeld directed huge munitions contracts for Mexican revolutionaries to his friend. In addition, Olin benefitted from the German corner of smokeless powder and hydraulic presses needed to produce cartridges. The Midwestern businessman thus built the only new cartridge factory in 1916 with hydraulic presses from German sources under the condition that he supplied neutrals in the World War. From the windfall profits of the war, Olin had set the Western Cartridge company on a path so powerful, that it swallowed up the Winchester Repeating Arms Company in 1931. Franklin Olin became a multi-millionaire, philanthropist, and defense industry powerhouse. Felix Sommerfeld had given Olin a huge boost when he convinced the entrepreneur to compete against Remington and enter the profitable 7mm munitions market. Without a doubt, the German agent opened the Mexican market for the small and unknown powder company from East Alton, Illinois. He did not stop there. The rise of Olin's companies in and beyond the First World War is intricately linked to Sommerfeld's work in 1914 and 1915, as well as, the German government's efforts to combat the Entente supply lines in the United States.

CHAPTER 3:
SOMMERFELD, BOY-ED AND VON PAPEN

AS EARLY AS MARCH 1914, Franz von Papen established a so-called "Kriegsnachrichtendienst," the "war intelligence agency," on orders of the General Staff.[58] Von Papen's superiors wanted to put Hans Tauscher, the Krupp agent in New York, in charge of the office. For reasons unknown, maybe because Tauscher was not interested in taking a $238 per month job, von Papen suggested finding someone else.[59] His next choice was Wolf Walter Franz von Igel.[60] The twenty-six year-old German from Posen, Germany had worked as a banker for the German investment bank, Conrad Donner, in the city.[61] Von Papen also suggested three vice consuls to his superiors to run the "Nachrichtendienst" in strategic U.S. cities. The consuls, he most likely referred were Franz Bopp of San Francisco, Carl A. Luederitz of Baltimore, and Hans Kurt von Reiswitz of Chicago. All three, as well as scores of people working with and for them, ended indicted and convicted for their parts in Germany's clandestine operations in the U.S. between 1914 and 1916. By the outbreak of the war, the new organization definitely was in operation. In a request to Boy-Ed dated July 30th, von Papen asked his colleague to run the "Nachrichtendienst" while he was on his way back from Mexico.[62] Franz Wachendorf, alias Horst von der Goltz, also mentioned in his memoirs the existence of the "Intelligence Department of the General Staff."[63]

The intelligence agency transmitted critical, military-related information to several intelligence agencies in Germany. The department von Papen reported intelligence to and von der Goltz likely referred to was Abteilung IIIB. This office, the political section of the War Department, was interested in issues of policy, political developments, politicians, and activities of third countries. Papen wrote in his memoirs "... the whole responsibility for keeping Germany and her allies informed of politico-military developments in the North American continent devolved on me." [64] The *Nachrichtenabteilung des Admiralstabes* (Department N) under Commander Walter Isendahl was interested in any information related to third countries' naval operations, port installations, defensive positions, and the like. Department N also received copies of the military attaché's reports containing political and military intelligence. In countries where the German government did not station military attachés, the naval intelligence officer provided reports to both Department N and the political section of the War Department, Abteilung IIIb. Before the war, naval intelligence had been charged, for the most part, with intelligence operations on the American continent. The General Staff order from March 1914 clearly showed a change in intelligence strategy for the American continent.

Karl Boy-Ed, who ran his own intelligence agents, supplied his colleague, Franz von Papen, with pertinent data.[65] On the 11th of November, for example, he forwarded a report from Felix A. Sommerfeld to the military attaché with "compliments."[66] This report from Sommerfeld, who together with Hans Tauscher probably had the best intelligence on Entente purchases, seems to be one of the few remaining specimens of a weekly report, the German filed with the naval attaché. A second report to Boy-Ed with further information on arms contracts for the Entente reached von Papen's desk on November 29th.[67] Agents of the American Bureau of Investigations, who came into possession of these reports, later accused Sommerfeld of having been in contact with von Papen. Sommerfeld emphatically denied the charge. He had addressed the second report as "Geehrter Herr Kapitän." The American translator made this into "My dear captain," which is technically correct, but the naval rank of "Kapitän" (Commander) referred to Boy-Ed not to von Papen. If Sommerfeld had addressed von Papen, he would have written "Hauptmann," which refers to the rank of army captain. Sommerfeld, indeed, never reported intelligence to von Papen, as far as the archival files reveal. Of course, he still gathered intelligence, just for the naval intelligence. This fact, he lied about in his interrogation on 1918.[68]

Sommerfeld was one of the most important German agents in the United States who seemed connected to the scheme but was not identified. Wachendorf claimed in his memoirs and sworn statements that it was German Consul Kueck who sent him to New York. However, the German agent had likely worked for Felix Sommerfeld in Mexico. Sommerfeld shifted his base of operations from El Paso to New York in the summer of 1914. While Kueck could have possibly supplied the ever-penniless Wachendorf with traveling money, it is unlikely that Wachendorf would not report to Sommerfeld in New York before contacting von Papen. Indeed the time lag of an entire month between Wachendorf leaving El Paso and connecting with von Papen in New York suggests the likelihood that Sommerfeld had been involved. [69] According to Sommerfeld, something happened between him and von Papen in the beginning of the war which poisoned their relationship. The German agent told American authorities in 1918 that in the "very beginning of the war ... he would state I had broken my word of honor to the Germans."[70] According to Sommerfeld, von Papen had bad-mouthed him to the crowd in the German Club. "He said I had given my word of honor to the German Minister of Mexico (von Hinsen [sic]) that I would not mix in Mexican politics... "[71]

Sommerfeld's explanation of his trouble with von Papen was of a slightly different sort. As the chief of Mexico's secret service under President Francisco Madero, Sommerfeld had the task to stop insurgencies against Mexico's central government. Two of the primary arms dealers in the American Southwest and northern Mexico were Krakauer Zork and Moye and Ketelsen and Degetau. Both companies were owned by Germans. In Mexico City as well, members of the German community supported efforts to dislodge the revolutionary Madero administration. Sommerfeld certainly did his utmost to interrupt the reactionary agitation of the German and any other community. Adolph Krakauer even received death threats from Sommerfeld.[72] According to prominent members of the German community in Mexico City, Sommerfeld caused the black-listing of fourteen Germans, as well as the arrest of six of them. "Following the example of other famous leaders, Madero also created a 'black cabinet.' Leading this useful institution was a certain Sommerfeld, an arch scoundrel and – alas – a German citizen... Unbelievable but true: – Mr. v. Hintze, who could not or would not protect decent Germans in Mexico, granted this scalawag not only the protection of the embassy but even whisked him out of Mexico under the immunity of the German flag, where he was to face court martial for embezzling public funds."[73]

Indeed, von Hintze saved Sommerfeld's life in the *Decena Trágica* when General Victoriano Huerta had issued a warrant for his arrest. It is also likely that members of the anti-Madero German community faced difficulties as a result of Sommerfeld's agitation. Franz von Papen spent the spring and summer of 1914 in Mexico City, as Mexican revolutionaries and Sommerfeld played an important part in finally ousting the usurper president, Huerta.[74] Von Papen's close connection with the pro-Huerta German community in Mexico City likely influenced his assessment of Sommerfeld's character. When von Papen returned to New York in August 1914, he met Sommerfeld as one of his colleague Karl Boy-Ed's agents. Apparently, while being forced to work with Sommerfeld, who provided the key research on Allied arms contracts, von Papen voiced his opinion of the German agent in the German Club. Sommerfeld would not forget von Papen's insults. Von Hintze battled accusations of dereliction of duty brought in a lawsuit by the leader of the German community of Mexico City, Gustav Pagenstecher, in 1914.[75] The lawsuit in German courts even caught the attention of the emperor and Chancellor von Bethmann Hollweg. In the end, von Hintze's name was cleared and he moved on to an important war assignment in China. Despite his detractor's efforts, von Hintze's career reached its zenith in 1918 when he briefly became imperial foreign secretary.

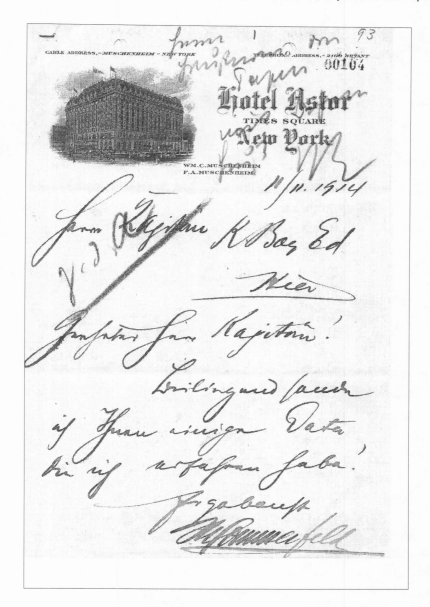

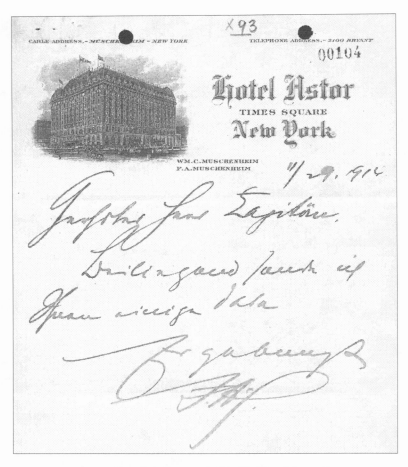

Letter from F. A. Sommerfeld to Karl Boy-Ed, 1914 [76]

Since the U.S. armament production capacities in the beginning of the war were relatively small, the German officials in the U.S. became convinced early on that a cornering of the munitions and explosives markets was feasible. Count Bernstorff sent a report to the Foreign Office, seconded by von Papen, reporting to the German General Staff on September 10th and 12th, 1914 respectively, and requested the go-ahead to "preempt purchase [by Entente of total annual production of artillery shells]." [77] Von Papen claimed in his memoirs that he requested to "take over the total production of the munition [sic] factories of the United States." [78] The cost of this venture amounted to "around $20 million" ($420,000,000 in today's value).[79] Count Bernstorff, who clearly supported the request, notified both Bernhard Dernburg and Heinrich Albert on October 17th: "Please tell Mr. von Papen that I am trying to prevent the purchasing of munitions by the Allies in a different way, since we are not receiving a go-ahead with respect to this option from Berlin."[80] The long-awaited but disappointing answer came on October 27th: "Munitions purchases are not viewed as practical."[81] Papen considered the decision a huge mistake.[82] In his opinion, and clearly those of Count von Bernstorff and Albert, and most likely including those of Tauscher and Sommerfeld, an early contracting of American munitions factories would have effectively closed the U.S. market to Entente purchases. Albert wrote in his unpublished memoirs, "Undoubtedly the decision from Berlin... was a mistake from any point of view. At that time we could have achieved three things with a relatively small sacrifice: first, the supply of the Allies with ammunition would have been made more difficult; second, the American government would have been pushed into a neutrality that was not just theoretical; third, business connections with influential American companies would have been created, which [the companies] naturally would have been on the German side."[83]

Albert and his colleagues correctly ascertained that this strategy would have worked, however, only for a short period of time; namely, the exact time it would take to add industrial capacity. Munitions factories rose from the ashes of the American recession in large numbers by 1915. In hindsight, von Papen's idea might appear crazy and naïve. However, considering the small munitions capacity of U.S. plants and the prevailing opinion among German officials that the war would be over in a matter of months lends credence to the realism of the idea. American manufacturers in the beginning of the conflict seemed hesitant to build too much capacity, with which they feared to be straddled after a short war. They decided instead to increase prices of their products. However, once construction of new factories began, this brief window of opportunity came to a close. The New York team went back to the drawing board.

The intelligence gathering activities of the two attachés in New York did not break American law "in the strictly legal sense." However, Koenig and the regional consulates also vetted the scores of volunteers and reservists for use in clandestine operations. "... when strangers used to approach us with claims of having carried out this or that act on behalf of the Fatherland, Koenig was instructed to check up on them."[84] Once the "strangers" checked out as viable candidates for a clandestine mission, the German military attaché organized their finances and sent them on their way. The regional consulates supported the operations as best as they could. Von Papen's and Boy-Ed's secret service staff, including the detective agency of Koenig's, served only to a small degree the legal collection of intelligence. The main purpose of the German organizations became the execution of the mission of "hurting the enemy."

CHAPTER 4:
DIPLOMACY AND WAR IN MEXICO

WHEN "CONSTITUTIONALIST" REVOLUTIONARIES OUSTED THE Mexican dictator Victoriano Huerta in July 1914, the political situation in Mexico was far from stable. The rivalry between the victorious Mexican rebel commanders Pancho Villa and Venustiano Carranza coincided with the outbreak of World War I. Mexico subsequently became a strategic interest in the war because of its oil wealth and proximity to the United States. German agents, most notably Felix A. Sommerfeld, Dr. Arnold Krumm-Heller, and Frederico Stallforth, infiltrated the inner circles of the Villa and Carranza factions, as well as the large community of exiled Mexican leaders.[85] In the fall and winter of 1914, the imperial German government had not yet decided upon a strategy to use the unsettled political situation in Mexico against the United States.

However, in the beginning of May 1915, German naval intelligence agent Felix Sommerfeld proposed to his German superiors to single-handedly create an American military intervention in Mexico.[86] The intervention would have caused the American military to use arms and munitions for its own forces, thus curbing the exploding exportation of military supplies to Germany's enemies. Sommerfeld stated to the former German colonial minister turned propaganda chief in Washington, Dr. Bernhard Dernburg, that he, Sommerfeld, had had the chance to create such an intervention in the winter of 1914/15, at the height of the border tensions at Naco, Arizona.[87] The only reason he refrained, declared the agent, was that he was unsure of German intensions. Dernburg wrote to Admiral Henning von Holtzendorff, "Felix A. Sommerfeld had misgivings at the time to force an intervention through General Villa since he did not know the intentions of Germany towards the United States."[88]

Sommerfeld's role in the stand-off at Naco has indeed been overlooked.[89] He used his connections to the highest echelons of the U.S. government, as well as his status as Pancho Villa's representative in the United States to precipitate the end to the crisis. One year later, between January and June 1916, after the German government had accepted Sommerfeld's offer to create a war between the U.S. and Mexico, the German agent used his experience and connections from Naco to the opposite effect; namely, to bring the two countries to the brink of war.[90]

After the ouster of the common enemy, Victoriano Huerta, in the middle of July 1914, the rivalry between Pancho Villa and Venustiano Carranza, superficially patched at Torreón, re-ignited later in the summer of that year.[91] The revolutionary factions in Mexico split along several political lines. Pancho Villa, now at the zenith of his power, commanded the largest army of the revolution. Although, personally, he had no interest in becoming president of Mexico, Villa deeply mistrusted Venustiano Carranza's commitment to land reform, redistribution of wealth, and constitutional government.[92] Above all, according to the *Plan de Guadalupe* and the agreement between the two warlords in Torreon, Carranza had to step down as provisional president and call for free elections. The agreements specified that he could not run for office. However, in the months after Huerta's demise, the First Chief Carranza gave no indication of calling elections or stepping aside. The opposite was the case, as not only Pancho Villa but also other generals like Alvaro Obregón, Pablo Gonzalez, and Emiliano Zapata noticed. Carranza ruled as provisional president through decree. With Villa as his only viable challenger, rumors ran rampant that Carranza attempted to turn other revolutionary chieftains against the northern general.

Aligned with Villa's camp were several conservative leaders, chief among them general Felipe Ángeles, the former secretary of war and brilliant strategist of Villa's military campaigns in 1914. Felix Sommerfeld and a select group of American business leaders had proffered the idea of Ángeles becoming president of Mexico.[93] They believed that of all the revolutionary chieftains, he was the closest to the ideals of Francisco I. Madero, the slain Mexican president who set the spark that ignited the revolution in 1910. Ángeles, without doubt, commanded significant respect from international, particularly

American, political and business circles. However, in Mexico the former federal general had forfeited his cabinet post as Secretary of War in Carranza's provisional government and sided with Pancho Villa in the spring of 1914. Therefore, he attracted the ire of virtually all Mexican factions other than Villa's.

Another conservative leader who aligned himself with the fortunes of Pancho Villa was José Maria Maytorena, the governor of Sonora. Maytorena was less a military man than a cunning political boss. After Victoriano Huerta toppled President Francisco Madero in February 1913, Maytorena declared himself against the usurper. He did not await the fate of his colleague in Chihuahua, Governor Abraham Gonzalez, who Huerta's henchmen brutally murdered. Rather, the governor fled to Tucson, Arizona and from there to Los Angeles. Maytorena returned to Sonora in July 1913. He reclaimed the governorship after the forces of Alvaro Obregón liberated Chihuahua from Huertista control. Widely regarded as a coward among revolutionaries, the Sonoran politico now depended largely on the military power of Obregón's army. Even while in exile, the governor only gave token support to rebel leaders who took up arms against Huerta. Villa, who saw Maytorena in Tucson in the spring of 1913, received a measly $1,000 from the governor to start a fighting force in Chihuahua. Nonetheless, Villa succeeded in building the largest military force of the revolution. Controlling most of the north of Mexico, he considered the Sonoran governor an important pawn in the struggle to curb Carranza's power. Villa began sending Maytorena supplies, including arms and ammunition, in order to break the governor's reliance on Obregón.

Maytorena had assembled a force of two thousand, mostly Yaqui fighters known for their fearlessness and brutality by June 1914. The governor managed to consolidate his power in the aftermath of Huerta's ouster mostly as a result of Villa's support. In a secret agreement between Maytorena and Huerta's beleaguered federal army at Guaymas, the governor managed to take the city in August 1914 without a fight and established virtual control over Sonora.[94] Flexing his muscle against the Carrancista commanders Colonel Plutarco Elías Calles and General Benjamin Hill, Maytorena forced a showdown with Venustiano Carranza. The governor's gamble worked. Instead of subduing the independent governor militarily, Carranza had to yield to

Pancho Villa, who threatened to invade Sonora with his army in support of Maytorena.[95] The battle lines were drawn. Although Villa could not exercise more than token control over the fiercely independent Maytorena, the clash between Maytorena and the Carrancista forces in Sonora became an important proxy war in Villa's attempt to dislodge Carranza from power. Maytorena took the border city of Nogales on August 24th 1914, a key supply port for the Carrancista forces.

The Sonoran situation threatened to escalate into an all-out shooting war between the revolutionary factions. Carranzista General Alvaro Obregón stepped in at this juncture, hoping to save Mexico from renewed civil war. In a daring move, the Carranzista commander decided to come to Villa's headquarters in Chihuahua on August 25th 1914 "with a small escort of no more than 20 men."[96] It is unclear whether Carranza ordered Obregón to meet with Villa or if he came on his own accord. According to Villa, Carranza asked Obregón to see Villa and formally asked him for safe conduct in advance of the general's arrival in Chihuahua.[97] Villa respected courage and welcomed the general with full military honors, organized traditional fiestas, and guaranteed his safety. As a gesture of good will, and since Maytorena now held Nogales, Villa agreed publicly to order Maytorena to halt his offensive in Sonora.[98] This was not much of an accommodation. He wrote to the Sonoran governor: "Obregón and I will leave here in several days. Wait until we arrive. Avoid fighting in your advance on Nogales. We will have a conference on our arrival, and you can be sure that your rights will be granted and nobody will obstruct the work of your government."[99]

Observers hoped that after much haggling and positioning, the victorious rebel leaders would reach an accommodation that was the prerequisite for a pacified nation. Naturally, the U.S. government saw it as its vital interest to advance the peace talks and solve the ongoing destruction of life and property on the American side of the border. When Villa asked the U.S. government whether he and Obregón could travel through U.S. territory from El Paso to Nogales, the opportunity arose for President Wilson to broker talks between his government, Obregón, and Villa. He instructed Secretary of War Lindley M. Garrison and Hugh L. Scott, his Army Chief of Staff, to organize the meetings and ensure safe conduct for the two generals while on U.S. soil. The Wilson administration used Felix A. Sommerfeld as a

direct line to Villa in order to receive first-hand updates on the negotiations. The German agent had been in constant contact with the
U.S. Secretary of War Garrison for months. On August 26th 1914, the
day of the scheduled meeting in El Paso, Sommerfeld informed the
Secretary,

> Aug. 26. 1914
> Dear Sir:
> Referring to our last conversation I beg to
> inform you that I telegraphed to General Villa yester-
> day, asking him whether he had transmitted to Mr.
> Carranza his demands – I refer to the ones sent to
> Washington – In my opinion it is absolutely necessary
> for the establishment of government and peace in
> Mexico to end this uncertain situation and come to a
> definite understanding with Mr. Carranza. General Villa
> wired me today, that he would present his demands to
> Mr. Carranza as soon as he returned from Sonora.
> It seems that Villa has come to some kind of
> an understanding with Obregón in this matter and I
> therefore retain my optimistic opinion that everything
> can and will be arranged in a satisfactory and speedy
> manner.
>
> Thanking you for past favors
>
> I am
> Very respectfully yours,
>
> F. A. Sommerfeld.[100]

Given Sommerfeld's report on the progress of the meetings,
the conditions for a successful meeting between American authorities
and the revolutionaries had been set. Garrison thanked Sommerfeld
a few days later, "... am much obliged for the information contained
[in your letter of the 26th]."[101] The responsibility to receive Villa and
Obregón as they crossed from Mexico fell on General John J. Pershing.
Villa and Obregón arrived in Ciudad Juarez around noon after stopping

at Tierra Blanca where Villa had won a decisive battle against the federal army under José Inés Salazar only three years before. The two
generals walked the battlefield with Villa enthusiastically recounting
the details of his attacks. In a half-serious challenge, Villa competed
with Obregón in a shoot-out using glass bottles as targets.[102]

Álvaro Obregón, Pancho Villa, John J. Pershing.
Over Pershing's right shoulder second row is Lieutenant George S. Patton [103]

In the evening of August 26th, with great fanfare and cheers
from the citizenry of El Paso, the commander of Fort Bliss, General
John J. Pershing, welcomed the famous Mexican generals on the
international bridge between Ciudad Juarez and El Paso. Robert
Runyon's photograph of the meeting imprinted itself as one of the
most widely recognized images of the revolution. The picture shows
Villa, Obregón, and Pershing. Lieutenant George S. Patton, the future
World War II army commander, is the fourth person from the right.
"... As the procession, which included some twenty automobiles,
drove through the street, thousand [sic] who gathered to obtain a
view of Mexico's famous military leaders, cheered heartily and shouts
of 'Viva Villa' were frequent along the line of march. The Mexicans
responded by lifting their hats and bowing and smiling to the assembled throngs."[104]

Obregón endeared himself to the American hosts by commenting admiringly on the "appearance of the city, with its towering buildings and miles of handsome residences."[105] It was the first visit of the Mexican general to El Paso. Dressed "in the gold lace and regalia of the full dress uniform of the Mexican army," Obregón drew a sharp contrast to Villa and his staff who appeared in "mufti."[106] Pershing took the guests to the local country club, where a reception in their honor introduced Villa and Obregón to the elite members of El Paso's society, such as Zach Lamar Cobb, the customs collector of El Paso and local politician, and Tom Lea, the mayor of El Paso. The party then proceeded to Fort Bliss.

> General Pershing had arranged a reception in honor of the visitors and the officers of the local garrison were drawn up to receive them at General Pershing's headquarters. Military band was present and played the Mexican national anthem as Generals Villa and Obregón arrived. Refreshments were served to the visitors at General Pershing's home, and toasts to the United States and to Mexico, to the chief magistrates of the two countries, to the visiting military commanders and the [sic] General Pershing were drunk. The reception was entirely informal and for half an hour the officers remained conversing before they returned to the city. It had been planned to hold a view at the post, but as the party did not arrive until after dusk this feature was eliminated. At the close of the reception the military band played the 'Star Spangled Banner,' and with the American officers, Generals Villa and Obregón and their staffs stood at attention.[107]

After the reception the two Mexican generals "were the guest[s] of honor at a ball given by military and civil officials at the customs house."[108] After only a few hours of sleep by daybreak, Villa and Obregón, escorted by detachments of the twentieth infantry regiment, boarded a special train that took them to Nogales via Tucson, Arizona. The governors of Texas, Oscar B. Colquitt, of New Mexico, William G. McDonald, and of Arizona, George W. P. Hunt extended special permission for the traveling party. The U.S. Departments of War and State had also consented. Maytorena met the two men in Nogales, Sonora, on August 28th. The talks dragged on for two days. "...the leaders could find no solution, which was wholly acceptable to all parties. An initial agreement permitting Maytorena to continue as governor and giving him command of all constitutionalist forces in the state was annulled on the protest of Carranza partisans, and subsequently was modified to make Maytorena, in his capacity as military commander, subject to the national authority of Obregón... Maytorena refused to accept this solution... Villa and Obregón nevertheless signed the accord over the governor's abstention."[109] The conference did little to pacify Sonora. Maytorena continued to pursue his plan to consolidate military and political power in his state.

Obregón and Villa returned to El Paso on September 1st. They agreed that the only solution for peace in Sonora would be a removal of the warring commanders on both sides. Villa committed to supporting a new candidate for governor and withdrawing his support from Maytorena. Obregón agreed to elections in which Carranza would not be a presidential contender. Publicly, the two commanders showed unity and satisfaction with their mission. Secretary of State William Jennings Bryan sent a congratulatory telegram to Villa, thanking him for his efforts to maintain peace. Felix Sommerfeld underscored the impression that a satisfactory arrangement had been made between Maytorena and the Carrancistas. Sommerfeld answered Secretary Garrison's repeated requests for news on September 3rd in the form of a translated message from Pancho Villa: "In answer to your code message of 1st and 2nd I inform you that the relations of the Division of the North with Mr. Venustiano Carranza are satisfactory. We are procuring our demands on the basis you know."[110] It is curious to note that Sommerfeld transmitted Villa's answer without further comment. Clearly, the German agent was trotting Villa's public policy line. He had been pushing Villa for months to assert his position against the First Chief but tried his best to portray Villa as the responsible statesman and defender of democracy.

Sommerfeld acknowledged in his messages to Secretary Garrison that he had transmitted Villa's demands of Carranza beforehand to the U.S. government. These demands are listed in Pancho Villa's memoirs: Villa accepted Carranza's position as interim president. He demanded immediate appointment of a functional judiciary. Within a month of the appointment of judges, the governors of the Mexican states were to call elections for local governments. After new state governments were democratically elected, national elections would be held. Neither Carranza nor any of the revolutionary governors and commanders would be allowed as candidates.[111] This outline for a democratic transition of government in Mexico is a litany of items President Wilson would support enthusiastically. Carranza was sure to reject the demands since they precluded his candidacy. In that case, Villa would appear to the American government as a democrat and the only viable leader of the Mexican people. The plan to achieve U.S. diplomatic recognition, which Villa had hatched with Sommerfeld and Sherburne G. Hopkins in the spring of 1914, now could come to fruition.[112] The only danger for unraveling the relationship of Villa with the U.S. government was the border disturbances Maytorena was causing. As a result, it was very much in Sommerfeld's interest to foster an accommodation between the Mexican leaders, which ended the fighting close to the border and, at the same time, made Pancho Villa appear as the reasonable broker of peace and stability.

Secretary Bryan's telegram to Pancho Villa on September 1st bore witness to the favorable impression the State Department had of Villa. Lindley Garrison's attitude towards Villa is unknown; however, Carranza certainly had few friends among the American military brass. Hugh Lenox Scott commented in his memoirs on Carranza, "Carranza, finding Coahuila too hot to hold for him [in the spring of 1913], fled across Mexico to Hermosillo on the Pacific, where he occupied himself in dancing and dining…"[113] And, "This plan, of course, would leave him [Carranza] out in the cold, where he belonged."[114] General Tasker Bliss, commander of the army's Southern Department wrote to Hugh Lenox Scott on August 26th 1914, the day of Villa's visit to El Paso: "I never had any belief in the sincerity of Carranza. He would use the old rallying cry [land for the people] as long as it served his purpose to get into power, but once in power, I doubt if he will or can do any more than Madero did. His disposition not to carry out the promises made to the peons is shown in his efforts to thrust aside Villa after he has climbed into power on the latter's shoulders… his [Villa's] proposition to immediately do away with military government will make him popular in the United States… If a 'Conference of

Generals' should ... decide that a Constitutionalist General could be a candidate [for president], it seems to me that the chances would be decidedly in favor of Villa."[115]

Obregón returned to Mexico City, in the company of former Secretary of Education and Villa's foreign policy adviser Miguel Díaz Lombardo. Carranza rejected the proposals as expected. So did Maytorena. When the Sonoran governor realized that Villa had sold him out by agreeing to support General Cabral as governor, tempers flared. Villa retreated from his commitments to Obregón and sent a telegram in support of Maytorena's continued ambitions on September 3rd. "Do not heed my telegrams concerning the suspension of hostilities... since they have been sent under special circumstances."[116] Villa also sent Felipe Ángeles to confer with Maytorena around the same time. Ángeles assured the governor of Villa's support in the fight against Calles and Hill. As the Sonoran governor renewed his military campaign he quickly pushed the Carrancistas into a narrow corridor between the border towns of Nogales and Naco. By September 15th, the situation for the Carrancistas in Sonora seemed hopeless. Obregón decided to meet Villa a second time. He arrived in Chihuahua on September 16th. However, this time Villa bore no likeness to the hospitable and cooperative host of two weeks prior. The discussions between the two generals deteriorated into a fight. Villa accused Obregón of having broken his promise to withdraw General Hill's forces. Obregón argued that Maytorena and Villa had broken their word. An enraged Villa "... ordered a firing squad to stand by so that Obregón could be executed as soon as Villa gave the order to do so... Hearing of the planned execution, Raul Madero and Ángeles attempted to dissuade Villa. Ángeles went to Luz Corral [Villa's wife] who, with great difficulty, persuaded Villa that executing Obregón in his [Villa's] own home would brand him in the eyes of future generations as a man incapable of respecting the rules of hospitality."[117] Villa relented. Under the threat of execution, Villa forced Obregón to send an order to General Benjamin Hill to retreat to Casas Grandes, away from Maytorena's domain. Only then did he allow Obregón to return to Mexico City.

On the train Obregón recanted the order to his commander. The Villistas intercepted the countermanding order. Still in Villista territory, the train's engineer received instructions to stop and return to Chihuahua. This time, Villa was determined to execute Obregón.

Again his commanders and advisers convinced him to refrain. Finally, on September 21st, Obregón boarded a special train to Mexico City. However, he was not out of danger. Villa had made arrangements for the train to be stopped and Obregón executed. The plan failed. Several of Villa's commanders intervened and shuttled Obregón to safety. The Carrancista general reached Mexico City the next day having barely escaped Villa's deadly wrath. Villa, unable to eliminate the most important men of his inner circle, Raul Madero and Felipe Ángeles, forgave them for having helped Obregón. However, in the coming battles with Obregón, Villa would never waste an opportunity to remind his commanders that it was their fault Obregón still walked the face of the earth. On September 23rd, Villa declared war against Carranza. The most violent phase of the revolution had begun.[118]

Hearst press headlines on September 26th 1914 read: "Carranza Force Is Defeated."[119] The articles described the desperation of Benjamin Hill's forces retreating from the quick pursuit by Governor Maytorena's irregulars. The papers quoted an interview with Pancho Villa. In it, Villa raged against Carranza, recalled the meeting between him and General Obregón in late August, in which the Carrancista general supposedly refused to join forces with Villa to oust Carranza. Villa lamented that he spared General Obregón's life and let him return to Mexico City. It is unclear whether the interview ever happened, contained different facts, or had been transcribed accurately. However, the day before the publication of the interview, Villa directed Sommerfeld to "deny them [Villa's declarations against Carranza] categorically." Sommerfeld did so in a letter to Secretary of War Garrison:

> Sept. 27th 1914
> Dear Sir:
>
> I enclose herewith a clipping from one of the Hearst's papers with a supposed interview given by General Villa to the correspondent of the Hearst's papers, John W. Roberts.
> I wired to General Villa on September 25th, transcribing to him the contents of this supposed interview.

I have the honor to transmit to you the original telegram and translation, containing the answer of General Villa to my telegram, and beg you, to transmit same to his Excellency the President, as the supposed interview contains some references to the President.

Thanking you for this and past favor,

I am

Very respectfully yours,

[Felix A. Sommerfeld]

Translation [of Villa's telegram]

Noted contents of your telegram of today with reference declarations which Hearst's papers publish as made by me through John W. Roberts. I manifest to you that they are absolutely false and that you can deny them categorically. I am ordering already that said Roberts shall be expelled as obnoxious individual. Best regards.

The Commanding General,

Francisco Villa. [120]

While Villa probably gave the interview on the record and failed to recant it, it likely was Sommerfeld and Sherburne G. Hopkins who did not want to publicize this final break between the two revolutionary factions just yet.

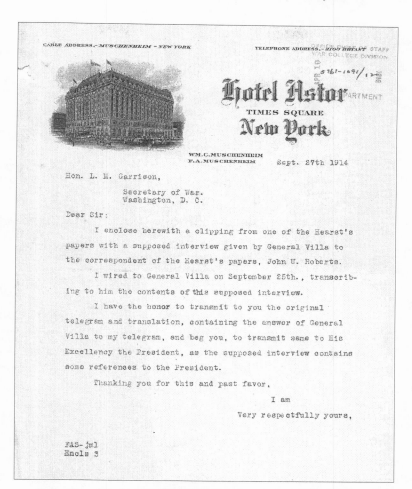

CABLE ADDRESS,-*MUSCHENHEIM - NEW YORK*

TELEPHONE ADDRESS.-*2100 BRYANT* STAFF
WAR COLLEGE DIVISION

APR 10

576/-/09/, /

Hotel Astor ARTMENT

TIMES SQUARE

New York

WM.C.MUSCHENHEIM
F.A.MUSCHENHEIM

Sept. 27th 1914

Hon. L. M. Garrison,

Secretary of War.
Washington, D. C.

Dear Sir:

I enclose herewith a clipping from one of the Hearst's papers with a supposed interview given by General Villa to the correspondent of the Hearst's papers, John W. Roberts.

I wired to General Villa on September 25th., transcribing to him the contents of this supposed interview.

I have the honor to transmit to you the original telegram and translation, containing the answer of General Villa to my telegram, and beg you, to transmit same to His Excellency the President, as the supposed interview contains some references to the President.

Thanking you for this and past favor,

I am

Very respectfully yours,

FAS-jml
Encls 3

Letter from F. A. Sommerfeld to Lindley M. Garrison, September 1914

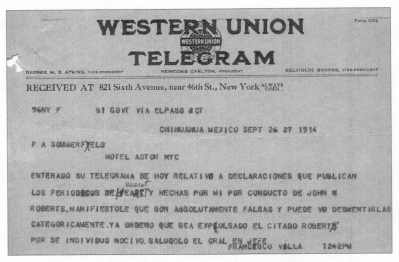

Telegram from Pancho Villa to F. A. Sommerfeld, September 1914 [121]

Maytorena's offensive threatened Villa's favorable relations with the Wilson administration. As the fighting further intensified along the Mexican-American border, stray bullets threatened the civilian population of Nogales, Arizona. U.S. cavalry units took positions along the American side of the border to prevent Mexican units from crossing the border and violating the neutrality of the United States. By the beginning of October, Maytorena had pinned down the Carrancistas under General Benjamin Hill in the town of Naco, Sonora. Heavy fighting on the Mexican side prompted the 10th U.S. Cavalry with enforcements from the 9th to take up positions on October 7. The 12th Infantry from Nogales, Arizona joined the cavalry units that had been dispatched from Fort Huachuca near Tucson and Fort Douglas. The commander of the Southern Department of the U.S. army at Fort Sam Houston, Brigadier General Tasker Howard Bliss, had overall command. The American units dug in and observed the fighting. Stray bullets – some were occasionally not so stray – pounded the American positions and American onlookers, some of whom came from as far as Bisbee to see the fighting. Naco, Arizona sustained heavy damages as a result of the continued shelling. "From their trenches and rifle pits, the men of the 10th and their comrades from the 9th Cavalry watched the fighting. It was a dangerous business; the Buffalo Soldier regiment [10th Cavalry] had eight men wounded while the Ninth 'had some killed and wounded.' They also lost a number of horses and mules from gunfire straying across the border."[122] Unlike the previous battles in Sonora, in which Maytorena consistently defeated the Constitutionalist opposition, Naco did not turn into a rout. During fierce combat, General Benjamin Hill dug in along the border and supplied his troops from the American side. "Three lines of formidable trenches and earthen breastworks interspaced about 200 yards apart were thrown up around the entire perimeter to the border. Barbed wire and whatever other obstacles could be found were erected to impede the expected attack... the town [of Naco, Sonora] was transformed into a virtual fortress..."[123]

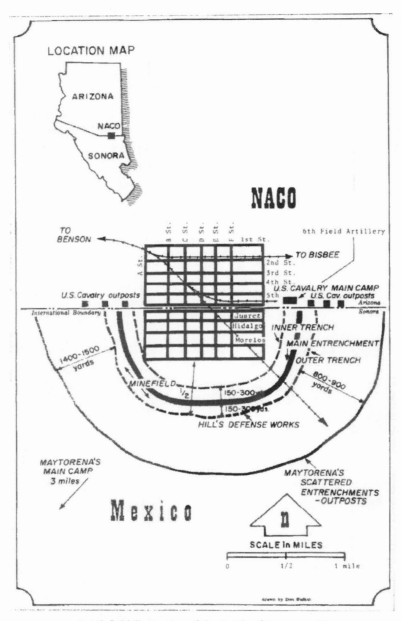

Battlefield illustration of the Battle of Naco, 1914 [124]

American customs officials had no means to stop the flow of arms and ammunition to the two warring factions. The Bureau of Investigations agents along the border recorded the influx of American munitions. "... 625,000 7 m/m ammunition ... was shipped ... by the Winchester Repeating Arms Co., on September 14th and 15th last... on the 30th of last month [September] Walker Bros/ Hancock Company of this city exported to Matamoros, Mexico through this port [San Antonio], 1,350,000 7 m/m cartridges... This ammunition was ordered for the Constitutionalists in Mexico and has been delivered to them."[125] Since the border officials in September and October 1914 did not distinguish between the Constitutionalist, Villista, and Maytorena factions, this shipment could have gone to any Mexican force. However, Carranza had closed the port of Tampico to Villa's supply chain in June. As a result, shipments for the Division of the North were routed through Bagdad, the port of Matamoros.[126] B.I. officials in the middle of November 1914 estimated that "some 50,000 rounds of ammunition was [sic] fired by both factions [Maytorena and Hill]" in a single day.[127] Maytorena's siege of Naco turned into the longest battle of the Mexican Revolution, lasting 119 days. Repeated attempts of the attackers to break through the defenses of the Carrancistas resulted in heavy casualties on both sides.

The American troops were under orders not to return fire. As the siege dragged on, the restraint of the U.S. army turned into admirable acts of self-discipline. Colonel William C. Brown of the 10th Cavalry confided in a letter to a friend in October of 1914,

> About 12:25 a.m., on the 17th [Maytorena] made the most determined attack yet made [sic] –]--- first from the west, then from the east and lastly from the south, the direction which would send the high shots into our camp and of which he had previously been warned. On the night of the 10th four shots hit the little R.R. station where I had my headquarters; on the night of the 16th-17th, 14 shots hit the same building and I should say that the shots (probably several hundred) dropped in our camp in about the same proportion. Fortunately nearly all men and animals had been moved out for safety but notwithstanding

this our casualty list was as follows: Four troopers wounded, one will probably die, and another lose his eye-sight [sic]. One horse and one mule killed one horse wounded besides at least two natives shot on the U.S. side of the line. It is a surprise here that the U.S. takes no notice of such an outrageous pro-ceeding. Does the U.S. Government propose to sit complacently by and allow such deliberate firing per-pendicular to the boundary that our soldiers are shot in their own camps? This after repeated warnings of the effect of such firing. If this be true I am having my eyes opened, and getting an entirely new idea of the protection afforded by the U.S. flag.[128]

Sommerfeld had his hands full to prevent further aggravation among the American forces on the border. In a diplomatic effort, the German agent steadfastly maintained to the American government that reconciliation in Mexico could still be accomplished. On October 1st, Carranza summoned a conference in Mexico City, ostensibly to create an agreement between the warring factions. However, the real purpose was a publicity stunt in which Carranza offered his resignation to the members of the convention. Heavily stacked in his favor, the participants rejected the motion unconditionally.

However, in the meantime, a sincere meeting of all the Mexican factions took shape in the city of Aguascalientes on October 10th 1914. Representatives of Villa and Obregón had agreed to meet on neutral ground, halfway between Carranza and Villa's domains to work on a plan for national unity. All factions participated except the Zapatistas. "...in all 57 generals and governors and 95 representatives of revolutionary leaders, all of them either colonels, lieutenant colonels, majors, captains, or lieutenants, participated. At first glance, it could be called an unrepresentative military gathering. No common soldier participated and no election of delegates took place."[129] Venustiano Carranza had publicly declared that he would not recognize Zapata's *Plan de Ayala* that mandated extensive land reform. The Zapatistas made the acceptance of their plan a precondition for participating. In a message Sommerfeld sent to General Scott to inform the U.S. president about Villa's disposition, the German agent wrote "...understanding [of Villa is] that Carranza would retire from office and ... want to discuss the personality [sic] of Carranza with view of his remaining in the presidency, which we [Villistas] will not accept..."[130] Three days later Sommerfeld telegraphed, "If we would not obtain the retirement of Carranza, we would go to war....."[131]

Initially, Villa was successful in curbing Obregón's control of the proceedings and displacing Carranza. Many of the First Chief's commanders had vowed to support the decisions of the convention. While he put pressure on his generals to submit to his command, the First Chief now feared that the troops protecting him in Mexico City would try to arrest him. On November 1st, Carranza fled to Puebla, holding out there until the American government turned the city of Veracruz over to him three weeks later. Carranza quickly shored up his sway over the revolution. The commander of the Division of the Northeast Gonzalez, and the commander of the Division of the Northwest Obregón, joined him and declared the results of the convention null and void. President Gutiérrez gave Carranza a deadline to fall in line behind the decisions of the Convention. After it passed, he announced that the First Chief was "in rebellion."[132]

General Obregón declared war on Pancho Villa on November 19th. He issued a statement, in which he called on all Mexicans to join him. "The perfidy of Villa, Ángeles, and Maytorena nullified the efforts of all honest men to establish permanent peace, following the triumph of the revolution. American gold helped to make their actions effective. All patriots must fight against the domination of Villa..."[133] The next day, he abandoned Mexico City, since it was too costly to defend. The Convention government appointed Villa as the commander of President Eulalio Gutiérrez' so-called conventionist forces. Zapata joined the forces of the new government, as well, as did Maytorena.[134] Zapatista troops entered Mexico City on November 24th. After fighting Díaz, Madero, Huerta, and now Carranza, the rebel chief from Morelos and his peasant army took charge of the ancient Aztec capital. Zapata himself arrived by train on November 26th. Humbled as the Visigoth King Alaric I upon sacking Rome, Zapata stayed in the Hotel Lázaro rather than the empty presidential palace. Zapata's soldiers, dressed in traditional garb, barefoot or with sandals, armed with everything from machetes and muskets to modern repeating rifles, drove the fear of God down the spines of the capital's elites. Despite the worst premonitions, Zapata kept his troops in perfect discipline. Looters faced summary justice; soldiers protected the diplomatic corps and government buildings.

During the convention in Aguascalientes, the situation along the Mexican-American border continued to escalate. On October 11th, Maytorena attempted to rout the Constitutionalists. However, the attempt turned into an international incident. Maytorena's Yaqui forces tried to outflank the enemy and crossed into U.S. territory by night. The Americans opened fire and captured several of the Mexicans. According to the *New York Times*, the commander of the 9th U.S. Cavalry "... with difficulty ... has been able to restrain his dusky troopers from crossing the border and driving both Carranza and Villa troops back towards Cananea... Those who crossed were promptly interned by Lieut. Drake's command of the Ninth Cavalry. This angered the Maytorena forces, and many shots fell on the American side during the battle which followed... more than 500 bullets fell on Main Street here. In the handling of the cannon by a German gunner, shrapnel burst and fell in the Arizona border town. One struck the American Custom House, another fell on a mercantile establishment, a third struck an occupied residence..."[135] The firefight across the border lasted the better part of the day, aggravated by the unscrupulous targeting of a German mercenary. Two Americans, one of them a civilian, were shot, bringing the casualty list to a total of five U.S. citizens.[136] Governor Hunt of Arizona threatened to call up the National Guard if Washington would not act decisively. On October 23rd, Maytorena backed off and resumed the siege, having lost hundreds of fighters. Hill re-supplied his troops from the American side of the border.[137]

However, the calm proved to be an illusion. The breakup of the Convention of Aguascalientes and Obregón's declaration of war against Villa intensified the struggle at the border. Maytorena, now a member of the Convention fighting the Carrancista "rebellion" pounded the defenses of General Hill. American Justice Department agents reported in Mid-November, "The faction defending Naco may be able to hold out indefinitely. They are well equipped with ammunition, machine guns, and some artillery. The attacking force under Maytorena are [sic] equally well supplied with munitions of war and men, but they are at a disadvantage in using their artillery because of the proximity of the enemy to the international border line."[138] The

American side of Naco turned into a virtual battlefield, terrorizing the citizens and provoking angry calls for military intervention by Governor Hunt and Senator Albert B. Fall. Hugh Lenox Scott, the American Army Chief of Staff, described the situation: "The Mexicans had done great damage to the town of Naco, having fired into transcontinental trains and killed or wounded fifty-four persons on our side of the line, and the people of Arizona were becoming very restless, asking for arms to defend themselves and talking about taking their defense in their own hands and invading Mexico."[139]

The real and perceived violation of U.S. sovereignty became a rallying cry for those in Washington who considered President Wilson's Mexico policies weak and ill conceived. This is, in fact, what Governor Maytorena intended. Since he could not take the Carrancista forces by military means, he now enlisted the American military to his ends. Purposely, Maytorena's snipers fired on the American side in order to draw the U.S. army into Mexican territory, all the while claiming to return fire from the encircled forces. With General Benjamin Hill encircled from the Mexican side, an American military action would undoubtedly have led to clashes with the Carrancistas, who had to either fight and lose against the Americans or flee straight into the Villistas' arms.

Benjamin Hill complained bitterly to the American government via Carranza's envoy in Washington, Rafael Zubarán Capmany, "I again call your attention to the convenience of energetically protesting to the American Government against the irritating discrimination of the military authorities at Naco, Ariz., whose good graces have been won by the Maytorenistas. Bullets from our enemy are constantly causing damage to the American town, but we are held responsible for it..."[140] Secretary of War Garrison had to admit to the press on December 7th, that the situation in Naco "baffled" him.[141] The siege and Maytorena's overt attempt to involve the U.S. military in destroying the Carrancistas turned into a huge embarrassment for the administration. Armed intervention was not an option to the Wilson Administration. The U.S. government had just abandoned the port city of Veracruz on November 23rd after seven months of occupation. Mexico's political landscape was in shambles. American forces retreated from Veracruz without any tangible results that justified blood and treasure spent there. Now, the acute border troubles in Arizona made the Wilson administration look incredibly weak and disorganized to the American public. War with Mexico seemed virtually assured, should the situation deteriorate further, for example, through another cross-border incursion.

General Tasker H. Bliss inspected the situation in Naco on December 11th. According to the *New York Times*, Mexican rebels took potshots at the American general. "... Two bullets fired from the Mexican side of the boundary passed perilously near the General and his staff as he was examining a bomb-proof [shelter] near the immigration station, about 100 feet north of the international line. Soldiers guarding the immigration station are protected by three bomb proofs and by a line of loaded coal cars drawn before the American town and the border, but a break in the line of coal cars had been left to permit access to the border. Gen. Bliss was near this break when the bullets whistled."[142] Whether Mexican snipers targeted General Bliss on purpose or whether the incident was accidental, the Wilson administration's decision to dispatch a larger military force was affirmed. The next day, the U.S. military moved heavy artillery from Fort Bliss, Texas into Naco.[143]

The entire 6th Brigade with 4,750 soldiers headed from Galveston, Texas to Naco on December 15th, bringing the total American troop strength there to 6,215 men.[144] The American army had assembled a full invasion force, larger and with more firepower than the troops dispatched to Veracruz in April, complete with cavalry, infantry, and heavy artillery. Following the blessing of the War Department, General Bliss issued an ultimatum on December 16th: "If for any reason a single shot falls on American soil after this ultimatum has reached you and has been translated, I will be forced to use extreme measures to end this useless danger to innocent lives in a neutral and well-intentioned country."[145] Simultaneously, Secretary of War Lindley Garrison ordered the Army Chief of Staff General Hugh Scott to Naco in person to find a solution. All options were on the table. According to Scott's memoirs, he had virtually begged the Secretary of War to go. "I can't stand this anymore! If Mr. Bryan won't do anything I'll go down there and drive those Mexicans away myself!"[146] The order finally came from the president himself. Scott arrived during the evening of December 20th 1914.[147] Enforcing the negotiation team were two heavy hitters: Felix Sommerfeld had arrived at the border from New York and Sherburne G. Hopkins came from Washington.[148] George Carothers observed the negotiations from El Paso for the State Department.[149]

The Army Chief of Staff did not lose much time. He submitted a settlement agreement to the two opposing forces. The port of Naco would remain closed while the contending forces would withdraw from the border, Maytorena to Nogales and Calles to Agua Prieta. No fighting near the border would be permitted to prevent "endangering the friendly relations of the United States."[150] The negotiations began immediately. Scott camped in Osborne, Arizona at the headquarters of the 6th Brigade. Sherburne Hopkins shuttled between the Carrancista headquarters in Naco and General Scott. He headed the negotiations with General Hill and Colonel Calles for the Army Chief of Staff. Carranza's secret service chief and personal representative, Roberto V. Pesquiera, stood by in El Paso where he negotiated with Sommerfeld. Sommerfeld represented Pancho Villa, who was tied up consolidating his control over Mexico City. Early results sounded very promising. Calles and Hill seemed willing to sign on the dotted line. However, Maytorena refused, on the grounds that if he retreated, Calles' forces would get away. He firmly believed that the battle of Naco was his to finish.

Torrential rainstorms set the town of Naco and, especially, the flats between the Arizona and Sonora towns under water on December 21st. The whole negotiation team, Hopkins, Sommerfeld, Scott, and Pesquiera had descended on the tiny Hotel Naco on the American side.[151] Both Calles and Hill stood by on the Mexican side of town to meet with General Scott. Hopkins reported to Scott, "was in Naco, Sonora, and had long talk with Generals Hill and Calles along the lines you told me. Left them both in a happy frame of mind and Hill will be very guarded in his conversation, especially with newspaper men..."[152] Sommerfeld made arrangements for General Scott to cross the border and meet with General Hill and Colonel Calles to have them approve the proposed accord. However, the Department of War forbade Scott to cross into Mexico. Instead of going himself, he dispatched Sommerfeld.[153] Maytorena was to come to Scott's camp at Osborne, Arizona in the afternoon and also sign the agreements. However, Maytorena used the effects of the rainstorms to his advantage. He claimed to Sherburne Hopkins that his health would not permit riding or walking across the border and his car could not maneuver through the mud.[154]

Sommerfeld took charge and asked General Tasker Bliss to provide an ambulance that could bring the Sonoran governor to General Scott's camp, but to no avail.[155] The governor refused to cross the border. "Owing to mud here it was impossible for me to leave for the line by auto or by horse... I regret very much that I have put you to any inconvenience in this matter... Another condition which must be taken into consideration is the fact that the constitution of Sonora does not permit of my crossing the line, which would necessitate our holding the conference in the open which would be most disagreeable in this weather."[156] On the 23rd, Scott finally met Calles and Hill on the U.S.-Mexican line. They signed the agreement with the stipulation that Maytorena would lend his signature.[157] Nonetheless, Maytorena avoided meeting with Scott. A frustrated Scott telegraphed to the War Department on December 23rd, "Interview arranged for tomorrow morning eleven o'clock... Will wire details after final interview."[158] The "final interview" remained elusive. On Christmas Eve, Maytorena again cited the weather as a reason to cancel his appointment with General Scott.[159] Instead, the Sonoran governor attempted to create a fait accompli and attacked the besieged Carrancistas. Again, bullets rained down on the American side, making a mockery of General Scott's negotiation efforts. Finally, in the afternoon of Christmas Eve, both Sommerfeld and Scott met with Maytorena in Osborne.[160] Reportedly, the meetings were heated. Still, Maytorena did not budge. "... Our talk was most friendly but he refused to sign agreement giving as his sole reason that he had not the necessary power to conclude such an agreement but offered to take it up by telegraph with his government at Mexico... Maytorena says he will carry it out [the agreement] if he gets the necessary orders from President Gutierrez... "[161]

Felix Sommerfeld proposed the only viable solution to the problem. Pancho Villa had to put pressure on Maytorena. The German left for El Paso to arrange meetings with Villa. Scott reported on Christmas Day, "Shots from both sides still fall in Naco, Arizona, and American camp."[162] On December 26th, Maytorena made good on a promise to stop the bombardment and move his forces away from the border.[163] General Scott reported to the Secretary of War "... I state for your information that Sommerfeld wires me noon today that proposition has been accepted in City Mexico. Period. Maytorena has withdrawn his forces from trenches heretofore occupied and burned his shelters and is said to have gone eight kilometers [approximately five miles] south."[164] Governor Maytorena agreed to confer with Villa.[165] Sommerfeld awaited the arrival of Villa, scheduled for the 27th of December. However, the German agent was dealt a difficult hand. Just as the German agent negotiated for Villa's support, the actions of American consul Leon L. Canova in Mexico City threatened to derail the negotiations.

A sensitive diplomatic situation had developed in the Mexican capital, which greatly affected Pancho Villa's productive relationship with the United States and the Department of State in particular. The main cause of consternation was Colonel Eduardo Iturbide, a far rela- tion of the first Mexican emperor. He had been police chief of Mexico City, as well as governor of the Federal District. After Huerta chose to go into exile in July 1914, Iturbide kept order in the capital. He enjoyed widespread admiration among the foreign colony. A very wealthy socialite and accredited "nobleman," Iturbide was handsome, charm- ing, a member of all the right clubs, and a successful polo player. The American government especially appreciated Iturbide's courage to stay behind and wait for the forces of Obregón to take control of the capital. American officials and the large colony of foreign businessmen shuddered at the thought of Zapata's "wild hordes" ransacking the city and murdering foreigners for entertainment.[166] Iturbide kept his commitment. The capital remained calm even after interim president Francisco S. Carvajal chose to evade the risk of a confrontation with the Carrancistas and fled. For Iturbide to keep order included, among other things, that he ordered police and federal army units to the out- skirts of Mexico City to check the advance of the encroaching Zapatis- tas. According to press reports, fifty Zapatistas died in the clashes.[167] When Álvaro Obregón finally entered the capital in the middle of August, the American colony demanded that Iturbide remain unmo- lested. Under pressure from the American embassy, Obregón had to guarantee the police chief's security. A week later, Carranza seconded the decision, deferring a "trial" of Iturbide for serving under Huerta and killing Constitutionalist soldiers to a later, unspecified date.

However, all that changed in November, the moment Obregón left the city and allowed the Zapatistas to take over. The colonel's fate threatened to parallel that of his famous ancestor, Emperor Itur- bide of Mexico: Execution. Fearing for his life, he went underground, protected by the American diplomats Silliman and Canova. He hid in the residence of H. Cunard Cummins, the British charge d'affairs.[168] As the new government under Eulalio Gutiérrez settled in, both the Villa and Zapata factions began rounding up former federals, members of the Huerta government, supporters of the Carranza government, and a whole host of people noted on wanted lists as "enemies of the state."[169] According to American reports, 155 men had been executed in the week after Christmas alone.[170] Without question, Iturbide featured prominently on Zapata's blacklist. President Gutiérrez did not support the wonton acts of violence Villa and Zapata's henchmen were committing. However, he had little sway over the likes of Villa's notorious executor, Rodolfo Fierro, settling old debts. "Representations were made to the authorities in Mexico City by both the American and British government, asking that he [Iturbide] be given passports to leave the country. These were granted by provisional president Gutiérrez and immediately resulted in a vigorous protest from Gen. Palafox, the Zapata leader in Mexico City."[171]

American special envoy Leon L. Canova with the help of American consul John R. Silliman convinced Mexican President Gutiérrez on December 21st to issue a safe conduct pass for Iturbide.[172] Both diplomats acted on orders of the State Department. In the previous week, on December 13th, Secretary of State Bryan had instructed Silliman: "Do everything in your power to save Iturbide. He acted for Carvajal [sic] and turned the city over to the Constitutionalists thus saving much loss of life as well as preventing disorder. It would be most unfortunate if he were dealt with harshly."[173] Accordingly, Silliman created a passport for "a citizen of Mexico sojourning in the United States."[174] With Zapata hot on Iturbide's heals, Silliman and Canova decided to smuggle him out.

Canova had scheduled a trip back to Texas in order to be home for Christmas. He decided to hide Iturbide in his special railcar, in which he enjoyed diplomatic immunity. None other than Pancho Villa himself saw Canova, and even briefly chatted with him, at the train station in Mexico City on December 22nd.[175] It is unclear why Villa was at the station. Most likely, he arrived from a trip. Severe fighting had erupted in Guadalajara, Veracruz, Saltillo, and the area around Tampico. This was a very busy time for Villa, the de facto master over much of Mexico. The rebel leader who had entered Mexico with a handful of men less than two years earlier now had reached the zenith of his military and political power. After the train left, Villa's secret service reported to him that Iturbide had been observed with Canova and that he had disappeared.

Villa put together what had occurred and, after throwing one of his well-known fits, issued a call for Iturbide's arrest. Cables went out to garrisons all along the rail line to stop Canova and search his compartment. The situation grew tense. Villa had ransacked a British consulate to get Luis Terrazas Jr. three years earlier. Certainly, he was capable of extracting Iturbide from Canova's railcar. In fact, he vowed to get Canova and Iturbide himself if his commanders would not dare to. Villa's secret service agents boarded the train in Aguascalientes. Canova refused to allow a search and managed to fend off the Villistas. A few hours later, the train stopped again, this time in Zacatecas. The next day at Torreón, Canova intimidated a whole company of troops and demanded to complain directly to Pancho Villa. Not knowing what to do the officer in command permitted the train to continue.[176] In Chihuahua City, the Villistas evacuated the whole train, claiming a defective car. A search party finally entered the compartment when Canova exited his railcar. Iturbide was gone! He had exited the train just south of Aguascalientes hours before the first attempt to search the compartment, and was making his way up to the American border on foot. Canova had so misled Iturbide's pursuers by refusing a search, that they lost his trail. As the train with the American consul arrived in El Paso on Christmas day 1914, Iturbide relied on his skills and sheer luck to make it across the border to safety.[177] "I rode on that train... just one day for I realized that the secret service men were trailing me and that an order for my arrest would come at any minute. I wrote my will and gave it to Mr. Canova and slipped off the train just south of Aguascalientes. I walked around aimlessly for sixty miles and finally got a horse on a ranch. For fifteen days I rode, disguised as a rancher and made my way to the American border, eluding troops and police by traveling mostly at night and sleeping by day."[178]

Villa was furious. He declared Canova a persona-non-grata. The new president, Eulalio Gutiérrez, had locked horns with both Villa and Zapata over the widespread persecution and execution of public and personal enemies. This episode brought the tensions to a boil. Villa accused Gutiérrez of corruption and treachery; Gutiérrez leveled charges of insubordination on the northern general. The split between Gutiérrez and his two main rebel leaders was by no means a surprise. However, the Iturbide affair certainly added fuel to the fire. The embattled Mexican president sent his wife to safety on the 9th of January, before he evacuated the capital for San Luis Potosi. Canova's expulsion from Villa's territory prompted Secretary of State Bryan to reinstate George C. Carothers as the personal envoy to Villa.[179] Carothers had resigned in early December as a result of disagreements over policy with the State Department. Consistent rumors of corruption, coming from State Department sources, that have never been proven or litigated, implanted themselves in the historical portrait of the special envoy.[180] Carothers's career in the State Department ended in 1916. Undoubtedly, Villa's already shaky relationship with William Jennings Bryan also deteriorated as a result of this episode. Rather than ruining Canova's diplomatic career, Villa's refusal to let him come back to Mexico got the native Floridian a huge promotion: Secretary Bryan decided to appoint Canova to head the Latin American desk of the State Department. The decision would have tragic consequences for both Mexico and the United States.

Nonetheless, Sommerfeld succeeded in getting Villa to push for a conclusion of the border conflict on December 27th, at the height of Villa's outrage over the Canova affair. Acting Secretary of War, Henry S. Breckinridge, notified General Scott "Number three thirty eight dash a the secy of state has just informed me by telephone that Villa's Confidential agent [Enrique Llorente] here [Washington D.C.] has informed him that Villa has approved the agreement set forth in your number three sixty nine dash a."[181] Scott replied, "… Sommerfeld goes tomorrow to Maytorena's camp to secure formal compliance with Villa's order to accept agreement period. Maytorena's other advisers are opposing signature period… "[182] The problem with Villa's agreement to General Scott's proposal was that while he agreed to the terms, he did not instruct Maytorena to sign. Scott sent George C. Carothers, freshly reinstated as an envoy to Villa, to try his magic.[183] The rebel commander played hard to get. Sommerfeld returned from El Paso on New Year's Eve to join General Scott in Osborne. The Army Chief of Staff reported to the Secretary of War, "… Sommerfeld returned from his voluntary and unofficial mission as Villa's agent … to secure Villa's order to sign period."[184] Suddenly, pandemonium erupted in the middle of the night on the Mexican side of the border. "...rifles, bombs, and cannon were all employed."[185] The American forces expected another incursion of Maytorena troops and started firing across the border. It became apparent the next morning that the Mexican soldiers had celebrated the arrival of a new year with volleys of shots into the night sky in lieu of fireworks.[186] Sommerfeld impressed on Villa that refusing to conclude an agreement would endanger the "friendship of General Scott" apart from the danger of further escalation.[187] In a telegram to Villa, which was copied to the Secretaries of War and State and landed on the desk of Woodrow Wilson, Sommerfeld related to Villa at 10:00 am on December 31st, "...it is necessary that a settlement is concluded immediately since General Scott told me yesterday that he would wait until this afternoon and, in case he would not receive an answer from you that you would sign the settlement, he would notify Washington that we do not want to conclude a settlement."[188]

Villa as Commander-in-Chief of the Convention government not only rejected the ultimatum but also, to the alarm of President Wilson and his cabinet, proceeded to give General Scott a taste of old-fashioned Mexican machismo. He answered Sommerfeld: "I have mobilized eight thousand cavalrymen and they left yesterday under the command of General Cabral who will be in Casas Grandes within two days and they will proceed to Naco immediately period... if he [Scott] will permit us the time of eight hours Naco will be taken and the situation will be concluded... the assault will be rapid, uniform and effective period. Please cause General Scott to know this and ask him to have patience for four days..."[189] While Villa's chest thumping might appear just to be that, the situation could not have grown tenser. Villa threatened war! Moving eight thousand troops to northern Sonora, which was almost completely in the hands of his forces, clearly aimed at the American army assembled on the other side of the line. The combined forces of Maytorena and Villa, numbering approximately 9,500, would trump the assembled American army units.

Scott took Villa's threat at face value. He cabled the Secretary of War for permission to "...stop movement of Villa's troops in this direction before leaving the railroad or failing this that all Americans be brought out of Mexico and General Bliss be instructed to protect the town of Naco by repelling the attack by force of arms. General

Bliss desires that he receive his instructions in time to bring field hospital from San Antonio and make other necessary dispositions."[190] Villa assembled two full cavalry brigades to assault the border town of Naco while between six and seven thousand American troops readied themselves for a military expedition into Mexico. Acting Secretary of War Breckenridge approved the field hospital to be moved in place on January 2nd 1915. Carranza added fuel to the fire when he issued a statement warning the American government of an invasion. "Any use of whatever force... would have to be considered by this Government as an act of hostility... The [American] Department of State does not appreciate to the fullest extent the seriousness which the use of force ... would entail."[191] None other than the President of the United States stepped on the brakes at this point and rebuked his Army Chief of Staff. Through the acting Secretary of War, Breckenridge, he ordered Scott to step away from the brink and to arrange a meeting with Pancho Villa at the Mexican general's convenience: "The President was struck with the statement in Summerfeld's [sic] telegram to Villa that quote it is necessary to arrange the matter immediately because General Scott told me yesterday he would wait until this afternoon... I think the President felt that your alleged mention of a time-limit for an answer... might be fraught with serious possibilities and he does not desire that at present you insist upon any day certain for a final answer."[192]

The Secretary of State cabled to President Gutiérrez most likely on the orders of President Wilson that same day. He warned against the consequences of a movement of Villa's troops to the border. Rather, Gutiérrez should use his good offices to push his commander to meet with General Scott. Sommerfeld received a copy of the message with the instructions from Hugh Scott to "... communicate the foregoing [the U.S. will defend the life and property of its citizens by force of arms] to General Villa and tell him that the Secretary of War directs me to endeavor to arrange through you [Sommerfeld] a meeting between myself and him [Villa] as soon as possible in El Paso... "[193]

Villa was scheduled to arrive in Ciudad Juarez across from El Paso on January 6th 1915. Finally, on January 8th, he did and promptly came to El Paso to sit down with General Scott and his aide de camp, Lieutenant Colonel Robert E. Lee Mitchie. They "met in a little back room of the Immigration Detention Station at the American end of the international bridge... "[194] Felix Sommerfeld and Rodolfo Fierro accompanied the Mexican general. The two generals exchanged pleasantries, and after talking for an hour, agreed on a follow-up meeting in Ciudad Juarez the next day. Villa commented to the waiting press corps that he was "proud of the friendship with Gen. Scott, and that he would do anything the General wished that was reasonable."[195]

Scott crossed the border on January 9th with the explicit permission of President Wilson, and saw Villa in Juarez.[196] Villa quickly relented on the issue of Villista forces moving to the border and attacking the Carrancistas. However, letting the Carrancistas evacuate Naco was a different issue. "Villa did not want to give the order to Maytorena to sign and we locked horns there, like two bull elk, for two hours swaying now this way, now that, until his neck at last got tired and he agreed to make Maytorena sign."[197] Scott and Villa shook hands in front of the cameras during a small ceremony in front of the government offices in Ciudad Juarez.

From left Lieutenant Colonel Robert E. Lee Mitchie,
General Hugh Lenox Scott, General Francisco "Pancho" Villa.[198]

Sommerfeld, who had the thankless task of shuttling between Villa and Maytorena, received the long awaited signature from the Sonoran strongman on January 9th.[199] General Hill had already left Naco for Galveston, Texas the previous day by train to join up with Carrancista forces fighting in Veracruz. The situation was diffused. Villa had scored a huge diplomatic success. Not only had he positioned himself again as the statesman who would broker a reasonable solution to an international problem, but he also showed President Gutiérrez the full might of his military prowess that prompted even the president of the United States to ask for help. The Americans' fear of Villa coming to the border was well founded. After the battle for Guadalajara, Villa was moving troops to shore up the border between Sonora and Arizona, a vital supply line for his army. Carrancista General Ramon Iturbe had retaken the port city of Guaymas on December 3rd 1914, and headed up the west coast of Sonora towards Nogales.[200]

General Scott and the entire American government, including the president himself, greatly appreciated the efforts of Felix Sommerfeld. Scott noted in his memoirs, "The influence of Felix Summerfield [sic], a former soldier of the German Army, was exerted often with success... I owe him gratitude for services to our Government in Mexico when I was not allowed to cross the border, which he freely and faithfully rendered without thought of compensation, as a duty to our Government and in friendliness to me."[201] Sommerfeld reinforced Scott's feelings in a flattering Christmas note a year later on December 23rd 1915. He wrote to the Army Chief of Staff:

> My dear General:
>
> About a year ago or better just a year ago (Dec. 24) we were trying to keep warm under an army tent somewhere near Osborne, Arizona, making strenuous efforts to convince Governor Maytorena that it was necessary for him to sign a peace agreement. In those trying days I learned to admire your wonderful patience, tact and ability to deal with men and your determination to stand for the "square deal" idea. I deem it my greatest pleasure and honor to have been with you at that time and to have been able to be of some assistance to you and the cause you represented. You spent Xmas eve under a water coated tent

somewhere in an army camp in Arizona and I had to listen to the wonderful music of the shrieking wheels of
a railroad coach between Naco and El Paso. But I know
that you did not mind those inconveniences [,] neither
did I. We were on a mission to preserve peace and we
accomplished something worthwhile...

I hope that this Christmas will be a very pleas-
ant and merry one for you, Mrs. Scott and your family.

> With kindest regards,
> I beg to remain
> Most sincerely and gratefully
>
> Yours,
> Felix A. Sommerfeld[202]

In the course of a year, Sommerfeld had witnessed the United
States on the brink of war three times. The first episode resulted from
the murder of William S. Benton. Sommerfeld and Hopkins carefully
maneuvered their protégé, Villa, away from the brink and, conse-
quently, soured the relations of the U.S. with Carranza.[203] The arms
delivery aboard the German steamer SS Ypiranga in April precipitated
a full-scale U.S. invasion of the port city of Veracruz. Again, Sommerfeld worked with the American government to diffuse the tension.
Pancho Villa, in fact, forced Venustiano Carranza to mute his bellig-
erency on the advice of Sommerfeld and Hopkins.[204] Now, for a third
time in one year, the German agent not only witnessed, but also took
an active part in diffusing tensions along the Mexican-American border. This incident brought the U.S. and Mexico closer to the brink
than either the Benton affair or Veracruz had. This time, there was no
usurper president in the person of Victoriano Huerta serving as a common enemy to align U.S. and Constitutionalist foreign policy. An intervention at Naco with six to seven thousand American troops could
have galvanized the splintered forces of the revolution into an all-out
war. Villa alone commanded an estimated forty thousand men. The
results of a military showdown can hardly be fathomed. Sommerfeld
saw firsthand when the threshold for the American government to
act with force would be crossed.

Despite President Wilson's reluctance to commit troops to the Mexican theater, partly because of the lack of a Mexican political structure, and partly because the U.S. army was ill-prepared for a mission that would require a majority of the available regular forces, the United States could easily have been pushed into a war against Mexico. An armed incursion of Mexican raiders and the killing of American civilians would have driven the interventionists in Washington to win the upper hand. Sommerfeld could have arranged such an outcome at Naco. This knowledge would become the basis for Sommerfeld's future actions in 1915 and 1916 to create just such a war. The border remained a powder keg that Sommerfeld and other German agents lit just over a year later.

CHAPTER 5: JUNTA "X"

SOMMERFELD HAD HELPED BROKER A cease-fire, thus averting a renewed American military intervention in Naco. President Wilson turned Veracruz over to Venustiano Carranza in November 1914 after a seven-month occupation. However, the Mexican border was hardly quiet. Lawlessness, banditry, shifting battle lines, and arms smuggling kept U.S. - Mexican relations at a tense simmer. German war planners kept a close watch on the southern border of the U.S. German activities in the United States took on a distinctly more violent character in 1915, as Mexico presented both a military target and a distinct opportunity to create troubles for the United States. The military target was the oil-producing region around Tampico. Most of the wells belonged to British and U.S. interests and, to a large degree, fueled the sizeable British fleet in Atlantic waters. The Admiralty also ordered the Secret War Council to disrupt the oil production there upon getting the authorization to commence sabotage against U.S. munitions production.

The newly appointed German envoy to Mexico, Heinrich von Eckardt, had supported the viewpoint of German businessman Eugen Motz in early January 1915, that "the Tampico oil fields could and actually should be almost completely in German hands... "[205] The German envoy seemed to endorse a more peaceful approach to keeping Mexican oil from the British fleet, namely financing a clandestine takeover by German capital, and interrupting supplies through strikes.[206] However, war planners in Berlin, who probably realized that there was no chance of acquiring the Mexican oil wells in a short period of time, ordered them dynamited instead. German records indicate that von Eckardt met "middlemen" who represented attachés von Papen and Boy-Ed in Galveston on February 22nd and in New Orleans on February 24th

1915, to finalize the sabotage plans against Tampico.[207] However, the German Admiralty instructed Captain Boy-Ed to call off the action on March 11th in a nebulous communication that read: "Significant military damage to England through closing of Mexican oil resources not possible. Thus no money for such action available."[208] Apparently, the German Admiralty was expecting the Standard Oil Company, which had strong financial ties to the Mexican Petroleum Company, "to show itself favorable" to the German Government.[209] The Admiralty's expectations seemed to upset Captain von Papen's simultaneous arrangements to have an agent named von Petersdorf "to create the greatest possible damage through extensive sabotage of tanks and pipelines."[210] Added von Papen, "given the current situation in Mexico, I am expecting large successes from relatively little resources."[211] Nevertheless, no noteworthy acts of sabotage occurred in Tampico during 1915-1916, perhaps due to Standard Oil's intentions, or perhaps due to miscalculation by the German Admiralty.

While the German war planners foundered with sending and then countermanding orders to sabotage oil production in Mexico, a relatively unknown American businessman named Andrew Meloy approached the German government with an outlandish scheme. The Irish-American business promoter boarded a ship in New York with his wife Alice on January 16th 1915 and sailed to Germany. He stayed in Berlin in the beginning of February and travelled around Europe until the middle of March.[212]

Meloy met with representatives of the Deutsche Bank in Berlin. Through his involvement with the Mexican Railways which were financed, in part, through this bank, Meloy had contacts high up, possibly even to its director, Franz Rintelen's father. According to a report the American ambassador to England prepared for the Secretary of State illuminating Meloy's subsequent trip to Germany in August, "Meloy's repeated statements ... are to the effect that his business in Berlin is to obtain financial support of the Deutsche Bank for a coalition of Mexican leaders... "[213] Immediately following the meetings in Berlin, Meloy traveled to Geneva and Paris where he conducted further negotiations between him and the former Secretary of War under President Huerta Manuel Mondragón.[214] "I decided then to make the trip to Berlin, confer with the Deutsches [sic] Bank and then come to Paris and arrange with Mondragón whatever was feasible."[215] Obviously, the information he received for his scheme in Berlin had been positive enough to warrant further negotiations with Mexican exiles.

Mondragón, who was exiled living in Spain, was working on a scheme to raise an army against both Venustiano Carranza and Pancho Villa to take back control of Mexico. He had been in contact with his old comrades, Victoriano Huerta, also exiled in Spain, as well as exiled General Aureliano Blanquet, and Felix Díaz for that purpose. These four had overthrown the democratically elected government of Mexico in the spring of 1913. The putschists had murdered the Mexican president, Francisco Madero, and his vice-president, José Maria Pino Suarez, in the process. As the usurper-president Huerta sought to consolidate his dictatorship, a powerful coalition of Mexican revolutionaries sprung up under the leadership of Venustiano Carranza and with the financial support of important U.S. interests. Following a furious and violent war that lasted fifteen months and caused the United States to occupy the harbor city of Veracruz, Huerta's government had capitulated in July 1914. The First World War was just about to begin. Despite the success of the revolutionaries, Mexico did not stabilize. Power struggles among the revolutionary leaders, most notably Francisco *Pancho* Villa, Emiliano Zapata, and Carranza continued to tear Mexico apart. The foreign community stood by helplessly as the revolution destroyed whatever remained of the sizeable foreign investments in mining, banking, ranching, and commerce.

Andrew Meloy was one of these distraught American investors. He owned rail lines in the mining areas of Northern Mexico with a group of financiers.[216] "All are familiar with the terrible ruin which has swept over Mexico during the past four years. No bank, no railroad, no property of any kind has escaped the burden of this ruin... My own personal affairs in common with the personal affairs of the Stallforths and other railways and banks have been compelled to endure the burden of this progressive ruin. My own personal investment in Mexico is more than $350,000 [7.3 million in today's value]. The total investment of my immediate friends through my office is more than $1,700,000 [$35.7 million in today's value]..."[217] If Meloy could convince banks and businesses such as the powerful railroad companies that he had a realistic plan to pacify Mexico, he believed he could raise the money needed for such an endeavor.

Barcelona, Paris, Havana, New Orleans, San Antonio, and New York became centers of intrigue during this time, with exiled members of the Mexican political elite plotting to enter the fray. Thousands of refugees, displaced civilians, former federal soldiers, and especially Orozquistas (who Pancho Villa executed mercilessly if captured) led lives of destitution in every major American border city. The Mexican general, Felipe Ángeles, who had served in the federal army under Presidents Porfirio Díaz and Madero, then as Secretary of War under Carranza, and finally as the strategic genius behind Pancho Villa's most successful military campaigns, moved to Boston, Massachusetts after a falling-out with Villa in May 1915. He remained in close touch with Mexican expatriates in New York City. Newspapers in the summer of 1914 had briefly traded his name as a potential candidate for the Mexican presidency. Also in New York was Eduardo Iturbide, a Polo-playing socialite who had bathed in the gratitude of the American colony in Mexico City, which he had protected from revolutionary furor in 1914. One of his best friends was Leon Canova who had smuggled him out of Mexico and who, meanwhile, had become the head of the Latin American desk in the State Department. Although Iturbide had little or no real influence in Mexican politics, his sway with the State Department helped keep his name in the mix of potential saviors for Mexico. Felix Díaz, the nephew of the former President of Mexico, cooled his heels in Havana but off and on came to New York to try to raise money for military expeditions against Carranza.[218] Most of the powerful Madero family lived in New York and San Antonio: The deposed president's father, the former Secretary of Finance, the former Secretary of Interior, two of Francisco Madero's uncles, as well as his widow. They kept fairly low-key because of the large investments that they hoped to recover in Mexico. However, not much went on with respect to Mexican conspiracies that the Maderos did not know about.

Whoever wished to listen to these expats would hear of grandiose plans to retake power in Mexico and finally create order. The only thing that seemed to be perpetually missing was money. Neither the American, nor French, nor British governments showed much willingness in the spring of 1915 to support ever-new revolutions and counter-revolutions. The members of Huerta's dictatorship, in particular, stood no chance of receiving American support since President Wilson had supported the powerful opposition that defeated the usurper. President Wilson was holding out for an eventual Mexican unity government that could count on popular support. The choice clearly lay between Villa and Carranza, not Huerta, Díaz, or Mondragon. Andrew Meloy had made powerful connections, not only with these exiled Mexican factions spoiling for a fight, but also with the Carranza representatives in the U.S., through his longtime friend, lawyer, and lobbyist, Charles A. Douglas, and Villa's envoy in the U.S., Felix A. Sommerfeld. Charles Douglas, in turn, was connected closely to the Counselor of the U.S. State Department, Robert Lansing. Lansing had mingled in Mexican affairs as a legal adviser to then-President Victoriano Huerta before he joined the State Department.[219] Ever an optimist, Meloy believed that he could combine the interests of all these factions with the goodwill of the American government, and the finance of German, as well as American banks.

Initial talks between Meloy, Sommerfeld, and Douglas in the winter of 1914/1915 seemed to have given Meloy the impression that a grand coalition of the different Mexican factions was indeed possible. By then, Villa and Carranza started to fight against each other in earnest, virtually guaranteeing a perpetuation of the civil war in Mexico for years to come. Meloy wrote, "When the Villa - Carranza split occurred ... the finances of Villa were directed in New York by Mr. Felix Summerfield [sic] and Frederick [sic] Stallforth. These two men came to wield a very considerable influence over Villa and immediately in my plans for a reorganization of Mexico assumed a position of great importance."[220] Frederico Stallforth, ever the promoter promised to "cultivate with Villa the possibility of an arrangement [to join Mondragón's group]."[221] Indeed, Meloy hoped that a new insurgency that was well-financed, thus having a powerful military presence, and was supported by the majority of the political factions in Mexico, would eventually receive the stamp of approval from the American government.

Sommerfeld and Stallforth seemed to have kept Meloy in the belief that such an alliance between Huerta, Mondragón, Blanquet, Díaz, Iturbide, and Villa would be possible. There certainly was a large incentive to keep this impression alive as long as possible: Intelligence. It was crucial for both agents to remain in the know of what the exile community was planning. The same held true for the representative of Carranza in the United States, Charles Douglas. He, too, seems to have egged on the naiveté of Meloy. "... I had conferences with him [Douglas] of exactly the same character as my conferences with Stallforth..."[222] The situation in Mexico in the spring of 1915 and the personal disposition of both Carranza and Villa towards these exiles makes Meloy's scheme seem unrealistic on the surface. Carranza, in particular, had no reason whatsoever to veer from his track of gaining total control of Mexico. His main commander, Alvaro Obregón, was continuously gaining ground against Villa. In April 1915, Villa had suffered his hitherto most devastating defeats in the two battles at Celaya. In another engagement in the first week of June, at the battle of León, Obregón again won decisively against Villa's Division of the North.

Observers noted admiringly that Obregón had studied German techniques in the battles raging in France. The German influence in the Mexican general's techniques came into the open through a Hearst reporter embedded with the Carranzistas. He handed a report from Captain Juan Rosales, a Carranzista living in El Paso, to the BI:

> General Obregón had his arm shot off early in the fifth, and then Krum [sic] Heller took charge. He had five German officers with him. None of them went into the field, but as every Mexican officer had been instructed by Obregón to obey Heller, he and his Germans sat in a little tent away from the firing line and made maps. On several occasions they rode out to hills and looked at everything through their field glasses. Then they would return to their tent. I was attached to Col. Heller's staff. Late that night Col. Heller sent for every Carranzista officer. Some of them regarded them as foolish and threatened to disobey, but Heller again produced an order signed by General Obregón commanding every Carranzista officer to obey him (Heller) [.] That settled the matter and the fight soon began. It did not last long. Villa was whipped and then retreated. Heller gave more instructions and our army advanced. Villas [sic] was whipped again and retreated. Heller again followed him and whipped him again. This was the end if Villa's army.[223]

Arnold Krumm-Heller was a German agent, of course, former doctor of President Madero, and the head of the Mexican Freemasons. While Obregón lay in his tent, reportedly suicidal over his debilitating injury, his commanders placed guards at his bedside to keep the general alive, and a group of German officers formed a command center from which they conducted Obregón's battles.

Krumm-Heller had been dispatched to both Zapata and Villa a few months earlier in January 1915, to offer military trainers to the revolutionaries, but both had declined. Villa not only rejected him, but asked the messenger who submitted Krumm-Heller's offer to tell him, "I give him [Krumm-Heller] 24 hours to get out of my country. If he is found here after that I will have him shot."[224] Krumm-Heller and his officers decisively defeated Villa's one-dimensional tactic of frontal cavalry assaults without keeping sufficient reserves. Villa came to regret rejecting the German offer. Carranza had no incentive to even consider sharing power in Mexico with the old guard as these battles decimated his forces.

Meloy's efforts seem less strange under scrutiny. Members of the State Department backed, maybe even concocted, Meloy's plan. President Wilson issued an ultimatum on June 2nd to the various Mexican factions to come to an agreement or the U.S. would intervene militarily.[225] A flurry of action started within the State Department as a result. William Jennings Bryan resigned as Secretary of State on June 9th over his frustration with Wilson's foreign policy towards Germany, which he believed would eventually drag the United States into the conflict. Robert Lansing came in his place, the Counselor of the State Department who had advised the President on a stricter course towards Germany. However, Lansing also believed that the continuation of the Mexican Revolution posed a national security risk for the United States.[226] His main adviser on Mexico was Leon Canova, the recently appointed head of the Latin American desk at the State Department.

Canova belonged to a group of American businessmen and exiled Mexican politicians who believed that in the end only an American military intervention or a faction of Mexicans with the full financial and political support of the United States could end the ongoing civil strife south of the border. This group included such men as the former Mexican Foreign Secretary Manuel Calero, Felix

Díaz and Aureliano Blanquet – two of the conspirators who over-threw President Madero in 1913 – and Villa's main military adviser, as well as the former secretary of war for Carranza, Felipe Ángeles. Manuel Esteva, the Mexican consul in New York under Porfirio Díaz and Victoriano Huerta, who Carranza fired in the fall of 1914, Andrew Meloy, and Frederico Stallforth all belonged to this group. Sherburne Hopkins, the powerful lobbyist for Madero, Villa, and Carranza in Washington D.C., and Felix Sommerfeld at least shared the group's ideas on resolving the Mexican civil war. Leon Canova, with the silent blessing of Robert Lansing, became the group's spokesman in the State Department.

Canova submitted a proposal to Secretary of State Bryan in May 1915, in which he claimed that Villa was ready to lay down his arms. A newly configured faction would be able to absorb his forces and pacify Mexico.[227] Canova claimed to be able to enlist former fed-eral officers (represented by Blanquet, Mondragón, and Angeles), rally the support of the Catholic Church (represented in the group through Felix Díaz and Eduardo Iturbide), receive financial support from the American oil and railroad industry (represented by Andrew Meloy, Charles Douglas, and Sherburne Hopkins), and mount this new opposition force quickly and efficiently. Mexico would be pacified by eliminating both Carranza and Villa.

The plan Canova submitted to Secretary Bryan and the plan Andrew Meloy pursued are almost identical. After his arrest in England, Meloy described his ideas for pacifying Mexico to the American Ambassador Walter Hines Page. Meloy's statement matched Canova's plan almost verbatim.[228] The American businessman claimed that through Sommerfeld and Stallforth, he had assurances that Villa would step aside, that he had broad support from different factions in Mexico, members of the old federal army, the Catholic Church, and important American financiers and industrialists. Even the informa-tion Meloy gave with respect to Carranza's refusal to be part of any unity government closely matched the known information about the Pan American conference between July 15th and August 8th. Charles Douglas apparently told Meloy, as well as Lansing and Canova after meetings in Veracruz, that Carranza would not yield nor participate in any unity government.[229] President Wilson not only followed Douglas' meetings personally; he had given Secretary Lansing instructions for the lawyer to take to Carranza. "I understand that Judge Douglas is going to start for Vera Cruz on Monday. Would it not be well to have a talk with him (not at your office, but at your house and as privately, as much away from the newspapers, as possible) and let him go down with a full understanding of our position, namely that Carranza must meet every honest advance half way if he expects to win our confidence, and that he must win our confidence, at least in some degree, if he hopes for ultimate recognition."[230] Carranza, certain that he would win the revolutionary war, refused to negotiate.[231] Further linking the Canova plan to Meloy, the arrested businessman perplexed the American ambassador in London by saying repeatedly, "Mr. Charles A. Douglas of Washington, whom he describes as 'Counselor to the Department of State for Latin American affairs.'"[232] That title belonged to Leon Canova. The embarrassment for Canova to have been involved in a scheme, in which German agents also participated, grew in the months to come. The head of the Bureau of Citizenship in the State Department told Canova in September 1915, "It appears to me that Meloy is engaged in a scheme of considerable proportions to foment a new revolutionary movement in Mexico, with German aid."[233]

Meloy pursued his plan in good faith with all the Mexican factions throughout the spring of 1915, with the sympathetic knowledge of members of the State Department. The Mexican factions all waited for whatever advantage they could gain from the scheme. Meanwhile, German agents plotted to use Meloy's idea as a smokescreen for introducing more strife into the border region than already existed. The American businessman traveled three times back and forth to Europe and met with expatriates in his office in New York. Boy-Ed wrote to Heinrich Albert in July, 1915, "I have repeatedly conferred with him [Meloy] and have received the impression that he is an honorable, trustworthy man. If he has a commercial failing, according to my observation, it is this one, that he is entirely too confiding and is easily made the victim of tricky businessmen."[234] The arrival of German naval intelligence agent Franz Rintelen in April and his participation in the plot on the behest of Boy-Ed beginning in May 1915 made a joke of the naïve Meloy.

Rintelen's opportunity to subvert the plot for his purposes arose when Mondragón proposed to arrange the purchase of U.S.

rifles from government surplus through a Russian military attaché, Colonel Ignatieff, in Paris. Since the U.S. government would not sell arms directly to belligerents, Mondragón offered to arrange for the purchase.[235] However, Mondragón's plan seems to have been to deliver these rifles to Mexico to support his envisioned military campaign. The Mexican general traveled to New York in April to make final arrangements just around the time when Franz Rintelen arrived. The two men met through Meloy or Stallforth. Posing as a wine merchant with the name E. V. Gates, Rintelen proposed to finance the purchase.[236] He had hoped to entice the Russian government to place more orders with his front company. Taking down payments and then defaulting on the contracts would not only have hurt the Russian government financially, but also tied up American munitions plants with dummy orders as indeed, Albert and his agents were doing while this plot unfolded. U.S. Ambassador to Britain Page mused, "Ignatieff was being used as a catspaw [sic] to supply the money for the purchase of the rifles which were not to go to Russia via Sweden as Ignatieff desired, but in reality to Mexico."[237]

Little over one week after the arrival of Franz Rintelen, on April 12th 1915, ex-president Victoriano Huerta, Manuel Mondragón, Enrique Creel, the former governor of Chihuahua, and Huerta's secretary General José Delgado stepped off the steamer *Antonio Lopez* in New York. Enrique Llorente, Villa's representative in Washington who reported to Sommerfeld, filed a protest with the Wilson administration before the ship had even docked in the harbor. He alleged what most believed to be true at the time: that the former dictator of Mexico came to insert himself in Mexican affairs once again.[238] Before letting Huerta enter the United States, immigration officials made the exiled dictator give an oath to the effect that he would stay out of Mexican affairs.[239] Despite the oath and public pronouncements, New York's newspapers continued to speculate about the true purpose of Huerta's trip.[240] The general informed reporters smilingly that he was on a "pleasure trip" and had no intention of mingling in Mexican affairs. He settled in a suite on the fifth floor of the Hotel Ansonia, on Broadway and 73rd Street, in New York. Reporters watched closely as Huerta received hundreds of visitors, generals of the Porfirio Díaz era, former governors, and exiled politicians, all hoping to join the new movement.[241] The old general basked in the attention, freely granted interviews with journalists, and pleasantly ignored direct questions regarding his purpose in New York. Claiming that he had "fallen in love with this country," Huerta rented a large villa on Long Island in the beginning of May. His wife and children and servants joined him in the new home, a household of thirty-five.[242]

Huerta's private secretary Jose C. Delgado, Victoriano Huerta,
his confidential agent ithe U.S., Abraham Z. Ratner, in New York, April 12th 1915.[243]

The line of Mexican luminaries visiting the ex-dictator did not decrease. One of Huerta's secret visitors was General Pascual Orozco. The notorious revolutionary had first supported President Madero, then participated in uprisings against him.[244] Sommerfeld had hunted the former mule driver turned revolutionary general for years without success. His followers, known as "Red Flaggers" because of their identifying red bandanas in battle, constituted the largest group of potential fighters in a new revolution. Orozco was the avowed enemy of Pancho Villa and his faction of revolutionaries.

Orozco came to Meloy's offices sometime in May and met with Franz Rintelen.[245] Stallforth describes what happened next: "... a peculiar incident occurred, that required considerable maneuvering on his [Stallforth's] part to keep Summerfield [sic] who was in his office from coming into contact with Orozco... being in the office of Meloy at the same time, knowing that Villa and Huerta followers were at the same time dead enemies."[246] With Orozco on board, Huerta, Mondragón, and Blanquet, and the seemingly agreeable Villa and Ángeles, "Meloy told Stallforth that he had all of the factions in Mexico under his control except Carranza's party, but he hoped perhaps to bring pressure to bear on Carranza through Germany in some way."[247] Felix Díaz, despite his fruitless entreaties with Villa in the past, also became part of the group and arrived in New York sometime in June. Díaz supposedly had financial support from the leaders of the Catholic church of Mexico. Father Francis Clement Kelley had founded a seminary on the outskirts of San Antonio with the purpose of organizing Mexican clergy to countermand the anti-clerical undercurrent of the Mexican Revolution.[248] In the end, Father Kelley did not, or could not, support the Huerta plot financially.

Evidence that Felix Sommerfeld (and by extension, Pancho Villa) did not support the Huerta-Orozco-Mondragón plot surfaced in El Paso in the first week of May 1915. Sommerfeld had traveled to the border in secrecy where he still operated Villa's secret service on the American side.[249] His intelligence chief in El Paso was Hector Ramos who worked hand in hand with federal agents of the Bureau of Investigations. The well-known soldiers-of-fortune, Sam Dreben and Emil Holmdahl, as well as retired policeman Powell Roberts, even former agents of the Bureau of Investigations, filled the ranks of this powerful organization.[250] It is unknown whether Sommerfeld had come to confer with Villa, but he certainly came to focus his secret service organization on sabotaging the "Científico" plot. American agents of the Bureau of Investigations reported on May 3rd "... Felix Sommerfeld and [illegible], both very active heretofore in revolutionary matters, had been seen a few days ago, just about daylight, coming from the direction of the foothills north of El Paso."[251]

The effort to dismantle the plot paralleled the cooperation between Sommerfeld's people and U.S. authorities in 1912. Kramp, Dreben, Roberts, Ramos and many more had fought another Orozco uprising and had brought it to its knees at that time.[252] A satisfied U.S. official reported to B.I. Chief Bielaski, "I am assured the hearty cooperation of mayor, sheriff, and United States military. All are working harmoniously together. Villa agents rendering valuable assistance..."[253] Here again, Sommerfeld's men covered every angle of the conspiracy, submitted daily written reports to the U.S. authorities, pointed out suspects, and in some cases, arrested them, and turned them over to U.S. authorities.[254] Sommerfeld's men, with the help of Villistas from Ciudad Juarez in an all-out war against the conspirators, identified suspects and places where arms, munitions, and explosives were stored. The suspects ended in jail, and on several occasions, the secret service men stole the supplies and took them across the river to the Villa garrison.[255] Lázaro De La Garza, who worked with Sommerfeld and the Maderos in Villa's supply operation, gave intelligence on the conspirators in New York, while Sherburne Hopkins worked the Washington side with reports directly to the U.S. State Department.[256] The noose around Huerta's conspirators was tight.

There is little doubt that Villa was not in favor of any plot that included Orozco or Huerta. Sommerfeld had been spotted near El Paso on the day Abraham Ratner disparaged the Mexican rebel general in the press in New York, "'General Huerta,' he said, 'had ordered Villa executed, and when Villa was brought before him he stretched himself at General Huerta's feet and made a piteous appeal for mercy. He caught General Huerta around the legs, tried to kiss him, and humbled himself in every possible way. 'Please, please spare me,' he whined as he cringed before the General,' said Ratner."[257] Comments like these did not play well to the man who had raised an army of 40,000 men and defeated Huerta on the battlefield and helped send him into exile. Villa and his men in the United States now did anything in their power to foil the conspiracy.

The Huerta-Orozco-Mondragón plot featured prominently in the headlines of New York's papers for weeks. And it was real. Federal agents all along the border checked every nook and cranny for conspirators, money, arms, and ammunition. The Secretary of War personally addressed the issue with the Attorney General in a memorandum on May 6th,

Sir:

I have the honor to quote for your consideration and such action as you deem advisable, the following extract from a letter I received from the Intelligence officer, U.S. forces at Douglas, Arizona:

'Indications in El Paso point to the assembling there of many supporters of the Científicos composed mostly of soldiers and officers who came across the line after the battle of Ojinaga. A large part of these men are at present in El Paso and can be seen any day at the Hotel El Paso... The Villa forces at Juarez have been fearing that an attack might be made and it is thought that should Villa be unsuccessful a new revolution will be launched at or in the vicinity of Juarez with the object of taking that port from the Villa faction. All of this points to preparations for General Huerta to re-enter Mexico.'

Very respectfully,
(signed) Lindley M. Garrison
Secretary of War[258]

The fact that Secretary Garrison admonished the Justice Department to do something is significant. Military Intelligence had filed few reports on the issue in April. Felix Sommerfeld seems to have been the source of the most pertinent information. He wrote to the Secretary on April 23rd, the week before he went to the border,: "I was very sorry not to have had the pleasure of seeing you in Washington last week, but I hope to see you in the near future, in order to tell you all I know about the latest developments in Mexico."[259] The timing of Garrison's note to his colleague coincides exactly with Sommerfeld's return from El Paso.

The entire group of conspirators arrived in New York in the middle of June. Manuel Mondragón, who had gone to Europe in May, returned together with Aureliano Blanquet on June 15th.[260] Felix Díaz came from New Orleans. Andrew Meloy arrived on the 21st from Europe. Feeding rumors about a split between him and Villa, Felipe Ángeles, as well, turned up in New York to confer with the Maderos and members of the former Madero cabinet. Naturally, papers speculated that he, maybe even Villa himself, contemplated joining the Huerta movement.[261] Pascual Orozco also came briefly around the 20th and returned to El Paso on the 24th.[262] He mostly stayed at the border, frantically organizing the incursion and supplies for the conspirators.[263]

Rumors of fantastic supplies or arms and ammunition ran rampant all along the border. However, in most instances, these were supplies going to Villa and Obregón's forces, not the "Científico" opposition.[264]

According to British intelligence, intensive meetings occurred in and around Huerta that involved Franz Rintelen, Franz von Papen, and Karl Boy-Ed. Boy-Ed, who claimed steadfastly never to have met Huerta other than in Mexico in 1914, might not have been involved but still professed his sympathies with the exiled dictator in his memoirs.[265] "His forced removal by the Americans I always thought it [the ousting of Huerta] to be a calamity for Mexico," he wrote in 1920.[266] It became clear in these meetings, very likely involving Franz von Papen, that the Meloy "Peace Plan" for Mexico was failing miserably.

First Chief Carranza had announced publicly from the beginning that he would have no negotiations with Pancho Villa, Huerta, or anyone else for that matter. His chief of the artillery and secret service agent, Arnold Krumm-Heller, who was the head of the order of Freemasons in Mexico, went as far as expelling Huerta, Díaz, "and about eighty other Mexicans, who have been prominently identified with the political affairs of Mexico."[267] Carranza sent an official document to Washington D.C. and had it published, signed the "Masonic Grand Orient ..." bearing the Masonic seal of "Progreso y Libertad Orden de Mexico."[268] While no one showed much surprise that Carranza refused to participate, other leaders bailed as well. Both Felipe Ángeles, who may never have been committed to the insurgency, and Manuel Mondragón, the centerpieces of Meloy's plan, quit. The U.S. State Department agents who analyzed Rintelen's correspondence concluded that "Mondragón had refused the offer [of the Catholic Church to finance him] because the idea of re-establishing the power of the Catholic Church in Mexico was futile. He had also refused 100,000 dollars and the Secretaryship [sic] of War, which he was offered if he would accompany Huerta to the border... apart from Mondragon, Diaz and the Catholic Church will remain impotent."[269] Meloy's idea had come apart at the seams.

Despite these setbacks, Huerta and Orozco kept pushing their plot. Significant amounts of supplies poured into the border region throughout May and June, consigned to small dealers in and around Texas. The sudden influx, evidenced by Sommerfeld's activities and enlistment of his friend, the Secretary of War, combined with the rampant rumors that a conspiracy was afoot, caused great alarm with both the American officials and the Villista secret service.[270] It was very difficult to separate these shipments from deliveries to Villa and Obregón, who imported millions of cartridges for over 60,000 soldiers in active duty. The source of these weapons, as well as the finances behind them, became the looming question. The next chapter offers evidence that proves that throughout the preparation time of this plot, Felix Sommerfeld was sending millions of cartridges from the Western Cartridge Company, Peters Cartridge Company, and Winchester Arms Company to the border.

Felix Sommerfeld pointed to a large cache of arms and ammunition in an interview with B.I. Agent Cantrell that the Mexican government had supposedly bought in 1913.[271] According to him, this cache had been stored in the Navy Yard of New York ever since Huerta's demise and belonged to the Mexican government. According to Sommerfeld, however, Huerta, through the Ratners and the Russian-Jewish-Mexican merchant, Leon Rasst, had laid his hands on these supplies and shipped them to the border. U.S. State Department documents support the main facts of Sommerfeld's claim. In April 1915, the SS Monterrey stopped in New York.[272] Customs officials impounded a large load of rifles, machine guns, and ammunition and stored them in the New York Navy Yard. Leon Rasst tried to have the impounded shipment released. However, U.S. authorities determined that the true owner was Abraham Ratner, who subsequently received the rights to the arms.[273] Officials in El Paso tried to find out on May 12th, who had received eight carloads of munitions, approximately matching the size of Ratner's cache. The Villista secret service further confirmed that the consignment was not theirs.[274]

U.S. authorities and Sommerfeld's organization tried their best to stop the conspiracy. Despite their efforts and the lack of support from the other Mexican factions, Victoriano Huerta and his immediate followers decided on June 24th to go ahead with their plan. The exiled general and a group of his closest advisers took a train to San Francisco on that day, ostensibly to visit the World Fair exhibition. However, in Chicago they switched to a train to Kansas City, where they changed destinations again and headed for El Paso.[275] The train stopped in the early morning hours of June 27th, right across the Texas border near Newman, New Mexico, a small hamlet between New

Mexico and Texas and only twenty miles from El Paso. Pascual Orozco and a small group of Huertistas had waited at the station with two cars to take their leader across the Mexican border. Customs Collector Zach Lamar Cobb and a detail of soldiers from Fort Bliss arrested Orozco and his men. As the train stopped on the Texas side of the border Huerta greeted Orozco before U.S. authorities arrested him, as well.[276] Huerta seemed completely surprised. Not so surprised was the American public. Even before agents arrested Huerta, New York papers had reported that the general was on a train bound for El Paso to start a new revolution.[277]

He and Orozco posted bail within hours and remained in El Paso, freely continuing to plot their insurgency. Orozco escaped from house arrest on July 3rd 1915. Reports indicated that he entered Mexico where three hundred of his followers awaited him. It turned out he went into hiding on the American side of the border, without men or equipment or money. An American posse hunted him and four companions down, shot and killed them on August 30th.[278] Huerta, who had been re-arrested after Orozco's escape, remained incarcerated at Fort Bliss. A lifelong alcoholic, the death of Orozco caused him once more to seek solace in Cognac and other spirits. After falling ill, being released, rearrested, and falling ill again, he died on January 13th1916. The official cause of death read cirrhosis of the liver, an entirely reasonable explanation. However, reports of two botched medical operations leading to his final decline fueled conspiracy theories ever since that someone, maybe even the American government, had murdered him. The border remained unsettled for months to come. Felix Díaz tried his own insurrection from New Orleans in the coming months. The Bureau of Investigations uncovered several small filibustering operations in August. About $10,000 worth of arms and ammunition fell into the hands of American officials.[279] However, the plot of the "Científicos" under the leadership of Huerta and Orozco had been ended effectively with the arrests near Newman, New Mexico.

Felipe Ángeles conducted meetings with Secretary of the Interior Franklin K. Lane and Hugh Lenox Scott, Wilson's Chief of the Army in July. In these meetings, Ángeles proffered former members of the Madero administration as candidates for a unity government in Mexico.[280] He also reiterated the stated commitment from Villa that he would go into exile if Carranza would.[281] Secretary Lane thought enough of Ángeles' foray that he informed President Wilson of the conversations.[282] Wilson had been especially impressed with Ángeles and considered him a potential candidate for the Mexican presidency. However, none of the Mexican factions shared his admiration. *The New York Herald* reporter Alexander Williams phrased the likelihood of an Ángeles administration in Mexico a few months later: "Felipe Angeles is the enemy politically of every faction in Mexico other [than] that headed by Villa. Every other faction considers him a traitor. None of the important Mexicans would under any conditions affiliate with him."[283] However, Ángeles presented a new approach to the Wilson administration, one that revived the idea of a unity government without either Villa or Carranza as its head. Sommerfeld and Army Chief of Staff Hugh Lenox Scott supported Ángeles' foray. It would have been a sensible solution had Secretary Lansing and Leon Canova not shifted gears by then. Facing a continuing decline of Villa's power in Mexico, and despite their shared belief that Carranza was impossible to deal with, both were now pushing for a government under his auspices.

The details of the Huerta-Orozco-Mondragón plot and many of the facts remain obscured to this day. The links between Meloy, the State Department and Leon Canova, in particular, have never been explored. However, Secretary of State Robert Lansing certainly knew of Canova's activities, if he did not participate in meetings with the Mexican exile groups and their lawyers and lobbyists himself. As soon as the arrest of Andrew Meloy uncovered the fact that he had been linked to German agents, Leon Canova suddenly seemed absent from the front lines of policy making. This fact is particularly apparent because in August and September 1915 there was a flurry of activity regarding Mexico, such as several meetings of the Pan-American Conference and tough negotiations with Pancho Villa over confiscated American property. However, the conniving Canova remained at his post, quietly manipulating the fluid situation in Mexico to his ends. By the middle of September 1915, Villa's fate was sealed. Secretary Lansing and his head of the Mexican desk had convinced President Wilson to recognize Venustiano Carranza as the de facto president of Mexico over Pancho Villa's faction. The decision would have grave consequences for the United States.

English propaganda helped Lansing and Canova sweep their embarrassing link to German secret service activities under the rug.

Instead of embarrassing the U.S. government, the pro-English press went into high gear to sensationalize another plot of the "Huns" trying to hurt the United States. Since the failure of the plot coincided with the arrest of Franz Rintelen and the resulting feeding frenzy of the American press, most historical treatments of the conspiracy are fraught with factual mistakes. Virtually all historians dealing with this topic repeated claims of the *Providence Journal* and other British propaganda, with the notable exceptions of Reinhard Doerries and Alan Knight.[284] The English misinformation campaign started with a report in the *New York Times* on August 4th beginning with the ominous words, "The *Providence Journal* will say tomorrow morning... "[285] The *Providence Journal*, of course, was the British counterpart of Sylvester Viereck's *Fatherland*. The article went on, "Large sums of money have been paid to Huerta since his arrival in this country directly through German hands, and it is known that some of this money was used for the purchase of rifles which were subsequently sent by water from New York to Yucatan."[286] Most importantly, there are no records in German archives that substantiate Barbara Tuchman's claim repeated in virtually every book on the conspiracy since, namely that "eight million rounds of ammunition were purchased in St. Louis... and a preliminary sum of $800,000 deposited to Huerta's account in the Deutsche Bank in Havana as well as $95,000 in a Mexican account."[287] These "facts" came from the *Providence Journal* and have never been corroborated with any archival evidence. While German financing of the Secret War Council, transfers of funds to Boy-Ed, Albert, and Count Bernstorff are all well documented in German archives, the funding of the Huerta plot is nowhere to be found.[288] Also, Rintelen's correspondence, which British authorities confiscated in August of 1915, contained evidence to the effect that he was trying to find sources of funding for Mondragón but did not have them at the time. Investigators of the State Department summarized the information in the letters with respect to the Mexican plot. "He [Rintelen] doubts whether the Germans will want to extend their investments in Mexico just now."[289] Also, "he [Rintelen] was working to provide arms for Mexican revolutionists."[290]

Considering that Rintelen's accounts showed an unexplained deficit of $125,000 in August, it is possible, theoretically, that some of this money financed the Mondragón-Huerta plot. According to the testimony of Rintelen's banker, the notorious "Wolf of Wall Street" David Lamar "tried to get money out of him [Rintelen] to 'bear' the market so as to pay him back the money he had used," a more likely explanation of where Rintelen's funds could have ended.[291] Neither the B.I., nor the investigators of the Justice Department in the 1917 trial of Rintelen, nor the lawyers of the Mixed Claims Commission that closely investigated the Rintelen mission in the 1920s and 1930s, could come up with a single check or money transfer between Huerta and his co-conspirators and Rintelen, Boy-Ed, or Franz von Papen.

The arms buyer for von Papen was Hans Tauscher. His records indicate that, indeed, he owned a large cache of U.S. army surplus rifles that were supposed to have gone to Indian resistance fighters. However, in June 1915 U.S. authorities impounded those supplies when the arms of the *Annie Larsen* came to light.[292] Investigators looking into Tauscher's affairs determined that he had significant amounts of munitions in storage in New York in 1917.[293] Tauscher also shipped "500 cases of 7 millimetre [sic] cartridges... consigned to the Guatemalan government" around the middle of August 1915.[294] However, these munitions came from the Western Cartridge Company, since the caliber was not 45/70 but 7mm. The details follow in the next chapter. Whether the shipment to Guatemala found its way to Mexico, and if so, to whom, is not documented. Despite all the allegations, British propaganda claims, and multiple investigations for decades, the only documented money Rintelen disbursed for the Huerta-Orozco-Mondragón conspiracy is $10,000, paid on July 16th 1915.[295] This check to Andrew Meloy could have covered expenses for bribing officials and paying recruits or defectors, which happened on a large scale.[296] It was too small for significant munitions purchases. Many other possibilities for Meloy receiving this money exist, such as Meloy paying himself for various services to Rintelen.

The U.S. Justice Department solved the mystery of where most of Huerta's funds had come from on July 7th 1915: Huerta himself.[297] Huerta had cashed several hundred thousand dollars of his own money, as Felix Sommerfeld had explained to B.I. Agent Cantrell a few days before. According to Sommerfeld, this money came from Mexican bonds Huerta had on deposit in New York. Agents of the B.I. confirmed Sommerfeld's allegations that Huerta sold Mexican bonds to finance his conspiracy.[298] According to the captain of the German warship that took Huerta to Jamaica into exile in 1914, "Huerta and General Blanquet were well supplied with travelling money, and the women similarly with jewelry. Huerta had roughly half a million marks in gold with him. Additionally, he had a much greater amount in checks and other paper [i.e. treasury bonds]."[299] José Vasconcelos, Mexican lawyer, member of the Madero and Gutiérrez governments, testified on June 30th, "When he [Huerta] left Mexico it was estimated that he took out with him around five million [in] gold [approximately $2.5 million, which in today's value would be $52 million]."[300] In short, Sommerfeld and Vasconcelos both estimated that Huerta had access to millions of dollars of his own money while in New York.[301]

The arrest of Huerta on June 27th and the collapse of the "Científico" conspiracy brought to light some astonishing facts about the Secret War Council. Around the beginning of May, Sommerfeld, Bernhard Dernburg, and very likely Karl Boy-Ed made the decision that the Huerta-Orozco-Mondragón plot was not worth supporting. This decision stood in stark contrast to the continued efforts of Franz Rintelen, Frederico Stallforth, and Andrew Meloy, as well as the "Oliver North of the State Department," Leon Canova, to push on with the plot.[302] The extent of Robert Lansing's knowledge or involvement in the plot is unknown. Clearly, he supported a solution that eliminated Villa and Carranza as players in a pacified Mexico. He knew Huerta and had worked for him as a lawyer several years before, but it is unlikely that he involved himself actively in the plot or took a special interest in it.[303]

Felix Sommerfeld worked closely with Boy-Ed through the fall of 1914 and spring of 1915. His regular intelligence reports to the naval attaché attest to Sommerfeld's job description.[304] It is highly unlikely to assume that Sommerfeld acted without approval from Boy-Ed when he took apart the Huerta plot at the border. A much larger and much more effective German clandestine project was under way when Rintelen inserted himself into Mexican affairs. Sommerfeld, who the American government considered an honest broker, who had personal access to the highest levels of the Departments of Justice, War and State, and whose connections to the American business elite greatly exceeded those of Andrew Meloy and Rintelen, undertook the most ambitious German project of the period: Create a war between the United States and Mexico through the manipulation of U.S. government officials, American businesses, and the only real power in Mexico to cause war, Pancho Villa. Sommerfeld proposed to the German Admiralty through Bernhard Dernburg on May 10th 1915 to create an intervention in Mexico. "He [Sommerfeld] is completely sure that an intervention of the United States in Mexico can be provoked... let Mr. Sommerfeld through me [Dernburg] have a clear 'yes' or 'no.'"[305] When Sommerfeld received a clear "yes," Rintelen stood in the way.[306]

Sommerfeld took him out without hesitation. Two weeks after he went to the border, and the week after he conferred with Lindley Garrison, Sommerfeld leaked Rintelen's identity to James F. McElhone of the *New York Herald* on May 17th.[307] McElhone's boss was Editor-in-chief William Willis, one of Sommerfeld's closest friends.[308] Willis not only published his reporter's scoop on the German agent but also reported Sommerfeld's information to the Chief of the U.S. Secret Service, William Flynn.[309] The *New York Sun* carried an article on May 26th mentioning a mysterious German agent named "Hansen" (Rintelen's alias).[310] Not knowing how he had been identified, Rintelen moved his office in with Meloy and Stallforth, where Sommerfeld reportedly was a frequent visitor. According to witnesses, Sommerfeld not only watched Rintelen's every move but also "advised" him. Rintelen had presented Sommerfeld a letter of introduction from Peter Bruchhausen. Bruchhausen, a German commercial attaché attached to the legation in Argentina, had been Sommerfeld's intelligence handler in Mexico between 1911 and 1913.

Rintelen himself participated in his downfall as the American secret service began to hone in on the German agent. Rintelen had contracted the publicity agent John C. Hammond for $10,000 to make propaganda against the Allies as early as the end of April.[311] The effort to show Bernhard Dernburg and the others in the German Press Office how propaganda is done backfired badly. Hammond reported Rintelen's identity, as well as his activities to President Wilson's secretary, Joseph Tumulty.[312] Rintelen also blundered in his social activities. He invited Anne L. Seward, a young and pretty school teacher who he knew from Berlin, on several dates in the first week of June. In order to impress her and other dinner guests, Rintelen spoke of "unlimited funds" at his disposal and made disparaging remarks about the "policy of the United States and the action of the

President."[313] The niece of former Secretary of State, William Seward, found "the actions and general conduct of Captain Rintelen ... so suspicious that ... she determined to and did write the President upon the subject."[314] This letter went to President Wilson's secretary Joseph Tumulty, as well.

Rintelen had become a tremendous liability for the Secret War Council by the time the Huerta affair came to light. British and American agents began to close in on his location and activities. French police discovered the first cigar bombs on the SS Kirk Oswald in Marseilles on May 10th. The New York Bomb Squad was hot on the heels of Rintelen's sabotage team. Likely upon the request of his direct superior, Karl Boy-Ed, the German Admiralty issued an order for his recall on July 2nd.[315] The strike at Bridgeport began on July 15th and aroused further suspicions about this mysterious agent in New York. Albert lost his briefcase in the "El" on July 24th, exposing most intelligence operations conducted through the Secret War Council. His environment became so restrictive that without the ability to obtain a new passport, Rintelen booked a voyage back to Europe on the SS Noordam. He had decided to use the Swiss passport with which he had come to America. Meloy, his wife, and his secretary joined Rintelen on his trip. Even then, on the ship back to Europe, Rintelen showed little restraint and aroused suspicions from other passengers. British patrols took Rintelen off the ship during a routine check on August 13th at Ramsgate. He successfully hid his true identity under questioning for a few days until he caved. He remained in England as a prisoner of war until 1917 when the American government won his extradition. Frederico Stallforth alluded to the real attitude in the Secret War Council concerning the Huerta-Orozco-Mondragón plot in a report to Heinrich Albert in the middle of August. Celebrating the fact that Meloy had accompanied Rintelen to Europe, Stallforth wrote, "All that which might have been especially suspicious has vanished and we have put out of the way all relating to the Mexican business... Perchance [sic] you will decide... to hold our friend M[eloy] over on some pretext or other so that he will not again make such a furor here [referring to the discovery of the Huerta plot]. You can imagine how well everything is going here since he [Meloy] has been eliminated from this stage [and gone to Europe]."[316]

Halfhearted German efforts to affect a prisoner exchange for Rintelen in 1918 did not work, mainly because a few months after his arrest in England, the German government through Ambassador Count Bernstorff disavowed him.[317] The war between Germany and the United States Rintelen had helped to provoke was in full swing when he came back to the U.S. in 1917. New York courts convicted Rintelen because his offenses occurred in the neutrality period, and passed several sentences aggregating to four years of incarceration for procuring a false passport, conspiracy, firebombing ships, and causing labor unrest.[318] The Huerta plot did not figure into his conviction. There simply was not enough evidence of a German-Mexican conspiracy.

Rintelen sued the German government for damages for years after returning to Germany in 1921. Disenchanted and bitter about the war Rintelen wrote his memoirs called *The Dark Invader*.[319] The German government tried to stop its publication. After years of wrangling a British publisher accepted the manuscript. Fearing for his life, Rintelen moved to Great Britain permanently in 1931 and renounced his German citizenship. *The Dark Invader* hit the stands in 1933 and was a great success. He followed up with a sequel, *The Return of the Dark Invader* in 1935.[320] His books, as well as multiple interviews he gave to promote them, contain exaggerations that even exceeded those spread in the British propaganda of World War I. He claimed to have been in charge of everything: propaganda, sabotage, thousands of agents, even the sinking of the *Lusitania* and sabotage acts that happened a year after his departure.[321] An honest discussion of what really happened in the United States during the spring and summer of 1915 did not come forth because of the ongoing legal action between Germany and the United States through the 1920s and 30s. An admission of the existence of sabotage, and a revelation of the chain of command, would have negatively affected Germany's position in the negotiations.

A final analysis reveals that Rintelen had serious personality issues that thwarted his career and put those assigned to work with him in danger. Clearly, the navy commander had an inferiority complex that caused him to constantly exaggerate his importance. Adopting a false title of nobility, he claimed to Americans that he was a member of the imperial family.[322] Like Horst von der Goltz, another megalomaniac character of the time, Rintelen insisted that he reported to the Kaiser who had sent him personally.[323] He swore during a spat with

Bernhard Dernburg that he would make sure that the Kaiser would never receive him again.[324] Dernburg was a personal friend of Wilhelm II and a former cabinet member. Rintelen honestly seemed to believe that if he could just get in front of President Wilson, he could convince him to institute a weapons embargo against the Allies. While still in Berlin and desperate for the attention of his superiors, he attacked two of the most powerful players in the German empire, Max Warburg and Albert Ballin.[325] He hid under the coattails of Secretary von Tirpitz when the backlash swept over him, and recklessly invoked his boss' power. Though his superiors in the Admiralty may have considered this youthful daredevil useful, his activities in Berlin were a harbinger of the damages he caused when he came to the U.S.

Impulsive action and reckless ambition followed Rintelen like a bad smell. His failure was not to follow the orders under which he had come to the U.S., namely to create labor unrest and stop munitions shipments. The true failure was his indiscretion and lack of respect for the people and projects the Secret War Council had so carefully put in place. He told anyone who wanted to listen that his powers exceeded those of the German ambassador.[326] He believed he could do a better job than Dernburg, Albert, Boy-Ed and von Papen together and, as a result, he inserted himself into their projects. The result was disastrous. Not only was he discovered within weeks of his arrival, but anybody who came in contact with him in the three months of his stay found themselves in the interrogation rooms of American authorities within months. The expulsion of Karl Boy-Ed in December 1915 resulted to a large degree from Rintelen's discovery. The government found out in October 1915 that the $508,000 Rintelen had at his disposal came from the naval attaché. Two months later, Boy-Ed received his passport.

Rintelen's brashness and miscalculation of power and influence would haunt him all his life. No one came to his rescue while he served out his prison sentences in a Georgia penitentiary. When he returned to Germany, he received a medal for his wartime service but otherwise was shunned. The recognition he so desperately sought remained elusive. The only place where he could be the hero he wanted the world to see was in his books. A tragic conclusion of his career was that his chosen country of residence, Great Britain, arrested Rintelen in 1940 and interned him for the duration of the Second World War.

A U.S. Secret Service agent remarked: "The causes of his failure were typically Prussian – he had no understanding of men and conditions and he thought he was a superman."[327] His friend and co-conspirator in New York, George Plochmann, had an even better characterization of Rintelen: "Excellent talker, with the cast of a man who lives his life as in the penny dreadful novel. He lives in that kind of style at home or wherever he goes. Either he does something exceedingly foolish, or can pull off a very big task."[328] Franz Rintelen died in London on May 30th 1949, of a heart attack.

CHAPTER 6:
TWENTY-SEVEN MILLION CARTRIDGES

THE CREDIBLE DOCUMENTS THAT MIGHT have revealed the exact point in time when Franz Rintelen ran afoul with the Secret War Council have not been uncovered. However, all indications suggest that Rintelen's insertion into Mexican politics ran counter to a project that had been underway since April 10th 1915, one week after he came to New York. Heinrich Albert noted in his diary on that day, "In this connection a conversation with Meyer-Gerhard at the office of Dernberg [sic] took place, in which the present political situation and the measures to be adopted, especially those in the M. question were discussed."[329] The "M" question undoubtedly concerned Mexico. The diary entry also places Bernhard Dernburg at the center of the "measures to be adopted" with respect to Mexico.

Despite Rintelen's alleged efforts to support a Huerta insurgency in Mexico, the lack of German funding of the plot, as well as subsequent significant funding of Pancho Villa and Venustiano Carranza, suggests the evolution of a new strategy for Mexico in the middle of April 1915. The purpose, namely perpetuating unrest in Mexico and forcing a U.S. military intervention, had much better chances of success if the Secret War Council supplied Villa and Carranza rather than foment a conspiracy with Huerta. This did not sit well with Rintelen who, witnesses recalled, referred to Dernburg as "a pig and an imbecile."[330] It was Villa on who the German agents mostly placed their bets, since one of their own was in charge of supplying his army. Felix Sommerfeld made the argument in conversations with Bernhard Dernburg that an American military intervention could easily be provoked, and likely also the German ambassador himself. However, a defeat of Villa through Carranza would carry with it the danger of a sudden end to the Mexican Revolution. Cleverly, Sommerfeld combined his interest as the main arms buyer for Villa with the strategic interests of the German government. The "present political situation" in Mexico, which Albert mentioned in his diary, referred to the falling of Mexico City to Carranza's forces in late January. As interim President Eulalio Gutiérrez fled the scene, the situation in the ancient Aztec capital degraded into utter chaos. Hunger, pestilence, lawlessness, wonton executions, and a complete breakdown of central authority marked the hitherto worst period of the revolution for Mexico City. The new German envoy to Mexico, Heinrich von Eckardt, arrived in the capital as this situation unfolded.

One month after Carranzista forces occupied the capital, General Obregón evacuated and left Mexico City's desperate citizens to fend for themselves. Emiliano Zapata took control within a short time, but was not able to set up an effective administration of the city. The capital changed hands four times between January and June.[331] According to von Papen's reports to the Imperial War Department on the situation, "The circumstances in Mexico have come to a head lately so much so that under pressure from the diplomatic representatives [there] the State Department for better or for worse will have to gather itself up to take more energetic steps. As a first step several warships have been dispatched to Veracruz. Since there it is said that there is complete anarchy in the capital, the Department of War believes a decision to undertake a second intervention will be made soon."[332] By the time Albert made the 'M' question entry in his diary, Villa's army had suffered over 2,000 casualties at the first battle of Celaya, April 6th to April 7th, and prepared for a second encounter with Obregón's forces, which would be an even worse rout. Villa stood the danger of being completely wiped out.

Villa had made entreaties to the German government shortly after Obregón took the Mexican capital and made a mess of it. On February 16th 1915, Ambassador Count Bernstorff sent a telegram he had received from Villa's envoy in Washington D.C., Enrique Llorente, to the German Chancellor von Bethmann Hollweg.[333] The message likely originated as an idea from Sommerfeld.

Agencia Confidencial del Gobierno provisional
de Mexico, Washington D.C.

February 16th, 1915

Excellency,

The attitude of the so-called Carranza Government towards the diplomatic agents of friendly nations residing at the city of Mexico, in ignoring the rights, privileges and immunities accorded them by international law and usage, meets with strong disapprobation on the part of the Provisional Government under whose authority General Francisco Villa has, for the time being, assumed political power in the Northern and Central States.

In view of the circumstances, and in order that the Government of Your Excellency may be assured of amicable disposition of the Provisional Government, which now controls the greater part of the Mexican republic, I am desired by General Villa to convey to Your Excellency the assurance that, in case the diplomatic agent of your Excellency's Government in the city of Mexico finds it desirable, at any time, to depart from the Capital, he would be most hospitably received at Chihuahua, or at any other city within our lines, where every courtesy, facility and guarantee will be invariable [sic] extended to him.

Please accept, Excellency, the assurances of my highest consideration.

Signed C. c. [sic] Llorente.[334]

Pancho Villa not only invited the newly arrived German envoy to meet with him, he also presented himself as the pro-order candidate in the Mexican struggle. Realistically, he was.

Von Eckardt had arrived in Mexico City from Havana in the beginning of February.[335] Indeed, he left the Mexican capital to meet with "representatives" of the naval and military attachés, von Papen and Boy-Ed, in Galveston and New Orleans on February 22nd and 24th 1915 respectively.[336] The sabotage campaign against the Mexican oil wells in Tampico was at issue. One of the identities of the mysterious "representatives" seems to have been von Papen's designated sabotage agent for Mexico, von Petersdorf.[337] Sommerfeld likely represented the other, in charge of Karl Boy-Ed's interests. If von Eckardt took the opportunity to meet with Villa while at the Mexican-American border, Sommerfeld would have accompanied him to the general's headquarters. However, the German envoy did not file a report about meeting Villa, which favors the conclusion that the encounter never took place.

Sommerfeld's efforts to enlist German support behind the Villa faction continued in the following months. Intensive meetings with Bernhard Dernburg led to an astonishing communication of the ideas of his "friend, Mr. Felix A. Sommerfeld" with the German War Office which would have grave consequences:[338] The Sommerfeld-Dernburg memorandum went to Admiral Henning von Holtzendorff on May 15th 1915 (to shortly become the head of the admiralty), and made the rounds in the German government, including Foreign Secretary Gottlieb von Jagow, Chancellor von Bethmann Hollweg and members of the German Admiralty. Next to the sabotage order from January 1915, this document is perhaps the most remarkable piece of evidence regarding German strategy towards the U.S. in the neutrality period between 1914 and 1917. Historian Friedrich Katz first discovered its existence in the 1970s.

> Because of my friend, Mr. Felix A. Sommerfeld,
> German citizen, did I gain knowledge of the different
> [munitions] contracts [of the Allies in the U.S.] in the
> beginning of the war... Felix A. Sommerfeld proposed
> to have the infantry cartridge 7mm... manufactured.
> The infantry cartridge Mauser 7mm could then be sold
> off to South American countries and Spain, which are
> all using this make, and that profitably... Felix A. Sommerfeld is intimately familiar with Mexican politics for
> the last four years, was adviser and confidential agent
> of President Madero in all diplomatic missions and currently holds the same position with General Villa and
> had since been commissioned to procure munitions
> and war supplies here in the United States [for him].
> As a result, he knows all factories and their capacities.
> Ever since Sommerfeld, who is an excellent patriot,

has been trying his best to find out what can be done to support Germany.

All contracts of the arms manufacturers contain a clause, which relegates the agreement null and void in the event of the United States entering into a war. The policies of the United States towards Mexico are widely known and one can be completely sure that the government of the United States will do whatever it can to prevent an intervention in Mexico. The military leadership of the United States, however, is very much in favor of an intervention, as well as the state governments of Texas and Arizona, that are bordering on Mexico. A few months ago an incident occurred at the Mexican border in Arizona [Naco] that almost resulted in an intervention. At this time the chief of the General Staff [Hugh Lenox Scott] at the insistence of Secretary of War Garrison was sent to the border to negotiate with General Villa. These negotiations took place through the mediation of Felix A. Sommerfeld, and at that time, as he told me multiple times, it would have been easy to provoke an intervention. Such an event at this time would mean the following for Germany:

An embargo on all munitions for the Allies, and since everyone knows that the Allies are completely dependent on American munitions and war supplies, [it would mean] a quick success for Germany, credits for the Allies would be restricted and, additionally, the policies of the United States would be distracted, another fact that would be to Germany's advantage.

... Felix A. Sommerfeld had misgivings at the time to force an intervention through General Villa since he did not know the intentions of Germany towards the United States...

This issue seems to become relevant again in the near term and Felix A. Sommerfeld discussed it with me. He is completely convinced that an intervention in Mexico by the United States can be provoked...

> After acknowledgement of this report I request that through any means at your disposal or through me Mr. Felix A. Sommerfeld be given a simple 'yes' or 'no' [for his proposal to provoke an intervention]...[339]

The answer arrived a few days later, after the Foreign Secretary Gottlieb von Jagow saw the report:

> In my opinion, the answer is absolutely 'yes.' Even if the shipments of munitions cannot be stopped, and I am not sure they can, it would be highly desirable for America to become involved in a war and be diverted from Europe... an intervention made necessary by the developments in Mexico would be the only [emphasis added] possible diversion for the American government. Moreover, since we can at this time do nothing in the Mexican situation, an American intervention would also be the best thing possible for our interests there.[340]

Sommerfeld had presented a plan that the German Imperial Foreign Secretary and, most likely as a result of the importance of the proposal, the German Chancellor von Bethmann Hollweg personally had signed off on. The answer from Henning von Holtzendorff underlines the timing of Sommerfeld's proposal. The Imperial German cabinet was mired in discussions on how – or if – to proceed with the commerce war using the submarine. Hardline proponents guaranteed a victory over England within six months, while the moderate wing of the cabinet, including Chancellor von Bethmann Hollweg, doubted that the submarine fleet even had enough boats to effectively blockade England. The logical consequence of an American declaration of war in case of unrestricted submarine warfare seemed too risky to the moderates, given the uncertainties of the strategy's effectiveness.[341]

The debate raged even louder in May as a result of the sinking of the *Lusitania*. The hardline group saw the *Lusitania* sinking as *Abschreckung*, a means to scare commerce traffic away from British harbors.[342] The subsequent guarantees of the German government to President Wilson that submarines would, henceforth, observe cruiser rules and not sink passenger ships, led to a rift in the cabinet. Chief of the Admiralty Bachmann and Grand Admiral von Tirpitz openly opposed von Bethmann Hollweg and the Emperor and offered their resignations, which the Kaiser did not grant, initially.[343] He was fired in August when Admiral Bachmann opposed the moderates again, while von Tirpitz was put on ice.[344] The new Chief of the Admiralty was Admiral Henning von Holtzendorff.

Just as tempers flared in Berlin, Sommerfeld proposed a way out of the dilemma. Rather than having to decide now whether to risk a war with the United States or give up the unrestricted submarine war the navy demanded, he sought to create certain conditions in the United States that would end the threat of an effective American impact on the European war. Dernburg chose von Holtzendorff, who was then still retired, because his views regarding the submarine fleet were moderate and acceptable to Wilhelm II and von Bethmann Hollweg. Von Holtzendorff explained to the chancellor and the foreign secretary that if Sommerfeld's proposal worked, American attention would be diverted and munitions kept from the Allies at the same time, while unrestricted submarine warfare could be re-launched. He wrote that an American intervention in Mexico would have an added benefit of also reestablishing order of whatever definition. The appointment of von Holtzendorff in August insured that Sommerfeld's plan would be enacted. The Secret War Council was to create a strategic window in which unrestricted submarine warfare could be enacted and the war brought to a favorable conclusion.

The former Secretary of Colonial Affairs left the United States within a month of the Sommerfeld proposal.[345] Public remarks in defense of Germany's torpedoing of the *Lusitania* had created such uproar that Ambassador Count Bernstorff decided to send Dernburg home. Sommerfeld's project came under the auspices of Heinrich Albert and his assistant, Carl Heynen, a close friend of Sommerfeld and Stallforth's, as a result. Almost giddy, Frederico Stallforth reported to Heinrich Albert on August 13th 1915, the day Franz Rintelen and Andrew Meloy were arrested in England, "In Mexico, the thing is working quietly there, and I believe that it is now possible that it must come to a decision. The President [Wilson] has run ahead so firmly [in trying to force the Mexican factions to come up with an agreeable government] that nothing more is to be done, either fight, or the people will blame him horribly."[346] Doubtless, the German agent alluded to the German mission under way to force the U.S. president's hand and cause an intervention – the plan that Sommerfeld had proposed to Admiral von Holtzendorff.

Sommerfeld had mastered the art of coalescing various seemingly unrelated interests into cohesive strategies over the years as a secret agent. He was a master manipulator. He acted as a go-between for Francisco Madero and the American military in El Paso that was worried about stray bullets in 1911.[347] A few months later, the German agent connected German envoy to Mexico Paul von Hintze with the Mexican Secretary of Finance, Ernesto Madero, in order to facilitate negotiations over a reciprocity treaty between Germany and Mexico.[348] In return, Sommerfeld made sure that the German government, looking at the revolutionary government with suspicion, gained insight into its policies and received valuable contracts to sell arms to the Mexican military.[349] When Mexican rebels murdered several German citizens in an textile mill in Puebla in 1912, Sommerfeld pushed the Madero administration to track down the perpetrators, and helped German envoy von Hintze negotiate a financial compensation which was actually paid out.[350] No other foreign government received reparations for their murdered citizens under Madero. Sommerfeld mounted the largest secret service operation a foreign country ever organized on U.S. soil when Pascual Orozco rose against Madero in 1912.[351] How did he do it? He supported the quest of the Wilson administration to pacify the Mexican border, which also coincided with the interests of American corporations in Mexico that lobbied for an arms embargo. He eliminated the most significant threat to Madero's government at the same time.[352]

In Sommerfeld's world, all interest groups he represented stood to gain. He had no qualms about working at the same time for American corporate interests, the American government, Mexican revolutionaries, and the German government. His masterful manipulations of seemingly opposed interests are at the heart of understanding how Sommerfeld could work the secret plots to provide arms to Pancho Villa in 1915. The German agent had to come up with a scenario, like he had in the years past, in which all parties benefitted from working with him.

As a result of the placement of unsecured German war bonds among a wide range of clientele in the United States, Heinrich Albert opened bank accounts in April 1915, presumably in every region where these bonds were sold.[353] The purpose, according to Albert's accountant, was to give confidence to the banks selling these bonds that the German government was actually backing up the face value with cash reserves.[354] Each of those accounts, therefore, received deposits of $50,000 to $150,000, depending upon the value of war bonds traded in each region. The bond sales ended abruptly with the sinking of the *Lusitania* on May 7th 1915. Albert quietly retrieved a portion of his deposits in the next weeks and months to use for other purposes. These transfers of significant amounts of money, according to American investigators, became the vehicles for shifting money to German agents and Felix Sommerfeld, in particular. Especially suspicious were accounts in the Mississippi Valley Trust Company of St. Louis. On April 1st 1915, Albert established business with this bank (there was a significant German-American population in St. Louis that bought German war bonds) and deposited $100,000.[355] April 1st coincided with the day the German bonds became available for purchase. Felix Sommerfeld opened an account in the same bank on April 3rd, with a deposit of $15,000 and used it to pay for munitions shipments from the Western Cartridge Company in East Alton, Illinois to Pancho Villa's forces.[356]

Years later, investigators of the Justice Department inter-viewed the staff of the bank, looked at the transactions in both accounts, and, despite their best efforts, could not find a firm connec-tion between Sommerfeld and Albert's accounts other than the suspi-cious timing.[357] However, the connection existed. Albert's accounting records reveal how much Sommerfeld's project had cost up to the point of Dr. Dernburg's departure. On June 11th 1915, the day before Dr. Dernburg sailed for Norway, Albert's Amsinck and Company accounts showed a credit: "June 11 Refund in 'M[exico]' matter by Dr. Dernburg [$] 206,735.10 [$4.3 Million in today's value]."[358] The amount matches almost exactly the deposits Sommerfeld had received in the same time period on his account at the Mississippi Valley Trust Company.

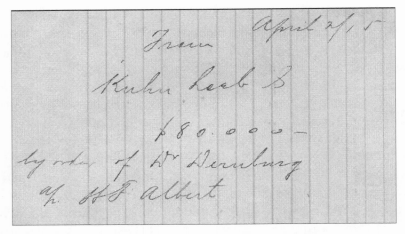

Evidence of Dernburg's transfers can be found in this note in the Albert Papers.[359]

Sommerfeld paid out a total of $381,000 ($8 million in today's value) from this account over the next six months.[360] U.S. investigators mixed up the two accounts that Heinrich Albert owned in St. Louis and missed four others he controlled in Chicago, Cleveland, and Milwaukee, thus losing the money trail that connected Albert with Sommerfeld and Pancho Villa.[361] After Heinrich Albert moved portions of his deposits back to New York, the German agent's remaining funds in St. Louis, Milwaukee, Cleveland, and Chicago from June to December, for which his books show no accounting, amounted to between $200,000 and $250,000.[362] The most viable explanation of why no accounting exists in Albert's papers is that the German fiscal agent destroyed the records before he left for Germany in 1917. The reason: Sommerfeld's deposits for the same time period between June 14th and December 15th show $182,385 ($3.8 Million in today's value), a striking semblance to Albert's secret funds left in the various regional banks. The combination of the initial funding from Dr. Dernburg's accounts and, after his departure, the continued money transfers from Albert's account marked *Kriegsministerium* (War Department), both showing parallel deposits in Sommerfeld's account for Pancho Villa's munitions purchases, can hardly be explained as mere coincidence.[363] American investigators had simply failed to follow Albert's various money transfers between banks and correlate them to Sommerfeld's accounts in St. Louis.

Pancho Villa's organization in the United States faced serious consequences, as well, as his fortunes declined on the battlefields of Celaya and León. Throughout 1914, three of the slain president Madero's uncles, Alberto, Alfonso, and Ernesto Madero (the former Secretary of Finance), as well as Raphael Hernández (the former Secretary of Justice and Madero's brother-in-law) handled the majority of Villa's purchases in the United States. The Maderos received funds for purchases through the Department of the Hacienda (Villa's treasury department). Some orders the Madero uncles handled themselves; however, most concerned arms and munitions, which was Sommerfeld's domain. He received money transfers from Villa's financial agent, Lázaro De La Garza. On a few occasions, funds also came directly through Pancho Villa's brother, Hipólito, who controlled the sales of confiscated cattle in the United States, as well as the racetrack, gambling joints, and brothels in Ciudad Juarez for his brother. The Maderos, as well as De La Garza also pursued their own business in the United States, separate from that of Pancho Villa. They sold ore, cotton, rubber, and bullion from the various businesses their families owned in Northern Mexico. Although hard to discern, Villa's finances, those of the state of Chihuahua, and proceeds from various exports comingled in a very complicated set of arrangements that opened doors to corruption and fraud. Legal battles between the Maderos, De La Garza, and Hipólito Villa that dragged on into the 1930s are ample evidence for the existence of unhealthy financial arrangements.

Much of the land and possessions of the Maderos and most of De La Garza's came under the control of Carranza's administrators when Villa had to retreat from the territories around Torreón and the Laguna region. The First Chief immediately confiscated the properties of the two families, alleging treason.[364] Not that these families had much of a choice! When Pancho Villa controlled these regions in the summer of 1914, as the rupture between him and Carranza occurred, the Madero and De La Garza families had to make a choice: Side with Carranza and Villa's revenge would be awful. Side with Villa, the chance of him winning control over Mexico on the battlefield was significant at the time. In fact, historian Katz labeled Villa's defeat in 1915 a "defeat snatched from the claws of victory."[365] His demise proved a disaster for the families who had sided with Villa. De La Garza, whose level of loyalty seemed to depend largely on the

padding of his pocketbook, removed himself from the Villa organization in July 1915. He founded his own merchant house, the L. De La
Garza & Co. Inc., "Import, Export and Commission Business," located
at 115 Broadway, together with Francisco Madero's brother-in-law
Raphael Hernández.[366] Alberto, Alfonso, and Ernesto Madero's trading company, Madero Bros. Inc., occupied offices in the same building,
115 Broadway, as the Mexican consulate and De La Garza's business.

As soon as Obregón handed Villa the disastrous defeat at
Celaya in the beginning of April, Sommerfeld scoured the U.S. market for additional large munitions contracts. The clandestine German
establishment of the Bridgeport Projectile Company in April, that
had allowed the conclusion of an exclusive contract with the Aetna
Explosives Company, changed the munitions market in the United
States profoundly. Manufacturers scrambled to find supplies. Prices
for any munitions, whether shrapnel or rifle cartridges, sky-rocketed.
Mexican revolutionary forces, in particular, felt the pinch. Delivery
contracts to Mexican revolutionaries dwindled under the weight of
Allied munitions demand. Sommerfeld had been successful in placing
large munitions contracts with Remington as a result of his impecca-
ble reputation for prompt payment. Using De La Garza as an intermediary, he offered to buy 25 million 7mm cartridges from Remington
Arms Co. in Bridgeport for $50 per thousand. Behind on orders as a
result of Rintelen-induced strikes, the company declined, even after
De La Garza offered a $250,000 down-payment.[367]

Despite the difficult market situation, Sommerfeld closed several large contracts in that time, some of which have been thoroughly
documented.[368] One member of his network that diverted arms and
munitions was his friend, Manuel Esteva. The Mexican career-diplomat
had served as Mexican vice-consul in New York under Porfirio Díaz,
then became President Madero's consul in San Antonio, and finally
served President Huerta as Consul General in New York. Needless to
say, Esteva maintained a large network to the entire Mexican exile
community, as well as to the revolutionary factions in Mexico.[369]
He also hated the leader of the Constitutionalists, Venustiano
Carranza, who fired him in the summer of 1914.[370] Officially "retired"
from Mexican affairs, the former Mexican consul now mingled with
Sommerfeld and others in the profitable munitions trade. Esteva
received funds through Frederico Stallforth, who had just started to

handle Rintelen's finances. "Knowing the good connections he had in Mexico, we [Stallforth Brothers] agreed to help him finance some of his exports... I may mention that Esteva is one of the close friends of Felix Sommerfeld."[371] Indeed, Sommerfeld, Esteva, and Stallforth were friends. In July of 1915, as German money streamed through Sommerfeld's bank accounts in St. Louis, both Esteva and Sommerfeld wrote into Stallforth's guestbook:

> Today as we meet as expatriates, far from our beloved homelands, I earnestly yearn for that day when we all can call ourselves brothers and when countries know no borders. Ma. Esteva.[372]

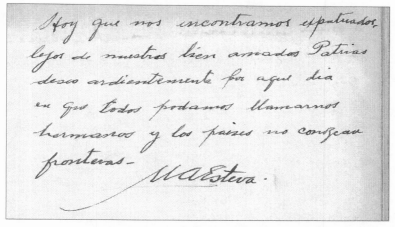

Entry from Manuel Esteva in Frederico Stallforth's guestboook

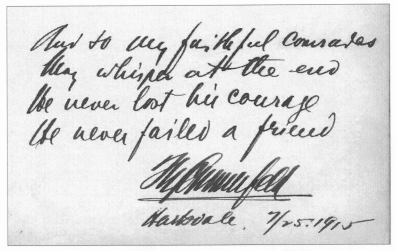

Entry from F. A. Sommerfeld in Frederico Stallforth's guestbook

And to my faithful comrades
May whisper at the end
He never lost his courage
He never failed a friend

F. A. Sommerfeld
Hartsdale [NY], 7/25. 1915[373]

One of the shipments Manuel Esteva purchased with funds provided through Stallforth is documented in De La Garza's ledgers: Esteva bought 500,000 cartridges and 500 rifles and sold them for $28,500 [$600,000 in today's value] to De La Garza who shipped them to Villa on May 3rd 1915.[374] The pervasive odor of Esteva's close relationship with Sommerfeld and German money is undeniable. In addition to these profitable contracts, Sommerfeld knew everyone and everything that had anything to do with the U.S. munitions industry, for the decided benefit of Karl Boy-Ed and Franz von Papen.

Sommerfeld began shipping on a $420,000 contract on April 1st 1915 for 12 million 7mm cartridges he had closed on behalf of Villa in February 1915.[375] The Mexican general had provided a down-payment of $50,000. For this order only the initial deposit appears in the accounts of Lázaro De La Garza, who had financial control of all New

York funds of Villa's supply chain.[376] This leads to the unanswered question, who paid for the balance of this contract? The entire order was produced, paid for, and shipped to Villa between April and August 1915. The price per thousand cartridges was an astonishingly low $35, while Remington and Winchester charged $50 for the same product, and Peters Cartridge Company between $55 and $60.[377]

Sommerfeld closed another arms contract on May 14th 1915, this time for 15 million cartridges at the same price as his earlier contract, $35 per thousand, valued at $525,000 ($11 Million in today's value). There are several astonishing aspects to Sommerfeld's deal. First, the price Sommerfeld got for the munitions was, again, at least thirty percent below market value. How did he get such an outstanding deal? Second, he managed to occupy the entire capacity of Franklin W. Olin's factory in Alton, Ill for the year 1915 with this second order. Sommerfeld was now on the hook for $945,000 ($20 Million in today's value), as Villa's fortunes declined, and the Villista fiat money was rapidly losing value. All the while he managed these huge contracts as a German in the middle of a huge spy scare. The German agent also stood to make 2% commissions, $18,900 if both contracts were fulfilled ($400,000 in today's value).

2168   BREWING AND LIQUOR INTERESTS AND GERMAN PROPAGANDA.

storff from the beginning, whereas the other was an individual account of Albert's to begin with?

Maj. HUMES. That is correct.

This is the significant matter: On the same day, April 5, 1915, there was an account opened in the Mississippi Valley Trust Co. of St. Louis in the name of F. A. Sommerfeld, who was an alien enemy and who is now interned as a German alien enemy; and in order that you may understand the exhibits which are attached, I ask that this whole bank account be made a part of the record, to show the amounts at various times.

(The account referred to is as follows:)

F. A. Sommerfeld In Account Current with Mississippi Valley Trust Company.
Saint Louis.

Deposits		Withdrawals			
Date of deposit	Deposit	Date paid	Checks	Date paid	Checks
April 5, 1915	15,000.00	Apr	2,838.80	Jun	5,421.50
Apr 20	5,000.00	Apr	684.82	Jun	1,756.42
Apr 21	10,000.00	Apr	1,852.62	Jun	6,210.50
Apr 26	20,000.00	Apr	1,768.41	Jun	4,210.50
Apr 29	20,000.00	Apr	2,588.25	Jun	1,721.00
Int	12.84	Apr	2,128.41	Jun	
May 4	15,000.00	Apr	2,273.07	Jun	
May 7	15,000.00	Apr	2,357.88	June	4,210.50
May 11	10,000.00	Apr	2,563.14	Jun	
May 17	10,000.00	Apr	2,789.45	Jun	
May 17	12,168.75	Apr	4,278.92	Jun	
May 21	2,831.25	Apr	7,157.85	Jun	
May 24	20,000.00	Apr	3,596.92	Jun	
May 27	20,000.00	Apr	3,452.91	Jun	
Int 28	21.38	Apr	3,199.98	Jun	
Jun 1	8,000.00	May	5,398.44	Jun	
June 4	5,000.00	May	3,873.00	Jun	
Jun 7	8,000.00	May	3,334.92	Jun	
Jun 9	8,000.00	May	3,875.00	Jun	
Jun 14	25,000.00	May	2,863.14	Jun	
Jun 15	13,000.00	May	4,847.34	Jun	
Jun 18	8,000.00	May	1,713.18	Jun	4,210.50
Jun 21	5,000.00	May	4,294.77	Jun	
Jun 23	5,000.00	May	3,705.34	Jun	
Jun 23	5,000.00	May	3,326.92	Jun	
Jun 24	5,000.00	May	3,596.92	Jun	
Jun 25	5,000.00	May	3,636.92	Jul	
June 28	6,000.00	May	3,118.77	Jul	
Int 29	8.42	May	4,397.97	July	8,421.00
Jun 30	8,000.00	May	3,897.97	Jul	
Jul 2	13,000.00	May	3,421.08	Jul	11,010.00
Jul 9	4,233.00	May	4,042.00	Jul	4,210.50
July 9	8,000.00	May	3,210.50	Jul	1,000.00
Jul 11	3,000.00	May	3,279.00	Jul	
Jul 13	3,000.00	May	3,395.21	Jul	16,000.00
Jul 14	1,000.00	May	3,894.70	Jul	17,555.00
July 28	17,000.00	May	3,210.50	Jul	
Jul 27	15,000.00	May	4,210.50	Aug	10,529.00
Int 30	2.43	May	4,210.50	Aug	10,529.00
Aug 20	31,000.00	May	4,210.50	Aug	
Aug 20	5,500.00	May	4,210.50	Aug	8,160.00
Int 30	0.74	May	1,693.00	Sept	5,000.00
Sep 8	6,000.00	May	4,210.50	Sept	5,000.00
Int 29	0.45	May	4,210.50	Nov 26	
Int Oct. 28	1.04			Dec 7	2,500.00
Nov 12	6,935.96			Dec 10	
Int 29	0.61			Dec 11	654.10
1915 Dec 11	None				

Sommerfeld's account at the Mississippi Valley Trust Company shows a total $381,000 flowing through it from April to December 1915.[378]

Only days after closing on the second contract for the fifteen million cartridges, on May 17th 1915, he signed the contract over to Lázaro De La Garza.[379] De La Garza provided the down-payment of $65,000, which went to the Western Cartridge Company. The money came from the Maderos, probably profits from sales of goods from the area Villa controlled in Northern Mexico, such as bullion, cattle, rubber, or cotton. De La Garza also logged a deposit "en B[an]co St. Louis" in May for $30,000.[380] This amount does not show up on Sommerfeld's account. However, Albert withdrew that exact amount in May from his account at the St. Louis Union Bank. Obviously, not just Albert, but also Sommerfeld maintained accounts in the St. Louis

Union Bank, which were connected. Assuming that Sommerfeld paid for both contracts, his St. Louis Union Bank account showed transactions of roughly $400,000, similar to his Mississippi Valley Trust account. Only $145,000 of the total $945,000 appeared in the books of De La Garza. The French government bought $265,000 worth. The Carranza faction took $150,000 of the munitions. The Western Cartridge Company refunded $65,000. This leaves $385,000, almost the exact sum of Sommerfeld's Mississippi Valley Trust transactions and what the U.S. government alleged to have come from Heinrich Albert ($381,000).[381] The $385,000 also matches the funds believed to have remained on Albert's various accounts in Milwaukee, Cleveland, St. Louis, and Chicago.

Another question looms large as well: Why would Franklin W. Olin sell munitions to Sommerfeld thirty percent or more below market value? Even if Olin would have sympathized with the German cause to the point that he refused to produce munitions for the Entente, he still could have commanded a higher price from the various Mexican factions, even Villa's. Incidentally, De La Garza's accounts show payments to Peters Cartridge Company for the same ammunition in May 1915 priced at $55 per thousand.[382] The answer to this riddle may have revealed itself in the spring of 1916 when, out of the blue, and, without much fanfare, F. W. Olin opened a brass casing factory next to Western Cartridge Company in Alton, Illinois.

Olin was a businessman who believed in vertical integration. He started his business in 1892 when he founded the Equitable Powder Manufacturing Company. The company's blasting caps served mostly the coal industry in the Midwest. He expanded the production to include small arms ammunition in 1898, changing the name to Western Cartridge Company. He also founded a company that manufactured targets in the same year to better serve his sporting and hunting rifle customers. The Western Cartridge Company had managed to carve out a nice slice of the U.S. ammunitions market dominated by the large arms manufacturers such as Winchester Rifle Company and Remington by the early teens.[383] Since the outbreak of the Mexican Revolution in 1910 the company thrived. The success resulted from the fact that Western was willing to produce 7mm Mauser cartridges widely used in Mexico. The Western Cartridge Company had sold millions of cases of ammunition through Sommerfeld to Madero, Carranza, and Villa over the years.

President Franklin Olin and his son, John, liked doing business with Sommerfeld. His clout over the past years had made the transportation of shipments across the international border smooth. When the U.S. government instituted various embargos, Sommerfeld called on his friends in very high places, such as Lindley Garrison, Secretary of War, or William Jennings Bryan, Secretary of State, or Hugh Lenox Scott, the General in charge of border troops and later President Wilson's Chief of Staff of the Army. Sommerfeld also stood by his word. He was very well organized, understood proper specification, had the customer contacts, and, most importantly, he always paid on time.

The savvy businessman chomped at the bit when Sommerfeld asked Olin to quote on the two largest munitions orders in the company's history. An order of that size would allow Olin to install his own brass mill to produce the cartridge cups. However, where to get the all-important presses for such a production? Enter Carl Heynen and the Bridgeport Projectile Company. The Secret War Council had signed contracts in the spring of 1915, locking up the entire capacity for hydraulic presses in the United States. Where did Olin get this equipment that allowed him to open a brass mill in the spring of 1916? The difference between the sales price and market price on twenty seven million cartridges that Sommerfeld contracted amounted to approximately $405,000 ($8.5 million in today's value).[384] Heynen accounted for the cost of hydraulic presses he had ordered and which were actually produced: "$417,550 for presses which had actually been produced."[385] A striking coincidence! If true, the German government supported Olin's plans for a brass mill with the understanding that he would not produce for the Entente; hence, the contracts with Sommerfeld at a price far below market value. The new factory would prove to be a boon for Olin. He came out of the war with tremendous financial strength. In 1931 he bought Winchester. Olin Industries is one of the largest corporations in the United States to this day, partly thanks to Franklin Olin and the connections of his good friend, Felix A. Sommerfeld.

Not all went smoothly with the shipments from Western Cartridge Company. Frustrated telegrams between Sommerfeld, De La Garza, and Villa in the end of May document the financial straits of the *División Del Norte*. Sommerfeld wrote on May 27th 1915, "... if you do not send me thirty-five thousand dollars by Thursday, we will not get the shipment from the factory..."[386] Sommerfeld's shipments from the Western Cartridge Company in Alton, Illinois to the border tell the story: In April, 2.2 million 7mm rounds left the factory ($78,400 at $35 per thousand), in May slightly more, 2.5 million rounds ($88,515 at $35 per thousand).[387] Sommerfeld shipped 3.3 million rounds ($115,465 at $35 per thousand) in June, when reports suggest that Villa was running out of cash.[388] Franz von Papen received $115,304 ($24.2 million in today's value) from Albert for a non-specified, munitions-related purpose on June 18th 1915.[389] It was definitely not for the Indian resistance or the Bridgeport Projectile project. The deposit was almost exactly the dollar amount of Sommerfeld's shipments between May 15th and June 15th 1915.[390] Sommerfeld sent the angry telegrams to De La Garza when Villa's army could not supply the funds to continue shipments. He used German government funds to ship an average of 120,300 cartridges per day, a total of 3.3 million between mid-May and mid-June, amounting to $115,500.

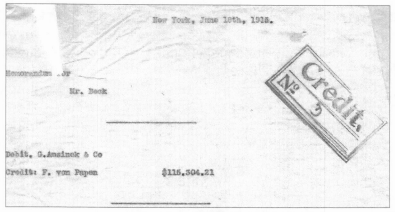

Credit memo from Heinrich Albert concerning Franz von Papen funds, June 1915 [391]

July shipments amounted to 2.6 million rounds. Shipments stopped abruptly in August, when the second contract for fifteen million cartridges was supposed to start. The contract had called for one million cartridges per week, Olin's full plant capacity. Since he also committed to a large Spanish contract and the brass mill was not yet operational, the shipments fell well below the call-off commitment by August. Western Cartridge did not ship anything between August 1st and August 24th. Apparently, the production manager had thought that he could benefit from less set-up times and more production continuity since Spanish Mauser and Mexican Mauser used the same cartridge. What he had not counted on were serious problems with quality, which caused twenty-eight percent of the production to misfire or not fire at all.[392] The quality problem was severe enough that production came to a virtual standstill. It is feasible that the dependence of Western on brass cups, which were in rare supply, caused the problems. A certain indication is the investment the company made in its own mill, which produced the first cups by May of 1916.

The financial woes of Villa exacerbated the delivery problems of Western Cartridge. De La Garza seemed incapable of handling the situation. Since Sommerfeld had signed the orders over to the Mexican merchant, thus releasing himself from all financial responsibility, he should not have cared. Yet, the opposite was the case. Sommerfeld organized meetings with F. W. Olin in New York and sent inspectors to Alton to help fix the quality problems. Although his personal money was not at stake, he stood to lose his reputation, his commissions, and, most importantly, would be blamed by Albert and von Papen for losing the investment the Secret War Council had made in Western Cartridge. The Secret War Council decided to take over the operation from De La Garza around the middle of August. It was not without a fight. The Mexican merchant complained bitterly to one of his best friends Emilio Madero, a brother of Francisco Madero, and at the time one of Villa's generals. De La Garza blamed Sommerfeld for the disastrous outcome of the order:

> The last time I was in New York I entered into a contract on behalf of the Division of the North for 15,000,000 cartridges and had to provide some of my own money as collateral. When I closed the contract with the factory I instructed Summerfield [sic] to stay in New York and adequately attend to this contract, in the same way he had done in the past. As I began to worry that Summerfield [sic] did not give the attention to this matter it deserved I sent a telegram to Los Angeles asking if the agency there had funds to make the shipments. They said no and I feared a fight with the Agency. I IMMEDIATELY notified General Villa

about this matter, however he has not responded to date… Now Señor González, representative of the Agency, approached me and told me to come to an understanding with Summerfield [sic]. These guys will stop at nothing, because if this friend [Sommerfeld] is wrong for any reason, as has happened, I would bear the responsibility, which I want to avoid under all circumstances and prefer to spend my time in this business arrangement to see it completed satisfactorily, and to avoid the consequences that I might find. Well, there is much that has worn on me, such as what they are claiming I stole in the five months I was in the Agency… [393]

The fact was that De La Garza, who had founded his own company in the end of July, had offered the balance of the order to Carranza.[394] Now, De La Garza feared Villa's wrath, especially since the "Agency" (Villa's administration) had ordered him "to come to an understanding with Summerfield [sic]."[395]

The specifics of this "understanding" became immediately apparent. A Jewish-Rumanian immigrant and German agent, James Manoil, became the front man in the management of the munitions contract with the Western Cartridge Company. Who was this mysterious agent? Manoil was twenty-seven years old and worked with his brother Maurice (or Morris according to Census records) in a suite on 60 Broadway, New York.[396] James Manoil and Company produced a "manophone [phonograph] and other musical instruments."[397] Likely on a secret mission for Karl Boy-Ed, Manoil travelled to Argentina in January 1915.[398] The trip coincided with the end of the remaining German fleet at the battle of Falkland, as a result of which hundreds of German sailors were stranded in Argentina. Not much more is known about Manoil, other than he did not possess significant wealth. According to a statement by the Assistant Treasurer of the Guaranty Trust Company of New York, "concerning Mr. James Manoil … we have known him for some time and have extended him accommodation in small amounts on notes … We have never had a statement of his financial affairs, but we are inclined to think his means are moderate."[399] This man purchased several hundred thousand dollars' worth of munitions from the Western Cartridge Company in the next weeks. Manoil's address also happened to be that of the office of the German military attaché, Franz von Papen.

Von Papen's offices housed the management of the Bridgeport Projectile Company. Its manager was Carl Heynen, the former HAPAG representative in Mexico. His main job was managing the purchase of smokeless powder, hydraulic presses, and other items that would create shortages in the American munitions industry. Heynen would have been von Papen's ideal go-to person to help with the mess at Western Cartridge Company. Heynen was not only a well-honed manager, he knew Mexico and Mexican culture better than anyone, was an experienced logistics man, and a personal friend of Felix Sommerfeld. It is safe to assume that Manoil's main purpose in 1915 was to lend his name and business as a cover for the Secret War Council.

Almost immediately after the Villa administration told De La Garza to submit to Sommerfeld, the project righted itself, if only briefly. De La Garza's "office" dispatched an inspector named Thomas Rhein to Alton.[400] Similarly to Manoil, there was only a handful of Thomas Rheins in the United States. Only one lived in the vicinity of New York and worked for the railroads there. He had no known expertise in testing ammunition. Rhein was the alias of another German agent, most likely dispatched from Hans Tauscher's office where the real technical expertise for munitions resided, a clear choice for von Papen and Heynen. Also in August, the German government sent money to cover shipments of one million cartridges.[401] However, Villa still did not have enough funds to buy the rest of the munitions. Sommerfeld testified in 1918 that in the summer of 1915 "... he [Villa] stopped sending money..."[402] Heynen decided to approach Carranza's arms buyer in Los Angeles, L. E. Hall.

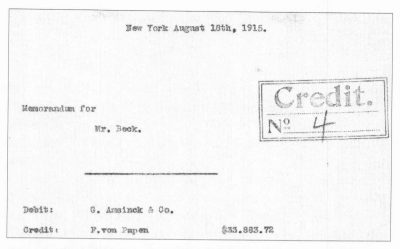

New York August 18th, 1915.

Memorandum for

Mr. Beck.

Credit.
No. 4

Debit: G. Amsinck & Co.

Credit: F. von Papen $33.883.72

*Credit memo for Franz von Papen at exactly the same time when
James Manoil bought one million rounds of ammunition for $35,000[403]*

The B.I. agent who interviewed Hall around that time noted,

> Hall stated that he was purchasing 7m/m shells
> from James Manoil, with DELA Garcia [sic] brokers
> located at 115 Broadway, New York City. Hall stated
> that Manoil had ordered these shells for Villa and had
> put up a large payment with the Western Cartridge
> Company at Alton, Illinois, part payment of a three
> million round order. Due to Villa not being able to
> put up the money Manoil is going to sell this order to
> Carranza. Hall alleges that Arthur Gonzalez, purchas-
> ing agent for Carranza, is expecting a draft from New
> York for $53,000.00 to pay for one million rounds of
> 7m/m shells and thereafter will receive $53,000.00
> once a week for two weeks to pay for the total of
> three million rounds of 7m/m shells.[404]

A few days later the same agent noted,

> Today agent was informed... that Gonzalez
> has not yet placed the money in the Bank for the large

> shipment of ammunition which has been ordered through Mr. F. A. Sommerfeld in the three million round order from the Western Cartridge Company... [405]

The German agents in New York, with the help of De La Garza, were able to sell three million cartridges to Carranza for a profit of $15 per thousand ($45,000) on September 13th.[406] De La Garza received an additional $2 per thousand in commissions.[407] Only 1.8 million were shipped. Apparently, General Obregón stopped the shipments in the beginning of October, citing that the price of the cartridges was "excessive."[408] In reality, he had won decisive battles against Villa and captured millions of rounds of his munitions, weapons, rolling stock, and other supplies. The remaining cartridges of the order, therefore, went directly to New York, filling the warehouses that Tauscher rented on behalf of the German government. Sommerfeld and De La Garza, as well as Alberto Madero, another staunch Villa supporter and financial backer, Felipe Ángeles and a dozen of Villa's military commanders all deserted the hapless revolutionary chieftain in September 1915.[409] The German agents decided to drop the project by October, after an investment of $405,000 in presses and $381,000 in investments.

There was further trouble with Western Cartridge Company. The cartridges still had quality problems and, in addition, the machinists suddenly went on strike. Carranza refused to take any more shipments and the Bureau of Investigations was hot on the heels of the German agents. Tauscher had been indicted for the mishap with the *Djember* in July, when agents discovered him shipping arms and ammunition to Indian resistance fighters. Albert had the contents of his briefcase plastered all over New York's dailies also in July. The British arrested Rintelen and Meloy in the middle of August. Police arrested Robert Fay and started to unravel the fire bomb plot in October. New York's newspapers again beamed with a scandal on October 28th: Felix Sommerfeld had been arrested on an old warrant and paraded in handcuffs through the Astor hotel.

De La Garza and his German backers signed the contract for the remaining five million cartridges over to the Standard Stoker Company on October 14th 1915, an arms merchant dealing with France. The price for the cartridges in the new contract with France was $48.50, a $12.50 per 1,000 profit windfall for De La Garza.[410] What Sommerfeld most likely knew, but what De La Garza and the arms dealer had not considered, was the fact that 7 mm cartridges are different for different guns. The French government had actually sourced the munitions for the Serbian army. However, since the Serbians did not use the same Mauser rifles that were common in Mexico, the cartridges did not work. De La Garza and J. P. Morgan, who had to pay for the order, battled over the problems with the shells over the course of the next six months.

The trouble of selling the contract and dealing with the very unhappy, new customers was worth it for De La Garza. As soon as the French had signed the delivery contract, De La Garza sued the Western Cartridge Company for the return of his deposit of $65,000 ($1.37 million in today's value). Olin "refunded" the money to him without much hesitation. However, the down payment belonged to the Madero brothers who, in turn, owed that amount to the División Del Norte, then under the leadership of Pancho Villa. De La Garza was unsure what to do with the money. He kept it in his account for three months. Nobody claimed it. He carefully evaluated the ownership of the funds. De La Garza paid $5,000 ($105,000 in today's value) to Sommerfeld at the end of December, the remainder of his commission. By the summer of 1916, the contract had made De La Garza $65,000 deposit money (paid by Villa and the Maderos) and $75,000 commissions ($1.6 million in today's value) from the French. De La Garza had some minor expenses for legal fees and the administration of the contract. De La Garza made somewhere around $140,000 ($3 Million in today's value) in total through this arrangement. Immediately after the contract came to its conclusion in the summer of 1916, De La Garza moved himself and his family, including his brother, Vidal, to Los Angeles. There, he bought a $100,000 ($200,000 if one believes *the Los Angeles Times*) mansion with cash and settled down. His wife, Esther, brought over $93,000 (close to $2 million in today's value) with her in cash from Torreón. It is likely that this money represented earnings and other cash assets from his investments in Mexico. Most of his property had been expropriated by Carranza, who by the fall of 1915 had full control over Chihuahua and Torreón. As a Villista, De La Garza could expect no mercy and no reimbursement.[411] He officially "retired" from the Revolution when he moved to Los Angeles. Retirement treated De La Garza well: He settled in his mansion in a well-to-do foothills neighborhood and lived lavishly on the interest of his "savings," a whopping $5 million in today's money.[412] The revolution had made him an even richer man than he already was in 1911.

It did not take long for Villa and the Madero brothers to catch onto the fact that De La Garza had made off with the deposit. Alberto Madero sued him in Los Angeles in June 1916.[413] The case dragged on until 1918, when it was dismissed. The dismissal was based on a technicality, namely that Pancho Villa was an enemy of the United States and, therefore, could not recover any money north of the border. Villa was furious. He sent De La Garza a letter in 1919, asking him to work for him again and that everything would be forgotten.[414] While he did not ask De La Garza to come to Mexico for a meeting, ultimately, that would have been what Villa intended. Then, he could arrest and execute his former treasurer.

However, De La Garza was no dummy. He wrote to his friend, Leon Canova, that he would stay as far away from Villa as he could. His friend agreed. Canova had smuggled Eduardo Iturbide out of Mexico in 1914. Villa had pursued the then-American consul all the way to the American border but could not arrest and execute Iturbide. An irate Villa had publicly vowed to kill Canova if he ever set foot into Mexico again. "I think you are right in regard to General Villa," Canova mused, "and that your safest line is to keep clear of him... If I could meet Villa at a time when he was in good humor I would not hesitate to do so – BUT, I think that if the meeting occurred when he was in one of his rages, he would order me to be shot forthwith. I imagine he would follow the same line of conduct with you. So, in a case of this kind it is best to 'watch your step.'"[415]

De La Garza was holed up in his mansion, fearing for his life. He had outfoxed el General. When Villa realized that he could not touch De La Garza, he threatened to kidnap twelve Americans that he would trade for the merchant.[416] Neither did the kidnappings happen, nor did Villa get to have his revenge. Villa died in 1923 from an assassin's bullets in Hidalgo de Parral, Mexico. His brother, Hipólito, kept up the pressure and sued De La Garza into the 1930s. A court in Ciudad Juarez finally convicted De La Garza in 1933 and issued a warrant for his arrest. De La Garza defended himself with all means at his disposal all the way to the Mexican Supreme Court, which overturned the conviction.

He cited needs for "personal security" with the Mexican government, which gave him permission to carry a concealed weapon during his journey to the Mexican capital.[417] Undoubtedly, the embattled businessman feared for his life.

While De La Garza succeeded in keeping the stolen money, he paid a hefty, non-material price for his crime. Alberto Madero and Hipólito Villa ruined De La Garza's reputation with continued lawsuits and negative press coverage. Headlines in Mexico such as "The man who robbed 10 Million Dollars from Pancho Villa" branded the former financial agent a traitor to the revolution.[418] His reputation was forever tainted. Later in life, he tried to re-establish a meaningful business in Mexico, but his effort came to nothing. Not even a network of American politicians and financiers, including President Harding, Vice President and encumbant President Coolidge could help him overcome the reputation of a swindler who had sold out his country. Lázaro De La Garza died in Torreón in August of 1939.[419]

The twenty-seven million cartridge orders with all their repercussions and strange twists also presented a number of lost opportunities for the American government. Authorities missed their greatest chance to uncover the machinations of the German secret service in the United States. There is no other conclusion than to call the failure of U.S. authorities to investigate James Manoil one of the greatest intelligence blunders in the World War. James Manoil would have been easy to investigate. There was only one person with that name in the United States. A quick visit to his office on 60 Broadway would have revealed that this person neither had the funds nor the wherewithal to buy millions of cartridges in the United States. Shadowing the man would have revealed his work for Franz von Papen and the Secret War Council. The link between Villa and von Papen that the MID and BI records fully documented would have uncovered Sommerfeld's responsibilities and would have likely led to his arrest long before the attack on Columbus, New Mexico in March 1916 occurred.

The Military Intelligence Division investigated Manoil in 1918 after he had moved to Mexico. The American military attaché interviewed him, found him to be "very shrewd, intelligent [,] not well educated... of a rather aggressive character."[420] Investigators never connected Manoil with Sommerfeld, De La Garza, or the German government despite the documentation they had on the fifteen and the twelve million cartridge contracts. Researchers, as well, failed to understand Manoil's role as a patsy for German secret agents.[421]

Felix Sommerfeld's skill as a secret agent was nothing short of impressive. Despite the discovery of Franz Rintelen and indications American investigators had that Sommerfeld had at least conferred with him, and despite being arrested on a trumped-up charge in the end of October, Sommerfeld concluded these large contracts, and managed their execution, while removing his fingerprints almost entirely. No investigator ever suspected German involvement in the arms deliveries to first Pancho Villa, and then to Venustiano Carranza. Neither the Mexicans who sued De La Garza for the next twenty years, nor the American Bureau of Investigations, the Military Intelligence Division, nor the Secret Service, all of whom were investigating German activities in the United States at the time, ever traced the payments that James Manoil effected to the German government. If they had, they would have shone a spotlight on Heinrich Albert, Felix Sommerfeld, and the rest of the Secret War Council.

Germany's material support of F. W. Olin's company with hydraulic presses as a quid pro quo for not supplying the Entente fulfilled its intended purpose to a large degree. The Western Cartridge Company filled the remaining orders for the French government with cartridges that were unusable on the battlefields of Europe. This was exactly what Sommerfeld had proposed to the German government in May of 1915. Only a few months after the Secret War Council turned the munitions contract over to the French government, the Mexican border exploded with an unprecedented incursion into the U.S. by Pancho Villa's forces in March of 1916. The German government had invested $786,000 ($16.5 million in today's value) as a first installment to force the hand of the U.S. government and remove available munitions from the coffers of the Entente. As a matter of fact, more than half ($405,000) of the investment consisted of hydraulic presses that the German government already owned. The remainder was the $381,000 that flowed through Sommerfeld's accounts in St. Louis. A large portion (about $119,000) of that, the profits on shipments to the French government, lined the pockets of Lázaro De La Garza.[422] Albert recovered approximately $45,000 from sales of munitions to Carranza. As Sommerfeld had predicted, Olin and most of his competitors began producing munitions by the spring of 1916 for the

American military that built up its strength as a result of tensions on the Mexican border.

A significant piece of Sommerfeld's strategy to create a war between the United States and Mexico fell into place in October of 1915. Woodrow Wilson decided to extend diplomatic recognition to Venustiano Carranza as a result of the declining fortunes of Pancho Villa. The decision was based, in part, on the intent to reduce tensions in Mexico and to strengthen the dominant faction in the civil war. However, the head of the Latin American desk in the State Department, Villa's sworn enemy Leon Canova, had much to do with swaying the President to change policy towards Mexico. The American government underestimated the extent of Pancho Villa's fury in the process, and did not count on the manipulative genius of Felix Sommerfeld to take advantage of this new situation.

CHAPTER 7:
AND THE WINNER IS...

WHILE FELIX A. SOMMERFELD WAS busy shipping millions of cartridges to Mexico with German government support and financing, he also worked diligently on maintaining his important connections to the Wilson administration. The machinations of Leon Canova in promoting the creation of a unity government for Mexico under the leadership of a powerful coalition of Mexican military and civilian leaders had backfired in June 1915. The destruction of the Huerta-Orozco-Mondragón plot and the subsequent arrest of Andrew Meloy in England had brought the new Secretary of State Lansing and his adviser Canova dangerously close to being implicated in a German plot. The manipulating hand of Leon Canova disappeared briefly from the public eye as negotiations with the warring Mexican factions of Villa, Zapata, and Carranza continued. American foreign policy towards Mexico took an unexpected turn, one that favored German secret strategy to destabilize the border and tie up American resources and attention. After removing Canova from the driver's seat of Mexican policy, Secretary of State Robert Lansing, at the insistence of President Wilson, mobilized an old war horse, and Wilson confidante, Army Chief of Staff Hugh Lenox Scott to head to El Paso and negotiate with Pancho Villa.

General Scott had successfully settled serious border disturbances with Villa throughout the Mexican Revolution, most recently the standoff at Naco in the winter of 1914. At issue now were Villa's desperate moves to raise funds for his dwindling army. Villa resorted to expropriating foreign, mostly American assets, and blackmailing the international business community in Chihuahua as Carranza's forces closed in on the *División Del Norte*. Dangling the prospect of recognition of a Mexican government under his auspices, Secretary Lansing dispatched Villa's "friend" to the border to negotiate for the release of millions of dollars' worth of American assets. Though Villa had been weary of the U.S. State Department and their representatives Canova and Silliman, in particular, he agreed to meet with the Army Chief of Staff in El Paso in the middle of August 1915.

The situation in Northern Mexico had become precarious as a result of Carranza and Obregón's successful campaign against Villa. The stakes were as high as ever. President Wilson had issued an ultimatum to all the warring factions that they should end their quarrels in due time or risk an intervention to force pacification on American terms on June 2nd 1915. The speech resulted in a flurry of activity in all quarters of the Mexican community, most notably among the exiles who had gathered around Victoriano Huerta. President Wilson made clear to anyone willing to listen that Huerta, or anybody associating with him, would not be part of a solution for Mexico. Felix Díaz, the expatriate conspirator and nephew of the former dictator Porfirio Díaz, pronounced his willingness to support the American President's efforts as an alternative to "the scoundrel" Huerta.[423] All he needed was sufficient funding and the promise of recognition once his military takeover of Mexico would be successful. Of course, no one but Díaz alone believed that the exiled politician had any significant following, support from other powerful factions, or the wherewithal to mount a military campaign of any significance. Both the American and the German governments snubbed his attempts to insert himself into Mexican politics.[424] American agents arrested Huerta when he attempted his military intervention in the end of June, effectively ending the conspiracy. Pascual Orozco, although arrested at the same time, managed to flee. However, he died in July while on the run from American authorities. After Huerta's arrest, Manuel Mondragón returned to Spain and ended his quest for power in Mexico.

Most remaining exiles gathered around either the Carranza or Villa faction, as President Wilson and the new Secretary of State Lansing publicly embraced a solution that did not include either revolutionary chieftain as president of Mexico. Unofficially, however, feelers went out to Carranza by way of Charles Douglas, Carranza's main lobbyist in the U.S., asking Carranza to support a Pan-American Conference that would select a president for Mexico acceptable to all warring factions. Douglas, a well-known lawyer and judge in Washington D.C., had close

connections to the State Department and Robert Lansing, in particular. Wilson saw a possibility in using Douglas as an "unofficial channel" to proffer the possibility of recognizing Carranza as president in
return for his cooperation.[425] Lansing seemed to be less excited than
his boss to consider the possibility of recognizing Carranza, whom he
viewed as "stubborn" and hard to work with. In this opinion, Lansing
joined a group within the administration, including Secretary of War
Lindley Garrison, Secretary of the Interior Franklin Knight Lane, and
Army Chief of Staff General Hugh Lenox Scott. Scott characterized
the First Chief as a coward in his memoirs, who instead of fighting,
"occupied himself in dancing and dining, far out of harm's way."[426]
While Garrison, Scott, and others actively lobbied the President for a
solution that excluded a Carranza presidency (Villa had excluded himself voluntarily), Wilson kept pushing to explore ways for finding a
working relationship with the revolutionary leader.

The President could not deny the fact that Carranza was winning the competition with Villa by the end of June, and that a future
peace would undoubtedly have to include Carranza.[427] President
Wilson gave marching orders to Douglas via his Secretary of State on
June 18th 1915, "I understand that Judge Douglas is going to start for
Vera Cruz on Monday. Would it not be well to have a talk with him
(not at your office, but at your house and as privately, as much away
from newspapers, as possible) and let him go down with a full understanding of our position, namely that Carranza must meet every honest advance half-way if he expects to win our confidence, and that
he must win our confidence, at least in some degree, if he hopes for
ultimate recognition..."[428] However, the result was disappointing.
Douglas returned from his meetings confirming Carranza's position
that no country, especially the United States, had any right to inter-
fere in domestic Mexican affairs. The First Chief refused to recognize
the Pan-American Conference as an institution with any but advisory
power. However, Carranza did commit his former Secret Service Chief
Roberto Pesquiera as an observer to the conference that was scheduled to start in July 1915.[429]

Not one to back down easily, and an equal to Carranza
concerning stubbornness, President Wilson appointed Paul Fuller, a
prominent international lawyer, on July 7th as the mediator between
the Mexican factions.[430] Wilson's special envoy tried to convince the

Mexican revolutionary chieftain to commit to a unity government during meetings with representatives of Carranza. Again, Carranza refused. Aside from his principled stands against foreign interference in the affairs of Mexico, Carranza was on a firm path to military supremacy in Mexico. He also had well-founded suspicions as to the real motivations behind the American entreaties. Fuller was not the only official working on a Mexican settlement. Wilson's special envoy was negotiating with Carranza's representatives at the same time General Scott went to El Paso to meet Villa. Two "independent" negotiators, James Garfield, a prominent Republican lobbying for U.S. oil companies in Washington and the son of President James A. Garfield, as well as Nelson Rhoades, a businessman from Los Angeles, simultaneously sought to enlist exiles, as well as Carranza and Villa generals, to back the plan for a unity government in Mexico. According to historian Friedrich Katz, these U.S. government officials and semi-official businessmen fanning out among the various Mexican revolutionary factions pursued a solution for Mexico that excluded Carranza entirely. Behind the First Chief's back but not without his finding out, Fuller, Garfield and Rhoades approached Carrancista generals Alvaro Obregón and Pablo Gonzales. General Scott, with the help of special envoy George Carothers, negotiated with Pancho Villa at the same time. Fuller and Interior Secretary Lane spoke with Villa general Felipe Ángeles.

Felix Sommerfeld attended most of these meetings as Villa's representative in the United States.[431] He had complete access to the American negotiating team under Scott, while scouring the situation for an opportunity to make good on his commitment to the German government, namely creating a border incident that would provoke an American military intervention. Sommerfeld's quest, with this goal in mind, was pretty much in line with the prevailing opinion of American businessmen with interests in Mexico, as well as key members of the Wilson cabinet and the State Department; namely, that an intervention would solve the Mexican quagmire once and for all.

In what historian Katz called the "Canova plot," Paul Fuller and Leon Canova, with the backing of important American business leaders, Wilson's various envoys, and members of his cabinet, dangled recognition in front of the by-then ever more desperate Pancho Villa.[432] Unsurprisingly, Villa grasped the last straw of his waning power in

Mexico and reiterated his long held determination to not ever run for president of Mexico. He announced that he was willing to go into exile if Carranza would do the same.[433] General Scott, the main negotiator because of his close relationship with Villa, described the meetings in August 1915 in his memoirs:

> A scheme was worked out with Mr. James Garfield, one-time secretary of the interior [sic] in the Roosevelt cabinet, and with Mr. [Nelson] Rhoades of Los Angeles that gave great promise of stabilizing conditions in Mexico, provided our State Department would give its consent. The plan was primarily upon the fact that a member of Madero's cabinet [Vázquez Tagle, Secretary of Justice], then living quietly in Mexico City with the respect of all parties, had never resigned after the deaths of President Madero and Vice-President Suarez, and the succession made him the *de jure* president of Mexico. It was proposed that both the Villista and Carrancista factions be brought to agree that he be recognized as the *de facto* as well as *de jure* president with a bi-partisan cabinet, half Carrancista and half Villista, and that our State Department immediately stabilize this composite government by recognition and allow it to import arms and munitions of war with which to maintain itself. Villa agreed to this, and it remained to secure the adhesion of one or two men – General Obregón or General Pablo Gonzales. The power of the Carrancistas rested upon those two men... This plan, of course, would leave him [Carranza] out in the cold, where he belonged.[434]

The plan had one serious flaw: Carranza, the *de facto* main military and political power in Mexico in July 1915, simply refused to have any part of it. His generals were not willing to risk a confrontation with the revolutionary leader as they finished off the last remnants of Villa's army. General Scott blamed the State Department, which during the entire month of July "would not say either yes or no" to his request to see the two Carrancista generals behind the First Chief's back.[435] Scott complained, "I almost had a nervous prostration, feeling like a dog tied up in the back yard, longing for my collar to be taken off."[436] While the State Department "procrastinated" over a decision on whether or not to risk alienating Venustiano Carranza, the most powerful man in Mexico, by going behind his back, Villa's military situation went from bad to worse. Simultaneously, closely following the power shift in Mexico and behind the scenes, President Wilson reined in his new Secretary of State. The President thus stopped the effort to artificially create a solution for Mexico other than the one that was organically evolving that summer.

This fundamental shift in American policy towards Mexico happened in the isolation of the Oval Office without any public pro-nouncements or consultations with anyone within or outside the U.S. government. Secretary Lansing still clearly supported a solution without Carranza in the beginning of July.[437] He informed President Wilson as late as August 6th, "in the discussions [in the Pan-American Conference] I found that there was unanimous agreement that Carranza was impossible... "[438] The people involved in finding a solu-tion for Mexico, State Department officials, special envoys, Mexican exiles, and the ranking members of the Pan-American Conference meeting in New York in the beginning of August, had no reason to doubt that a unity government for Mexico was the ultimate goal. *The New York Times* reported on August 2nd under the headline "Wilson Peace Plan Ready for Mexico," that the American president would "recognize some member of the Madero cabinet approved by fac-tions."[439] The article mentioned in detail the candidate the Villa fac-tion was promoting and people like Scott, Canova, Lane, and Garrison were supporting: Manuel Vázquez Tagle.

Vázquez Tagle had been a member of the Madero admin-istration. Enthusiastically, *The New York Times* published a full page spread on the former Secretary of Justice under the title, "Vasquez [sic] Tagle, Mexico's Hope."[440] The hope was not just Mexico's but as the article explained, Vázquez Tagle was against confiscation, "a stanch [sic] defender of the law," "Villa could not for one moment control him," and, most importantly, he had the "backing of President Wilson."[441] He could be expected to respect foreign property. The for-mer Secretary of Justice also had never resigned after Huerta's bloody coup d'état in 1913. While other members of Madero's cabinet never resigned either, Vázquez Tagle had remained in Mexico and thus was constitutionally next in line for the Mexican presidency.

However, in reality, Wilson had already settled on a Carranza presidency. President Wilson instructed Lansing on August 11th not to insist on the elimination of Carranza in the next meeting of the Pan-American Conference.[442] That was all it took to reverse the entire foreign policy towards Mexico. Only a week after informing President Wilson that Carranza was "impossible," Robert Lansing suddenly entertained a de facto recognition of the First Chief. This change of heart not only baffled Paul Fuller and General Scott, the latter wondering why the State Department would not move on his proposals, but also all members of the group supporting a solution that included the Villa faction, most notably the Villista negotiators Miguel Díaz Lombardo, Roque Gonzalez Garza, Felix Sommerfeld, and Manuel Bonilla.

President Wilson's thoughts in this crucial time are not well documented. He retreated to Cornish, New Hampshire from the end of July until the beginning of the Pan-American Conference on August 4th, ostensibly to contemplate a solution for the Mexican problem. It appeared to most observers that he sincerely tried to look at all options. He conferred periodically with Robert Lansing; however, he did not disclose his thought process to him. The President clearly arrived at a different conclusion while at Cornish, all the while keeping Robert Lansing and his various envoys in the belief that a unity government for Mexico remained the stated foreign policy goal. As a result of the extraordinary interest the President took in Mexican matters in the summer of 1915, he arrived at the conclusion that a unity government excluding the man who led the strongest faction in the Revolution and who had gained the upper hand against Villa was doomed to fail.[443] By the beginning of the Pan-American Conference on August 4th, Wilson had made up his mind to recognize the victorious Carranza as the next president of Mexico. Despite his change of heart, Wilson continued to allow the Pan-American Conference to proceed under the false assumption of finding a unity solution. He also made no effort to stop a multitude of interest groups lobbying his administration. In the end, all of them felt deceived, most notably Pancho Villa and the people that had supported him.

While the President contemplated his approach to Mexico throughout June and July 1915, well-seasoned manipulators of Mexican politics such as Sherburne G. Hopkins, Andrew Meloy, and Charles Douglas all worked their networks to find potential candidates linked to the democratically elected and deposed Madero administration that could be agreeable to all factions, especially the United States. Publicly, President Wilson showed particular interest in two men, Felipe Ángeles and Manuel Bonilla. He asked Robert Lansing to ascertain the opinions of these two men on July 8th. "What did Ángeles and Bonilla have in mind? I suppose they are still in Washington, or near at hand; and it seems to me that, directly or indirectly, we ought to know everything that is in their mind..."[444] Wilson wondered in the same letter if perhaps Ángeles should be the favored candidate of the U.S. government.[445]

Ángeles, a close ally of the murdered President Madero, had gone to Washington with Pancho Villa's approval to meet with the Secretary of State and other members of the Wilson administration. President Wilson, General Scott, as well as Secretaries Lane and Garrison liked Ángeles and thought him to be a viable presidential candidate. Scott wrote in his memoirs, "Ángeles was the most cultivated and loyal gentleman I have known in the history of Mexico and he was Villa's candidate for president, as he was mine so far as I had a right to have any."[446] However, fielding Ángeles as a candidate was a non-starter. *New York Herald* reporter Alexander Williams aptly defined the probability of an Ángeles administration in Mexico a few months later: "Felipe Ángeles is the enemy politically of every faction in Mexico other [than] that headed by Villa. Every other faction considers him a traitor. None of the important Mexicans would under any conditions affiliate with him."[447] Ángeles had started his career as a federal officer, and then joined the Madero revolution in 1911. After the president's murder in 1913, the general sided with the Constitutionalists and became Carranza's Secretary of War. When Villa and Carranza split, Ángeles sided with Villa. As a result, both the reactionary factions who could not forgive him for joining Madero, and the Constitutionalists, who Ángeles had dealt devastating military defeats, considered the formidable politician, tactician, and intellectual a traitor. Undoubtedly, President Wilson recognized the fact that Ángeles carried too much baggage to be a viable candidate for the

Mexican presidency. He kept these opinions to himself. The Mexican general remained an important source of information for the administration and a link between President Wilson and Pancho Villa.

Manuel Bonilla had been Secretary of Communication, then Secretary of Development in the De La Barra and Madero administrations respectively, and thus seemed to have the potential to succeed the slain president as a legitimate successor. Bonilla had joined the Constitutionalists after the murder of President Madero in the spring of 1913. After Villa split with Carranza in 1914, he joined the Villista movement. However, precisely because he identified with Villa, there is no evidence that Bonilla had any real support from the Wilson administration.

Pancho Villa sent another heavy-weight in Mexican politics to Washington: Former Secretary of Education Miguel Díaz Lombardo. Díaz Lombardo spent most of the time the Constitutionalists fought to unseat the usurper president Huerta as their ambassador to France. Díaz Lombardo joined the Villista movement as the Minister of Foreign Affairs when he returned in 1914. A towering intellectual of the Mexican Revolution with an aristocratic background, he was a powerful voice in support of the Villista faction.

Roque Gonzalez Garza, one of the most important intellectuals of "Villismo" and one of Villa's closest advisers, also joined the team. Gonzalez Garza, Díaz Lombardo, Bonilla, and Ángeles pushed for the candidacy of Vázquez Tagle, all the while all four had personal ambitions for the Mexican presidency. Another intellectual leader in the exile community was José Vasconselos. A philosopher, lawyer, and politician, he had served under the Gutiérrez administration as Secretary of Education until the government collapsed under the weight of Carranza's military successes. In exile, he maintained close ties with Sherburne Hopkins and the American oil industry. These links came to light in June of 1914, when burglars ravaged Hopkins' offices and gave sensitive files on the relationship between Mexican revolutionaries and American oil barons to the press. Wholly unacceptable to a host of Mexican factions, he, as well, was not a viable unity candidate for the presidency. Sherburne Hopkins, meanwhile, pushed another potential candidate: Emilio Vasquez Gomez, the Interior Secretary in Madero's cabinet. He wrote to the exiled politician on June 7th, "I think you ought to offer your impartial services... For my part I am ready to do anything whatever [sic] that is reasonable and proper."[448] However, Vasquez Gomez' role in destabilizing the Madero presidency in an uprising in the spring of 1912 made him unacceptable to a host of Mexican exiles.[449]

While all the positioning and posturing engulfed the meetings of the Pan-American Conference between August 4th and August 15th, and as President Wilson had made up his mind to support Carranza as the rightful successor to the Mexican presidency, Hugh Lenox Scott and George C. Carothers negotiated with Pancho Villa and Felix Sommerfeld in El Paso, Texas. Taking at face value the pursuit of a unity government for Mexico, the American officials made the recognition of a Villa-backed presidential candidate contingent on important concessions. General Scott described the stakes in his memoirs: "Early in August, 1915, I was sent for by Assistant Secretary of War [Henry C.] Breckinridge to meet him in the office of Secretary of State [Robert] Lansing where I met also Mr. Paul Fuller. Secretary Lansing told me that he was in dire trouble... the secretary asked in such a pitiful way that I had to say 'yes'... "[450] At issue were confiscations of American businesses in Mexico.

Villa had always refrained from touching American property in order to maintain good relations with the U.S. until now. However, as his fortunes declined rapidly and since northern Mexico had endured half a decade of looting, confiscations, "special" taxations, and destruction, there was little Mexican property left to confiscate. Villa announced in the beginning of August that he intended to levy a special "tax" on American mining companies.[451] Companies such as ASARCO (American Smelting and Refining Company), the largest smelting operation in Mexico, immediately raised alarm in Washington. Many mines had already ceased operations and pulled out their employees because of the chaotic environment in Northern Mexico as Carranza's armies pushed Villa ever further north. Villa needed these businesses to operate in order to generate income from export duties for Chihuahua. He threatened companies that did not resume operations with confiscation. He seized several mines in southern Chihuahua and operated them with his own men in July 1915 to make his point. Although these forced operations did not legally constitute confiscation, Villa's mine operators probably sent the bullion to their broke chieftain rather than the legitimate owners of the

mines. The *New York Times* reported on August 2nd that Villa had confiscated numerous foreign businesses and expelled "an entire train-
load of foreigners."[452] The Chihuahua merchants had refused to take
the worthless Villa currency for payment by customers. It was a desperate and ineffectual attempt to curb inflation and the devaluation
of his currency.

When Scott met with Villa in the beginning of August, the
Army Chief of Staff made the argument that Villa would forfeit his
chances to have his faction recognized as the legitimate power in
Mexico if he would not release these businesses. Secretary Lansing
instructed Scott to tell Villa "the United States would never recognize Carranza."[453] While Scott later claimed that he did not relay this
statement to Villa, Sommerfeld, who as a confidante of both Villa
and Scott was undoubtedly informed, certainly did.[454] Much to the
surprise of observers, but not so surprising giving the assurances of
the U.S. State Department, Villa acceded to all of Scott's demands.[455]
"In all, there was more than six million dollars [Villa returned to
American businesses] for which I had no equivalent to offer to Villa
or promises to make, and he gave them up because I asked him; no
more and no less."[456] Scott did offer to allow Villa the exportation of
cattle (with questionable ownership) to the U.S. for cash. However,
when Secretary Lansing mentioned the proposal to the President,
he stopped it. "Do you think it wise to put Villa in the way of getting
money just at the moment when he is apparently weakest and on the
verge of collapse?" the President questioned, clearly showing that he
had, by then, already changed his mind.[457] To be fair, the real value of
what Villa conceded to Scott was only the value of the production revenue of these mines and the confiscated merchandise in Chihuahua.
However, with his fiat money devalued and his area of control shrink-
ing by the day, Villa's concessions did constitute a major sacrifice on
his part. Not surprisingly, Villa's cession of the mining properties coincided with him not sending any more funds to Sommerfeld and De La
Garza to pay for the munitions he had under contract in the U.S.

As Scott, Sommerfeld, and Carothers sealed the deal with
Villa on August 19th, Carranza's ten million cartridge contract with the
Western Cartridge Company was put on hold.[458] He would receive
three million cartridges sold through "James Manoil" in September
1915, exactly when Villa needed those most. Although the Army Chief

of Staff did not detail the promises he made to Villa, since he had nothing "to offer," recognition of a Villa-backed Mexican government was the very least General Villa expected. When it did not happen, Scott had unwittingly participated in sending the revolutionary chieftain into the arms of German secret service agents while at the same time speeding up his demise.

Scott and Fuller's missions in August of 1915 were a resounding success if viewed from the perspective of achieving a unity government acceptable to most factions of Mexico. Not only did Villa agree to everything the negotiators had presented to him, his commanders, as well, supported the unity government solution. Even Emiliano Zapata, the commander who had fought presidents Díaz, Madero, and Huerta, with all his generals agreed in the end of August to send delegates to the Pan-American Conference which was to reconvene in September.[459] Carranza and his commanders remained the only holdouts. Robert Lansing, with President Wilson's agreement, made one last effort to get Carranza to officially join the conference. Lansing sent David Lawrence in the middle of August, a well-respected journalist and editor with lots of experience in Mexico, to make one last ditch appeal to the First Chief. Lawrence had been an AP News reporter on the border for years, as a result of which he also became a personal friend of Felix Sommerfeld.[460] Lawrence met confidentially with Eliseo Arredondo, Carranza's envoy in Washington, and then travelled to Veracruz in the end of August. He returned from meetings with the "stiff-necked First Chief" empty-handed.[461]

Carranza gave an interview on the day of Lawrence's departure on September 1st 1915, which was published in the New York Times. In it, he summarized his attitude towards a unity government: "The fact that Villa is steadily beaten... shows that the Mexican people as a whole are supporting the Constitutionalist Government."[462] In other words, he challenged the American government with the de facto situation on the ground. Visibly frustrated, Lawrence published a detailed spread in the Century Magazine in September 1915. He argued for a military intervention in Mexico "for the beneficent cause of humanity" as the best way to bring the various factions to settle on a unity government.[463] Fellow journalists seconded his analysis in the New York Times on September 8th. Despite Carranza's victories on the battlefield, the situation in Mexico seemed to deteriorate by the day. Reports from

Mexico City filled newspaper columns with tales of starvation, looting, and chaos.[464] The Mexican-American border was on fire, as well, when Lawrence published his piece.

The deteriorating situation at the border stemmed from what became known as the *Plan de San Diego* and the *revolución de Texas*. Issued in the town of San Diego, Texas in January 1915, the *Plan de San Diego* called for an uprising of the Mexican-American populations in Texas, New Mexico, Arizona, Colorado, and California against the "Yankee tyranny."[465] Among other stipulations, the manifesto included passages that alarmed American officials who first saw a copy of the plan in the end of January 1915. Objective number 5 read: "It is strictly forbidden to hold prisoners ... they shall be shot immediately without any pretext." Number 6: "Every foreigner [i.e. any non-Chicano in the states to be liberated from the Yankee tyranny] who shall be found armed and cannot prove his right to carry arms, shall be summarily executed..." Number 7: "Every North American [sic] over sixteen years of age shall be put to death..."[466]

While local sheriffs carefully watched the mood among the Mexican-American population, not much happened as a result of the plan until June 1915.[467] "Bands of outlaws" raided ranches throughout the lower Rio Grande Valley within weeks of President Wilson putting pressure on the Mexican revolutionary factions in his ultimatum of June 2nd, 1915. Propaganda, spread through agents of the Carranza administration, proclaimed a "Texas Revolution," an uprising that called for Mexican-Americans freeing themselves from the "shackles of Anglo supremacy." The first American, an eighteen-year-old farmhand, died from the bullets of a Chicano raider in the end of July. During July and August hundreds of attacks occurred, some of which had nothing to do with the *revolución de Texas* but undoubtedly, people took advantage of the situation to settle old scores.[468] Short of personnel and hesitant to get involved, the U.S. army reluctantly reinforced the overwhelmed Texas Rangers and local law enforcement authorities in September. Raiders not only robbed banks, shops, and ranches but also blew up railroad bridges and cut telegraph lines. The Mexican Revolution finally seemed to be spilling over into U.S. territory in a deadly and disturbing way.

Some American newspapers quickly blamed the disturbances on German agitation. These suspicions seem to have pressured

Secretary Lansing and possibly also President Woodrow Wilson to find a solution for stabilizing Mexico as quickly as possible. Lansing wrote in his diary, "Germany does not want one faction dominant in Mexico; therefore we must recognize one faction as dominant in Mexico... It comes down to this: our possible relations with Germany must be our first consideration; and all our intercourse with Mexico must be regulated accordingly."[469] While German archives do not reveal any obvious financing or organizing of the border troubles, there are indications that the Secret War Council, and Heinrich Albert in particular, could have been involved. Maurice Leon, a member of the French embassy in Washington who handled financial and legal affairs for the Allies, suggested to the U.S. State Department two days after Villa's attack on Columbus, New Mexico in the spring of 1916, "heavy sales of German marks on Wall Street 'seem to point to the possibility that Villa and his band not only received a part of their proceeds, but also that the great part is to be utilized to induce Mexican 'leaders' to oppose by force [U.S.] operations to suppress border outlawry."[470] This allegation is partly correct. Albert and the German government, indeed, engaged in heavy trading to prop up the devalued German Mark in March and April 1916. However, although not impossible, there is no indication in Albert's financial records that any of these funds went to Mexico.[471] Historians Harris and Sadler's research, as well, shows that on the surface the unrest was conceived, organized, and financed through the Carranza administration in Mexico. However, there are links to German agents that have been overlooked. German agents had infiltrated the Carranza administration. While Sommerfeld organized munitions supplies for Villa at the same time that he supported the efforts of the U.S. State Department to wrest important concessions from the revolutionary chieftain, a sinister plot developed in South Texas.

Der Verfasser in Dienst-Uniform

"The author in service uniform." Colonel Arnold Krumm-Heller, 1915 – Mexican revolutionary or German agitator? The mustache gives it away.[472]

Colonel Arnold Krumm-Heller, the physician and German agent, who had engineered Villa's most devastating defeat at Celaya, suddenly appeared in freemasonry lodges, saloons, and gatherings of Mexican-Americans around Brownsville, San Antonio, and El Paso, Texas between June and August 1915, giving inflammatory anti-American and pro-Carranza speeches. *The El Paso Herald* reported on June 22nd 1915, "Dr. Krumm-Heller, formerly professor of literature in the University of Mexico, Will [sic] deliver a lecture Friday night on 'The

Origin of the war in Mexico and the method of pacification by the Mexicans themselves,' at the old Fraternal Brotherhood hall... No admission is charged to the lectures, which favor neither faction."⁴⁷³ The target audience of Krumm-Heller's "lecture" tour through the Southwest, which started in the middle of June and lasted into August, was mainly German-Americans and Mexican-Americans.

Though supposedly "not favoring" any faction in the revolutionary struggle, Krumm-Heller was a devout Carrancista and fanatic German nationalist. The German envoy to Mexico, Heinrich von Eckardt, reported to the German Chancellor von Bethmann Hollweg in 1916, "K. H. [Krumm-Heller] has been whenever possible extremely helpful to Germans throughout the Mexican Revolution until now. Since the beginning of the European war he has engaged tirelessly in propaganda for the German cause through lectures, articles, and leaflets in Spanish, while relentlessly proceeding against the Allies... As Grand Wizard of the Mexican Freemasons (about 20,000 strong) he is influential in all layers of Mexican society... Krumm-Heller reports directly to Carranza. His goal is to support the pro-German tendencies here [in Mexico] and reduce the influence of the Allies in Mexico."⁴⁷⁴ Historian Mark Cronland Anderson traced lavish financial support of Krumm-Heller's lecture tour to Carranza: Krumm-Heller's "efforts were successful, and his [propaganda] work apparently did not lack funding [from Carranza]."⁴⁷⁵ The financial records of the German legation in Mexico City have been lost. It is therefore not clear when Krumm-Heller might have received money from von Eckardt for his pro-German propaganda and how much. In May 1916, von Eckardt confirmed to the German chancellor that "the necessary funds [for a one year assignment in Germany] have been officially made available [by von Eckardt]."⁴⁷⁶ Krumm-Heller left no doubt as to his disposition to the U.S., the Mexican Revolution, and his propaganda mission in the Southwest in the summer of 1915.

He wrote in his book *Für Freiheit und Recht: Meine Erlebnisse aus dem mexikanischen Bürgerkriege (For Liberty and Justice: My Adventures in the Mexican Civil War)*, which was published in Germany in 1916:

> Against my wishes I had to go back to the United States, which I so hated. I got there in the beautiful spring time and luckily into a state [Texas],

in which millions of Mexicans, millions of Germans, and fewer American [Anglo] elements were present. Once-in-a-while one finds cities, **which are 80 percent German** [emphasis in the original]. Nevertheless have the Germans that have settled there wound up in the same dependency as the Mexicans that settled there or have remained there as the original inhabitants [before the U.S.-Mexican war of 1846 to 1848]. As overlords the Americans driven by their boundless need for speculation have succeeded in settling on the once large Mexican haciendas through the creation of the notorious lumber- and land companies. The Germans that had immigrated there received land for colonization under ostensibly favorable conditions. They were promised anything that a settler can dream of. But as a result of the inadequate legal circumstances it was easy for unscrupulous lawyers to add clauses to the contracts that made the settlers utterly dependent. Did one of those inexperienced hapless devils have difficulties making payments the issue was twisted in such a way that while faking leniency and sympathy he was given extended deadlines. In reality, he was allowed to work a little longer, until in the decisive moment everything was taken away and the land sold a second time, this time for a higher price than before since all the cultivation had already been done making the land arable. Thus the Germans and the Mexicans, or whoever else got caught in the Yankee web, were exploited and driven in many cases to suicide. What else could such a man start, who had lost everything without a way to go back home. Much has been written about these unhealthy speculation deals and the so-called revolutions in these regions are nothing but momentarily flaring acts of revenge that the terrible pressures of these circumstances created.[477]

Krumm-Heller's idea that there was a natural alliance between the sizeable German and Mexican populations in the Southwest had little basis in fact. German immigrants in the Southwest had done quite well as merchants, farmers, and craftsmen. The radical, separatist Mexicans who called for uprisings, strikes, property destruction, and murder, hardly appealed to the order-loving and authority-accepting German communities of Texas and Louisiana. However, the natural alignment of interest existed in the disappointment of German-Americans in the political attitude of the United States towards Germany in the war. As such, German-American companies such as Hayman-Krupp Company, Krakauer, Zork, and Moye, or Ketelsen and Degetau, some of the largest arms dealers in the region, could possibly be convinced to materially support elements in the Mexican-American community that caused unrest along the border. U.S. special envoy George Carothers alluded to the loyalty of German-American merchants in March 1917 in a letter to the Secretary of State, "The men referred to in my telegram are on their way to Brownsville, to secure aid from some Germans who are to meet them in a hardware store... The [German] owners of the hardware store have an extensive system of distribution all along the border."[478] Helping the German cause in this case certainly was also good for business.

A key question regarding the *revolución de Texas* is whether or not a deliberate effort of the German government supported it. Two facts stand out in considering this theory. There was a connection between Felix A. Sommerfeld and Arnold Krumm-Heller. Both had been in the inner circle of the slain president of Mexico, Francisco Madero. Krumm-Heller acted as his spiritual adviser, personal physician, and worked in the Mexican secret service in 1912. Felix Sommerfeld, a personal friend of the president, worked first as his chief of staff, then as head of the Mexican secret service. According to the American Military Intelligence Division, Krumm-Heller worked "in conjunction with Felix Sommerfeld, who was at that time in charge of the Mexican Secret Service in El Paso, Texas."[479] Both Germans reported to the German legation in this time period. It is no accident that when Villa and Carranza split after the ouster of Huerta and started the latest round of civil war, Sommerfeld stayed with Villa, while Krumm-Heller stayed close to Carranza.

As German envoy Heinrich von Eckardt reported to his superiors in 1916, Krumm-Heller had performed valuable services as a staff member of Carranza. Karl Boy-Ed reported the same about

Sommerfeld. While no direct link can be established between Sommerfeld and Krumm-Heller, Sommerfeld traveled to El Paso throughout the summer, first to direct the fifteen million cartridge order for Villa, then to assist General Scott's negotiations with Villa, and report "on the latest developments in Mexico" to Secretary of War Garrison. Unquestionably, the two agents could have been, and likely were, in personal contact. The second important fact is that Sommerfeld received orders from the Imperial War Department at the end of May to proceed on his proposal to instigate an American intervention in Mexico. The German agent, Krumm-Heller, appeared in the border region as a pro-German and pro-Carranza propagandist to incite the Mexican-American population against the "tyranny" of the United States within weeks of this order. The timing of Krumm-Heller's trip coincided not only with Sommerfeld's order to produce a military intervention in Mexico, but also with the labor unrest in America's war industry, planned, financed, and executed by German agents in remarkable parallels.

The Pan-American Conference reconvened on September 18th 1915. The decision to recognize Carranza framed the assembly. As a member of the administration, General Scott knew firsthand that President Wilson had adjusted his views despite the "pig-headedness" of the victorious Mexican leader, Carranza. A week before the conference and the day after Villa's forces lost control over the important railroad hub of Torreón and retreated north, General Scott, alarmed by Villa's deteriorating negotiation power, rallied the pro-Villa faction. "I told Bonilla and Llorente to get busy now to combat this Carranza propaganda here [that Villa was beaten] and regain the standing for Villa that has been lost... I told [Felix] Sommerfeld the same thing and urged him to do it. ... I do not know what we can do further as I have done everything I can think of."[480]

Scott's dread was well justified. Two days before the Pan-American delegates reconvened on September 15th, the State Department ordered all U.S. consuls out of Mexico. Americans residing in Sonora and Chihuahua received word to get out, as well.[481] British and French officials also scurried to safety on the American side of the border. No one really knew what to expect from Villa once he realized that he had been outfoxed. Although Secretary Lansing had notified the press that Carranza would be recognized, some members of the

Pan-American Conference, possibly through the last-minute efforts of Díaz Lombardo, Gonzalez Garza, Bonilla, Llorente, and Sommerfeld, refused to give their agreement. Rather, the group's announcement on September 18th proclaimed that whichever faction was deemed militarily stronger by the middle of October would be recognized as the *de facto* government.

Meanwhile, the unrest on the border took on crisis proportions. Carrancista irregulars engaged soldiers of the 12th Cavalry in Brownsville, Texas, on August 3rd, leaving one soldier dead and two wounded.[482] Mexican raiders engaged the 3rd Cavalry and Texas Rangers again in Brownsville on September 6th in a shootout that left two Mexicans dead.[483] U.S. authorities involved in battling the uprising and arresting the organizers behind the *revolución de Texas* left no stone unturned. Dozens of Mexican-Americans faced arrest and detention. Reprisals by the local Anglo population and the Texas Rangers raised the specter of a race war. As the battle for diplomatic recognition intensified in Washington and New York, so did the war in Texas. By the time the raids ended in October, six Anglos and approximately three hundred Mexicans and Mexican-Americans had died.[484]

The raids ended as suddenly as they had started. They stopped on October 1st, shortly after the American government announced that it would recognize Carranza's faction as the legitimate government of Mexico. General Funston reported to his superiors in Washington on October 13th that "it had been ten days since the last hostile shot had been fired."[485] Historians Harris and Sadler concluded in their analysis of the uprising, "once Carranza withdrew his support, the insurrection in Texas collapsed like a punctured balloon... Viewing Mexican-Americans as a useful fifth column, Carranza skillfully played on their hopes and fears as a means of exerting pressure on the United States. When his [Carranza's] policies shifted [and those of the United States], they were cynically abandoned... The Plan left a legacy of racial tension in south Texas that has endured to the present."[486] Carranza once more resurrected the *Plan de San Diego* in the summer of 1916, when, indeed, the United States and Mexico marched to the brink of war. And again, this time only partially achieving his objectives, Carranza shut down the unrest.[487]

Villa faced an impossible task on the run with decimated forces and General Obregón hot on his heels. Not one to back down even with impossible odds, Villa went on the offensive. He decided to plan a sweeping campaign into Sonora and capture the important border state with its all-important customs houses in Agua Prieta, Naco, and Nogales. However, this time, his military commanders, notably Felipe Ángeles, did not follow their leader. After personally appealing to Villa on September 24th to end his fight instead of marching into Sonora, Villa's most powerful commander took exile in the United States.[488] Sommerfeld, fearing for the life of his old friend, wrote to General Scott, "It is absolutely necessary that General Ángeles leave Villa territory in order to save his life."[489] Rafael Buelna, Villa's military commander in Tepic, as well as Sonora's Villista governor José Maria Maytorena, the Madero family, including two that served as Villa's division commanders, and more than a dozen of Villa's comrades left the sinking ship.[490] Villa himself dealt with one of his oldest and most corrupt *compadres*, Tomás Urbina, who he had killed. The executioner, Rodolfo Fierro, himself one of the most brutal of Villa's henchmen and a member of his inner-most circle, died on October 14th 1915 in the Sonora campaign. He fell off his horse and drowned in a sinkhole with his soldiers idly standing by, watching the demise of their hated commander. Significantly, and understandably in view of Sommerfeld's true mission from the German Naval Intelligence, the German secret agent maintained his loyalty to Villa.

The week before the Pan-American Conference would render its final decision, effectively rubber-stamping President Wilson's decision, Villa's most powerful representatives met with Robert Lansing on October 5th.[491] Although Sommerfeld does not appear to have joined Manuel Bonilla, Roque Gonzales Garza, and Enrique Llorente, he undoubtedly maintained close contact with the group and helped prepare the meeting. The Secretary heard the delegation's arguments, their professions of imminent military successes, of being the only guarantors of constitutional order, and their claim of having support from the majority of Mexico's factions. The Mexican negotiators emerged discouraged. There was nothing they could have said to change the decision of the American president. Pancho Villa himself spoke to reporters on October 8th, ominously threatening that recognition of Carranza's faction "would bring revolution after revolution, and revolution in its worst forms. Existing conditions in Mexico are bad enough, but if Carranza be recognized, those conditions would become tenfold worse…"[492] If anyone should doubt as to who would be initiating those revolutions, he vowed: "I am here in Juarez, but this is as far as I shall go north… Here I shall fight and here I shall live…"[493]

The conference reconvened on October 9th as expected. Robert Lansing told reporters after a three-hour session at the State Department, "The conference, after careful consideration of the facts, have [sic] found that the Carranza party is the only party possessing the essentials for recognition as the de facto government of Mexico, and they have so reported to their respective Governments."[494] The U.S. government officially extended an invitation to the "*de facto* Government of Mexico, of which General Venustiano Carranza is the Chief Executive," on October 19th, to exchange diplomatic representatives.[495] American battleships raised the Mexican flag and fired a twenty-one-gun-salute in the harbor of Veracruz. General Scott, clearly disgusted, commented, "The recognition of Carranza had the effect of solidifying the power of the man who had rewarded us with kicks on every occasion… I did what I could to prevent this but was not powerful enough. I had never been put in such a position in my life."[496] Despite the many claims that Villa was wholly unaware of these developments, the American decision did not surprise the revolutionary chieftain. He knew that realities on the ground, his losses to the Carrancista forces, had precipitated the American decision. What he had not anticipated, however, were the swift actions with which the Wilson administration now pursued his complete annihilation. The State Department issued an embargo for arms and munitions on October 20th against any faction in Mexico other than the recognized government.[497] Returning to the old days of having to smuggle arms and munitions across the border, Villa suffered another devastating blow. It would not be the last.

General Scott, as well as most Mexicans who had supported the unity government idea, could not understand how the Wilson administration could have reversed its policies from June 2nd, when President Wilson appealed to all factions to come to the table or else – to October, when Carranza became the *de facto* president of Mexico. President Wilson "did not reveal his intentions then [when General Scott met him in the end of August] but he recognized Carranza in a few months… I never knew why. I asked the officers of the State Department, junior to the secretary [likely Leon Canova], why such a thing had been done and they said they did not know... That information has always made the President's step even more of a mystery to me."[498] President Wilson never explained his motivations, even to his closest associates.[499] Like most mysteries, this one created a host of speculative conspiracy theories but that also would have grave consequences for the United States. What did the Carranza faction concede to the American government to sway the President's opinion?

The fertile ground of the unknown provided a golden opportunity for Felix Sommerfeld to churn the rumor mill with "opinions" that implicated Canova and the State Department in a secret plot to take control of Mexican sovereignty. After all, there were clear indications that such a secret agreement with Carranza and the Wilson administration existed. Sommerfeld had been a negotiator on Villa's behalf in August with General Scott and Leon Canova, who as a State Department representative directed Scott in his meetings with Villa. Sommerfeld also had other important connections in the Wilson administration. Sommerfeld sent one of over a dozen letters and telegrams, preserved in Secretary of War Lindley M. Garrison's papers, on September 7th 1915. He included a clipping from the New York Evening Post concerning the "attitude of the A.B.C. powers [Argentina, Brazil, Chile, the leading members of the Pan-American Conference] in case of a possible intervention in Mexico, which I sincerely hope, will not occur."[500] Apart from the fact that Sommerfeld apparently maintained an open and direct channel of communication with the Secretary, he also alluded to previous discussions on the Pan-American Conference. "It [the article in the New York Evening Post] verifies my statement to you..."[501] Sommerfeld, more than any other member of the Villa faction in the United States, had been privy to the wrangling within the administration and the sudden, unexplained shift of policy towards Carranza. Villa, who used Sommerfeld's direct access to the Secretary of War, as well as to Secretary of State Bryan on multiple occasions, thus knew of the German agent's connections to the Wilson cabinet.[502]

Sommerfeld's relationship with Secretary Garrison was more than just casual. There was a regular and frequent exchange of information. A few months before his latest message, Sommerfeld wrote to the Secretary, "I was very sorry not to have had the pleasure of seeing you in Washington last week, but I hope to see you in the near future, in order to tell you all I know about the latest developments in Mexico."[503] Sommerfeld had also been in contact with Secretary of the Interior Franklin Lane in the fall of 1914. Secretary Lane asked General Scott to contact Sommerfeld and research the disappearance of the American writer, Ambrose Bierce, in Mexico in January 1914.[504] Villa and his envoys, Bonilla and Díaz Lombardo, must have relied on Sommerfeld's insights into the decision-making process, especially in a key issue such as diplomatic recognition. It did not take much for a manipulating mind such as Sommerfeld's to reinforce the suspicion that Wilson's decision was the result of secret concessions from the First Chief Carranza. Even General Scott suspected that something unseemly must have happened. Typical for Sommerfeld's *modus operandi*, he did not leave any overt fingerprints on the campaign that convinced Pancho Villa beyond doubt that such a secret agreement indeed existed. Instead, he used Miguel Díaz Lombardo, Manuel Bonilla, Roque Gonzales Garza, Felipe Ángeles, and others close to Villa to convey the message.

Pancho Villa, in a desperate effort to change *status quo* of the superiority of Carranza's military in Mexico, prepared a new campaign into Sonora in the end of September. He believed that occupying the two most important states along the Mexican-American border, Chihuahua and Sonora, would tilt the decision of the American government to his favor. Throughout the revolution, whoever occupied Chihuahua and Sonora could not be easily dislodged. The American border, even under an arms embargo, provided ample possibilities for smuggling of arms, munitions, and supplies. If the U.S. government's intention was pacification of Mexico, Villa's control over the all-important border crossings and customs stations could not be ignored. Sonora also harbored far more resources to sustain a large army since it had not been fought over as intensively as Chihuahua.

The northwestern state contained fewer than three thousand Carrancista troops when Villa made his decision. The Villista governor, Maytorena, held most of the state with his forces made up of fierce Yaqui Indian fighters. Twelve thousand strong, a far cry from the proud army of forty thousand men of just a few months earlier, Villa's Division of the North split forces. Approximately ten thousand soldiers set out across the Sierra Madre Occidental in the middle of October with only a few hundred left behind to defend positions in Chihuahua. Villa's demoralized and spent army units wound their way through the valleys and passes of an extremely hostile environment without having the benefit of rail transportation through the mountains. In order to save food and increase speed the army left their *soldaderas*, who typically provided food, medical care, and logistical support, behind. Villa also could not take the cattle herds, which in the past had provided milk and food. Ox carts and donkey trains carried artillery and supplies through the unforgiving terrain.

Villa's first target was Agua Prieta, the Sonoran hamlet across Douglas, Arizona, a city of 20,000 souls with important smelters serving the mining industry. While Villa's main force crossed the Sierra Madres, Villista General Urbalejo with a force of seven hundred took the border hamlet of Naco, Sonora. Another Villista detachment under General Beltrán took the copper city of Cananea. Beltrán and Urbalejo continued to march east, chasing the dislodged Carrancista troops commanded by Plutarco Elías Calles to the Agua Prieta garrison. The Villista forces in western Sonora combined with Villa's main body of troops at the outskirts of Agua Prieta on October 30th. Sommerfeld's employee and head of the Villa munitions supply organization in El Paso, Sam Dreben, arrived in Douglas on the same day.[505] He told State Department envoy George C. Carothers, "There was considerable ammunition being smuggled in the vicinity of El Paso."[506] These munitions seem to have come from stocks of the failed Huerta insurgency that Dreben now shipped to Villa, but that failed to reach him in time. Four days before the official recognition of Carranza, on October 15th, U.S. authorities detained the schooner *Lucy H.* loaded with munitions for Villa in Pensacola, Florida. The captain decided to try his luck and left the port for Tuxpan, Veracruz on the 20th.[507] When the *Lucy H.* returned, she was impounded and the captain charged,

> ... that the said schooner *Lucy H* on the 14th day of September AD 1915 within the navigable waters of the United States and within the jurisdiction of this court was then and there unlawfully furnished fitted out and supplied and armed with a military expedition of 15 armed men more or less with intent to be employed in the service of the Villistas certain insurgents in the country called Mexico with whom the United States were and are at peace with intent

to cruise and commit hostilities against the subjects citizens and property of first, the people of Mexico, second Gen. Carranza, a foreign prince, third the colony of Mexico, fourth the district of Mexico, fifth the republic of Mexico, sixth the de facto government and the forces of Gen. Carranza with whom the United States then were and now are at peace...[508]

The tide had really turned against Villa. However, Dreben's presence in Douglas, and the continued efforts to supply Villa with munitions, underlines the fact that Felix Sommerfeld remained one of the few supporters the Mexican revolutionary chief had left. Sommerfeld claimed to American authorities in 1918 that he had ceased all relations with Villa after Carranza had been recognized.[509] That was a lie. He supported Villa throughout 1915 and 1916 to the detriment of the United States.

While Villa's progress in the north seemed on schedule, Carrancista units under General Manuel M. Diéguez took the important port city of Guaymas in southern Sonora on October 13th. Reinforcing his army from the sea, he marched north with twelve thousand troops. Hermosillo, the state capital in the center of Sonora, fell on October 20th. The remaining Villista forces retreated northward, blocking the railroad for their Carrancista pursuers. The Carrancista forces dug in at Agua Prieta and, constructed long trenches. Machine gun emplacements and barbed wire secured the perimeter of the town. The mayor of Douglas desperately tried to get the U.S. army to prevent the impending battle on the American side of the border, fearing for the safety of his residents.[510] Brigadier General Thomas F. Davis commanded the U.S. army forces securing the border. Davis had "three regiments of infantry, a regiment of field artillery, and several troops of cavalry" in a force of roughly six thousand men at his disposal.[511]

Villa surveyed the battlefield. His scouts had estimated the opposing force to be somewhere between twelve hundred and three thousand. Despite the heavy defenses, minefields, barbed wire, and entrenchments, the Mexican general decided on a "softening" with artillery, then a frontal night attack with cavalry. He had used this strategy many times before. However, General Calles had learned his lesson. He was inspired by the European war, where trench warfare, minefields, and electrically charged barbed wire secured perimeters that were covered with machine gun emplacements and defended battle lines even against an overwhelming force. Villa only knew one way to attack, usually without even retaining reserves. An eyewitness described the ensuing battle:

> Villa's artillery started firing at 1: 15 Monday afternoon and continued intermittently all day. The defenders' guns answered when there was a target. It shortly became clear that a daylight assault would not come against such a formidable defense. During that night, actually the next morning at 1:50 a.m., the main attack on Agua Prieta began. There was continuous noise from artillery fire, the bursting of shells, and both rifle and machine gun shots. For this battle the whole area was lighted by large carbon-arc lights, provided, it is reported, by the U.S. Army Engineers. These lights were among the early casualties; all were finally knocked out and two of the six operators were killed. It was over soon and suddenly. At about four in the morning the attacking guns fired three rounds of shrapnel over the town, then ceased.[512]

The Villista attack turned into a rout. The main charge around midnight failed to overrun the Carrancista trenches. Villa originally claimed, and stubbornly maintained, that U.S. forces provided the battlefield illumination. While the claim is still in debate, the power to run the lights as well as the electrification of the perimeter barbed wire, which claimed a few of his soldiers' lives, most definitely came from the American side. The result was disastrous for Villa as the frontal cavalry attack ran up against the deadly machine gun positions. Villa ordered a total of five assaults on the enemy defenses and was repelled every time. Virtually no one managed to breach the trenches. Though Villa knew that there were more soldiers on the Carrancista side than he had originally expected, he did not adjust his strategy. General Calles had more than 7,500 men at his disposal, which he effectively brought to bear on Villa's attacking force to the latter's detriment. Also surprising for Villa was how well his opponents were armed. Calles had twenty-two cannon and sixty-five machine guns, a deadly long- and medium-range defense covering the entire depth of the battlefield. Train cars loaded with ammunition to re-supply the defenders waited on the American side of the border with U.S. soldiers providing security.

While Villa contemplated further frontal assaults for the morning of November 2nd, his attack crumbled, mainly because his troops threatened mutiny. Having left behind his supplies and the supply train of *soldaderas* that usually took care of the provisions for the *División Del Norte*, the Villista soldiers had not eaten in days, and even ran low on water. The last issue might have been the benign but real reason Villa decided to quit the attacks: his forces had been cut to pieces by the time Villa ordered retreat in the early morning hours of November 2nd. Bodies, hundreds of dead, and even more wounded without the famous hospital train to care for them, littered the battlefield. He had failed, not only because of the formidable preparations and fortifications of the Agua Prieta garrison, but also because he had fought without a discernible strategy: No utilization of the element of surprise, no attack plan utilizing even the faintest hint of creativity, and the inexcusable lack of logistical support. It is questionable if under these circumstances an opposing force of three thousand or even less, which would have been the defending force without American aid, would not have been able to hold the town. Dislodging a well dug-in force, backed to the American border as a supply base, was virtually impossible, as General Maytorena had experienced in Naco ten months earlier.

Some historians and contemporary news reports have made much of the claim that Villa learned of the large reinforcements of the garrison only after the battle. As a matter of fact, on October 23rd, the U.S. government had allowed 4,500 reinforcements for Agua Prieta to travel via railroad through American territory.[513] According to Hearst reporter John W. Roberts, Villa was completely unaware and surprised. "He saw me [on the American side of the border fence] and walked up quickly. 'My God, Roberts, what happened?'... I told him in as few words possible [and] explained the situation. Villa said nothing... Just then, General [Frederick] Funston... rode up with a number of officers. I told Villa who he was. Villa merely stared. Funston dismounted and came forward. 'Is this General Villa?' he asked me, I nodded and introduced the two chiefs. Each stood in their own country and they shook hands over the barbed-wire fence."[514] John W. Roberts was a reporter prone to exaggeration. Villa had expelled him "as an obnoxious individual" from his territory because he published an interview that he had never given.[515] The same seemed to be the case here. American newspapers reported on the transfer of Mexican soldiers through U.S. territory to Agua Prieta on October 25th.[516] The Villista governor of Sonora, Carlos Randall, officially launched a protest with the American State Department on October 30th.[517] That same day, Villa met up with the Yaqui contingents under General Urbalejo, who would have known all about this issue. According to historian Carl Cole who interviewed veterans of the battle, Villa had learned of the reinforcements for Agua Prieta that came via U.S. railroads two days before the battle.[518] He simply failed to make adequate adjustments to his attack plan. It is also unlikely that it took an American reporter to introduce Villa to General Funston. If the general had wanted to see Villa, a U.S. army liaison officer would have contacted Villa's staff or the other way around, as Funston indeed claimed.

Frederick Funston, the Commander of the Southern Department of the Army, had just arrived from El Paso on November 2nd to take control of the uneasy situation.[519] He met with Villa outside of Agua Prieta, about one mile to the east.[520] There was ample reason to talk. Nine Americans had been wounded, and one killed, on the Douglas side of the border.[521] A hail of bullets and shrapnel had been raining down over the American town for two days. It was unclear if Villa would resume his offensive. Reportedly, Villa assured Funston that he did not want to draw the American military into the conflict.[522] Despite the assurances, however, Funston cabled the War Department for permission to pursue Mexican forces across the border in case of an attack on U.S. territory immediately after the meeting.[523] The *Plan de San Diego* raids, as well as the heap of stray bullets and shrapnel that had hit the American town and its residents, had worn Funston's patience with the Mexican revolutionaries precariously thin.

Despite the disastrous attack strategy that cost Villa the last chance to re-kindle his military prowess in northern Mexico, the fact remained that the United States had actively intervened in the revolution. The Bureau of Investigations agent Steve Pinckney reported on November 2nd, "There is much ammunition in Douglas for General Calles, all of it being guarded by the local [U.S.] military authorities...

The local railroad officials, express companies, and officers are work-ing in harmony with the US authorities."[524] The U.S. Treasury Depart-ment reported to the Department of State on the day before the battle, October 30th, 1915, "Collectors at Laredo, Texas and Nogales, Arizona instructed to facilitate movement of 1,000,000 rounds of ammunition for Carranza government to Agua Prieta."[525] Villa not only suffered from the arms embargo that gave Carranza advantage, but U.S. customs in El Paso also stopped all cattle imports from Chihuahua to the U.S. for "examination of brands."[526] Zach Lamar Cobb, the U.S. customs collector in El Paso, added coal to his list of items to be held up at the border.[527]

Cobb was determined to do what he could to aid in the demise of the *División Del Norte*, despite serious threats from Villa's people in the U.S. and instructions from Secretary McAdoo to refrain from his activities. Cobb, despite his official employment in the Treasury Department, was an agent of the State Department's Intelligence Service. As such, he clearly executed the wishes of Robert Lansing, destroying what were the last remaining avenues for Villa to supply himself, and raise cash for munitions. Pancho Villa's reaction to the aid his opponents had received from the U.S. government was remark-ably measured on the surface. Known for violent outbursts of rage and emotionally charged decisions, the embattled Mexican general now weighed his options carefully. Villa initially talked openly about attacking the American side of the border.[528] In response, General Funston moved his forces away from the border the day after the bat-tle should Villa decide on shelling the town with his artillery. However, facing a combined American and Carrancista force of close to 14,000 troops, Villa only vented his anger but refrained from committing his remaining troops to a suicide mission. Instead, he took four Ameri-cans hostage and threatened to execute them. He released them a few days later. Villa retreated to Naco, Sonora, on November 4th, where his troops received a reprieve from the fight. His troops raided and pillaged Cananea on the way. The full weight of Carranza's recog-nition as the *de facto* Mexican president seemed to finally sink in while resting at Naco. Agua Prieta had been a setup. The U.S. government had done everything in its power, short of engaging its own military, in an unprecedented move to make sure Villa would be defeated. According the special U.S. envoy George C. Carothers, who had been with Villa for the past years, the Mexican general appeared now "irresponsible and dangerous. He was subject to violent fits of temper and was capable of any extreme."[529]

Villa issued a damning proclamation against Carranza on November 9th 1915, against Carranza with the gist that he had sold out the revolution and his country to the United States.[530] Villa had become convinced that a secret pact between Carranza and the Wilson administration had precipitated his demise. He charged that Carranza had agreed to eight concessions: 1. Amnesty for all political prisoners; 2. U.S. rights over Magdalena Bay, Tehuantepec, and an oil zone for 99 years; 3. Mexico's Interior, Foreign Affairs, and Finance ministries would be filled with candidates supported by Washington; 4. All paper money issued by the revolution would be consolidated; 5. All just claims by foreigners for damages caused by the revolution would be paid and all confiscated property returned; 6. The Mexican National Railways would be controlled by the governing board in New York until the debts to this board were repaid; 7. The United States through Wall Street bankers, would grant a $500 million loan; 8. Pablo Gonzalez would be named provisional president and would call for elections within six months.[531] Historian Friedrich Katz, the premier scholar on the topic of Pancho Villa, researched the existence of this secret agreement thoroughly. He found evidence that Carranza agreed to examine U.S. claims for damages and that Speyer and Company had offered to support a new Mexican government with $500 million.[532] The historian still concluded, "There is no evidence that Carranza ever signed such a pact."[533]

However, there was much more evidence than historian Katz and others cited bolstering the judgment that most of these eight points were indeed part of a secret understanding, even if it was never formally put to paper. Pancho Villa did have ample reason to believe that this agreement existed. John R. Silliman, the U.S. consul in Saltillo, approached the revolutionary chieftain in December of 1914, and offered recognition of his government for "the use of lower [sic] California [by the American navy], Magdalena Bay [as a naval station], and the Tampico oil fields."[534] Villa declined. The American lawyer, James M. Keedy, approached Villa with a message from Leon Canova, the head of the Mexican desk in the State Department in September 1915, after Villa had conceded to General Scott whatever the State

Department required to recognize his faction. Canova demanded the power to name Villa's cabinet in case of recognition.[535] As it turned out, Keedy was a German secret service agent, whom Sommerfeld likely had dispatched. Sommerfeld, whose mission was to create an American military intervention, thus maintained his distance from the plans of a conspiratorial faction within the State Department, while remaining intricately involved.[536]

General Scott's papers are incomplete insofar as to the total list of demands as a prerequisite to recognition he presented to Villa in August. It could well have contained items such as the use of Magdalena Bay and American control over the Mexican railways. Undoubtedly, there were more attempts to wrest territorial and financial concessions from Villa as he grew more desperate in the fall of 1915. Villa cited such attempts to his confidantes, for example to the Chihuahuan Secretary of State, Silvestre Terrazas.[537] However, Villa had clearly rejected any such proposals. Given the knowledge of the State Department's desires for territorial and financial concessions one cannot blame Villa and his supporters, including General Scott, for wondering what Carranza had offered that got him such prompt recognition. Roque Gonzales Garza, one of Villa's closest advisers and negotiator in Washington and New York, wrote to his Mexican chief on October 29th, "… you have always been miserably deceived… I do not entirely know what has been decided concretely, but I am convinced that something very dark has been agreed on; for I have no other explanation for the sudden change in U.S. policy against our group and in favor of Carranza."[538]

The New York Times reported that the new Board of Directors of the National Railways of Mexico had been elected on the day after Gonzales Garza wrote to Villa that there must have been foul play.[539] Wrangling over control of the railroads had driven American support away from Porfirio Díaz to Francisco Madero, and now to Venustiano Carranza. It was stacked with favorites of Charles Flint and Henry Clay Pierce. Alberto Pani remained the head of the board. He had been installed through Sherburne Hopkins for Henry Clay Pierce in 1914.[540] Carranza clearly was cooperating in this for the U.S. critical industry and point six of Villa's charges. Carranza released some political prisoners and immediately started to return confiscated properties.[541] He allowed that American financiers stacked the National Railways'

Board in their favor. The First Chief also immediately began eliminating all fiat money and issued a new currency in the spring of 1916.[542] Fascinatingly, although maybe just a fluke, the *El Paso Herald* printed right below the article reporting on the new Board of Directors for the Mexican railways that Carranza had not signed any secret agreement: "Denies That U.S. Imposed Any Condition on Carranza."[543] He might not have signed anything concrete. However, his actions subsequent to the U.S. recognition in October tell a story much in line with Villa's accusations. Whether formally committed to paper or through informal channels, Villa had ample reasons to believe that Carranza had offered concessions to the United States that put Mexican sovereignty into question, especially if advisers close to him including Felix Sommerfeld told him so.

The avalanche of reports in the American press of Villa's rage against the United States and President Wilson, in particular, precipitated the last known letter from Felix Sommerfeld to Secretary of War Lindley M. Garrison in defense of Pancho Villa. Sommerfeld wrote on November 12th 1915, "I am enclosing a clipping from today's *N.Y. American* with an alleged interview of one of the Hearst reporters [John W. Roberts] with General Villa... I do wish to protest most emphatically against these intentionally and willfully false statements created in the mind of an irresponsible reporter who might have received instructions from headquarters to write such stuff in order to conform with [sic] the political tendency of the paper."[544] Roberts had written under the heading "Whiskers Tie Mexico's Fate, Writes Villa... Tell Mr. Wilson that he is not a democrat. Tell him I say he prefers whiskers [i.e. Venustiano Carranza] to valor, egotism to personal honor, shamelessness to the welfare of the Mexican people."[545] There was nothing left to do for Sommerfeld other than to let the tragedy of Villa's demise play out. Personally, he had to tread carefully since on October 28th New York police arrested him, paraded him in handcuffs through the lobby of the Astor Hotel, and later released him on bail. He had been warned.

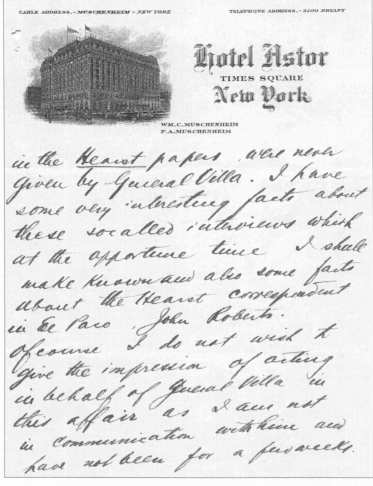

CABLE ADDRESS.- *MUSCHENHEIM - NEW YORK*   TELEPHONE ADDRESS.- *2100 BRYANT*

Hotel Astor
TIMES SQUARE
New York

WM.C.MUSCHENHEIM
F.A.MUSCHENHEIM

in the <u>Hearst</u> papers, will never given by General Villa. I have some very interesting facts about these so called interviews which at the opportune time I shall make known and also some facts about the Hearst correspondent in El Paso, John Roberts. Of course I do not wish to give the impression of acting in behalf of General Villa in this affair as I am not in communication with him and have not been for a few weeks.

Letter from F. A. Sommerfeld to Lindley M. Garrison, November 1915

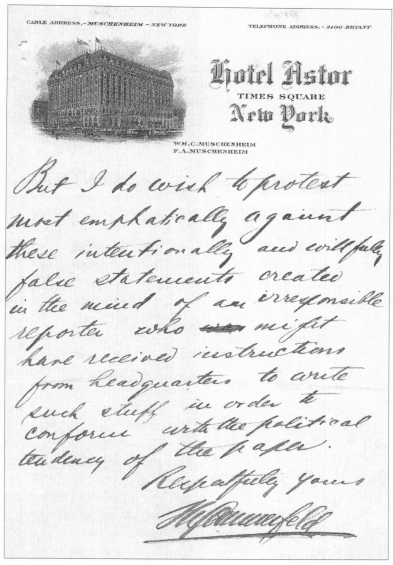

CABLE ADDRESS,-*MUSCHENHEIM - NEW YORK*
TELEPHONE ADDRESS,- *2100 BRYANT*

Hotel Astor
TIMES SQUARE
New York

WM.C.MUSCHENHEIM
F.A.MUSCHENHEIM

But I do wish to protest most emphatically against these intentionally and willfully false statements created in the mind of an irresponsible reporter who ~~was~~ might have received instructions from headquarters to write such stuff in order to conform with the political tendency of the paper.

Respectfully yours

546

After resting his troops in Naco and re-supplying, Villa decided to march on Hermosillo, the capital of Sonora. He attacked the defending force under General Diéguez head-on with close to six thousand troops. The once invincible general had to order retreat on November 22nd, again without the element of surprise, and with a force still reeling from the disastrous defeat at Agua Prieta.[547] This time, the Yaqui

Indian contingents defected to Carranza rather than volunteering as cannon fodder for the hapless Villa. In disarray, the Villistas made for the U.S. border city of Nogales. However, the American government had again allowed Carrancista troops to move through U.S. territory.[548] Closing the border to prevent the Villa garrison from supplying itself, Nogales fell without much of a fight on November 25th.[549] Villa retreated into the Sierra Madre, however, not before engaging the 10th Cavalry and the 12th U.S. Infantry with sniper-fire, killing one U.S. soldier and wounding two.[550] Bands of infuriated Villista cavalry rode up and down the border fence in Nogales challenging the U.S. military to come across for a fight. U.S. troops picked off several Mexican attackers but did not enter Mexican territory.[551] Unable to fault himself for the tragic losses on the battlefield, Villa vented his frustration on the rural populations of Sonora. He personally commanded and participated in a horrible massacre, killing over sixty villagers in San Pedro de las Cuevas.[552] The revolutionary chieftain crossed the mountains back into Chihuahua with less than a third of his original army to defend his last stronghold against the advancing armies of General Alvaro Obregón.

Villa had suffered a decisive defeat at Agua Prieta, which he repeated at Hermosillo. The wily revolutionary tried to impress newspapermen and the opposition with his remaining strength as his troops retreated back into Chihuahua. One troop train after another arrived in Chihuahua, discharging thousands of soldiers. In reality, the troops left the rail station and took their horses a few miles down the road to be loaded again and brought into Chihuahua.[553] The only strategy left for Villa was to turn up the propaganda in the United States. The *New York Tribune* reported on September 21st, "The Villa agency [in the United States consisting of Bonilla, Gonzalez Garza, Díaz Lombardo, Llorente, and Sommerfeld] has become suddenly active, and in statement after statement asserts that the army of the north is preparing a mighty campaign. Obregón is to be led north as far as Chihuahua, far from his base of supplies, and is there to be slaughtered. Zapata, taking advantage of the necessary withdrawal of troops from the vicinity of Mexico City to reinforce Obregón, will rush in and drive the Carrancistas from Chapultepec. Flying columns will be sent along the principal railroads to cut Carranza's communications."[554] The propaganda could not mask the realities on the battlefield. Obregón was coming into Chihuahua, but not to be slaughtered.

Pancho Villa addressed his remaining followers and the world in a sweeping speech from a balcony of the municipal palace in Chihuahua City on December 17th 1915. He repeated the accusations he had leveled against Carranza in November. Villa declared that the famed *División Del Norte* was dissolved but he would continue to fight. Villa issued an unmistakable declaration of war against the United States. "Villa said, he was not willing to spend even one cartridge to fight against Mexicans but would reserve all of his forces to combat the Americans once they attempted to take over the country."[555] The *New York Times* reported that Villa had vowed to "destroy American property wherever it was found, and that no American life would be safe in his territory. His feeling for the United States grows more bitter [sic], and it is feared that a massacre of Americans may occur at any time in Chihuahua State or city."[556] He had convinced himself that a U.S. invasion was imminent as a result of Carranza's "treachery." Despite multiple rumors that Villa would join many of his commanders and seek exile in the United States, the revolutionary chieftain retreated into the mountains with a handful of his elite "Dorados" in mid-December. He told the few remaining friends who wanted him to come to the U.S., "they [the Washington Government] have double-crossed me many times and if I go to the United States they will double-cross me again. I will fight to the last."[557] Ciudad Juarez fell to the Carrancistas on December 23rd without much of a fight. The last battle between Villistas and Carranza's forces occurred on the day before, in Mapula, on the outskirts of Chihuahua City.[558] Villa's family, his wife, and his brother, Hipólito, went into exile in Cuba at the end of the month. The famed Villa army and its leader, the Centaur of the North, had been defeated, or so American and Mexican authorities hoped.

Villa's fall from preeminence in Mexico in the spring of 1915 to utter destruction nine months later was nothing short of astounding in what historian Katz termed "defeat snatched from the jaws of victory."[559] Unquestionably, Villa's military training was informal, and acquired in the field. He was able to gather important advisers such as Felipe Ángeles with ample formal training to lift Villa to military prowess. Villa's losses are directly attributable to Ángeles' waning influence after the battle of Celaya. However, other factors contributed to Villa's demise, as well. German military advisers under the leadership of Arnold Krumm-Heller had much to do with engineering Villa's losses in the summer of 1915. Military defeat translated to lack of recruitment and money in the Mexican Revolution. Sommerfeld's attempt to bridge Villa's financial woes in the summer of 1915 failed to make much difference. The extraction of serious financial concessions from Villa in August, to which Sommerfeld was part and parcel, ended the Mexican revolutionary's chance to fill his munitions accounts with loot. His fate hung in the balance once the Secret War Council decided to drop Villa and instead favor Carranza with arms shipments. President Wilson and, once on board, Secretary Lansing, Leon Canova, and Zach Lamar Cobb finished him off. Villa's bitterness towards the United States, therefore, cannot be surprising.

Felix Sommerfeld wrote to General Scott on December 23rd 1915, the day Ciudad Juarez fell, "'Sic transit gloria mundi [Thus passes the glory of the world].' I am very sorry for General Villa. I am convinced that he in his own way wanted to do right. He did not know how [to] do it. But nobody can take away from him the glory which is his and in spite of all vehement accusations against him at this moment, the history of Mexico must and will do him justice and give him his place as one of the ablest soldiers of Mexico."[560] General Scott, who wanted Villa to come into exile to the United States, vented his frustration and disagreement with the role he played personally in Villa's downfall.

> After Villa had given up millions of dollars at the request of the State Department, expressed through me, they made him an outlaw. He was a wild man who could not be expected to know the difference between the duties of the State and War Departments, and might very well have thought that I double-crossed him, had he not had the confidence in me that he did. No white man, no negro, no Indian, no Moro nor any person, however humble, ever had as much right as Villa to believe I had turned against him, yet he telegraphed a mutual friend in new York [Felix A. Sommerfeld] that General Scott was the only honest man north of Mexico – he had once included the President but now he dropped him altogether.[561]

While the old Indian fighter remained an apologist for Villa until his death, the Wilson administration had cast its lot against the revolutionary chieftain in favor of Venustiano Carranza. The choice would prove to play into the hands of German agents in the United States and Mexico. Secretary Lansing's decision not to intervene militarily in Mexico under any circumstances, even as Villista soldiers fired at U.S. army units, temporarily blunted German efforts to create an intervention. Neither fiery speeches in meeting halls along the border, nor supplying Villa's disintegrating army with millions of rounds of ammunition, had the desired outcome. It was the unexplained and misguided reversal of U.S. foreign policy towards Mexico that unexpectedly created the volatility for a major upheaval along the vulnerable Mexican-American border. Carranza turned out to be a bad choice for the United States. He played German and U.S. interests against each other for his own favor during the remainder of the war, while preparing a constitution that squarely aimed at U.S. financial interest in Mexico. Simultaneously, a marginalized Villa, blinded by the perceived injustice of his downfall, would produce the intervention that Germany so much desired. The U.S. would be virtually at war with Mexico within six months of Carranza's recognition; most of the U.S. army would be on the Mexican-American border or in Mexican territory. Wilson's choice for Carranza, in combination with the ruthless elimination of Villa, became a boon for German strategists.

CHAPTER 8:
"AN ENRAGED ROOSTER"

VILLA TOOK TO THE SIERRA Madres in the end of December, vowing revenge on the perceived treachery of the United States. Paul Keane, an employee of the Hearst ranch near Barbicora, died on Sunday, January 9th 1916, after Villa allegedly ordered his execution. The next day, about six miles south of Santa Ysabel, Chihuahua, a derailment in a curve leading through Box Cañon blocked the passage of a following train on the way to Cusihuriachic, a mining town in the south of Chihuahua. Villa commander Colonel Pablo López, a loyal Yaqui Indian officer of Villa's famed *Dorados*, with an estimated seventy Villista troops quickly surrounded the second train.[562] The train carried among its passengers seventeen American employees of the Cusihuriachic Mining Company, one Canadian, and a British citizen. The conductor described in an affidavit what happened:

> The train arrived at Santa Ysabel at 1:15 P. M. Arriving at Kilometer 68, eight kilometers beyond Santa Ysabel, we encountered a train, engine No. 57, off the track. When I got off to see what had happened the shooting started. Afterward General [sic] Reyna came up and placed us under guard, searching us and also searching the car. All the money on the passengers and in the car was taken. After this had taken place we left, the Americans having been killed. Some of the foreigners were first shot on the train, and a number, including one Mexican [M. B. Romero, an American citizen of Mexican heritage from New Mexico, the Cusi Mining Company auditor], who were wounded in the car, were later taken off and murdered. Some of them

jumped off the train and ran toward the river. These included [Charles R.] Watson [the general manager of the Cusi Mining Company]. They were followed and fired upon."[563]

Thomas B. Holmes, the only American who survived the massacre, described the crime in especially graphic detail:

"Watson, after getting off, ran toward the river, Machatton [actually Richard P. McHatton of El Paso] and I followed. Machatton [sic] fell. I do not know whether he was killed then or stripped. Watson kept running, and they were still shooting at him when I turned and ran down grade, where I fell in some brush, probably 100 feet from the rear of the train. I lay there perfectly quiet and looked around and could see the Mexicans shooting in the direction in which Watson was running. I saw that they were not shooting at me, and, thinking they believed me already dead, I took a chance and crawled into some thicker bushes until I reached the bank of the stream [the Ysabel river]. I then made my way to a point probably 100 yards from the train. There I lay under the bank for half an hour and heard shoots by ones, twos [sic], and threes. I did not hear any sort of groans or yells or cries from our Americans...[564]

The bodies that arrived at Chihuahua City on the following day showed single bullet wounds to the forehead, except for the corpse of supervisor Charles Watson whose entire head had been blown off. A funeral train delivered the victims' bodies to El Paso on January 13th. American mining companies immediately evacuated hundreds of their employees from the Northern Mexican mining centers of Madera, Cusihuriachic, and Parral.[565] Settlements of Mormons in Chihuahua with mostly American expatriates refused to heed the call of evacuation and requested Carrancista troops for protection instead.[566] The reaction to this massacre was predictable: Pablo López, who the Mexican passengers on the train had clearly identified as the leader of the raiding party, immediately became the obsession of outraged El Pasoans who wanted to hunt him down in Mexico and bring him to justice. El Paso police arrested Miguel Díaz Lombardo, the Villa Secretary of Foreign Affairs, who still professed loyalty to his chief, for "vagrancy" and expelled him from the city.[567] Díaz Lombardo complied and went to Los Angeles.[568] Tensions between Mexican and Anglo residents of El Paso ran so high that an altercation between two American soldiers and several Mexicans on Broadway in downtown El Paso caused a mob of eight hundred to one thousand men to challenge the police and U.S. cavalry detachments. Barely able to contain the angry crowd, Carrancista soldiers from the Ciudad Juarez garrison prepared to cross the international line in order to help their Mexican brethren in El Paso. Thankfully, cooler heads prevailed. General Pershing ordered all U.S. troops to return to Fort Bliss. The local sheriff arrested nineteen men while clearing the streets.[569] The city government of El Paso cancelled a mass meeting planned for the next day, January 14th, as a result of the explosive mood on the street.

The El Paso Herald and other papers in cities along the border, as well as the entire Hearst press, clamored for action and decried the ineffectiveness of the Carranza administration in finding the perpetrators of the massacre. Conservative voices long opposed to President Wilson's Mexico policy, such as former president Theodore Roosevelt, former ambassador to Mexico Henry Lane Wilson, Senators Fall, Borah, Poindexter, Gallinger, Works, and Lewis, joined in the interventionist chorus.[570] German Ambassador Count Bernstorff reported to his superiors in Berlin, "It is significant to note about the debates [in the U. S. Senate] that none of the speeches excluded the possibility of military intervention."[571] Count Bernstorff also noted the potentially devastating political impact of this latest Mexican outrage on Wilson's reelection campaign in 1916. "The Republicans all agreed [despite diverse opinions on what to do] in the condemnation of the policy of 'watchful waiting...'" Despite the intense political and public pressure, Woodrow Wilson quickly announced that there would be no military intervention as a result of the slayings. A few weeks later, in Cleveland, Wilson explained, "The world is on fire and there is tinder everywhere. The sparks are liable to drop everywhere, and somewhere there may be material which we cannot prevent from bursting into flame. The whole influence of passion is abroad [sic] in the world, and it is not strange that men see red in such circumstances."[572]

Having disagreed with the president on military preparedness over the course of 1915, Secretary of War Lindley Garrison as well as Assistant Secretary of War Breckinridge offered their resignations on February 10th 1916. Both had been firmly on the side of military preparedness, seeking to strengthen the army and navy. They also openly favored American military intervention in Mexico. The shakeup at the War Department dealt a heavy blow to the administration. General Hugh Lenox Scott became the acting Secretary of War the next day. Count Bernstorff, a keen observer of the American political landscape, reported on a speech by Senate Foreign Relations Committee Chairman William J. Stone, a Democrat from Missouri. The Wilson advocate retorted to the Republican accusations of presidential weakness, that it was the best proof of the "human" strength of President Wilson by refusing to take the country to war despite the fact that his personal interest, namely re-election, would be better served by intervention.[573] Stone proposed to give Carranza one last chance to create order and concluded that no intervention would take place "unless there were further developments to force it."[574]

The "further developments" did not take long to materialize. Two Americans, a prospector and a ranch-hand, turned up murdered near Santa Ysabel three days after the massacre.[575] A group of Villistas crossed the international border at Hachita, New Mexico, on January 18th, about sixty miles northwest of Columbus. They raided a ranch and engaged a detachment of the 7th Cavalry Brigade. Also on the 18th, Villista raiders attacked a camp of the Alvarado Mining Company near Hidalgo de Parral, Chihuahua, and "killed the Chinese cook, wounded the [American] watchman and looted the company store."[576] The raids and the subsequent mass exodus of foreigners from Chihuahua all but stopped the important mining business in the region.[577] Carranza's government immediately felt the pinch from lost tax revenue and export duties. Desperately trying to impress the American public (and the U.S. government) with rigorous action, Carrancista commanders "eagerly" executed dozens of Villistas.[578] While Carrancista officials claimed that these executions dealt with men guilty of the Santa Ysabel murders, most had nothing to do with them.[579] Repeated false reports of the arrest of Pancho Villa and Pablo López incurred the mockery of El Paso dailies, citing the inefficiency of Carranza's pursuit of the rebels.[580]

Despite, or maybe because of the desperate attempts of the Carranza administration to prove its control over the border region, Villa retreated from public view, the headlines in the U.S., and the border during the month of February. Villa's disappearance from center stage presented a welcome break for the Wilson administration. It was already dealing with the threat of a renewed German submarine campaign, scheduled to start on March 1st, 1916, and trying to regain its balance after the vicious attacks from the right, the left, and the press. However, those who thought that the guerilla commander had given up his quest for revenge would soon be disappointed. Villa had sent a letter to Emiliano Zapata asking him to join forces against the United States on January 8th 1916, two days before the massacre at Santa Ysabel.[581] Villa wanted to provoke a military intervention. Pablo López encapsulated Villa's rational. The executioner of Santa Ysabel told a reporter on May 25th 1916, in an interview shortly before being executed,

> Don Pancho was convinced that the gringoes [sic] were too cowardly to fight us, or to try and win our country by force of arms. He said they would keep pitting one faction against another until we were all killed off, and our exhausted country would fall like a ripe pear into their eager hands... Don Pancho also told us that Carranza was selling our northern states to the gringoes [sic] to get money to keep himself in power. He said he wanted to make some attempt to get intervention from the gringoes [sic] before they were ready, and while we still had time to become a united nation... The Santa Ysabel affair partly satisfied my master's desire for revenge, but it did not succeed in satisfying his other wishes. So we marched on Columbus – we invaded American soil.[582]

López's recollection of Villa's strategy that led to a seemingly quixotic attack on the United States is fascinating on several levels. As Felix Sommerfeld had primed Villa's closest confidantes with "first-hand" witness information that Carranza had sold Mexico out to the United States, Villa had concluded that it was not a question of whether, but when, the United States would invade Mexico and take control of the land and resources Carranza had ceded for recognition. Rather than waiting for war, he decided to keep the element of surprise, while at the same time rallying Mexican popular support behind his efforts to save the fatherland.

Villa's arguments, namely that the United States purposely bled the country to death in its support of one, then another faction, appear almost verbatim in a report of German envoy to Mexico Heinrich von Eckardt to the Foreign Office. The report, originally sent on September 25th 1915, as the U.S. announced her intention to recognize Carranza, found unusually wide distribution in the German power structure. By mid-November, the Foreign Office sent von Eckardt's assessment to the main decision-makers in the then raging submarine debate: Emperor Wilhelm II, Chancellor von Bethmann Hollweg, Treasury Secretary Helfferich, the Reichsbank, Max Warburg, S. Bleichroeder, Dresdner Bank, Albert Ballin, and several other recipients.[583] The von Eckardt assessment of the Mexican situation outlined the exact points Villa stated to his commanders a few weeks later:

> Mr. Bryan told me, when he was still in office [as Secretary of State], that the revolution will be on going until the fighting factions have exhausted themselves... that a significant intervention [by the U.S.] was not needed could clearly be read between the lines... That the gentlemen of Wall Street had the cynicism and the power to cause the radical exhaustion of this wealthy neighbor state seemed so unbelievable to me that I decided to thoroughly investigate my understanding of the issue. In the meantime our consulates as well as other diplomatic missions and I realized in the past months that as soon as one of the two factions, the Carrancistas and the Villistas, became stronger, significant support from the United States, mostly with arms and ammunition, favored the weaker party. As a result, either Villa, then Carranza was able to take the capital, which then fell to the enemy for another

round of plundering after a few months. In the beginning of the year Villa actually dared to give a speech
to a group of officers, published in the press a few
days later, in which he outlined his fight against not
only Carranza but also an external enemy, namely the
Americans. The latter were systematically sowing dis-
cord among the revolutionary parties, so that they
would ruin the country, until Mexico would become
the easy prey of the Union [U.S.]. To achieve this end
Mr. Wilson employed confidential agents. He, Villa,
had been delegated Mr. Carothers, General Carranza
received Mr. Silliman. Both had been tasked to create
the impression that the Washington government preferred him, Villa, or Carranza, simultaneously and therefore each would be supported militarily and morally...
it became clear that the other side received the same
type of support... Moreover it is important to note
that as ruin envelops the country, real estate is depre-
ciated and landowners are impoverished thus increas-
ing the purchase of haciendas by Americans...[584]

Von Eckardt continued outlining the suspicion that the cooperation
of Wall Street financiers with the American government, as well as
the retreat of English capital as a result of the European war would
result in a *de facto* American takeover of Mexico.[585] The envoy's
assertions lacked refinement and contained more hearsay than facts.
Still, the memorandum is a significant document because it not only
detailed the fears Villa voiced in his declaration of war against the
United States but von Eckardt also outlined the message the German
secret service agent Sommerfeld likely communicated to Villa at the
time of Carranza's recognition. Virtually the entire power structure of
Germany thus saw how the current tensions in Mexico could benefit
a situation in which the United States' military could be preoccupied
with Mexico while Germany launched unrestricted submarine warfare
to bring England to her knees. It was exactly what Admiral Henning
von Holtzendorff and Foreign Secretary Gottlieb von Jagow had
emphatically supported when Sommerfeld offered to create a diver-
sion at the U.S. - Mexican border in May 1915.

According to historian Barbara Tuchman, "Villa, spoiling for a fight, with Germany whispering encouragement in his ear, danced up and down the border liker an enraged rooster trying to provoke the rush of a large dog."[586] The real fear of the American government in February 1916 seemed not so much the danger of more outrages by Villa, but the possibility of access to funding and his alignment with other factions, especially that of Felix Díaz. Numerous agent reports of the Bureau of Investigations in both, New York and Havana, Cuba, as well as requests for intercepting mail of suspected Díaz adherents, attest to these fears.[587] Díaz, the favorite of the Catholic Church which had supported him financially in the past, indeed seemed to be plotting another attempt to gain power in Mexico. The colorful revolutionary operator, Gonzalo C. Enrile, appeared in New York for meetings with Díaz in December 1915.[588]

A colonel in the Mexican federal army before the revolution, Enrile had joined in the diplomatic service, stationed in Costa Rica and in Clifton, Arizona as Mexican consul.[589] When the revolution formed, Enrile first supported the anti-reelection party of General Reyes. Under the first revolutionary administration of Francisco León De La Barra, Enrile went to Brussels as the Mexican consul.[590] He joined Pascual Orozco as his treasurer in 1912, when the latter challenged the presidency of Francisco Madero.[591] He was the key money connection between Orozco, the extremely wealthy Terrazas family, and the Díaz exile community in the United States which, to a large degree, financed Orozco's uprising. Not surprisingly, Maderista authorities arrested the former consul for attempting to foment "discontent among the men and to promote a hostile feeling against a friendly nation."[592] The colonel spent the last year of the Madero presidency as a consular employee in France in a deal to keep him away from Mexico.[593] After General Huerta took the reins of power in the spring of 1913, the forty-six year-old Enrile returned and joined the Mexican senate as deputy of the Catholic Party.[594] The Catholic Party supported Felix Díaz who Huerta had sidelined in his power-grab. Huerta had the deputy arrested as he ousted former Maderistas and Felicistas from positions of influence. Enrile spent the remainder of the Huerta presidency in Cuba, aligning himself with Felix Díaz and Aureliano Blanquet, who plotted a return to Mexico with other exile groups. Enrile lived in the Waldorf Astoria Hotel in New York, actively plotting with Andrew Meloy, Frederico Stallforth, and Franz Rintelen when Mexican exiles and American businessmen created the Junta X and tried to insert Victoriano Huerta, as well as Pascual Orozco, into the Mexican Revolution in 1915.[595] He had money and connections. All the usual suspects had descended on New York at the time, including Huerta, Orozco, Blanquet, Mondragón, and Díaz.

Two threads ran through Enrile's political career: he consistently worked against the interest of the United States, and he supported the reactionary side throughout the Mexican Revolution. His specialty remained fund-raising. The suspicion of all exile factions, as well as Pancho Villa and Emiliano Zapata, namely that Carranza had concluded some secret agreement with Washington that threatened the very sovereignty of the country, formed the background of Enrile's mission in December 1915.

Enrile arrived in New York from Havana around December 19th. It is difficult to determine exactly who sent him. There was a large exile community in Cuba at the time. Pancho Villa's wife and brother, Hipólito, settled there after the collapse of the Division of the North in mid-December 1915. Felix Díaz, who had operated out of Havana before he moved to New York, also had a large contingent of support-ers there. In addition, at the time former president of Mexico Fran-cisco León De La Barra lived at the Hotel Astor in New York, so did Felix Sommerfeld and Heinrich Albert.[596] Enrile himself claimed to Ger-man authorities that he represented the factions of De La Barra, Felix Díaz, Zapata, and Villa. Although historians have dismissed his claims as ludicrous, these factions all had a common enemy in Carranza, and a common conviction that the First Chief had sold out Mexico to the United States. Both Villa and Zapata expected a military showdown with the United States within a short time. B.I. agents along the bor-der who interviewed a Villista commander in April 1916 confirmed the development, "With the death of Orozco [in the summer of 1915] and Huerta [in January 1916] there has been a fusion of parties recognizing as leader Felix Díaz who, it is said, put himself in accord with Zapata... To invade American territory, to murder American citizens, burn American cities and cause all the possible depredations in American territory in order to bring a conflict with this nation [U.S.]."[597]

The U.S. government had hired one of Villa's secretaries, Dario Silva, in the fall of 1915. Silva reported to the Bureau of Investigations under deep cover, using the codename, "Avlis," and thoroughly documented the fact that the Catholic Church (who supported Felix Díaz, as well) "offered Villa three hundred thousand dollars for protection about September, 1915, and that they would continue to support him if he would take the side of the church."[598] It seems that money did indeed flow, as B.I. Agent Blanford reported from Los Angeles on March 22nd 1916.[599] The B.I. had discovered a retired U.S. army captain in Monrovia, California who held $55,000 ($1.1 million in today's value) for Villa. The source of the money remained obscure with the captain making the unrealistic claim that Villa had brought him the money personally.[600]

There was also the suspicion that the German government was financing Villa in his attempt to engage the U.S. in a war. A special agent of the B.I. in Pittsburg sent a letter to B.I. Chief A. Bruce Bielaski on April 12th 1916, with the information from a Wall Street investor that Hans Tauscher had told him about a payment of $320,000 to Villa.[601] This roughly matched the suspected financial support from the Catholic Church. Was the "Catholic Church" a cover and conduit for the German government? Was this the same money? It is established that Tauscher financed at least one arms shipment to Zapata, the other fighting force in the field against Carranza. Albert recorded a lunch meeting with "Stahl" on March 12th."[602] His luncheon partner was Aldolfo Stahl, a man "about 60 years of age, 5' 8", 150 pounds, gray hair, gray mustache, appears to be a Jew," and Tauscher's contact who bought arms and munitions for Guatemala.[603] The meeting, as well as its timing, indicates that Albert and Stahl discussed the financing of munitions shipments, further linking the Secret War Council to material support of the Junta that was trying to overthrow Carranza and create a war with the United States in the process.

Albert's financial records document a $300,000 transfer from a commercial account to the Mechanics and Metals National Bank, marked "K.M." at the end of November 1915. "K.M." stood for *Kriegsministerium* or Imperial War Department.[604] The ledger of the *Kriegsministerium* shows another $200,000 credit von Papen received in the beginning of December.[605] It was between November 23rd and December 4th, at the exact time when Villa's army was imploding, that von Papen received $500,000 from Albert. The use of these credits does not appear to have been for the Bridgeport Projectile Company or purchases of smokeless powder.

The ledgers are inconclusive as for what this money was used, and the accounts of the military attaché in 1916 do not document exactly how it was spent. However, in the months following the transfer, several suspicious payments stand out. Wolf von Igel, who took over von Papen's responsibility as provisional military attaché, received $25,000 on December 28th 1915, just one week after the Enrile-Papen encounter.[606] The Bureau of Investigations noted in the end of January 1916 that Adolfo Stahl had consigned four hundred cases of 7mm Mauser cartridges to the Guatemalan government, financed through G. Amsinck and Co.[607] A second order of four hundred cases of identical cartridges shipped at the end of February. The B.I. interviewed the Guatemalan consul about these large munitions shipments. He explained that the munitions the Guatemalan government had on-hand "deteriorate and are replaced from time to time by new stocks, and this explains the present shipments."[608] Stahl's two shipments amounted almost exactly to $25,000 at the going rate of $32 per thousand.

Von Igel's files do not contain a memorandum nor accounting for the purpose of the $25,000 expense. However, a clear link between his office and Adolfo Stahl exists. Albert's accounts of the War Department in this time period document an arms and munitions contract in March 1916 of ten Gatlin machine guns and 1.5 million cartridges, which Hans Tauscher sold for $53,115 [over $1 million in today's value] to Adolfo Stahl.[609] The American Bureau of Investigations was well aware of the shipment that left New York on the banana freighter *SS Sixiola* in May.[610] The shipment weighed one hundred tons.[611] A frustrated B.I. agent noted, "inasmuch as it [the shipment of munitions] was for the Guatemalan Government [sic] nothing could be done to prevent its leaving this port."[612] G. Amsinck and Co. handled the financial transaction just as they had the January and February shipments. The destination, of course, was a ruse. The *Sixiola* called on numerous harbors: New Orleans, Progreso on Yucatan, Mexico, Jamaica (British), and finally Puerto Barrios, Guatemala.[613] It is unknown where she discharged her munitions cargo in May, but B.I. agents considered it unlikely that the cargo of arms would have passed by British inspectors in Jamaica.[614] While Tauscher's memos indicated that the customer would transfer the money and that Tauscher would credit the military attaché with the proceeds, Albert's financials show no such credit throughout 1916, indicating that the shipment was a grant to Carranza or Zapata from the Imperial War Department.[615] The B.I. traced further shipments through Tauscher's office to Guatemala. American agents found out from an informer that "He [Zapata] has plenty of arms and ammunition. He gets it through Guatemala..."[616]

Carl Heynen is mentioned in Albert's books on January 10th 1916, as holding "advances aggregating [to] $132,000" for a "Mexican shipment."[617]Carl Heynen received $50,000 marked "Mexican Shipment" on April 4th 1916.[618] Heynen bought rubber "rosin" in Mexico for shipment to Germany in the summer and fall of 1915. However, in November 1915 English patrols seized the SS *Zealandia* off the coast of Mexico, the ship Heynen had leased for transporting the rubber.[619] The Albert files do not illuminate the question of what happened with the money for the rubber. Obviously, Heynen had not used it to pay for the rubber. Insurance companies were dealing with the losses from the British seizure. What did Heynen do with the money amounting to almost $4 million in today's value? There are other hints in Albert's accounts that point to a secret funding of the Mexican Revolution. These transactions appear in detail in a subsequent chapter.

There is yet another indication that the Catholic Church had a connection with Sommerfeld and the Secret War Council: Father Francis Kelley led the Catholic opposition to the Carranza government in the United States. Kelley had not supported the conspirators in the Huerta-Orozco-Mondragón plot for precisely that reason. According to historian Arthur Link, Kelley intervened with Sommerfeld on behalf of the treatment of the Mexican Catholic Church in February 1915. "Villa's chief agent in the United States, Felix A. Sommerfeld, obtained from Villa a promise not to molest the Church and negotiated with the Rev. Francis C. Kelley, the chief Catholic spokesman in the United States on Mexican matters."[620] In May 1916, B.I. agents received conclusive evidence that Fathers Kelly and Thierney "were active on behalf of Felix Díaz..."[621] Cryptically, and without providing any further detail, Sommerfeld told American investigators in 1918 that he had highly explosive information about Father Kelley. While the B.I. thoroughly investigated suspected German agents such as Sommerfeld, Heynen, Stallforth, and Albert, Father Kelley never appeared on their radar. Inadvertently, he might have been the financier behind Villa's attack on Columbus.

Enrile, equipped with $1,000 in travel money from Felix Díaz, returned to Havana before shipping out to Europe. He likely conferred with members of the exile community there, which in the meantime, also included Hipólito Villa.[622] Enrile travelled with the Mexico City lawyer Humberto Yslas to Spain on January 20th. Coincidentally, rumors abounded in New York and Havana that Villa had reached some sort of agreement with Felix Díaz.[623] George Carothers, the State Department envoy detailed to Villa until the Carranza recognition in October, wrote on March 3rd 1916, one week before the Columbus attack, "From very reliable source am informed that Villa has complete understanding with Felix Díaz, this understanding was reached last December [coinciding with Enrile's conferences in New York] and my information comes from person who saw letter from Villa to Díaz accepting condition. I anticipate renewed Villa activity in very near future."[624] It seems plausible that Sommerfeld was Carothers' "reliable" source and had indeed brought about the understanding between Díaz and Villa. Carothers' ominous expectation of "Villa activity in very near future" reflected the general mindset among people familiar with developments in Mexico.

The Enrile delegation went to Santander, Spain. Enrile met with the German ambassador, Maximilian Prince Ratibor, showed him a letter of introduction from Franz von Papen, and asked for permission to continue to Germany.[625] Again, historians have taken Ambassador Ratibor's cool reception as an indication that Enrile's mission had no import.[626] However, as members of the Secret War Council in New York could attest to, the Imperial Foreign Service was diametrically opposed to provoking an American entry into the war. Felix Díaz agents had approached Ambassador Count Bernstorff with similar proposals in July 1915. According to the ambassador, "the group gathered around Felix Díaz is putting itself at our disposal should there be a war between the United States and Germany [as a result of the *Lusitania* sinking]... This issue is clearly highly sensitive, and I therefore told the man that a war between the United States and Germany appears out of the question to me."[627] Despite his misgivings, he sent the Mexican envoy to von Papen. This establishes a clear relationship between von Papen and the Díaz faction in line with the Enrile mission as early as the summer of 1915, when the Sommerfeld-Dernburg proposal had been adopted as military strategy. Opposing the Foreign Service, the German military did not fear an American provocation as long as distractions, domestic or along the Mexican border, could be created. Thus, it is not surprising that Ambassadors Ratibor and Bernstorff, as well as their superiors in Berlin, stymied the Mexicans' efforts. After some back and forth, von Papen's letter of introduction and possible confirmation by the military attaché that Enrile was legitimate, the Mexican delegation finally continued on to Berlin via Switzerland.

Meanwhile, during the early morning hours of March 9th 1916, after a month of rumors and questions of what Villa's next move would be, the dreaded answer revealed itself. News of Villa approaching the border with a force of between five hundred and six hundred men, and the supposition that the revolutionary chieftain had finally decided to seek refuge in the United States, preceded the fateful night between March 8th and 9th. The *El Paso Herald* reported on March 8th, "With three American cattlemen presumably held as prisoner, Francisco Villa, the outlawed Mexican insurgent, was reported today with between 200 and 700 men at a point on the Boca Grande river in Chihuahua, 15 miles west of Columbus and 27 miles south of the border."[628] The three men had the bad luck of crossing Villa's path as his raiding party prepared to attack the United States. They did not survive the encounter. The next day, an American military unit found their bodies hanged and burnt.[629]

Despite the reports that Villa was at the border with a sizeable armed force, and despite the obvious fact that he did not appear to have changed his attitude towards the United States, rumors persisted that the Mexican rebel commander wanted to cross into the United States. The commander of the Columbus garrison, Colonel Herbert J. Slocum, who had given the information of Villa's whereabouts to the El Paso paper, seemed confident that Villa did not represent any danger. American intelligence, save for two agents, got it wrong. George Carothers, formally President Wilson's special envoy to Pancho Villa, cabled to the Secretary of State on March 3rd 1916, "I anticipate renewed Villa activity in the near future."[630] Zach Lamar Cobb, the tireless customs collector of El Paso and State Department intelligence officer, sent multiple telegrams to his superiors in Washington detailing Villa's whereabouts: He reported on March 3rd, "Villa left Pecheco Point, near Madera with three hundred men headed towards

Columbus, New Mexico..."[631] Cobb believed that Villa "intends to cross to United States and hopes to proceed to Washington."[632] He still cautioned as to Villa's intentions.

Col. Herbert J. Slocum on right. Photo courtesy Library of Congress, Prints and Photographs Division Washington, D.C.[633]

The rumor of Villa personally seeking to absolve himself for the Santa Ysabel murders in Washington was the result of communications between an AP reporter, George Seese, and Villa. Seese had advance knowledge of Villa's coming to Columbus and was supposed to accompany the revolutionary chieftain to Washington D.C. On February 28th he wrote a letter to his editor in Los Angeles: "I have reached Villa with proposition to come to United States secretly [and] go with me to see President Wilson... whether the president sees him or not we will have five or six days of fine exclusive stuff, and I have motion picture friend who would foot the bills for all expenses for the right to make pictures. ... My plan is to meet Villa somewhere near Columbus, run him up past Almagordo, N. M., to avoid eyes that might know him, board a train and scoot for Kansas City, thence via Chicago to Washington... "[634] Seese's boss immediately responded, "Do not at all approve plan... "[635] Seese wrote another message from El Paso on March 4th, "The Villa matter was dropped like a hot stove as soon as I received your message. I went after the proposition because I thought that having Villa in the United States would relieve the Mexican situation of one of its problems, afford the United States [sic] officials some satisfaction and give us a dandy story... Villa may come across the line any time now. By the time you get this he may already have crossed. I hope to put over a beat when he does, but the Associated Press is not and shall not be committed to anything."[636]

Seese did travel to Columbus on March 8th with an aide. It was never discovered who interceded with Villa on his behalf. While no archival smoking gun has turned up yet, Felix Sommerfeld did have all the right credentials to play the intermediary. He had worked for AP News and personally knew its general manager, Melville E. Stone, very well.[637] Sommerfeld also had a close relationship with Fred B. Warren, the general manager of Goldwyn Film Company. Warren, who lived in the Hotel Astor (just as Sommerfeld and Albert), would have been the person to promise funding of the project.[638] Albert, at the time, heavily invested in German propaganda films and his own film company. Finally, Sommerfeld was, albeit "unofficially" since October 1915, the loyal Villa representative in the United States. Sommerfeld told investigators in 1918 that he himself tried to get Villa to explain himself. "The only time I got in communication with Villa [after the recognition of Carranza] was the killing of the Americans at Santa Isabel [sic].

General Scott happened to be here in New York... I sent a long telegram, which I showed to General Scott, and sent it down to El Paso...
The murder of seventeen Americans is an atrocious crime. People
believe you have had something to do with it. In order to prove it, you
will have to get the man who did the killing and show that no foreigner's life has been, or will be, threatened by you."[639]

Clearly, under a purely military consideration, the rumor of
Villa's intention to explain himself personally in Washington blunted
the preparedness of U.S. forces at the border. Villa was approaching
the border with between five hundred and six hundred men, both
the State Department and Carranza officials warned the U.S. military
authorities, yet no one seemed alarmed.[640] Even the newspapers on
the day before the raid reported on Villa's kidnapping of American
cowboys. This certainly should at least have indicated the possibility
of a hostile intention of the Mexican force approaching the border.
Yet, Colonel Slocum did not post additional sentries anywhere, at
the border, the camp, or the town. He also did not employ scouts to
track Villa's movements. The 13th Cavalry Brigade at Camp Furlong in
Columbus was deep asleep in the early morning hours of March 9th.

Two detachments of Villistas, amounting to an estimated 485
men under the command of Candelario Cervantes and the infamous
Pablo López, simultaneously attacked the cavalry camp and the town
at approximately 4:30 am on March 9th 1916.[641] Villa himself stayed
behind in Mexico with a small reserve. The raiders stormed into town
shooting up the bank, and set fire to the Commercial Hotel, where they
executed its manager A. L. Ritchie, as well as several overnight guests.
The raiders proceeded to loot the town and fired indiscriminately at
homes, where unsuspecting residents were sleeping. A detachment
of Villistas sought to find and murder Sam Ravel. The owner of a local
hardware store located in the same building as the hotel had allegedly
cheated Villa sometime in the past. They looted the store. Ravel lived
to see another day because he was out of town that night.[642] However,
insurance refused to cover his losses of $10,000 [$210,000 in today's
value], a heavy blow for the businessman.[643] Simultaneously, the raiders attacked Camp Furlong.

Luckily for the surprised cavalry soldiers, the raiders mistook
the stables for the barracks and shot horses instead of men.[644] The
American soldiers mounted a counter-attack within a short time,

forcing the Villistas into retreat. Twenty-three Villistas died during intense fighting.[645] The raiding party withdrew into Mexico by 7:30 in the morning. Major Frank Tompkins chased the Villistas across the border with a squadron of fifty men and pursued them for five miles on Mexican territory. The Americans inflicted serious casualties on the rear guard of Villa's forces. There are no exact numbers of losses on the Villista side, but Major Tompkins reported seventy-five killed. The 13th Cavalry lost one man and two horses. Tompkins himself had to abandon his horse and "was shot through the hat."[646] Short of ammunition, without supplies for the horses, and to "get something to eat," he returned to Columbus later that day.[647]

The town was in shambles. Nine civilians and eight U.S. soldiers had died. Another nine soldiers had been injured; one of them succumbed to his wounds later.[648] The authorities apprehended thirty raiders. George Seese and his companion who had stayed in the Commercial Hotel made it out alive but sufficiently shaken. Seese, who believed that he might have caused this mess, and who had a warrant pending for his arrest for polygamy, fled to Canada. He finally gave interviews to American investigators when he turned up in New York a few months later. He had nothing to add other than he really believed he could have taken Villa to President Wilson. No one asked him about Sommerfeld.

Burning the bodies of dead bandits at Columbus, NM.[649]

Seemingly, the public outrage following the raid had no boundaries. The embarrassment of the military not to have been on guard as Villa approached was palpable. Reports of an overpowered, heroic 13th Cavalry that repelled up to one thousand raiders and killed hundreds of Villistas in the process could not distract from the painful truth.[650] Villa had successfully, and without paying a significant price, attacked the United States proper. Never before, and never since has a military force from a Latin American country invaded the territory of the United States.

March 9th was the first day on the job for Secretary of War Newton K. Baker in Washington. He immediately ordered his predecessor, Hugh Lenox Scott, to mount a punitive campaign. General John J. "Blackjack" Pershing would be in charge. The mission was to pursue "the Mexican band which attacked the town of Columbus, New Mexico, and the troops there on the morning of the ninth instant."[651] Much to the glee of the Secret War Council, the so-called Punitive Expedition would tie up a significant majority of the American military at the Mexican border and inside Mexico for the next nine months. It seemed virtually assured at the time that it would be only a matter of time when Carranza's forces would clash with American troops. A war between the United States and Mexico was expected in all quarters of the German and American governments when the situation became aggravated as a result of clashes with the U.S. military in May and June, 1916. The new American Secretary of War immediately ordered to look into expanding and equipping the military, forced to do what his predecessor could not implement and over which he resigned. The Columbus affair was a dream-come-true for the German military.

Countless books and articles since the attack speculated as to Villa's motivations, his finances, and his backers. The revolutionary himself never commented on his attack.[652] Why did he choose Columbus, New Mexico, a relatively unimportant town with little to loot and lots of military presence? The theories focused on Sam Ravel and Villa's attack as an act of revenge. However, killing a merchant did not require a major military attack. There were plenty of Villista agents who could have meted out the punishment. Another school of thought was that Villa indeed wanted to cross into the U.S. to justify himself. The theory argues that when the plan fell apart, Villa lost control over his forces. Hugh Lenox Scott promoted this idea.[653] However, Villa was no fool. He would have been arrested immediately for the murders of Americans in the preceding months. Many theories vaguely reference German agents as being behind Villa's attack. A German physician from El Paso, Dr. Lyman B. Rauschbaum, had been close to Villa in 1915 and 1916. There is no evidence that he did anything other than stay close to Villa.[654]

Suspicions also surrounded Felix Sommerfeld. It took some prodding from the editor of the *Providence Journal* and Carrancista representatives to get the B.I. to investigate Sommerfeld's whereabouts. Special Agent J. W. Allen asked the Military Intelligence Division on March 14th 1916, to "inform the secret service and get them to shadow him and secure his effects for incriminating evidence."[655] The Carranza representatives in the U.S. tried their best to pin suspicions on Sommerfeld. Carranza consul Beltrán in San Antonio told B.I. agent Beckham "... Sam Dreben, Sheldon Hotel, El Paso, and Felix Sommerfeld, New York City, were go-betweens for German interests and Francisco Villa."[656] According to the Carranza consulate in New York City, "Sommerfeld had told her [a woman without further description] in New York about 15 days ago that there would be intervention in a few days... Sommerfeld knew in advance about the Villa attack."[657] Bureau of Investigations Chief Bielaski took the Carrancista information seriously. He wired William Offley in New York City on March 14th, "Legal representative Carranza Government wires Felix Sommerfeld assisting Villa and suggest he be shadowed and effects examined for incriminating evidence. Please give Summerfield [sic] activities immediate attention and make best possible effort to see what he is doing."[658] Interestingly, despite Chief Bielaski asking New York agents to locate Sommerfeld, they did not actually contact him in the Hotel Astor until May 5th 1916.[659]

He may not have been there. The only evidence that Sommerfeld actually was in New York during the raid is a letter on Hotel Astor stationary he wrote to General Scott on March 10th 1916, in which he unequivocally condemned Villa's attack.[660] His actual whereabouts before and after the raid remain questionable. B.I. agents had interviewed the lawyer and Carranza lobbyist Sherburne Hopkins in Washington D.C. on February 28th. He told the B.I. agents that the Catholic Church was financing an uprising against Carranza. He suggested for them to speak with Sommerfeld, who was "stopping at the Waldorf Hotel..."[661] Sommerfeld had his office and regular living quarters in the Hotel Astor. Was he hiding from the prying eyes of those who knew where he regularly stayed? B.I. agents tried to locate Sommerfeld in New York at the end of April, but could not find him.[662] Instead, agents along the Mexican border in April reported Sommerfeld to be "in Los Angeles under an assumed name and evidently in disguise... on the street in Los Angeles dressed somewhat roughly."[663] B.I. Agent Barnes in El Paso also reported him "here under assumed name," and asked "is he wanted...?"[664] He was not. Most likely, Sommerfeld did go to the border before the raid to help supply Villa with munitions and to canvas the situation for the German secret service. Plenty of B.I. reports point to Sommerfeld remaining Villa's arms and munitions buyer with evidence of his purchases from merchants in Los Angeles, Boston, and New York abounding in the months before and after the attack on Columbus.[665] Using a disguise and fake names, at the very least, demonstrated apprehension on the part of the German agent. Many historians have tried to find a definite link between Columbus and the German agent over the years, but Sommerfeld was much too skilled to leave a smoking gun behind.[666]

The main theories of the motivation behind the raid all revolve around the fact that the Wilson administration had recognized Carranza and precipitated the violent reaction of Villa. Major Tompkins, the courageous cavalry officer who went after the raiders into Mexico, wrote a book about his experiences in which he also espoused this theory.[667] He seconded most of the interventionist supporters in the Senate who blamed Wilson's Mexico policy for the raid. All three theses, loot, vengeance, and German intrigue, contain what will ultimately prove to be a part of the historical truth. However, no one has yet fully explored the hard facts, the "how" in each of these theories. Villa certainly could have looked to Columbus as a source for loot, but there is no evidence or confirmation of this thesis. Vengeance against the American government proved itself a motivation, given Villa's speeches, the letter to Zapata, and his actions in the prior months. The articles historian Katz wrote about the role of Leon Canova are the best argued and supported analyses on the topic.

The elephant in the room was the German strategy to tie American forces down at the Mexican border, and the German interest in the American military having to use arms and munitions for itself rather than selling them to Europe. German agents, before and after the attack, had played a significant role in precipitating and supporting the border conflagration. The challenge of this theory is to prove who did what and how. Sommerfeld's mission to cause a war with Mexico and his role in helping convince Villa of an imminent danger to Mexico are well documented. The key to understanding the trigger of how German influence caused Villa to commence his attack lays within the background of the Enrile mission to Germany.

The Enrile delegation arrived in Berlin on April 10th 1916, one month after the Villa attack on Columbus, New Mexico, and while five thousand U.S. army troops were entering Mexico as part of the punitive expedition.[668] It is critical to understand the timing of this mission. Historians have discounted Enrile's efforts, since in May of 1916, when he finally met with Count Montgelas of the Foreign Office, the attack on Columbus had come and gone. The German government had, by then, markedly cooled to the proposal. However, Enrile's mission is critical for the understanding of Pancho Villa's motivation in the attack on Columbus, New Mexico. Enrile's proposal represented a clear rationale for Pancho Villa to attack the U.S. in the context of the German strategy to create a war between Mexico and the United States, which documentation supports Sommerfeld was actively pursuing. It is significant that this document had been drafted and approved by von Papen, Villista exiles, Felix Díaz exiles, and old-guard Científicos under De La Barra in December 1915.

The well-composed proposals of the Mexicans in perfect German reveal astounding similarities with the proposal which Dernburg and Sommerfeld had sent to Admiral von Holtzendorff back in May 1915. Additionally, Enrile's reasoning and argumentation mirrored the German military strategy towards the U.S., which the Mexicans knew little about. Without a doubt, Enrile had not only connected with von Papen while in New York and familiarized the latter with his backers and proposals, von Papen must have had a hand in drafting the proposals with Enrile and his friends. Enrile's initial memorandum to the German government dons the signature of the former military attaché, is undated and likely reached the German government before the Villa attack on Columbus.[669] The proposal Enrile submitted on behalf of the "National Party" of Mexico "whose Vice-president I am" completely matched the information of American Bureau of Investigations agents who had interviewed a Villa commander earlier:

The main proposal which I want to submit to the imperial government are the following:

Mexico needs weapons and munitions in order to defeat the reign of terror of the Carranza administration, as well as enough capital to recreate the old federal army. In addition the country needs the support of a large power such as Germany to resist the United States. In return we offer:

1) Installation of Mexican policies completely supportive of German policy, which is aimed against the interests of the United States.

2) Granting of concessions to Germany of railroads, petroleum, mines, and commerce.

3) Expulsion of American capital from the country through legal measures [i.e. expropriation].

4) Creation of an army strong enough to attack the United States in a for Germany and Mexico favorable moment.

5) Support of a separatist movement that already exists in several southern states of the United States: namely Texas, Arizona, New Mexico and the south of upper [U.S.] California.

6) Creation and support of a political race revolution in Cuba, Puertorico [sic], and Haiti.

7) Financial guarantees to Germany for weapons and munition in a for Germany agreeable form. The total sum, partly in cash, partly in weapons, munitions, and other war materials needed for an invasion of the United States amounts to 300 Million marks.

... any questions to be directed at Captain von Papen... [670]

Enrile laid out the rational for using Mexico to prevent the United States from entering the battlefields of Europe in another, more elaborate memorandum submitted to Count Montgelas of the Foreign Office (received there on May 15th 1916). The first paragraphs recounted the likelihood of an eventual war between Germany and the United

States as a result of the lopsided neutrality policy to the detriment of the Central Powers. Mexico was herself involved in a

> ... heroic and only because of her financial weakness desperate fight against the assaults of North America...
> A continuation of the conflict between Mexico and the United States [since the attack on Columbus] seem inevitable; Germany will be able to preserve the peace with the United States so long as the latter is fully occupied with the Mexican differences. Thus it could be achieved that:
> The United States will be weakened enough, to become ineffectual for further [military] excursions.
> a) The current manufacturing of weapons and munitions will end as a result of the United States requiring the same for herself [note the exact same argument in the Dernburg-Sommerfeld proposal].
> b) Mexico can save her existence as a result of the thus received support to defend herself.
> c) Should it come to a war between the United States anyway, the support of a Mexican army easily expanding to 200,000 men could help bring the defeat of the United States on American soil along a 2,000 kilometer long border... Signed Gonzalo C. Enrile, Colonel.[671]

Seven pages of details followed the memorandum substantiating the original proposal. The proposal found little support within the German government after the punitive expedition was underway.

There are very important aspects of the Enrile proposals that, so far, the large historiography on the Columbus attack has completely ignored. Villa, whose frame of mind in the months leading up to Columbus some contemporaries and historians have characterized as bordering on insanity, had a clear motivation and strategy for the attack. Historian Friedrich Katz assessed for the first time in 1978 that, indeed, Villa was not crazy when he selected Columbus, New Mexico, to provoke an American intervention.[672] Considering the rationale of the Enrile memorandum, Villa did not just attack the United States in a quixotic, one-time effort. The alienated Mexican exile community, with Villa as the "enraged rooster" leading the effort, believed that a military intervention into the United States would create a boon of German support. Enrile's proposal shows that, in his desperation, Villa clearly had aligned himself with factions of the old elite, especially that of Felix Díaz. Thus, Enrile's claims of representing diverse factions such as Villa, Zapata, Díaz, and De La Barra, which hosts of analyses ridiculed, was true. The suspected existence of a secret agreement between Carranza and the Wilson administration, whether in writing or not, promoted the existential fear among Mexican exiles and Villa that only a confrontation with the United States could either sever the friendly relations of the U.S. with Carranza, or rally the majority of Mexicans behind a defender of the homeland in the persons of Pancho Villa or Felix Díaz.

The timing of the document, namely that it had clearly been drafted and agreed upon before Santa Ysabel and Columbus, is crucial. Thus, Villa's venture was the beginning salvo of a much larger campaign that he was to undertake with the agreement and support of the other factions opposed to Carranza. Indeed, Villista incursions into the United States, small shoot-outs, and wholesale raids occurred several times between January and June 1916.[673] Ultimately, the pressure of the American military chasing him and the Carrancista forces preventing him from organizing ended his quest to start a war. The launch of Villa's attack before Enrile had received a German commitment of support is further evidence that initial funding from the Catholic Church and/or the Secret War Council was in place. The German government firmly supported Carranza after the United States launched the Punitive Expedition. The Mexican leader proved to offer a much better chance at causing a war with the U.S.

The German efforts to produce conflagrations along the Mexican-American border during 1915 and 1916 are thoroughly documented. The stated strategy of the Secret War Council since the Dernburg-Sommerfeld memo in May 1915 targeted the preoccupation of the United States with Mexico. It aimed both at diverting military forces and, at the same time, reducing availability of arms and munitions for the Entente in the face of an American military buildup. Both aspects of this strategy appear in Enrile's memorandum. Sommerfeld and others had succeeded in sufficiently infuriating Villa to contemplate his attack on

Columbus. While the Secret War Council through Felix Sommerfeld and Hans Tauscher supported Mexican efforts to set the border on fire, the decision to commit funds on the order envisioned by the conspirators required a sign-off in Berlin.

The critical decisions, however, had been made in December 1915 in New York. Sommerfeld had helped broker an understanding between Felix Díaz and Villa, German Military Attaché von Papen had promised to finance the resulting military action, and seemed to have shown his commitment through some preliminary funding or arms shipments. Albert's diary betrays that the head of the Secret War Council had a significant involvement in the Mexican situation. Franz von Papen, who had meanwhile arrived back in Germany, wrote to his former colleague in New York on March 9th, "I have talked with the chief about you a long time, and hope it will have a fine military result. You need not worry in any way [underlined in the original] – they know everything."[674] The cryptic message allows for some conjecture. Who was the "chief"? What was Albert worried about? The possibility that Albert had somehow collided with the Foreign Office over military matters (i.e. sabotage or blowing up the Mexican border) looms large. Von Papen seemed to have carried a message from Albert to the Chief of the Political Section IIIb of the General Staff, asking for an authorization of some kind that would trigger "a fine military result." The fact alone that the German military attaché for the United States and Mexico had approved the plan, and made a down-payment to a much larger commitment, would have been sufficient for Pancho Villa to initiate his campaign. Certainly, Villa had every reason to expect the full support of the German government as the campaign progressed. The "fine military result" tied down the majority of the U.S. military on the border and in Mexico.

The military buildup along the Mexican-American border and the intensifying U.S. incursion into Mexico triggered widespread excitement within all levels of the German government, the pro-German groups in the United States, and especially the members of the Secret War Council. Although Albert did not record his thoughts on the Mexican situation in the letters to his wife or in his diaries, a caricature he clipped out of the New York Evening Sun on April 12th 1916, and kept in his files, is a telling commentary. Albert's clipping of the New York Evening Sun showed a good measure of "Schadenfreude" (German for glee). The drawing depicts Uncle Sam looking helplessly at a lumbering, bearded Germanic warrior. The caption reads, "Go away. Don't you know my army is down in Mexico looking for a man?"[675] The lack of further commentary in Albert's files is curious. Albert commented on almost any topic, and even mentioned clandestine projects to his wife cryptically. Did he not care about the developments in Mexico or was this issue so sensitive that he did not dare to even touch upon it?

"Go away. Don't you know my army is down in Mexico looking for a man?!"[676]

Despite the failure of the Enrile mission as a result of bad timing, the idea of German military and financial support of Mexico remained prevalent within German government circles. The German military cheered and contemplated further assistance to fan the flames of war between Mexico and the United States when the attack did occur, and as it achieved, indeed, what German strategy had envisioned. The German government authorized the shipping of weapons and munitions to Mexico immediately after the attack on Columbus. Ambassador Count Bernstorff wrote on March 20th 1916, "the buildup of the military is proceeding with eagerness; currently, almost the entire regular army of the United States is in Mexico or congregating at the border."[677]

The German ambassador knew more about the plot than he ever let on. Ms. Catherine Birney, the sister-in-law of Sommerfeld's close friend and Doheny oil manager Harold Walker, married Wilhelm Albrecht von Schoen on February 12th 1916. Schoen was a German diplomat formerly stationed in Chile. The ambassador struck Sommerfeld from the guest list in Washington. "He said at once that it would not do to have him [Sommerfeld] appear at any function in connection with the German embassy, as it was important that his association with the Embassy should be kept secret."[678] If Sommerfeld had been retired from "Mexican affairs" by then, as he later claimed, the ambassador's action would have made little sense. As a matter of fact, Sommerfeld's fingerprints and evidence of German financial support were all over the Villa plot. American authorities, as well, had definite suspicions about Sommerfeld's involvement. They followed his every move in the months to come, while he infiltrated Pershing's punitive expedition with his agents.

CHAPTER 9:
FLIRTING WITH DISASTER

P RESIDENT WILSON AND HIS CABINET decided to mount a punitive expedition on the day of Pancho Villa's attack on Columbus, while the remains of downtown Columbus still smoldered, and while Major Frank Thompson chased the rear guard of the Villistas across the border.[679] The president was up for re-election in the fall. Letting the violation of U.S. territory go unpunished would undoubtedly have cost him the presidency. He feared the chorus of many voices that had clamored for intervention in Mexico for years, the likes of former President Theodore Roosevelt, Senators Fall of New Mexico, Gallinger of New Hampshire, and Works of California, newspaper mogul William Randolph Hearst, industrialists Henry Clay Pierce and Charles Flint, even former and current members of his cabinet such as Lindley Garrison and Franklin Lane. Historian Link succinctly described the conundrum of the president: "All Cabinet members agreed [in a meeting on the morning of March 10th] that Congress would adopt a resolution calling for armed intervention unless the government took vigorous action immediately... He [Wilson] realized that Villa had perpetrated the Columbus raid in order to force American military intervention."[680] President Wilson's hands were tied, despite his clear aversion to a military engagement in Mexico. The war in Europe was first and foremost on the president's mind. Mexico was a huge distraction and threatened to divert important resources from a potential involvement in the European War.

Scores of historians have searched through the details and archival documents related to the attack on Columbus in the quest to prove German involvement.[681] Not much has been uncovered. Theories about German agents surrounding Pancho Villa, and some-how prodding him to act on Germany's behalf, came and went in a flurry of studies between 1960 and 1980. Circumstantial evidence placed one of Pancho Villa's doctors, the German physician, Dr. Lyman B. Rauschbaum, in a position of influence with the Mexican revolutionary.[682] However, neither Rauschbaum himself nor anyone within Villa's entourage has ever confirmed any clear link to the decision to attack. There is no evidence in German archives that Rauschbaum was even a German agent. Lacking a money trail, a method, or any other tangible evidence of Rauschbaum's influence on Villa, the theory of his involvement remains just that, a theory.

Felix A. Sommerfeld remained a suspect throughout the historiography. However, neither his papers nor any papers connecting him definitively with Villa's decision to attack the United States, have surfaced. Still, the case of Felix Sommerfeld offers the most concrete evidence of German involvement, so far. Despite the fact that no one has yet been able to place him with Pancho Villa in this critical time, or near Columbus, Sommerfeld clearly was a German secret service agent and had offered to cause a border conflagration between Mexico and the United States. Unlike Dr. Rauschbaum, Sommerfeld behaved suspiciously in the weeks after the incident, appearing in El Paso and Los Angeles disguised and incognito. The aftermath of the Columbus attack offers key pieces of evidence as to how Felix Sommerfeld followed through on his orders from the German government.

The most common mistake in previous investigations was to look for a smoking gun, a specific order from the German general staff to Sommerfeld, an official letter or memorandum implying Sommerfeld's guilt, a statement from Sommerfeld himself, or the people near him. The historian has to assemble the many puzzle pieces without any direct evidence surrounding this crucial historical event, and still find a thesis that incorporates all these pieces. Only historian Friedrich Katz has passed that bar, so far.[683] Critical to the understanding of what happened, is the realization that intelligence missions, especially of the magnitude such as this, would have had to include a host of actors, most of whom had no idea that they were part of the plot. This explains the lack of direct evidence and the struggle to piece together the historical record. The undeniable facts that support German involvement are these: Germany had clearly embraced the strategy that tensions on the U.S. Mexican border would cause a pre-occupation of the U.S. government with Mexico rather than Europe. The badly equipped U.S. military would then have to source arms, munitions, and supplies in case of military intervention that, otherwise, would find their way to Germany's enemies in Europe. Felix Sommerfeld, the German secret service agent in charge of Mexico, had received clear orders to pursue this strategy in May of 1915. His subsequent actions, munitions purchases with German money, support for both Carranza and Villa, and manipulation of information reaching the Villa faction, are all consistent with his orders.

Precisely what German strategists had envisioned took place after the Columbus raid. German officials, especially German minister to Mexico von Eckardt, German ambassador to the U.S. Count Bernstorff, the head of the Latin American desk at the Foreign Office Count Montgelas, and other higher-ups in the German government were elated at the prospect of a U.S. – Mexican war. The only remaining mystery is whether or not the German agents tasked with precipitating that war actively participated in the preparations that led to the murders at Santa Ysabel, the attack on Columbus, as well as the results, namely the border raids as part of the *Plan de San Diego* conspiracy and the political, military, and diplomatic responses of the Carranza administration in the wake of the Punitive Expedition. Logic would support that they did. Certainly, President Wilson suspected German agitation and shuddered at the thought of having to fight a war against Mexico. Joseph Tumulty, President Wilson's secretary (Chief of Staff), recalled a conversation he had on March 15th 1916, the day American troops officially entered Mexico as part of the Punitive Expedition: "His [Wilson's] eyes flashed, and his lips quivered as he spoke. He rose from his chair and walked to the window of his study. He would not permit war; moreover, he went on, because German agents had been hard at work to stir trouble between the United States and Mexico in order to free Germany from the threat of American retaliation if she launched unrestricted submarine warfare."[684] If German agents indeed had caused the Columbus attack and fanned the flames of escalation, the critical question then arises: Who and how?

Sommerfeld, in addition to having extensive connections within the top tier of the U.S. government, was part of the inner circle of American-based foreign policy advisers around Pancho Villa, together with Miguel Díaz Lombardo, Enrique Llorente, and members of the Madero family. Thirdly, both Sommerfeld and Frederico Stallforth maintained close ties to a group of American businessmen, financiers, and politicians who favored a U.S. military intervention. These connections included Charles Flint, Andrew Meloy, Edward Doheny, Henry Clay Pierce, William Randolph Hearst, Sherburne G. Hopkins, and others. Sommerfeld cleverly exploited the motivations, fears, and influence within these associations for his mission without openly engaging any member of these diverse groups to his ends. Sommerfeld's close links within the U.S. government to Lindley Garrison, the Secretary of War, Franklin Lane, the Interior Secretary, and Hugh Lenox Scott, the Army Chief of Staff, and briefly Secretary of War, allowed him to understand the decision-making process and motivations of cabinet members. He was also aware of disagreements between the State Department, the U.S. military, the Senate Foreign Relations Committee, and the intelligence community. Through his frequently offered advice and actual assistance, Sommerfeld had the ability to manipulate the information these decision-makers used for reaching conclusions with wide-ranging import.

There were gaping disagreements and jealousies within the U.S. government, American business interests, and the Mexican exile community over the diplomatic recognition of Carranza, protection of U.S. interests in Mexico, and general military preparedness. Sommerfeld could relate to the voices of cabinet members Garrison, Lane, and Scott, opposition members of the Senate, such as Albert Fall and others, and members of the Mexican exile community, such as the Maderos, Felix Díaz, and former Científicos in open opposition to Carranza's recognition. No one else had this level of influence and in-depth knowledge of these diverse groups which, in turn, created a tremendous credibility for Sommerfeld with Pancho Villa. Villa did not just hear about the intricacies of the Carranza recognition, the perceived treason of Carranza, and the unfair support of his military campaign through the U.S. government from Sommerfeld. He heard it from all quarters, exile groups, politicians, and business groups. All Sommerfeld had to do was stoke the fires of opposition to Carranza from behind the scenes. It is highly unlikely that Sommerfeld had anything to do with the actual timing or planning of Villa's attacks. He simply helped pack the dynamite and prodded Villa to light the fuse.

Despite the lack of a smoking gun, evidence of German participation in the conflagration on the Mexican-American border in the
spring and summer of 1916 abounds. There is ample evidence that the
Secret War Council financed and shipped weapons and munitions to
Mexico through Hans Tauscher and Adolfo Stahl before the attack
on Columbus. More evidence of German financing and supplying
of Mexican factions in Mexico appeared after the attack. Carefully
watching the U.S. - Mexican conflict, the head of the Latin American
desk in the Imperial Foreign Office, Count Adolf von Montgelas, wrote
in a top-secret memorandum to his superiors on March 17th 1916, one
week after the attack on Columbus,

> ...the dispatch of 'money' [underline in the
> original] to Mexico in my opinion does not make
> much sense. As far as money could even have influ-
> ence, the Americans can always outspend us with
> ease, since they firstly have more money available and
> can distribute through many more channels than we
> can, since the Americans have been working with this
> tool [money] in Mexico for many years. It would be
> an entirely different proposition if we could funnel
> arms and ammunition (in the best case from American
> [underline in the original] sources) to Villa for his
> bands... [685]

Two important observations stand out in this memorandum: Obviously,
the Foreign Office and likely the Imperial cabinet had been discuss-
ing ways of aggravating the conflict between Villa and the U.S. One
of the proposals included funding Villa, to which Montgelas voiced
his opinion in this top-secret memorandum. Secondly, the fact that
the German government was willing to support Villa with arms and
ammunition from U.S. sources one week after the Columbus attack,
speaks to the involvement of Felix Sommerfeld. While Montgelas discounted money as a viable means of support, arms and ammunition
from U.S. sources became the preferred option. It is important to
consider that Hans Tauscher, the German agent in charge of storing
and shipping arms and ammunition in the U.S., was out of action as a
result of his trial, which only ended on June 30th 1916 with his acquittal,

when Montgelas mused about supporting Villa. Montgelas was likely thinking of Sommerfeld. And, indeed, it was Sommerfeld who immediately sprang into action.

The development of this "war" seemed well on its way immediately after the Columbus attack. The Wilson administration asked the First Chief for permission to enter Mexico with U.S. troops on March 10th 1916, in the effort to find and "disperse" the bands that had raided Columbus, New Mexico. Carranza replied that he would only allow U.S. military the pursuit of raiders into Mexico if the Mexican government could do the same and enter U.S. territory in hot pursuit of "bandits." He also stipulated that the reciprocity agreement applied to "future" raids, not the one that had occurred on March 9th. The U.S. government immediately interpreted the Carranza message to favor the intended punitive expedition, ignoring Carranza's exclusion of the Columbus raid and his request for reciprocity. Carranza ordered his commanders along the border and in Veracruz to prepare for a full-scale invasion of Mexico as more than four thousand American troops amassed in Columbus, and prepared to enter Mexico in pursuit of Villa.[686] Carranza asked, in a public appeal to the Mexican people, to "be prepared for any emergency... [the Constitutionalist government] will not admit, under any circumstances and whatever may be the reasons advanced and the explanation offered by the Government of the United States about the act it proposes to carry out, that the territory of Mexico be invaded for an instant and the dignity of the Republic outraged."[687] As soon as the Punitive Expedition was underway, U.S. officials on the border sensed an ambiguous attitude of the Carranza government, and reacted to the threat of further incursions into the U.S. by restricting arms and munitions shipments into Mexico. A month later, after a raid into Texas, an official arms embargo against all Mexican factions did take hold. The restricted arms trade not only cut off Villa but also Carranza, who turned to Germany for help.

War seemed imminent. Carranza sent a telegram to Secretary of State Lansing on March 11th 1916, warning of consequences: "There is no reason why, on account of the lamentable incident at Columbus, we should be carried to a declaration of war between the two countries... There would be no justification for any invasion of Mexican territory by an armed force of the United States, not even under the pretext of pursuing and capturing Villa."[688] General Funston, the commander of the Southern Department, requested the call-up of the militias of Arizona and New Mexico on March 12th in order to protect American towns along the border. The Secretary of War denied the request, at least for the time-being.[689] The fear of further raids into the United States all along the border was palpable.[690] Lansing replied to Carranza on March 13th, "The Government of the United States understands that in view of its agreement to this reciprocal arrangement proposed by the de facto Government the arrangement is now complete and in force and the reciprocal privileges thereunder may accordingly be exercised by either Government without further interchange of views."[691] Three U.S. army brigades with 4,800 soldiers entered Mexico from Columbus and Culbertson's Ranch, New Mexico, under the command of Brigadier General John J. Pershing on May 15th and 16th, almost one week after Villa's attack. Since the disposition of the Carrancista border commander at Palomas (across from Columbus) was in doubt, Pershing had arranged to create a peaceful border-crossing of American forces: He hired the Mexican border commander as a guide.[692] Carranza's newly appointed Foreign Secretary Acuña and Secretary of War Obregón faced the reality of having to yield "to superior force" on March 16th."[693] Both affirmed to General Funston that there would be no opposition to the American forces in pursuit of Villa.[694] Subsequent attempts by Carranza to limit the American troop levels and the depth of penetration came to naught.[695] Almost seven thousand U.S. troops roamed Northern Mexico by the end of the month, and the buildup kept coming.

John J. Pershing received command over the expedition on the recommendation of Army Chief of Staff General Hugh Lenox Scott. The logical choice would have been General Funston, the commander of the Southern Department of the Army; at least, he thought so. However, Scott chose Pershing, instead. According to the Army Chief of Staff, the expedition mainly used Pershing's troops from Fort Bliss and he was "nearly in El Paso."[696] The more likely reasons might have been that Funston had a short temper and lacked diplomatic finesse, counter to critical characteristics needed for this sensitive mission. It also seemed sensible to keep him in charge of the Southern Department in order to react firmly to further raids. Funston had been personally in charge of responding to the Plan de San Diego raids the previous summer.

Pershing had an impressive résumé for the assignment. Born in 1860 in Laclede, Missouri, Pershing chose a military career at age twenty-two when he entered West Point.[697] The West Point graduate rode in the last campaigns of the Indian Wars in the late 1880s. After a brief stint as a military science teacher at the University of Nebraska, Pershing joined the 10th Cavalry as an officer. He served with the so-called "buffalo soldiers" until 1897 when he returned to West Point as an instructor. During the service in the 10th Cavalry, he earned the nickname "Black Jack." Pershing fought in the Philippines the following year, where he acquired several languages including Spanish. He became Brigadier General in 1906, albeit under a cloud of suspicion that his wife's father, Senator Francis E. Warren, had something to do with the promotion. Pershing served in San Francisco in 1913, after another tour in the Philippines. He transferred to Fort Bliss, Texas from his West Coast assignment in 1915. His wife and three children died in a tragic fire in August of 1915, just as the family readied itself to join the general in El Paso. Only one son survived the accident. Stricken with grief, the general buried himself in his work, keeping mostly to himself as his worried peers looked on. Just before Villa's attack on Columbus in the spring of 1916, Pershing began dating Anne "Nita" Patton, George S. Patton's sister. George Patton, a lieutenant in the 8th Cavalry, used his "family connection" with the general to get appointed Pershing's adjutant for the Punitive Expedition. Brigadier General John J. "Black Jack" Pershing was as prepared, indeed, as anyone, to take on this "mission impossible."[698]

Although diplomatic rumblings continued between Mexico and the United States after the beginning of the American incursion, the Carranza administration grudgingly accepted the facts on the ground and did not risk an open confrontation with the U.S. forces. This development caught the German government by surprise. All indications had been that Carranza would resist the Punitive Expedition. Through Arnold Krumm-Heller, Minister von Eckardt's agent next to Carranza, and the diplomat's own understanding of the disposition of the Mexican government towards the U.S., Carranza was supposed to militarily oppose the American forces.[699] The immediate reaction of Carranza threatening war in case of U.S. forces crossing the border allows the supposition that, at least, the First Chief had contemplated resistance. However, promises of German arms and ammunition support were no match for the prospect of fighting the United States army along a border of twelve hundred miles.

Rumors of impending hostilities between the United States and Mexico ran rampant in Washington, which Ambassador Count Bernstorff dutifully related to his superiors in Berlin.[700] Despite the pressure from political opponents to mount a full military intervention, cabinet members, and Wall Street, even the customs agent, Zach Lamar Cobb, the Wilson administration had no interest in risking a quagmire of all Mexican factions uniting against a common enemy. To Wilson's relief, Carranza blinked first, mainly because he had decided on an alternate tactic to open confrontation. The First Chief knew when brinkmanship had to give way to acquiescence after the earlier *Plan de San Diego* raids in the summer and fall of 1915. He backed down from direct confrontation, but carefully monitored the progress of the American forces, limiting the supply lines by forbidding the use of Mexican railways. Carranza caged the Americans into a narrow north-south corridor between the Casas Grandes and Santa Maria rivers of Chihuahua while hunting down Villa with his own forces. Simultaneously, he re-activated the *Plan de San Diego* to pressure the American forces to leave.[701]

The German government in Berlin anxiously followed the situation in Mexico. The German ambassador in Washington, Count Bernstorff, accurately reported on the reciprocal agreement for hot pursuit that Carranza and Wilson had tentatively concluded, but added his impression that Wilson welcomed the Columbus attack for political reasons. "If some anti-German newspapers are claiming, we [the German government] had bribed Villa [to conduct the attack], one could with the same justification claim that the [American] president had bribed him [Villa]."[702] The German ambassador reported at the end of March that the public sentiment, as well as "the most influential circles" of the country expected a full-scale intervention.[703] Count Bernstorff noted, "If the president is able to continue to operate the same way, the country will slowly but surely slide into intervention without any domestic resistance. That," continued Count Bernstorff, "would in my own, humble opinion, secure the re-election of Mr. Wilson."[704] Despite the ambassador's factual reporting, his cynical opinion of President Wilson's motivation confirmed the hope of most German government officials that a war between Mexico and the

United States was becoming inevitable. Count Bernstorff added in his next report that rumors of Carranza troops defecting and joining Villa were false but that "Mexicans are observing the American incursion with quite some suspicion."[705] The ambassador added an important fact: "Almost the entire regular army of the United States is now in Mexico or congregating along the border."[706] Count Montgelas commented on Bernstorff's statement that accusations of Germany's involvement in the Columbus attack were "ridiculous" with the penciled remark "regrettably [i. e. "I wished we would have been behind the attack."]."[707]

A German naval intelligence commander, Captain Freyer, detailed Reuters news agency reports dated March 10th 1916 in a top-secret memorandum. According to the naval intelligence officer, the content was so explosive that British authorities had pulled it from publication in England. The Reuters correspondent supposedly reported (the original report is lost), "What is happening right now in Mexico is not an uprising but the beginning of a full-fledged war between the United States and Mexico, which under certain circumstances can be lasting. In Washington one is still trying to get an overview of the situation, recognizing the danger, but not the full consequences. At least one begins to doubt at this point (March 10) the attitude of Carranza... The situation for the United States is complicated by the fact that the Germans in Mexico are supporting Carranza with all means at their disposal, while Villa already has a few thousand Germans in his army."[708] Freyer continued to cite another Reuter's report from Washington D.C., "According to rumors Ojinaga [sic], the commanding officer of a company of Carranza troops, has been murdered in the attempt to quell an uprising of his troops. The soldiers had threatened a raid into the United States."[709] Count Montgelas signed the memo and responded on March 23rd with his suggestion to send arms and ammunition to Villa.[710] The German Foreign Office obviously agreed with the naval intelligence assessment of the situation. While the source of the Reuters information remains obscure, it is well-documented that Mexican federal troops, many of whom had fought in the Division of the North under Villa, engaged in sabotaging Carrancista attempts to catch the revolutionary. Further border raids, such as the slain Mexican army captain Ojinaga sought to prevent, seemed possible, indeed. Keeping Carranza at odds with the United

States, and somehow encouraging further trouble along the border, wholly fit the German strategy.

Thus was the environment the U.S. army faced in the latter part of March 1916: An elusive guerilla leader on his home turf; a mostly hostile civilian population in Mexico; the constant threat of open hostilities with the Carranza government; the likelihood of more border raids in the face of a loosely defended, two thousand-mile border; political pressures from Washington to show rapid success; and, the underhanded German agitation in support of both Villa and Carranza. Historian Frank McLynn remarked, "[Pershing's expedition] was the classic mission impossible. To catch Villa he had to fight a war of counter insurgency, and this meant burning villages, taking reprisals, shooting prisoners. Sooner or later this was bound to involve collision with Carranza's armies... "[711] The military operations into Mexico posed huge challenges for the badly-equipped and trained U.S. forces. Without permission to use Mexican railroads, supply of the American forces had to be trucked through the rugged and hostile terrain of western Chihuahua. The trucking fleet, often hailed in accounts of the expedition as a tremendous accomplishment of the U.S. army, was a standard on the European battlefields of the time. The reason the U.S. army could procure a significant amount of trucks in a very short time was the fact that American manufacturers long produced these vehicles for the British, French, and Russian armies.

The U.S. army was further hampered by its lack of good maps of the region. Supply truck drivers got lost in the Mexican countryside, while the cavalry forays deep into the Sierra Madre mountains depended on scouts, mostly local Mexicans, some Apache warriors of Arizona, even notorious soldiers-of-fortune, such as Sam Dreben and Emil Holmdahl. The local Mexican scouts, and also the soldiers-of-fortune, were of dubious loyalty. Dreben had worked for Felix Sommerfeld in El Paso for years as his local arms and ammunition representative supporting Pancho Villa's troops.[712] Dreben only stayed a short time with Pershing's forces and returned to El Paso in June, where he resumed smuggling arms and ammunition into Mexico.[713] Pershing's command informed the Bureau of Investigations on May 30th, "Dreben had been dropped by orders of Genl. Pershing for some sort of crooked work."[714] The B.I. suspected that Dreben worked for Sommerfeld all along, which leads to the suspicion that the wily German agent had effectively infiltrated the headquarters of Pershing's army.[715] However, Pershing would have none of it and, despite the documented security problems of Dreben, kept him under his personal protection between March and June 1916.[716] Holmdahl, as well, had fought under Pancho Villa and also worked for Sommerfeld. He owed the German agent for saving him from arrest and execution in Mexico on numerous occasions.[717]

The hostility of much of the civilian population in Chihuahua added to the often chaotic advances of American troops. Pershing enlisted several airplanes to serve as a means of communication and for observation. However, despite the novelty in military use, the squadron proved to be ineffective as a result of missing navigational aids, mechanical break-downs, and lack of experience and training of the pilots. Historian Welsome described the Curtiss JN-3 to have been as "flimsy as negligees and notoriously unreliable."[718] Communication between units in the ever-stretched supply lines remained a thorn in Pershing's side for the duration of the campaign.

The initial progress of the expedition seemed promising. The first columns of the American force reached Casas Grandes within a day and a half. Collector of Customs and secret agent Zach Cobb had reported on March 14th that Villa, with a force of approximately three hundred, camped "south of Corralitos and north of Casas Grandes last night."[719] As a matter of fact, Villa was camped out at Colonia Galeana, thirty miles south of Casas Grandes. There he assembled the entire town in the Zócalo and explained his attack on the United States in a rousing speech: "Brethren, I have called you together to inform you that in an endeavor to enter the United States I was stopped by the 'gringoes' on the line and was compelled to fight large numbers of them. I repeat to you, I shall not waste one more cartridge on our Mexican brothers but will save all my ammunition for the 'güeros;' prepare yourselves for the fight that is to come. I want to ask you to assist me in caring for the wounded I have with me, suffering for the good of our beloved country."[720] Villa repeated his claim in El Valle, some twenty miles south of Galeana, that a state of war between Mexico and the United States existed. He needed recruits but was facing a largely apathetic and war wearied population: "I have wanted you all present here to inform you that the Americans are about to come to Mexico to fight us. War has already been declared and I desire to see how many of you will join me; how many of you are ready to take up arms. I have soldiers with me from all the pueblos except from your own and it is essential that your pueblo be held above criticism. Fear nothing, I promise you not to fire a single cartridge against Mexicans and if one day I do so you may say I am a barbarian."[721] The invasion of American forces Villa had forecasted in December 1915 had become a self-fulfilling prophecy. However, the popular support Villa had expected remained elusive. These Chihuahuan villages had suffered through wave after wave of fighting. Many of their able-bodied men had died. They had nothing left to give for a lofty ideal. After all, it was not the spoils of a secret agreement with Carranza that the U.S. army pursued. It was el General himself, and his remaining forces.

Members of the 13th Cavalry Brigade found a former campsite of Villa's on the second day of the campaign with "a small expense booklet belonging to Rea Watson," the murdered supervisor at Santa Ysabel.[722] The U.S. cavalry was in hot pursuit six days behind the raiders. Both columns of U.S. army forces, 4,800 soldiers, 192 officers, and 4,175 animals, arrived near Casas Grandes in Colonia Dublán, a Mormon settlement friendly to the American troops, one hundred miles south of Columbus, New Mexico between March 17th and March 20th.[723] Intelligence reports indicated that Villa left the vicinity of Casas Grandes and was now making his way further south to the town of Namiquipa. Namiquipa had been one of the centers of Villismo.[724] Many of Villa's elite *Dorados* came from this traditional military colony, most notably Candelario Cervantes.[725] Cervantes had led the Mexican raiders into Columbus together with Pablo López, the infamous commander who had executed the American miners in Santa Ysabel. Witnesses identified Cervantes to have personally overseen the execution of the Americans in the Commercial Hotel.

The Carranza forces under the command of General Jacinto Treviño moved northwest from Chihuahua in order to cut off a southern escape of the Villistas. Pershing sent detachments of his cavalry at the same time to overtake the Villistas from the east and west. Detachments of the 7th Cavalry under Colonel George Dodd arrived in the vicinity of Namiquipa on March 24th, five days after a skirmish between Carrancista forces and Villistas there. To the chagrin of the American commander, Villa had slipped through the loose Carrancista lines and moved south to Guerrero. Villa took the city of Guerrero with its Carrancista garrison on March 27th, infuriating American and Carrancista pursuers with his show of utter contempt. Villa captured guns and ammunition. He also executed over 170 Carrancistas, many of them former members of the *Division del Norte*.[726] Having received news of Villa's attack, Colonel Dodd pressed on towards Guerrero, while Colonel Brown with troops of the 10th Cavalry charged slightly east to cut off Villa's path towards Chihuahua.

The attack on Guerrero, as daring and brazen as it was, proved to be a disaster for Pancho Villa. The stories of exactly what happened in the battle vary. It seems that one of the recruits Villa had pressed into service, accidentally – or more likely, intentionally – shot Villa in the leg from behind. The bullet struck just below the knee and shattered Villa's shin bone. Historian Welcome quoted a foot soldier, "'It was our intention to kill him and go over to the Carrancistas,' recalled Modesto Navárez. 'But just at the time when he was shot, the Carrancistas gave way and ran, leaving us with no possible way to escape, so we again assumed the pretense of loyalty and declared that if he had been shot by any of us it was purely accidental.'"[727] Villa knew that the Americans were hot on his heels. This injury, which excluded the possibility of him riding a horse, turned his cat-and-mouse game into a life and death threat. Perched up in a carriage with his last remaining *Dorados* and, shielded by his closest confidantes, Villa left Guerrero on March 28th. Villa's men took their injured commander towards Hidalgo del Parral in the far south of the state of Chihuahua. Parral, the home of Frederico Stallforth and his brothers, had been a Maderista and Villista stronghold throughout the revolution. However, the three hundred-mile trek through some of the most rugged regions of the Sierra Madre proved too ambitious a destination for the "Centaur of the North," who now was screaming in agony as his carriage bumped over the winding trails. Heavy sleet and snow slowed the progress of the Villistas. The party arrived at Cusihuriachic on March 29th, one hundred miles to the southeast of Guerrero.

Colonel Dodd encircled Guerrero that same day, poised for an attack. Villista commander Candelario Cervantes, with approximately two hundred Villistas, still occupied the town of three thousand souls. Dodd's troops swooped into town and killed thirty Villistas without losing one of their own.[728] Not entirely sure whether an existing force of several hundred troops holding up the Mexican flag were Carranza's soldiers, the Americans held their fire and let Cervantes take to the hills unharmed.[729] The Americans captured "forty-four rifles, two machine guns, and thirteen horses."[730] They also freed an estimated 175 Carrancista soldiers that Villa had slated for execution. The Americans did not pursue the Villistas. Dodd's units were exhausted, having covered two weeks of harsh marches. While charging the town, several horses had collapsed from exhaustion under their riders. The American cavalry had closed in on Villa within a twelve-hour gap, having started with a six-day lag behind the Columbus raiders. According to historian Welsome, Colonel Dodd could have possibly caught Villa, "the Jaguar," had he had better maps, scouts, or at least the hearts and minds of the local population.[731] Despite the failure to capture Villa, Dodd received a promotion to Brigadier General. His battle for Guerrero crowned the headlines of American dailies as a resounding success. Ebullient newspaper reports would fix the number of Villistas at five hundred, some even six hundred, proclaiming Dodd's victory to have been against "overwhelming forces." Villa's injury, which locals reported to American authorities, made his pending defeat or capture tangible.

General Pershing did not sit still while his cavalry chased Villa into the Sierra Madres. His command moved south from Casas Grandes and established headquarters in Namiquipa. Much to the chagrin of the Villistas, the people of Namiquipa welcomed the Americans. It was big business for the war-weary civilian population. American troops had to source food for themselves and grain and fodder for their animals. Local guides, translators, and workmen assisted the troops with anything they needed in exchange for American dollars. Checking the area for sympathizers of the elusive Mexican chieftain even turned up a large cache of arms and ammunition. Pershing headed thirty miles south from Namiquipa to San Geronimo Ranch near Bachiniva, almost three hundred miles from the American border. Talking with newspaper correspondents on March 29th, as Colonel Dodd fought his way into Guerrero, an optimistic General Pershing announced, "I think we've got Villa."[732]

Meanwhile, Villa headed south only hours ahead of the American pursuers, and under constant threat of discovery as Carrancista units scoured the mountains for the injured chief. He passed Cusihuriachic. Villa and a small group of bodyguards arrived at Ojitos on April 2nd, halfway between Cusihuriachic and Parral. The rest of his band had split up and was heading towards the Durango border. The 10th Cavalry under Colonel Brown killed two Villistas in an engagement at Agua Caliente, but had to let the majority of the Mexican soldiers escape into the rugged mountain terrain. Meanwhile, Major Frank Tompkins of the 13th Cavalry, who had chased the Villista raiders across the border after the attack on Columbus, and Major Robert Howze, with his squadron, headed south after Villa and his bodyguards. While Tompkins approached Parral from the northeast, Howze happened to follow exactly the trail Villa and his bodyguards had taken. He arrived at Ojitos on April 7th, just as Villa had been warned of a Carrancista force closing in, and had decided to leave. The Americans arrived at the hamlet of Santa Cruz in hot pursuit on April 11th where they were fired upon. After a short exchange in which two Mexicans died, Howze decided to camp just outside of town. "Lieutenant Summer Williams went into town to buy food and saw a group of Yaqui Indians, unarmed but wearing face paint, exiting from a ranch house a mile away... he became suspicious and returned to camp and urged Howze to attack the ranch house at once. 'No one of us could get him to listen to the possibility of Villa and a small band being in hiding in this house. He prohibited any of us from going to this ranch house, and the following morning we marched south,' the frustrated lieutenant would later write. 'I fully believe that this is where Major Howze and his column lost Villa and also lost our great opportunity.'"[733] Although it might never be known whether Villa had been in the ranch house for sure, he was in the area at this particular time. It would be the closest American forces ever got to capturing the Mexican revolutionary chieftain. Villa had now successfully evaded his pursuers for good since Major Howze missed the opportunity to check the ranch house. The small group of *Dorados* under Nicolás Fernandez that had shepherded their commander into safety, split from Villa and headed south towards Durango. The injured Villa disappeared into thin air with only two of his cousins at his side. None of the Villista deserters nor any local informants had any information as to Villa's whereabouts. He recuperated in a cave for the next two months, without any contact to the outside world, without a doctor, and was presumed to have died by many.[734]

*Army camp Columbus, N.M., auto truck supply train about to leave for Mexico.
Courtesy Library of Congress, Prints and Photographs Division.[735]*

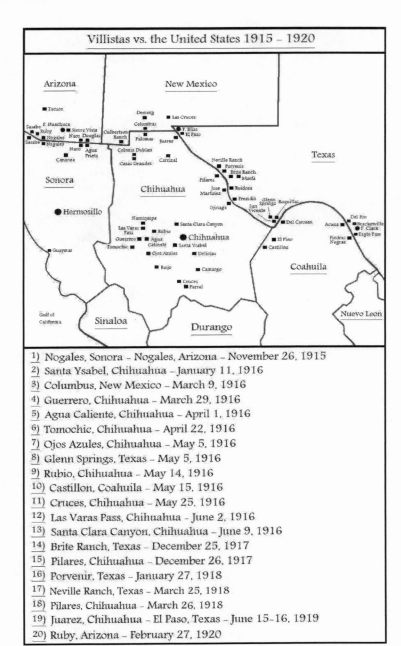

Map of battles during the Punitive Expedition [736]

An Army wagon pack train arriving on outskirts of Las Cruces, Mexico.
Courtesy Library of Congress, Prints and Photographs Division[737]

U.S. army camp at Colonia Dublan.
Courtesy Library of Congress Prints and Photographs Division.[738]

Brig. Gen. Pershing at headquarters near Casas Grandes, Mexico, March 26, 1916.
Courtesy Library of Congress, Print and Photographs Division.[739]

*Near Namiquipa, Mexico: Companies D, E, F, G and H
of the 6th Infantry after a six days hike arriving in camp,
Courtesy Library of Congress, Prints and Photographs Division.*[740]

*A supply truck stuck in the mud somewhere in Mexico, a frequent occurrence.
Courtesy Library of Congress, Prints and Photographs Division.*[741]

General John J. "Blackjack" Pershing in front of his command tent.
Courtesy Library of Congress, Prints and Photographs Division.[742]

Receiving wireless messages from the border near Casas Grandes, Mexico.
Courtesy Library of Congress, Prints and Photographs Division.[743]

The inevitable clash between Carranza forces and American army troops happened on April 12th, the day after the last known contact between Villa and the American pursuers. Major Tompkins, the officer who had so courageously hunted the raiders in the immediate aftermath of the

Columbus attack, led a column of 140 men to the outskirts of Parral. All intelligence assessments pointed to Villa having headed here. The Villista stronghold and hometown of Frederico Stallforth, over five hundred miles from the border, marked the farthest point south the Punitive Expedition would reach. The city of Parral, was eight hundred miles north of Mexico City and in the far Southwest corner of the state of Chihuahua.[744] Tompkins proceeded with a small detachment to the guardhouse when he arrived at the outskirts of the proud mining town. There, he asked to see the Carrancista commander. General Ismael Lozano as well as the *Presidente* of Parral, José de la Luz Herrera, obliged and invited the American delegation into the prestigious city hall. Major Herrera was the father of Maclovio and Luis Herrera, two of Villa's fiercest commanders who had recently switched sides and now supported Carranza. The Mexicans notified Tompkins that they wanted the American troops to leave town immediately. Tompkins brashly demanded supplies for his troops, which General Lozano arranged. However, while the men met in the city hall, "a huge mob led by a beautiful young woman named Elisa Griensen [from a prominent Parral family with Austrian background] had gathered. 'Viva Villa! Viva Mexico!' they shouted.

As the troops started out of town, other women leaned out of their second-floor windows and dumped their slop jars and spittoons onto the soldiers. Tompkins was infuriated and dropped behind to keep an eye on the crowd. One compactly built man, with a neat Vandyke beard and mounted on a very fine Mexican pony, seemed to be exhorting the mob to violence... Tompkins thought the man looked German and made up his mind to shoot this 'bird' first if violence did erupt."[745]

Elisa Griensen Zambrano[746]

Major (later Colonel, as in this photograph) Frank Tompkins, U.S. Army.[747]

As the Carrancista *jefe de armas* tried to ferry the American soldiers out of town, shots rang out. Despite the Carrancista troops shooting into the crowd and trying to protect the Americans, Tompkins immediately deployed his squadron on two hills overseeing the road into Parral, as well as in a railroad embankment. General Lozano "begged Tompkins to retreat at once. But Tompkins would not be budged: 'After we get our food and forage,' he responded."[748] A shootout between the Carrancistas and the Americans ensued. Tompkins had to withdraw and fight a rear guard action for five miles. In the end, the American cavalry detachment had lost two soldiers and suffered six wounded. Among the Carrancista casualties were forty deaths, with an unknown number of wounded and killed civilians in Parral.[749] General Pershing, upon learning of the firefight, decided to reinforce the American forces around Parral with more cavalry, a field artillery regiment, and two infantry regiments. Hundreds of American troops converged on the town.[750] Tompkins, whose action had precipitated the escalation of the conflict and, against orders, had provoked the clash with Carranza's forces, wrote in his memoirs, "We now felt as though our force was strong enough to conquer Mexico, and we were hoping the order to 'go' would soon come."[751] However, the order did not come. Under pressure as a result of stretched supply lines and the threat of more clashes with local Carrancista forces, General Pershing ordered U.S. forces to withdraw in the middle of April. Pershing mused in his memoirs, "the German Consul at Parral was instrumental in inciting the people."[752] While Frederico Stallforth's brother never hinted at his involvement, Alberto Stallforth was the German consular agent (Parral did not have a consulate) and could very well have been behind the angry mob in Parral. As a result of the clash, Pershing changed his strategy from flying columns pursuing Villistas in the region to organizing regional camps that conducted patrols and prevented the use of the covered territory as a base of operations for Villa.

After the shootout at Parral, Venustiano Carranza issued another stern demand to President Wilson that the Americans leave Mexico. The Wilson administration responded, and asked for a meeting between Secretary of War Obregón and Generals Funston and Scott in Ciudad Juarez. The military commanders met on April 30th. Obregón reiterated the unconditional demand of Venustiano Carranza for the Americans to withdraw. The meetings ended quickly because, according to Army Chief of Staff Scott, "General Funston allowed his real sentiments to be expressed so brusquely that he lost his influence in those conferences, and he thought it best for him not to attend anymore."[753] Scott's decision to choose General Pershing over Frederick Funston for the sake of diplomacy seemed to have been the correct one. Scott succeeded, during subsequent private meetings on May 1st and 2nd, in getting Obregón to back down somewhat.[754] Though the American troops were allowed to stay longer, Scott committed to a drawdown at an unspecified future date, and committed to pull back Pershing's main force to Colonia Dublan.[755] This move had more to do with overstretched supply lines and vulnerability in case of a conflict with Carranza, than with accommodating the demand of the Mexican government for withdrawal. Obregón signed the agreement with General Scott. "Wilson wholeheartedly welcomed the text of the agreement and instructed [Secretary of War] Baker to prepare a formal statement to be released once word was received of Carranza's acceptance. Anticipating a positive reply from the Mexicans, the draft announcement stated 'this agreement happily provides for the cordial cooperation between the two governments' and 'the ratification of this agreement by the two governments removes all controversy for their relations.' However, a response from the Mexicans was slow to arrive and Scott remained at the meeting site for another six days while awaiting official word from Carranza."[756] While President Wilson approved the accord on May 3rd, Carranza notified the American government a week later that he would not sign.[757] He wanted unconditional withdrawal of the Americans as soon as possible. He sent Obregón back to the border, this time with a Foreign Service official. The talks broke down for good on May 11th.

Carranza's suspicion that the American incursion into Mexico was just the beginning of an all-out occupation of Mexico received further confirmation after the Obregón-Scott meetings in El Paso. The American government strictly enforced the newly declared arms embargo. Despite General Scott's commitment to Obregón in their negotiations between April 30th and May 11th that the American troops would begin to withdraw shortly, American troop levels continued to build. Nearly ten thousand American soldiers with six thousand animals had entered Mexico by the end of April. Before the troops withdrew in January 1917, the buildup would reach over fourteen thousand soldiers. The conferences with the Mexican government took on a new tone on May 6th. Two Mexican raiding parties crossed into the big bend country of lower Texas in the middle of the night on May 5th 1916, and attacked the hamlets of Glenn Springs and Boquillas, shouting "¡Viva Villa!" and "¡Viva Carranza!" A small detachment of nine soldiers of the 14th Cavalry Brigade attempted to defend the town. The estimated ninety Mexican raiders killed one American civilian and three cavalry soldiers, wounded four men, looted the general store, burned several buildings, and destroyed the Candelilla wax factory.[758] On their way back into Mexico with two American hostages they also made off with the payroll of the Puerto Rico Mining Company on the Mexican side of the Rio Grande. Navidad Álvarez, a former Carrancista lieutenant colonel who led the raid on Boquillas, was captured.

Albeit on a smaller scale, the attack matched the pattern of the Columbus raid. It is not entirely clear to this day, who the attackers were. Early reactions from the Carranza government blamed American "interventionists" to have staged the raid to provoke a war with Mexico.[759] One of the two Mexican rebel officers in charge, Navidad Álvarez, had been a soldier in Carranza's army; the other, Captain Rodriguez Ramirez, was a Villista. Whether both had been out to provoke further American outrage on their own, had been sent by Villa to embarrass Carranza, or whether the raiders just sought to provision themselves, the historiography does not definitely establish. The only dead Mexican raider wore a Carrancista uniform.[760]

The result of the attack, however, clearly played into the hands of Villa and the German government, while torpedoing the talks between Obregón and General Scott. Rather than contemplating withdrawal, leaks from General Funston's command forecasted another punitive expedition with three thousand American troops.[761] American cavalry entered Mexico on May 6th in hot pursuit immediately after the raid. More detachments from Fort Bliss followed on May 10th. In response, Obregón authorized the Carrancista Commander Jacinto Treviño to engage the Americans if they moved further than fifty miles south of the border. The officer commanding the "flying columns" of the American cavalry was Major George T. Langhorne, the former American military attaché to Berlin, then stationed at Fort Bliss. When von Papen's suitcases had fallen into the hands of English investigators in January 1916, it became apparent that Langhorne had transported papers for von Papen in diplomatic pouches. Widely accused to be a traitor, the major had also had contact with Franz Rintelen who tried unsuccessfully to get a passport through him in 1915. The decision of whether or not the Department of War would court-martial Langhorne was pending when he set out on a second American punitive expedition. The major had ample reason to prove his worth – and he did. One hundred soldiers of the 8th Cavalry under Langhorne's command, and with the captured raider, Álvarez, as a scout, raced two hundred miles south into Mexico within a few days.[762] President Wilson activated the militias of Texas, New Mexico, and Arizona at the same time. Governors of other states, such as Florida and New York, sent units in assistance to the buildup on the border. One week after the Glenn Springs incident, another small group of raiders crossed the border and killed a rancher.

If Villa had intended to make his December 1915 forecast of an American invasion of Mexico a reality, he had come as close as ever. The U.S. Department of War now contemplated exactly that: a full invasion. An increasingly frustrated General Pershing advocated ending the cat-and-mouse game with the Carranza government after the clash in Parral. He wrote to General Funston on April 18th,

> In order to prosecute our mission with any promise of success it is therefore absolutely necessary for us to assume complete possession for time being of country through which we must operate and establish government therein. For this purpose it is imperative that we assume control of railroads as means of supplying forces required. Therefore recommend immediate capture by this command of city and state of Chihuahua also the seizure of all railroads therein, as preliminary to further military operations.[763]

General Scott also alluded to war plans against Mexico. His discussions with Obregón subsequent to Carranza's rejection of their agreement must have turned heated.

> Obregón began to talk about taking San Antonio in two weeks, knowing nothing more about conditions in the North than did General Weyler of the Spanish Army, who talked about landing in Charleston, S.C... I advised the President to call out the militia and put them along the border. He opposed this... 'The people of Mexico,' I argued, 'are ignorant and untraveled; they see a thin line twelve hundred miles long and believe they can break through it, as they easily can, but they have no idea of what will happen afterward...

Of course the militia cannot operate in those deserts – they would kill themselves in a short time if they were to try to march through them – but they can wear a uniform, carry a rifle, and occupy towns so as to release the regular troops for mobile purposes. Should Mexico actually try to occupy Texas in force and attack San Antonio, you will have a real war on your hands...[764]

Despite the pressure from the military, his cabinet, and the interventionist lobby in Washington, the president kept his cool. He did not authorize general mobilization of the state militias. However, the situation was as tense as a fused powder keg. Villa and Carranza, as well as Pershing, each held a lit match with which they could set the border ablaze. Without finding a trace of the injured rebel commander, American cavalry had dealt Villa several serious blows in April and May. Colonel Dodd's detachment of 7th Cavalry with 180 men ambushed two hundred Villistas under the command of Candelario Cervantes on April 22nd. The Americans killed thirty of the enemy and wounded at least twenty-five in a close-combat surprise attack before the Villistas withdrew.[765] Colonel Howze, with detachments of the 11th Cavalry, surprised an estimated one hundred Villistas under the command of Julio Acosta on May 5th as Mexican raiders terrorized Glenn Springs and Boquillas. Acosta had accepted amnesty from the Carranza government in January. Believing Villa's propaganda that the Punitive Expedition was the beginning of an all-out American invasion of Mexico, he recruited "resistance fighters" and prepared to attack American forces. His plan never came to fruition. Forty-one of his fighters died and several dozen were wounded in the engagement with Howze's troops. Acosta managed to flee.[766]

Pershing's aide-de-camp, Lieutenant George S. Patton, with a few soldiers and Emil Holmdahl as the scout, diverted from a shopping trip and surrounded the home of Julio Cardenas, a most wanted member of Villa's *Dorados*, on May 14th. The surprised Cardenas, who just happened to be there with two of his companions, made a stand but died in a hail of American bullets. Patton ordered the bodies of the three Mexicans strapped to the hoods of their Dodge touring cars, earning him the nickname "blood and guts." Excited newsmen in the

Namiquipa camp, about sixty miles to the north, celebrated the young army lieutenant as a hero. Patton, never shy when it came to publicity, showed off two notches on the butt of his revolver, marking the Mexican rebels he personally shot in close combat. Patton, likely at the insistence of Holmdahl or General Pershing, had to correct the record of what really had happened at the San Miguel Ranch on May 14th, a version quite different from the exaggerated newspapers reports:

> Headquarters U.S. Troops
> Somewhere in Mexico
> May 20th, 1916
> To Whom It May Concern;
>
>
> This is to certify that Mr [sic] H. L. Holmdahl, was the Government Scout with the U.S. troops under my command in an engagement with Villa Bandits, at San Miguel Ranch, Chihuahua, Mexico, on May 14th.
> I have highly recommended Scout Holmdahl, for his coolness, courage and efficiency while under fire, he personally killed General Julio Cardenes [sic], and Colonel Gildardo Lopez, in a pistol dual [sic]. At that time Holmdahl fought in the open, without cover of any kind, shot with great accuracy and deliberation his action being that of a man at target practice.
> I also wish to recommend him to any brother officer, who may wish a man who is thoroughly familiar with Mexico and its people or in any position of trust, as he is most reliable, and a Good Soldier.
>
> (sgd) Geo. Patton.
> 1st Lieut 10th, U.S. Cavalry.
> A.D. C. General Pershing.[767]

Despite official commendations from both General Pershing and Lieutenant George Patton, something led to Holmdahl being fired in July 1916.[768] Maybe his sudden discharge was not completely surprising, if indeed Holmdahl coerced Lieutenant Patton to pen this embarrassing "to whom it may concern" letter. Pershing testified in a memorandum in 1917 that "the information furnished by Mr. Holmdahl [as a scout in the Punitive Expedition] was mostly of vague and indefinite character and that his services as a scout were of no particular value; that Holmdahl was a very difficult man to manage on account of his desire to fight the Mexicans all the time and to open fire on them without regard for the consequences..."[769] Instead of bravery, Holmdahl's shootout, which netted Cardenas, earned him a discharge for recklessness.

Candelario Cervantes died on May 25th, near his hometown of Namiquipa in a clash with American infantrymen. Cervantes charged the American troops with a small detachment, killed one, injured three, and pinned down the rest of the soldiers. However, in subsequent exchanges of fire an American infantry private mortally wounded the Mexican commander. The news of Villa's right-hand man dying from the bullets of an American private became a sensation. Cervantes was the commander who had executed the Columbus attack. Another of Villa's commanders, Pablo López, the man who was responsible for the murders at Santa Ysabel in January 1916, and who also had been a leading officer of the Columbus attackers, fell into the hands of Carrancista forces on April 23rd.[770] He was the only of Villa's officers who explained the attack on Columbus from the perspective of an insider.[771] Carranza had him executed on June 5th, after the gunshot wounds through the hip he received at Columbus were sufficiently healed to face his executioners.

Locals from Namiquipa led American authorities on May 29th to a large cache of arms and munitions that Villa had hidden nearby in a cave.[772] The town would pay dearly for their cooperation with the American forces when Villa returned a year later and ordered all women of the town raped.[773] By the time Cervantes died in the end of May, Villa was severely wounded and hiding, most of his forces decimated and dispersed, his commanders on the run, arrested, or dead, and the threat of Villistas marauding the U.S.-Mexican border virtually eliminated. Cervantes' death marked the last perfect opportunity for the Wilson Administration to claim "mission accomplished" and withdraw the Punitive Expedition. General Scott, Secretary of War Baker, and others in the inner circle of the American president lobbied for withdrawal. The torpedoing of the SS Sussex in March and the subsequent crisis that made an American entry into the European war ever more likely, as well as the very real risk of a quagmire in Mexico, gave the withdrawal faction strong arguments. However, the president decided against his military's advice. Instead of withdrawal, Pershing's forces continued their buildup in Chihuahua, while American forces continued to patrol Coahuila in the wake of the Glenn Springs incident.

The only real change in strategy was a recall of American troops from the very edges of Chihuahua in order to shorten the supply lines and reduce the risk of isolating American units from the main force. Encountering ever more hostility from the Mexican population and Carrancista commanders, Pershing's main forces remained garrisoned in Colonia Dublán near Casas Grandes. Patrols kept Villista forces dispersed and on the run from regional camps such as Namiquipa. Troops had orders to keep a respectful distance from Mexican towns and the local Carrancista garrisons to reduce the potential for another clash. Still, after the execution of López, the deaths of Cardenas and Cervantes, as well as a few more Villa officers, Carranza and his closest advisers were firmly convinced that the American forces would remain in Mexico for the long-term. Carranza now executed his alternate strategy with renewed raids on the United States that were to precipitate an American withdrawal. The Mexican-American confrontation that had teetered on the edge of a major conflagration since the attack on Columbus now came to a head. German strategists watched in amazement and with great satisfaction as the seeds of conflict they had sown took on a momentum of their own.

CHAPTER 10: WAR CRISIS

THE *PLAN DE SAN DIEGO* raids that had plagued the lower Rio Grande valley in the summer and fall of 1915 suddenly resumed in the beginning of June 1916. The renewed border unrest coincided with the execution of Pablo López in Chihuahua. His death eliminated the second of the two Villista commanders of the Columbus attack. Nearly one hundred of the Columbus raiders, including the commanders other than Villa had died or been arrested. Despite the recent successes of the Pershing forces, and the forceful demands of the Carranza government for an unconditional withdrawal of American forces from Mexico, there was no end to the American incursion in sight. Carranza had exhausted most of his strategic options. After the Glenn Springs incident, he sent 15,000 additional troops under the command of General Jacinto Treviño to Coahuila and Chihuahua, building Carrancista forces up to 30,000. The addition of troops coincided with orders to all governors and commanders to prepare for war.[774] The Carrancista commanders at Matamoros and Nuevo Laredo received instructions to attack American forces on sight.[775]

At the same time, the U.S. called up and stationed the militias of Arizona, New Mexico, and Texas along strategic points on the border. Tens of thousands of well-armed military forces stood at the ready on both sides of the border, with another 10,000 American troops roaming western Chihuahua four hundred miles deep. While Carranza expected a full-scale American invasion, the American government feared attacks of the Carranza forces on the Punitive Expedition and unprotected Texas border towns. Carranza and his Secretary of War Obregón clearly realized that in case of an American invasion the military situation in this standoff would not favor a Mexican victory. The way out for the Carranza government was to somehow create a crisis within U.S. territory that would precipitate a re-allocation of forces and resources from Mexican territory into the U.S. In their trailblazing book, *The Plan de San Diego: Tejano Rebellion, Mexican Intrigue*, historians Harris and Sadler convincingly detail the active use of the *Plan de San Diego* organization by the Carranza administration to further its foreign policy goals against the United States.[776] The historians did not uncover a direct involvement of Germany in the organization and activities of the raiders in their exhaustive research of the *Plan de San Diego*. However, as Friedrich Katz stated in his book, *The Secret War in Mexico*, "it [was] certainly the type of plot the Germans would have liked to be involved in."[777] It was more than just a wish.

The question of whether or not the German government motivated Carranza in his revival of the raids in return for arms and ammunition remains open. Circumstantial evidence supports this possibility. Despite there being no smoking gun as usual, there are plenty of traces of residue. One week before Carranza released the organizers of the *Plan de San Diego* from prison on April 7th 1916, and charged them with resuming their activities on the American side of the border, German Minister to Mexico Heinrich von Eckardt wrote to the Imperial Foreign Secretary Gottlieb von Jagow, "I have the impression that as a result of the incursion of ever more [American] troops into Mexican territory (against Villa) it will come to a war between Mexico and the United States. General Carranza has now come to the conclusion that a war is inevitable and is trying to delay for approximately three months in order to procure weapons. He will likely ask me to seek permission from the Imperial government to **hand over** [emphasis added by the author, the German word "Überlassung" implies free-of-charge] weapons which we have in the United States. Washington has been notified [underlined in the original]."[778] Maybe the arms were not entirely "free of charge." A credit memo in the accounts of the office of the German military attaché in New York dated May 19th 1916, reads: "$44,649.87 [$94,000 in today's value] für Verkauf von Waffen, New York, 19 Mai, 1916, [for the sale of arms, New York, May 19th 1916], Heynen."[779] Subsequent actions of the Carranza administration speak for themselves, as well: Under the command of Carranza General Pablo González, the *Plan de San Diego* organizers, General José Maria Zuazua, Augustín Garza, and Luis de la Rosa received funding from Carranza and prepared a wholesale invasion of Texas.[780] Felix Sommerfeld, Carl Heynen (Heinrich

Albert's treasurer and manager of the Bridgeport Projectile Company), and Hans Tauscher (German agent and Krupp Arms representative in the U.S.) initiated significant and well-documented arms and munitions shipments to Carranza at the same time. The coincidence is striking.

The Bureau of Investigations carefully observed the arms trade along the border. In response to Villa's raid, the U.S. government had reinstituted an arms embargo against all Mexican parties, including that of the recognized government of Venustiano Carranza. Evidence indicates that this change in policy drove Carranza straight into the arms of Felix Sommerfeld and his fellow agents. There was only one significant source of 7mm Mauser ammunition available for shipment to Mexico: The daily production of the Western Cartridge Company in Alton, Illinois of approximately 100,000 cartridges. As Villa's fortunes declined in the summer of 1915, he could not pay for the deliveries of the two large orders Sommerfeld had placed with Olin's outfit. The Albert office jumped into the fold, and financed shipments between September and October 1915. The German agents, Tauscher and Heynen, managed to sell three million cartridges to the Carranza government (one month's worth of production of Western Cartridge), but in October 1915 Álvaro Obregón cancelled the orders. Villa was basically defeated, reducing the need for munitions.

No shipments to Mexico appear to have happened in November, which leads to the conclusion that "James Manoil" aka the Secret War Council purchased at least three million cartridges, which Hans Tauscher stored in New York.[781] Lázaro De La Garza sold the balance of Sommerfeld's twenty-seven million cartridge contracts (12.9 million cartridges) to J. P. Morgan, the representative of the French government at the end of October.[782] Shipments were to start on November 22nd. However, tests of the cartridges revealed that the specification of the cartridge did not work for the type of rifle used in the Serbian army, the ultimate destination of the ammunition. The Western Cartridge Company had warned De La Garza specifically of this potential issue.[783] However, he proceeded anyway, maybe at the insistence of "James Manoil" who certainly did not want Germany's enemies to receive additional munitions. J. P. Morgan, the French government purchasing representatives in the U.S., attempted to refuse shipments from the Western Cartridge factory in Alton, Illinois. Franklin Olin, under pressure from the French government, stood firm in the claim that his production specification matched the contract for "Spanish Mauser rifles."[784] Morgan had to take deliveries, while trying to solve the issue. One can only speculate how many cartridges went to Europe before it was obvious that the specification made them unusable. However, the very latest shipments stopped in April 1916 when an inspector of the Serbian army came to Alton, Illinois and rejected the ammunition.[785] De La Garza's correspondence with the Western Cartridge Company indicates that Olin, possibly at the request of the German backers of his production, refused to cooperate and faulted the Serbian rifle. J. P. Morgan officially cancelled the contract on May 16th 1916, and even had to pay commissions to De La Garza for the undelivered portion of the order.[786]

The question now begs, what happened to the Western Cartridge Company's production of 100,000 cartridges per day? Small amounts of cartridges reaching the Mexican border appeared in the investigative reports of the B.I. Federal agents reported in the end of March 1916, for example, that Leon Rasst, a notorious arms dealer and crook,[787] shipped 636 cases (1,000 cartridges per case) of cartridges from New York consigned to the "French Consul, Galveston."[788] B.I. Chief Bielaski suspected that the final destination of this shipment was Pancho Villa.[789] Felix Sommerfeld, who federal agents could not locate in New York for six weeks after the Columbus attack, reportedly negotiated with the merchant house Otis and Caulfield of Boston for the purchase of two million 7mm cartridges around the 16th of March.[790] The munitions Otis and Caulfield offered to Sommerfeld very likely came from the unusable stocks of Morgan's order. Sommerfeld's subsequent trips to the border in disguise likely served the purpose of organizing the smuggling into Mexico of these munitions. A corrupt American customs official in Galveston cleared multiple runs of the schooner Sunshine from Houston via Galveston, loaded to the hilt with ammunition declared as "barrels of beer" at the end of April.[791] The shipment Tauscher made to Guatemala via the steamer Sixiola in the same time period has already been mentioned.[792]

Given that the French government was stuck with millions of unusable cartridges, the smuggling trips of the Sunshine and the Sixiola, Rasst's shipment, and Sommerfeld's negotiations in Boston with subsequent trips to the border might just have been the tip of the iceberg. The papers of Lázaro De La Garza, the former purchasing agent of Pancho Villa and front company of the Secret War Council since the summer of 1915, reveal that the Western Cartridge Company indeed delivered, as contracted, between November 1915 and April 1916; just not to the French government. According to the former Carranza consul Jorge Orozco, Hans Tauscher had been shipping "100,000 [cartridges] per day and that the de facto [Carranza] Government are [sic] buying cartridges from him in small quantities... He [Orozco] is confident that that [Felix Sommerfeld] is the main source of the Villista's munition supplies."[793] The pattern of German support reaching both Carranza and Villa was apparent. De La Garza's ledgers show the shipment of 450,000 cartridges in November, 1.85 million in December, 1.3 million in January, 1.6 million in February, 1.7 million in March, and 1 million in April.[794]

All these shipments amounting to 7.9 million cartridges fall within the time period when J. P. Morgan could not use the munitions for the intended customer, and when Tauscher was rumored to ship 100,000 cartridges per day (the daily capacity of the Western Cartridge Company) to Mexico. According to the Western Cartridge Company, Carranza received shipments on a large scale in the same time period, an astonishing admission given that the French contract should have bound the entire production of the factory.[795] Alfred Joseph Norcom, Franklin W. Olin's secretary, "stated they [Western Cartridge Company] also have a contract with Carranza... just after the massacre of citizens at Columbus by Villa and his followers, he, [Secretary] Norcom, wired the State Department, telling them of this contract with Carranza, and asking if the company should hold up shipments of cartridges to Carranza, and the State Department replied to go ahead and ship Carranza all the cartridges desired."[796] The Western Cartridge Company official also told the B.I. investigator that "they [Western Cartridge Company] had a more recent [than the 15 million cartridge contract from May 1915] contract with Sommerfeld, but that only a few shipments had been made on it. They [Western Cartridge Company] cancelled this latter contract with Sommerfeld on account of his suspicious action. Sommerfeld wanted part of the ammunition contracted for in this latter contract shipped to the eastern coast... "[797]

The thirty-eight year old Norcom, who tried his best to get the Justice Department agents off his back, never produced either the communication with the State Department, or any information on

Sommerfeld's "more recent" contract.[798] Archival State Department records do not contain this correspondence from the Western Cartridge Company, either. It may never have existed since the U.S. government restricted arms supplies to Carranza immediately after the Columbus raid and re-instated an absolute embargo for munitions of war on April 15th 1916.[799] The Western Cartridge Company likely shipped on the "Carranza" contract, just not directly but via the Tauscher warehouse in New York. The claim that Olin cancelled Sommerfeld's contract because of "suspicious behavior" is also not documented. The opposite was the case. Sommerfeld was the man who could organize the smuggling of arms and munitions into Mexico on a grand scale.[800] He had smuggled Western Cartridge munitions into Mexico off and on throughout the revolution. His travels in disguise and the evidence of arms smuggling allow for the suspicion that Sommerfeld reactivated his old organization along the border.[801] The daily production of Western Cartridge indeed went to the East Coast, as secretary Norcom testified, just not to J. P. Morgan but Hans Tauscher who proceeded to ship "100,000 cartridges per day" to Mexico.

It should have been easy for the B.I. agents to follow up on Norcom's claims, but all they took was his word and delivery receipts for shipments on Sommerfeld's first contract up to September 1915.[802] The B.I. agents did have additional leads that pointed to the Secret War Council. However, it took until the end of June 1916 to get specific information. It appeared that the Mexican consul in New Orleans, Francisco R. Villavicencio, suddenly began spending large sums of money to outfit ships. The incident, which involved the smuggling journeys of the schooner *Sunshine* has already been mentioned. The *Sunshine* was only one of several ships that the Carranza government began acquiring and outfitting in May and June 1916. U.S. Naval Intelligence suspected, "In view of German activities in Mexico it is possible that that government supplied the money [for fixing up three schooners]."[803] The report listed deposits to the credit of Villavicencio in New Orleans, a former member of the Huerta Secret Service.[804] Between May 12th and June 2nd 1916, over $65,000 ($1.37 million in today's value) arrived from the Equitable Trust Company in New York, another $15,000 ($315,000 in today's value) through the Empire Trust Company of New York.[805] The Bureau of Investigations traced the payments to Juan T. Burns, the Mexican Consul General in New York, and Arturo Caturegli, the "Mexican financial Agent" for the Carranza administration whose bank account was listed as "Elias."[806] Both Francisco S. Elias and A. Caturegli appear in the files of Hans Tauscher and Franz von Papen in 1915, establishing them to have had business contacts with the Secret War Council.[807]

The plot thickened with the discovery that Burns opened an account at the Equitable Trust Company on March 10th, the day after Villa's attack on Columbus, New Mexico. He deposited $10,149.51. The account suspiciously closed the next day with the money transferring to New Orleans. Burns also maintained another account at the same bank, which showed deposits of $242,662 ($5 million in today's value). He had opened this account on March 22nd 1916. B.I. investigators wrote, "A number of the larger deposits … came through the Hanover National Bank and the Bank of Manhattan…"[808] The largest deposits were listed as follows:

May 10 Hanover National Bank	$ 25,000
May 11 Hanover National Bank	$ 11,400
May 17 Equitable Trust Co.	$ 50,000
May 31 Equitable Trust Co.	$ 10,000
May 31 Equitable Trust Co.	$ 40,000

Caturegli received the following deposits in the same time period:

April 12 Empire Trust Co.	$ 335,026
April 13 Hanover National Bank	$ 34,373

The deposits were traced to several dozen smaller deposits and a few larger ones:

April 12 National City Bank	$ 50,000
April 12 National City Bank	$ 50,000
April 12 National City Bank	$ 55,000
April 12 Chase National Bank	$ 3,280
April 12 National City Bank	$ 11,000

In summary, between April and the end of May 1916, Burns and Caturegli received deposits of $130,000 and $370,000, respectively.

Many more transactions amounting to close to three million dollars flowed through the accounts of these two Mexicans in the same time period.[809] However, many of those came from miscellaneous smaller deposits that appeared legitimate to the investigators and not exceptional for representatives of a country with major commercial relationships in New York. However, the large deposits amounting to $500,000 ($10 million dollars in today's value) that suspiciously flowed in and out of these accounts caught the attention of the American investigators. Were the Mexicans buying large amounts of ammunition in New York and shipping it through New Orleans into Mexico? The discovery of the *Sunshine*, the outfitting of three other ships, as well as the discovery of munitions shipments, such as Leon Rasst's, supported the theory. The investigators could not trace the origin of these Mexican funds but observed, "It will be noticed from the deposits that a number of the items are on German bankers."[810]

Heinrich Albert maintained accounts at the National City Bank, the Chase National Bank, and the Hanover National Bank, where many of the deposits for the two Mexicans originated. Two deposits in particular draw attention: Albert recorded a "Special Deposit" from the account of the German embassy of $300,000 on April 29th 1916.[811] On June 12th 1916, Albert sent a wire to his account at the Hanover National Bank amounting to $200,000 marked "K.M. Account" (*Kriegsministerium* – War Ministry).[812] Both transfers appear to have been "reimbursements" for money Albert had spent (for which there are no details) and for which he then received credit from the Imperial War Ministry and the Foreign Office. The two transactions match exactly the time frame and the suspicious amounts that the Bureau of Investigations tried to trace in the accounts of Caturegli and Burns. It appears from fragmented information in Albert's books that Frederico Stallforth and Carl Heynen disbursed the $500,000 in numerous unexplained draws to their credit suspiciously matching the deposits of the Mexican agents. These transactions appear as "Mexican Shipment," "Temporary Advance," "Currency Exchange," and "German Embassy, amounts handed to S.T. [Stallworth]."[813] June 1916 was the only occasion when Albert noted that money was "handed" to Stallforth in all his bookkeeping from1914 to 1917. The aggregate of these disbursals from Albert to the two German agents dealing with Mexico amounted to $444,153 between April 3rd and June 3rd, 1916.[814]

The notation in Albert's ledger: "amounts handed to S. T."[815]

The following threads all weave into a storyline that supports German involvement in the Mexican situation: information from the Western Cartridge Company; the evidence of Tauscher's involvement; the evidence of shipments of 7mm ammunition reaching the border; the numerous delivery contracts that exceeded the Western Cartridge production capacity by multiples; the fact that the French government could not use and rejected the Western Cartridge shipments; and, the suspicious money transactions in both Carranza and Albert's accounts. The facts support the intention Count Montgelas expressed in his top-secret memorandum; namely, that Germany wanted munitions shipments from American sources to increase the border tensions. There is enough convincing evidence in Albert's financial records, the B.I. investigative files, and in De La Garza's accounting of shipments that Sommerfeld, Heynen, and Tauscher engaged in shipping arms to Villa and Carranza before and after the Columbus attack. The Montgelas memo dated March 17th 1916, links this evidence to the official German strategy of provoking a war between Mexico and the United States.

The interests of the embattled Carranza government in Mexico and of Germany coincided in important ways in the months after the Columbus attack: Germany wanted the Americans to be busy on the border in order to keep them out of the European war both as a supplier and as an active participant. Mexico wanted the U.S. to spend her resources guarding the border rather than marching south. After the sinking of the French Steamer SS *Sussex* on March 24th, Germany surprisingly backed down from unrestricted submarine warfare in the so-called *Sussex pledge* on May 4th, agreeing to warn ships before attacking them.[816] There was a compelling reason: The German ambassador in Washington, Count Bernstorff, wrote to Imperial Chancellor von Bethmann Hollweg on April 4th, two weeks after the Punitive Expedition commenced, "As long as the Mexican question remains at this stage [on the precipice of war] we are, I believe, fairly safe from aggressive attack by the American government."[817] Count Bernstorff explained the German retreat from unrestricted submarine warfare even clearer on June 24th. He wrote to Imperial Foreign Minister von Jagow, "If intending to resume U-boat war in old forms [unrestricted], I am asking urgently to delay beginning until America should really be deadlocked in Mexico. Otherwise to be expected that President will immediately settle with Mexico and will use war with Germany to win elections with help of Roosevelt people."[818]

Faced with the potential of a full American invasion of Mexico, Carranza also wanted to keep the U.S. military busy with its domestic affairs. The vehicle for that, namely a concentration of U.S. forces along the border in order to quell an uprising of Mexicans and Mexican-Americans in the United States, seemed a daring but logical choice. The amount of forces the U.S. needed to secure the cities along a twelve hundred-mile border and guard against raids severely limited the resources and tactical choices of the Pershing command. Just as Germany suddenly backed down from the unrestricted submarine warfare in order to give the conflict between Mexico and the U.S. time to develop, Carranza successfully corralled the Pershing forces while trying to divert attention and resources to the border. It was now Carranza's turn to attack an American city with Villa in hiding and his forces dispersed. His target was Laredo, Texas.

General José Maria Zuazua, next to Augustín S. Garza aka León Caballo, Aniceto Pizaña, and Luis de la Rosa, the primary financier of the *Plan de San Diego*, received note on June 5th, 1916 that all was set for a major invasion of Texas on June 10th. Groups of rebels were to cut off the surrounding areas of Laredo, Texas, so that the Carrancista garrison in Nuevo Laredo could occupy the American border city.[819] The invasion had been meticulously planned. Carrancista General Pablo González, to whom General Zuazua reported, had ordered the release of Augustín Garza in April, and supplied money, as well as five thousand rifles, for the operation.[820] Garza aka León Caballo implicated who really was behind the operation in a revealing telegram to Zuazua: "Tomorrow the ready personnel leave for there [Piedras Negras] under Gerardo Garza González. Everything is arranged for the night of the 9th. All personnel are ready. Don Venustiano [Carranza] expects you to order that we receive all elements. Please do so. It is all arranged. Your orders are awaited. [signed] León Caballo."[821] In Monterrey, General Pablo González, one of Carranza's most loyal commanders, and officially assigned to protect the border and find Villa, gave orders to Esteban Fierros, a Carrancista officer with the rank of colonel born in Laredo, to command "a brigade of irregulars being formed to invade Texas."[822] Reporting directly to Garza, the head of the *Plan de San Diego* with the title, "General in Chief of the Liberating Army of Races and People in America," Fierros received the commission of Brigadier General.[823] The brigade of irregulars he commanded consisted of some 450 men, three "generals," dozens of colonels, captains and lieutenants, and a few handfuls of foot soldiers.[824] The unit prepared their mission in Monterrey, and then moved to the border. After the *Brigada Fierros* received orders to commence, its units infiltrated the U.S. between June 5th and 9th. Scouts went out at night to reconnoiter the region around Laredo and assisted groups of twenty-five to thirty men to cross the Rio Grande into the United States. General Fierros described the progress:

> Most of the cavalry [310 troops] have crossed into Texas to penetrate the interior of the State, disguised as vaqueros, and to date we have had no difficulty in crossing in parties of 25 and 30 men, dividing them into bands of 20 each [deployed] in different directions, designating Kennedy [Kenedy, southeast of San Antonio], Texas, as the assembly point. The Coup should break out tonight after midnight [June 10]. I expect we will soon have very good news to communicate to you [Augustín Garza]. I leave on Monday to put myself at the head of my troops, depending on the orders that Fortunato [Zuazua] gives me... [825]

While all these preparations took place, the American authorities did not sit by idly and watch the plot unfold. American agents had heard rumors of a conspiracy against the United States in Monterrey as early as January 1916. *Plan de San Diego* suspects Luis de la Rosa and others the B.I. had followed ever since the raids in the summer of 1915 appeared frequently in investigative reports as living freely in Monterrey and Tampico, despite the Carranza administration professing to have incarcerated them.[826] As the Fierros Brigade had started infiltrating Texas on June 7th, "Bureau agent Barnes reported that it was an open secret in Monterrey that the Carranza government was extending amnesty to all political offenders and ex-soldiers of the old Porfirio Díaz regime in order to enlist them for an invasion of the United States."[827] On the same day, General Funston reported that an invasion of Texas was imminent.[828]

The Military Intelligence officers along the border had seen more indications of trouble for a month. The former Villista General José Maria Morin, long known to the Bureau of Investigations as a recruiter for various revolutionary factions, ostensibly began recruiting "Mexicans for a projected uprising" in San Antonio.[829] B.I. agents found out that Morin issued commissions for an "army of liberation in Texas."[830] Witnesses linked Morin to Luis de la Rosa, who American authorities at the time suspected to have been the leader of the *Plan de San Diego* raids the year before. Morin's efforts not only involved San Antonio. One of his fellow conspirators organized Mexican and Mexican-American residents in Kingsville, Texas. On May 10th, federal agents arrested Morin and discovered among his papers a long list of officers under his command. They also arrested Victoriano Ponce, Morin's man in Kingsville. While federal agents prepared a trial for the two *Plan de San Diego* organizers, the two prisoners disappeared from their jail cells in Kingsville, Texas. As it turned out, Texas Rangers in charge of guarding the prisoners had murdered them on May 23rd.[831] Although the organizing of the Mexican community along the border in Texas and the plan to raid Laredo occurred in parallel, the murders ended the possibility of establishing a connection between Morin and the Brigada Fierros or the Carranza government.

The discovery of the invasion plan by the Military Intelligence Division and the Bureau of Investigations triggered a forceful demand to stop the conspiracy by the American Secretary of State Lansing on June 10th, the day the invasion was to take place.[832] Lansing's direct threat of war helped. Carranza pulled the plug. He ordered the Mexican border commander with headquarters in Matamoros, General Alfredo Ricaut, to once again stop the *Plan de San Diego* conspirators, as he had done so effectively the previous October. Fierros had no idea what was happening. Ricaut cancelled the attack plan and ordered Fierros to Monterrey. The *Brigada Fierros*, except for the forces already in Texas, returned to its barracks in Monterrey. The same day, General Ricaut met his American counterpart, Brigadier

General William A. Mann, on the international bridge between Nuevo Laredo and Laredo. Mann gave Ricaut the intelligence he had about the planned invasion and demanded an immediate arrest of Luis de la Rosa, the suspected leader of the *Plan de San Diego* and his co-conspirators.[833] The Mexican government reported the arrest of de la Rosa with forty co-conspirators on June 12th, and assured the U.S. border officials that there was no danger of raids.

The reality was quite different. The abandoned members of the *Brigada Fierros*, as well as pockets of raiders along the border and in Texas, executed a series of border raids. A large group of *Plan de San Diego* raiders attacked two ranches on the Mexican-American border close to La Jarita on June 10th, as General Ricaut hurriedly tried to shut down the invasion plan. After provisioning themselves with horses, the raiding parties crossed into the United States, and headed for Webb Station, a railroad stop twenty miles north of Laredo. The raiders had the objective of destroying a railroad bridge near Webb Station in order to prevent U.S. army reinforcements from getting to Laredo when the main attack was supposed to take place. Not only did the raiders not know that American law enforcement had discovered the invasion plans, but a Mexican cowboy who the band had captured at La Jarita, managed to escape and alerted the 14th U.S. Cavalry.[834] In a serious firefight on the night of June 11th, the Mexican commander, Lieutenant Colonel Pedro Villareal died.[835] The American deputy sheriff who shot him found a Carranza commission in Villareal's pockets.[836] He was also wearing a Carrancista army uniform, just like several prisoners that the American posse had taken.[837] The prisoners confirmed during questioning that they had been part of the de la Rosa command and that all their superiors were commissioned Carrancista officers.

Border officials reported another raid on June 14th. "A band of about 24 Mexicans crossed into Texas nine miles west from Brownsville at the place called Ranchito..." on June 14th.[838] The raid triggered an immediate chase by U.S. infantry and cavalry detachments into Mexico. The U.S. government recalled the units on the 18th of June. Carrancista forces shadowing the American troops fired on the rear guard of a cavalry unit on the way back into the U.S. The U.S. commander ordered a full-fledged attack on the Mexicans. American forces occupied the Mexican border city of Matamoros in the process. The American sacking of the border city caused a wholesale panic on the Mexican side. General Ricaut, desperate to prevent a showdown with the invaders, evacuated the town. Not only did the Mexican military abandon its positions, but Ricaut also ordered all women and children to flee the city. The situation was quickly diffused in meetings between the American commander and General Ricaut. However, on June 15th, this time near Laredo, "about one hundred Mexicans crossed from Mexico into Texas at San Ignacio... [they] fired upon two troops of the Fourteenth United States Cavalry as they lay asleep."[839] Three U.S. soldiers and six Mexican raiders died. The U.S. did not pursue the raiders into Mexico. The San Ignacio raid, according to later court proceedings, had been planned by de la Rosa with the blessing of the Carranza government.[840] The raids did not stop. Despite the assurances of General Ricaut that he had arrested the *Plan de San Diego* conspirators, and Luis de la Rosa in particular, the details are murky. According to historians Harris and Sadler, de la Rosa was only detained briefly, and soon continued plotting further raids.[841]

Bureau of Investigations detectives also uncovered plots on the Arizona border with Mexico. Special Agent Charles Breniman arrested Constantino Covani and an associate in Nogales, Arizona in the middle of April. Covani had been a member of the German sabotage team, which attempted to blow up the Welland Canal in the fall of 1914. He was now engaged in "pro-German" activities on the border. Also based in Arizona was Newenham A. Gray, a German mining engineer, former Sommerfeld employee in the Mexican Secret Service, and suspected German agent. He was en route to Columbus, New Mexico on the day before the raid and arrived only hours after the Villistas had retreated back into Mexico. No one seemed to question his sudden presence or the purpose of his trip. Gray had moved to New York and worked as an ordinance expert for Charles Flint when the European war started. Flint had a long history of involvement in Mexico, mainly because of his rubber business. He owned American Chicle. It is easy to imagine the strategic importance Gray's position with Flint had for the German government. While the BI covered Gray's movements on the border from time to time, he was never arrested nor questioned. He settled in Tucson, Arizona after the war, and engaged in mining. Details of his activities in the war on behalf of Germany have not surfaced.

The fact that agents of the American government stayed as

close to the conspiracies along the Mexican-American border was no accident. General Funston, who in 1915 had been in charge of battling the *Plan de San Diego* raids, reacted swiftly to renewed threats in the lower Rio Grande valley. Information from B.I. agents, as well as military intelligence, showed that Carranza's fingerprints were all over the raids. After the Scott-Obregón meetings in El Paso, Obregón had committed to sending ten thousand troops north to find Pancho Villa and stop raids into U.S. territory. The obvious threat to Pershing's supply lines and lines of communications became palpable when thirty thousand Carrancista troops moved towards the border.[842] General Treviño, the commander of the Chihuahua garrisons, wrote to General Pershing on June 16th that he had received "orders from my government to prevent, by the use of arms, new invasions of my country by American forces and also prevent the American forces that are in this state from moving to the south, east or west of the places they now occupy..."[843] The American commander sent a terse response to the Mexican general with the basic statement that, unless Pershing's superiors told him differently, he would move his forces as he damn well pleased. However, Treviño's message did nothing to alleviate the suspicion that, indeed, Carranza was preparing to wage war against the United States.

While the raids occurred in the lower Rio Grande, several violent demonstrations against the United States erupted in Cananea, Naco, Nogales, Monterrey, and Torreón. Demonstrators burnt down the American consulate in Durango on June 8th, and dragged the American flag through the streets of the city. "A mob of three thousand led by the mayor [of Torreón] stone[d] the U.S. consulate for several hours..." on June 18th.[844] American officials suspected Carranza as the agitator behind the outbursts of mob violence, as indeed he was.[845] "Mexican authorities at the port of Mazatlán fired on a tender from the *U.S.S. Annapolis* and seized members of the crew..." on June 19th.[846] One American sailor died in the ensuing firefight. A similar incident two years earlier had precipitated the American occupation of Veracruz. Virtually no one in the American government doubted that war was inevitable. President Wilson finally gave in to calling up almost the entire National Guard on June 18th, on the recommendations of both Generals Scott and Funston and in the wake of the Matamoros shootout. One hundred fifty-eight thousand troops were to take over the defense of the U.S. – Mexican border in order for the regular army to fight a war with Mexico. "When the rolls were taken at the peak of mobilization on 31 August 1916, they would count 7,003 officers and 133,256 enlisted men in federal service, which when combined with the number of regular troops on active duty... [amounted] to the most men in U.S. uniform since the American Civil War."[847]

The buildup of the National Guard units in June was an important part of a plan the War College Division had devised in the previous month on the order of General Scott. This full-scale invasion plan of Mexico now rolled out. "The plan was to invade Mexico on three lines, along the main railways... it was agreed with the secretary [Baker] that General Funston was to command the eastern column, General Pershing the central, and General Sage, then stationed at Nogales, the western... the President had directed that I should take command [of the entire invasion force] myself. Thus[,] had we invaded Mexico I would well have commanded the whole..."[848] It would indeed have been a remarkable irony of history that another General Scott would have commanded American forces taking over Mexico for the second time in sixty-eight years.[849] The situation for Mexico would have been dire. The plan's main strategic objective was the destruction of the Carrancista army, now concentrated in large parts in Northern Mexico. "Scott also instructed that the updated plan provide 'for the protection of the border, and an invasion on each of the lines of railway; a plan for taking over the railways as we go along, with personnel to manage them, repair gangs, bridge builders, etc.; the establishment of lines of communications; and the protection of American property in Mexico near the border that can be reached promptly.'"[850] The plan called for 70,000 American ground troops, as well as two naval squadrons transporting 10,000 infantry troops that were to take Tampico and Veracruz. The plan did not call for the occupation of Mexico City but rather a full occupation of Northern Mexico and a diplomatic settlement that likely would have cost Mexico half of her territory for a second time in history.[851] Virtually the entire regular U.S. army, except for one division protecting Washington D.C., as well as close to 108,000 National Guard troops with 50,000 under call-up and on the way, assembled at and beyond the Mexican border on June 23rd.

It is important to note that the call-up of the reserves, as well as the reinforcement of the border with U.S. troops, occurred as a direct response to the marauding Mexican raiders across the border. These raids continued even as these two formidable armies faced off along the Rio Grande. A railroad bridge east of Laredo burnt on June 19th. All eyes focused on the cause, which investigators could not definitively determine. Secretary of State Lansing issued a note to First Chief Carranza on June 20th. He demanded the arrests of *Plan de San Diego* organizers and an immediate end to the raids, or else. Although not publicly admitting to his change of mind, Carranza did indeed order the immediate cessation of cross border raids on June 20th. The First Chief also ordered the arrest of de la Rosa. The forces on both sides of the border held their breath, since now one little spark could set off the war. General Scott wrote on June 20th, "It looks to me as if war will be on in a few days."[852] Then, on June 21st, the fateful incident that the Mexican government had hoped to stop at the last moment, that American military commanders had prepared to react to, and that the German government was hoping for, occurred in the little Mexican hamlet of Carrizal.

In response to the demand of General Treviño for Pershing to move no other direction but north, the American commander not only defied the Mexican demands, but sent several detachments on reconnaissance missions into central Chihuahua. Pershing had to determine from an operational perspective where the Carrancista army concentrated its forces. However, the reconnoitering was a highly sensitive affair given the tense standoff. The largest concentrations of Carrancista forces were assembling around Villa Ahumada, Chihuahua, along the Mexican Central Railway, seventy miles south of El Paso. On June 17th, the day after Treviño sent his threatening telegram, Pershing simultaneously sent Troop C under the command of forty-six year-old Captain Charles T. Boyd and Troop K under Captain Lewis S. Morey, both of the 10th Cavalry to Villa Ahumada. Since the two units started from separate locations, they met up at the Santa Domingo ranch, seven miles outside of Carrizal on June 20th. While Pershing maintained in his recollections that he verbally instructed Boyd to prevent a clash with Mexican forces at all costs,[853] several historians considered the fact that he dispatched two cavalry units with the same orders to central Chihuahua "a highly provocative move."[854] No written instructions to Boyd and Morey existed, thus leaving the judgment of Pershing's intentions in the realm of surmise.

The forty-six year-old Boyd took command of the two troops of eighty-four buffalo soldiers on June 21st, and decided to move through Carrizal. He requested from the local Carrancista general, Félix Gómez, to be allowed to march through town. The general refused. General Pershing recounted in his memoirs, "even had such instructions not be given Boyd [as to preventing a clash] it is difficult to comprehend why, after reaching the outskirts of Carrizal and talking with General Gómez and seeing a large number of Mexican troops moving into position in his front and towards his flanks, he should have still adhered to his determination to go on."[855] Whether Pershing had purposely tried to deliver the first shot in a war with Mexico or not,[856] Boyd's tactical errors in this instance were undeniable. The American troops took up positions in an open field, facing two machine guns and an opposition of 150 well-entrenched Mexican soldiers on three sides. As the Americans advanced, the Mexican troops decimated the attackers. Captain Boyd and his second in command, Lieutenant Adair, fell within minutes. Twelve additional American soldiers died, twelve more were wounded, and twenty-four captured. The Mexican casualties amounted to over forty killed and thirty-nine wounded.[857] In Washington, President Wilson, who heard of the clash before even Pershing had all the details, assumed that the war had started.[858]

The U.S. government asked for an immediate release of the prisoners. At the same time, President Wilson started composing a message to the U.S. Congress asking for the authority to invade Mexico. Wilson proposed a joint Mexican-American Commission under the aegis of the ABC powers, Argentina, Brazil, and Chile in a last-ditch effort to prevent a formal commencement of hostilities. The commission was to settle peacefully the issues that had brought the two countries to the brink of war. Behind the scenes, both President Wilson and First Chief Carranza had decided not to go to war. Carranza released the American soldiers on June 28th and had ordered the raids into the U.S. to stop. Wilson, in return, ordered Pershing's troops to be garrisoned. As historian Welsome described the situation for the Punitive Expedition: "The Carrizal Incident was the last fight of the Punitive Expedition. Forbidden by his superiors to even send out patrols, Pershing had nothing left to do but await orders to withdraw which did not come for another seven months."[859] Pershing's aide de camp George Patton vented his frustration with President Wilson in a letter to his father: "He [Wilson] has not the soul of a louse nor the mind of a worm or the backbone of a jellyfish."[860] It was certainly to the credit of President Wilson that he could stand up to his military and not start a war that was the stated goal of Germany.

Captured U.S. soldiers of the 10th Cavalry Brigade

Pershing, however, did not rest entirely. While 10,000 American troops spent their days with military exercises, Pershing attempted to have Pancho Villa assassinated. Two Japanese, who actually were American secret agents, came to Villa's camp in Jimenez in July 1916. Meanwhile, the target of the Pershing expedition had sufficiently recovered to harass the Carrancista forces once again. Jimenez was the latest of his military successes. Villa's forces had swollen to 1,850 men.[861] One of the members of Pershing's intelligence department, Captain W. O. Reed, had outfitted the two agents with poison. They tried it on a dog first and then dropped the tablets into Villa's coffee. Villa, always suspicious of attempts to poison him, poured half of the coffee into the cup of another man. The poison did not kill the revolutionary chieftain. Pershing buried the story in an elaborate cover-up until historians Harris and Sadler uncovered the plot and published it in 1988.[862] The discovery was a sensation, covered in several newspapers at the time.[863] Villa captured the capital of Chihuahua in September 1916, proving to the world that he was alive and well.

The Punitive Expedition has received significant attention from military, Mexican, and diplomatic history scholars over the years.

There were many aspects of the expedition, not least that Villa eluded the U.S. troops for nine months, which led historians to declare the effort a failure. One of the earliest apologists for the expedition's results was Army Chief of Staff Hugh Lenox Scott. He argued in his memoirs that he personally had revised the mission from "catching Villa" to "dispersing the bands that had attacked Columbus."[864] This official mission, according to Scott, had clearly been accomplished. As a matter of fact, it had been accomplished by May 1916. With Villa holed up in a cave healing his leg wound, incapable of generating public support for his fight with the Americans, and his troops widely dispersed across Chihuahua and Durango, Scott recommended to President Wilson to pull the expeditionary forces out of Mexico.[865] Had punishment and dispersal of the bands that had attacked Columbus, New Mexico been the universally accepted mission, Wilson would have acted accordingly. Instead, Scott argued in his memoirs that the State Department never modified the public expectation of "catching Villa."[866] Scott's assessment of "mission creep" reflected, to a degree, the frustration the U.S. military must have felt with the mission in total. Clearly, Villa's capture and trial would have been a boon for the U.S. army and President Wilson's image. Just as President Bush tried to downplay the importance of catching Osama Bin Laden many years later, the American public expected the villains to be brought to justice in both cases.

EPILOGUE

THE ROLE OF GERMANY IN creating the tensions at the Mexican-American border has never been clearly determined. President Wilson, as well as Secretary of State Lansing, mentioned on many occasions that they suspected German influence in the deteriorating situation on the border. Certainly, plenty of newspaper articles also alluded to as much. General Pershing's mention of Alberto Stallforth of Parral as an instigator of trouble is one of the few instances of a high military officer considering German involvement. Historians such as Friedrich Katz, Michael Meyer, James Sandos, and others have intimated German manipulation of the border tensions but have not been able to find a definitive smoking gun. Harris and Sadler brilliantly analyzed the organization and money trail of the *Plan de San Diego* conspiracy. They did not find German involvement on this level, but did trace the command and control of the conspiracy to Venustiano Carranza.

With the Punitive Expedition roaming Mexico and the American government cutting off arms and munitions to all Mexican factions, Carranza did turn to Germany for help. It is on this level that German intrigue brought Mexico and the United States to the brink of war. The role of Sommerfeld in inciting the attack on Columbus, the smuggling of millions of German-financed rounds of ammunition to Carranza, and the propaganda in Mexico evidenced in Pershing's recollections, were all designed to acerbate the situation. Carranza sent one of his most influential German advisers, Dr. Arnold Krumm-Heller to Berlin in June 1916. The Berlin-Mexico City axis grew even closer and culminated in the miscalculated dispatch of the "Zimmermann Telegram" in 1917.

The German government was elated at the developments along the Mexican-American border in the spring and summer of 1916.

The friction between the two countries exceeded the wildest dreams of German war planners. Sommerfeld had delivered on his plan submitted in May 1915, namely, that he could help bring about a U.S. intervention, force the U.S. military to consume America's own production of war materials, and inhibit American flexibility to participate actively in the European war. Indeed, the United States military was unable to even consider involvement in the European war in June and July 1916. The historiography of this period has understated and underestimated how close the United States came to being hopelessly embroiled in a war that might not have taken long, in terms of conquering Northern Mexico, but that would have tied down U.S. military and economic resources for the long term.

The German gamble had high stakes. The longer the U.S. military supplied itself and trained its regular forces, as well as state militias, the more effective a fighting force it would become in case of an active role in the European war. It was a risk the German agents in the United States were willing to take. Internal dissentions within the German government as to whether to risk an American entry into the war led to discussions through the fall and winter of 1916. In the end, the strategy to tie up the American military on the Mexican-American border, while Germany brought England to her knees, backfired badly. Two years later, in 1918, American doughboys brought the German war effort to its knees. The Punitive Expedition undoubtedly resulted in concrete, positive effects on the preparedness of the U.S. military for its next, much larger challenge. Lengthy combat training in a hostile environment, the need to revamp and re-think supply lines, the testing of new technologies such as airplanes for combat, and a desperately needed enhancement of readiness, all contributed to an American expeditionary force deciding the fortunes of World War I. Sommerfeld, Heynen, Tauscher, Albert, as well as Minister to Mexico von Eckardt had created a short window of opportunity for the German government to reopen unrestricted submarine warfare in the summer of 1916, while the U.S. busied itself with Mexico. The window closed unused.

Sommerfeld played the stock market in New York from the summer of 1916 to June 1918 and, while undoubtedly maintaining his contacts, seemed to keep his head low. According to friends, he was working on his memoirs, which, sadly, have not been published.

American Justice Department agents finally arrested the German agent in June 1918. Sommerfeld gave away nothing during three days of exhausting interrogations. Without proof of wrong-doing, this German spy, who had brought the United States and Mexico to the brink of war, spent less than a year in the "dangerous alien" detention camp at Fort Oglethorpe, Georgia. Sommerfeld was released in 1919 and promptly resumed working at the behest of Mexican revolutionaries, at the urging of Sherburne Hopkins, Miguel Díaz Lombardo, General Hugh Lenox Scott, and David Lawrence. Archival files reveal little about Sommerfeld's remaining life. He traveled frequently across the border, and was rumored to have purchased arms for the de la Huerta faction in 1922. He shared an office with Frederico Stallforth at the Hotel Bristol in Berlin in 1928. His mail was addressed to "c/o Sara Perez de Madero, Mexico City," the slain Mexican president's wife, in the 1930s. The last known place of residence appeared in the World War II registration files. The sixty-three year-old "retired mining engineer" signed up for service in the U.S. military at San Antonio, Texas in 1942. Sommerfeld's brother in arms, Frederico Stallforth, signed up for the OSS also in 1942. It is likely, Sommerfeld once again joined his longtime comrade and intelligence partner. Maybe finally, after many years of service for German intelligence, and Mexican revolutionaries, Felix Sommerfeld decided to throw in his lot with the United States. His brother Siegfried, who had remained behind in Schneidemühl to run the Jewish family's business, committed suicide or was murdered by the Gestapo after he had organized the rounding up and transportation to the Nazi death camps of the entire Jewish community of his hometown. That could have finally turned the German agent against his Fatherland. However, as he meticulously did throughout his career as a secret agent, Sommerfeld kept his life after World War I and his death shrouded in mystery...

ENDNOTES

1   Library of Congress, Papers of Hugh Lenox Scott, Box 16, General Correspondence, Sommerfeld to Scott, December 23, 1915.

2   See Grams, Grant W., "Karl Respa and German Espionage in Canada During World War I, Journal of Military and Strategic Studies, Fall 2005, Volume 8, Issue 1, "p. 16, footnote 35 quoting several secondary sources making the claim that German agents acted unprofessionally, clumsy, and amateurish.

3   NA RG 165 Military Intelligence Division, file 9140-1754-44, April 26, 1919, Hanna to van Deman; Harris, Charles H., III and Sadler, Louis R., *The Secret War in El Paso: Mexican Revolutionary Intrigue, 1906-1920*, University of New Mexico Press, Albuquerque, NM, 2009, p. 75; Sommerfeld's height in Harris and Sadler is given as 5 feet, 6 inches, which is not correct.

4   Stallforth Papers, Private Collection, Courtesy Mary Prevo, Guestbook entry, March 11, 1911.

5   Examples are plentiful throughout this work, such as calling Senator Fall his "personal enemy" to his face, physically threatening Adolph Krakauer when he supplied arms to Orozco or corresponding with Hugh Lenox Scott and Lindley Garrison about helping American citizens caught in the revolution.

6   For a thorough biography of Felix Sommerfeld's life up to the beginning of World War I, please refer to Heribert von Feilitzsch, *In Plain Sight: Felix A. Sommerfeld, Spymaster in Mexico, 1908 to 1914*, Henselstone Verlag, Amissville, VA, 2012.

7   Hermann, eight years older, Julius, almost exactly six years older, and Siegfried, four years older. Felix also had two sisters, Hedwig and Rosa, but their birth and death records probably disappeared in the flames of the "Endlösung," which wiped out the Jewish history of Schneidemühl in 1942.

8   Felix Sommerfeld gave his residence as "Borkendorf" on his first trip to America in 1896. According to the Allgemeine Zeitung des Judentums, 1900, Heft 34 (August 24, 1900), Der Gemeindebote, p. 2. Borkendorf was half-an-hour from Schneidemühl (by horse).

9   See von Feilitzsch, *In Plain Sight*, chapter 21 for details on the Hopkins scandal.

10   NA RG 165 Military Intelligence Division, File 9140-1754-4, Richard Levering to American Protective League, December 4, 1917.

11   NA RG 60 Department of Justice, File 9-12-16-5305, Statement F. A. Sommerfeld, June 21, 1918.

12   Von Papen had publicly denounced Sommerfeld. He repeated claims of the German community in Mexico City that accused Sommerfeld of having persecuted German residents as Mexican secret service chief under Madero. Sommerfeld admitted to the charges, although whether his actions resulted in any serious repercussions for the Germans in question is dubious.

13   United States Senate, *Revolutions in Mexico, Hearing before a Subcommittee of the Committee on Foreign Relations*, Government Printing Office, Washington D. C., 1913, p. 393.

14   *The Washington Post*, July 6, 1914, "Rebel Cash Held Up."

15   Papers of Hugh Lenox Scott, Library of Congress, Washington, D.C., Box 16, General Correspondence.

16   See for example NA RG 165 Military Intelligence Division, file 5761-1091, Sommerfeld to Garrison, July 2, 1914; Sommerfeld to Garrison, August 26, 1914; Sommerfeld to Garrison, September 3, 1914.

17   Lázaro de la Garza Collection, University of Texas, Benson Library, Austin, TX, Box 5, folder B; Sommerfeld to De La Garza, June 4, 1914. Sommerfeld stated how the Carrancistas through Douglas "make my job impossible."

18   Lázaro de la Garza Collection, University of Texas, Benson Library, Austin, TX, Box II, Folder C, Extract of Cartridge Account. Jan. 31, 1916.

19   Lázaro de la Garza Collection, University of Texas, Benson Library, Austin, TX, Box 3, Folder E, Financials dated July 28, 1914.

20   Lázaro de la Garza Collection, University of Texas, Benson Library, Austin, TX, Box 1, folder F, De La Garza to Villa, June 2, 1914.

21   NA RG 65 M1085 Roll 862 file 232-311, Sommerfeld contract with Western Cartridge Company dated February 19, 1915. The price of 7mm cartridges rose significantly with the start of World War I. Bureau of Investigations records show the prices in 1914 to have been between $35 and $48 per thousand rounds depending on who bought and sold them.

22   The whole theory proffered in Tuchman's *Zimmermann Telegram* and Katz' *Secret War in Mexico* of Germany materially supporting General Huerta in 1913 and 1914 falls apart using the correct shipping amounts.

23   NA RG 65 M1085 Roll 856 file 232-98, Agent Barnes to Frederick Guy, September 5, 1914.

24   *The New York Times*, June 21, 1914, "Villa denies naming Angeles."

25   Ibid., June 28, 1914, "Carranza asks delay; his agent accuses ours."

26   Ibid., June 29, 1914, "Calderón in Washington."

27   Ibid.

28   *The New York Times*, July 3, 1914, "Rebel Mediators Gather."

29   NA RG 165 file 5761-1091, Sommerfeld to Garrison, July 2, 1914.

30   NA RG 165 file 5761-1091, Sommerfeld to Garrison, July 2, 1914. Lázaro De La Garza, a wealthy businessman from Torreón, headed the treasury of Pancho Villa's organization first in Mexico and then in the United States. In 1915, De La Garza split with Villa and was accused of stealing funds from the Mexican general (which indeed he did). The Mexican businessman moved to Los Angeles and spent the next twenty-five years defending himself against numerous lawsuits from Pancho Villa's brother and the Madero family.

31   Katz, Friedrich, *The Life and Times of Pancho Villa*, Stanford University Press, Stanford, CA, 1998, p. 361.

32   Scheina, Robert L., *Villa, Soldier of the Mexican Revolution*, Potomac Books, Washington D.C., 2004, p. 48.

33   Clendenen, Clarence, *The United States and Pancho Villa: A study in unconventional diplomacy*, Cornell University Press, Ithaca, New York, 1961, pp. 96-97.

34   NA RG 242 T141 Roll 19, Panselov to Imperial Navy Headquarters, July 21, 1914. *The New York Times*, August 17, 1914, "Huerta lands in England."

35   Cumberland, Charles C., *The Mexican Revolution: The Constitutionalist Years*, University of Texas Press, Austin, TX, 1974, pp. 149-150.

36   Library of Congress, Prints and Photographs Division, Washington, D.C., LC-B2-3170-2, public domain.

37   See von Feilitzsch, *In Plain Sight*, chapter 21, the Benton affair.

38   Clendenen, *The United States and Pancho Villa*, p. 97. Clendenen reported St. Clair's first name as Donald. All archival papers give his first name as George.

39   NA RG 59 Department of State, Division of Latin American Affairs, file 312.41/271, Sommerfeld to B. Long, July 4, 1914.

40   Ibid.

41   Clendenen and other historians have mistakenly thought that Villistas arrested Douglas, which is not accurate.

42   Lázaro de la Garza Collection, University of Texas, Benson Library, Austin, TX, Box 5, Folder B, Sommerfeld to De La Garza, July 2, 1914.

43   NA RG 59 Department of State, Division of Latin American Affairs, file 312.41/271, Cobb to State, July 6, 1914.

44   NA RG 242 Captured German Documents, T141 Roll 19, Bryan to Haniel von Haimhausen, July 6, 1914.

45   Von Feilitzsch, *In Plain Sight*, p. 202.

46   Holmdahl Papers, University of California at Berkley, Bancroft Library, C-B-921, Box 1, Holmdahl to A.M. Toler, February 27, 1914. Holmdahl's biographer Douglas Meed mentioned all the major Félix Díaz junta members but mistakenly considers them "Carranza" agents. See Meed, Douglas V., *Soldier of Fortune*, Halcyon Press, Ltd., Houston, TX, 2003, p. 115.

47   Papers of Hugh Lenox Scott, Library of Congress, Washington, D.C., Box 15, General Correspondence, F. A. Sommerfeld to L. M. Garrison, July 10, 1914.

48   Charles Ranlett Flint was a formidable Wall Street operator, nicknamed "father of trusts," with large financial interests in Mexican rubber and railroads. His companies included American Chicle (using Mexican rubber extract) and the Computing Tabulating Recording Company (the company that later became IBM). Flint supplied Mexican revolutionaries with arms and munitions before and during the World War.

49   Colby, Frank Moore, Williams, Talcott, eds., *The New International Encyclopedia*, Volume 24, Dodd, Mead, and Company, New York, 1918, p. 96. Although this seems an exaggeration, the general unpreparedness of Great Britain's munitions industry in 1914 is beyond question.

50   *Shrapnel and other War Material: A Reprint of Important Articles Presented in the American Machinist from January to June 1915*, McGraw-Hill Book Company, New York, 1915, p. 42.

51   Hardach, Gerd, *The First World War, 1914-1918*, University of California Press, Berkeley and Los Angeles, 1977, p. 150.

52   Hamilton, Douglas T., *Shrapnel Shell Manufacture*, The New Industrial Press, New York, NY, 1915, p. 19.

53   Hamilton, *Shrapnel Shell Manufacture*, p. 16.

54   Olin had a third son, Spencer, who eventually took over the business with John. Tragically, Franklin Jr. committed suicide in 1921.

55   Lázaro de la Garza Collection, University of Texas, Benson Library, Austin, TX, Box 5, Folder B, Sommerfeld to De La Garza, July 27, 1914.

56   Lázaro de la Garza Collection, University of Texas, Benson Library, Austin, TX, Box 3, Folder E.

57   http://iaaforum.org/forum3/viewtopic.php?f=8&t=8096&start=15, viewed 11-30-2011. Collectors in the U.S. have found 7mm cartridges made by Western Cartridge Company as early as 1913, although major production did not start until 1915 and with a new brass mill coming on line in May 1916.

58   NA RG 242 Captured German Documents, T141 Roll 19, von Papen to Auswärtiges Amt, July 30, 1914.

59   NA RG 242 Captured German Documents, T141, von Papen to Army General Staff, Political Section Section IIIb, No. 1610, March 31, 1914. Salary data is contained in NA RG 65 Albert Papers, Box 45, Selection from Papers found in the Possession of Captain von Papen, Falmouth, January 2 and 3, 1916, check No. 41, November 2, "W. von Igel (salary for October.)"

60   It is unclear from the archival sources, when von Igel was hired. *The New York Times* mentioned in an article on von Igel's arrest that "the crime for which von Igel is under indictment was committed in the first two months of the war..." See *The New York Times*, April 19, 1916, "Von Papen's Aid Arrested."

61   Reiling, Johannes, *Deutschland: Safe for Democracy?* Franz Steiner Verlag, Stuttgart, Germany, 1997, p. 127.

62   NA RG 242 Captured German Documents, T141 Roll 19, von Papen to Auswärtiges Amt, July 30, 1914.

63   Von der Goltz, Horst, *My Adventures as a German Secret Agent*, Robert M. McBride and Company, New York, NY, 1917, p. 56.

64   Von Papen, Franz, *Memoirs*, Translated into English by Brian Connell, E. P. Dutton and Company, Inc., New York, NY, 1953, p. 30.

65   Doerries, Reinhard R., *Diplomaten und Agenten: Nachrichtendienste in der Geschichte der deutsch-amerikanischen Beziehungen*, Universitätsverlag C. Winter, Heidelberg, 2001, p. 12. Doerries cites an agreement from May 1912, made between the German army and navy to share intelligence. Boy-Ed's reports that are shared with von Papen show that this cooperation seemed to work at least as far as these two officials were concerned.

66   NA RG 65 Albert Papers, Box 19, Sommerfeld to Boy-Ed, November 11, 1914.

67   NA RG 65 Albert Papers, Box 19, Sommerfeld to Boy-Ed, November 11, 1914, Sommerfeld to Boy-Ed, November 29, 1914.

68   NA RG 60 Department of Justice, File 9-12-16-5305, Statement F. A. Sommerfeld, June 21, 1918.

69   Miscellaneous No, 13 (1916), *Sworn Statement by Horst von der Goltz alias Bridgeman Taylor,* Harrison and Sons, London, 1916, p. 2. Wachendorf claimed in this statement that he first went to Washington, then hung around a few days and finally came to New York.

70   NA RG 60 Department of Justice, File 9-12-16-5305, Statement F. A. Sommerfeld, June 24, 1918.

71   Ibid., June 21, 1918.

72   NA RG 59 Department of State, file 312.11/752, Adolph Krakauer to Marion Letcher, July 3, 1912.

73   Bundesarchiv füer Militärgeschichte Freiburg (Hereafter BAMG), von Hintze Nachlass, RM 2, file 1780, letter of Eugen Knapp to Foreign Secretary Zimmermann, undated (April 1913).

74   See NA RG 65 Albert Papers, Box 45, Falmouth Papers, Boy-Ed to von Papen, May 25, 1914.

75   BAMG Freiburg, von Hintze Nachlass, RM2, file 1780.

76   NA RG 65 Albert Papers, Box 19, Sommerfeld to Boy-Ed, November 11 and 29, 1914. Notice in the first letter that Sommerfeld wrote "Herrn Kapitaen K. Boy-Ed." In the second he wrote "Geehrter Herr Kapitaen," clearly referring to the same person.

77   NA RG 65 Albert Papers, Box 19, von Papen to General Staff, undated; Von Papen quoted Count Bernstorff's telegram and added more details for his superiors. Also Box 23, Diary of Heinrich Albert, entry for September 10, 1914.

78   Von Papen, *Memoirs,* p. 37.

79   NA RG 65 Albert Papers, Box 19, von Papen to General Staff, undated; von Papen quoted Count Bernstorff's telegram and added more details for his superiors.

80   NA RG 65 Albert Papers, Box 3, Folder 10, Count Bernstorff to Dernburg and Albert, October 17, 1914.

81   NA RG 65 Albert Papers, Box 19, Prinz Hatzfeld to Albert, October 27, 1914.

82   NA RG 65 Albert Papers, Box 19, von Papen to von Falkenhayn, April 9, 1915, "The first proposal made by me... met very naturally with no consideration... "

83   NA RG 65 Albert Papers Box 8, "Massregeln zur Schädigung des Feindes." Quoted in Reiling, *Deutschland: Safe for Democracy?*, p. 125.

84   Von Papen, *Memoirs*, p. 36.

85   Felix Sommerfeld was assigned to Pancho Villa. The German agent became Villa's official representative in the United States as well as his chief arms buyer. Arnold Krumm-Heller was assigned to Venustiano Carranza. He accompanied Carranzista troops as an artillery specialist and military adviser. Frederico Stallforth worked in New York for the Madero family business, which mainly engaged in supplying Pancho Villa. Stallforth began working for the German commercial agency of Heinrich Albert in the fall of 1914. He maintained close connections to a number of other Mexican expatriates.

86   NA RG 242 Captured German Documents, T141, Roll 377, Document 735, Dernburg to Admiral Henning von Holtzendorff, Mai 10, 1915.

87   Ibid.

88   Ibid.

89   Only one article has appeared on the subject of the siege at Naco, see Mumme, Stephen P., "The Battle of Naco, Factionalism and Conflict in Sonora: 1914-1915," *Arizona and the West*, Volume 21, No. 2 (Summer, 1979), 157-186.

90   See Meyer, Michael C., "Villa, Sommerfeld, Columbus y los Alemanes," *Sobretiro de Historia Mexicana*, Vol. XXVIII, No. 4, El Colegio de Mexico, 1979; Sandos, James A., "German Involvement in Northern Mexico, 1915-1916: A New Look at the Columbus Raid," *The Hispanic American Historical Review*, Vol. 50, No. 1 (Feb., 1970), 70-88; Katz, Friedrich, "Pancho Villa and the Attack on Columbus, New Mexico," *The American Historical Review*, Vol. 83, No. 1 (Feb. 1978), 101-130.

91   See von Feilitzsch, *In Plain Sight*, chapter 23.

92   Villa announced many times, that he did not seek the presidency. When he had the chance, he did not take it. See for example *The New York Times*, November 30, 1914, "Villa puts Crown Aside."

93   See von Feilitzsch, *In Plain Sight*, chapter 23.

94   Katz, *The Life and Times of Pancho Villa,* p. 363.

95   *The New York Times*, June 14, 1914, "Villa saves Maytorena."

96   Katz, *The Life and Times of Pancho Villa,* p. 364.

97   Guzman, Martin Luis, *Memoirs of Pancho Villa*, translated by Virginia H. Taylor, University of Texas Press, Austin, Texas, 1975, p. 288.

98   Historian Friedrich Katz interpreted Villa's gesture as a ruse, citing Villa's countermanding order a week later as proof. However, the first message was sent when Obregón first arrived, the second after he left and Carranza refused to accept Villa's terms. There is no indication that Villa was not seriously attempting to solve the Maytorena-Obregón conflict to the satisfaction of the American government.

99   Guzman, *Memoirs of Pancho Villa*, p. 289.

100   NA RG 165 Military Intelligence Division, file 5761-1091, Sommerfeld to Garrison, August 26, 1914.

101   Ibid., Garrison to Sommerfeld, September 3, 1914.

102   *The El Paso Times*, August 26, 1914, "Street Throngs Cheer Torreón Hero."

103   Robert Runyon, August 27, 1914, copyright expired.

104   *The El Paso Times*, August 26, 1914, "Street Throngs Cheer Torreon Hero."

105   Ibid.

106   Ibid. Mufti refers to the comfortable civilian clothes, slacks, sweater, and riding boots in which Villa preferred to dress.

107   Ibid.

108   Ibid.

109   Mumme, "The Battle of Naco," p. 162.

110   NA RG 165 Military Intelligence Division, file 5761-1091, Sommerfeld to Garrison, September 3, 1914.

111   Guzman, *Memoirs of Pancho Villa*, 302-303.

112   Lawyer and lobbyist Sherburne G. Hopkins played a major role in the Mexican Revolution first as Francisco Madero's lobbyist in Washington, then acting on behalf of the Constitutionalists, both for Villa and Carranza. Hopkins had introduced Sommerfeld to influential members of the U.S. government. See von Feilitzsch, *In Plain Sight*, chapter 23.

113   Scott, Hugh Lenox, *Some Memories of a Soldier*, The Century Company, New York, NY, 1928, p. 497.

114   Ibid., p. 505.

115   Papers of Hugh Lenox Scott, Library of Congress, Washington, D.C., Box 15, General Correspondence, Tasker Bliss to Hugh L. Scott, August 26, 1914.

116   As quoted in Katz, *Life and Times of Pancho Villa*, p. 364.

117   Katz, *Life and Times of Pancho Villa*, p. 368.

118   Phase one was the fall of Díaz and Madero administration, phase two was the Constitutionalist war against Huerta, phase three was the fight between Carranza and Villa.

119   *The New York Journal*, September 26, 1914, "Carranza Force is Defeated."

120   NA RG 165 Military Intelligence Division, file 5761-1091-12, Sommerfeld to Garrison, September 27, 1914.

121   Ibid.

122   *Huachuca Illustrated, Volume 1, 1993*, by James P. Finley, Fort Huachuca, AZ, chapter 10.

123   Mumme, "The Battle of Naco," p. 164.

124   Originally published in *Arizona and the West*, Volume 21, No. 2 (Summer, 1979), pp. 157-186, "The Battle of Naco, Factionalism and Conflict in Sonora: 1914-1915," by Stephen P. Mumme, p. 168. Copyright Journal of the West ©1979, reprinted with permission of ABC-CLIO.

125   NA RG 65 FBI Case Files, M1085 Roll 855 file 232-37, Agent Blanford to Department, September 27, 1914.

126   See for example Lázaro de la Garza Collection, University of Texas, Benson Library, Austin, TX, Box 5 Folder B, Sommerfeld to De La Garza, June 8, 1914.

127   NA RG 65 FBI Case Files, M1085 Roll 855 file 232-37, Agent Blanford to Department, November 15, 1914.

128   As quoted from the Brown papers, James P. Finley, *Huachuca Illustrated, Volume 1, 1993*, chapter 10.

129   Katz, *Life and Times of Pancho Villa*, p. 375.

130   As quoted in Teitelbaum, Louis M., *Woodrow Wilson and the Mexican Revolution, 1913-1916*, Exposition Press, New York, NY, 1967, pp. 186-187.

131   Teitelbaum, *Woodrow Wilson and the Mexican Revolution*, p. 187.

132   Katz, *Life and Times of Pancho Villa*, p. 385.

133   *The New York Times*, December 7, 1914, "Obregon says Villa killed W. S. Benton." Obregon continues in the statement to levy fourteen specific accusations against Villa.

134   For more information of the Convention of Aguascalientes, see Quirk, Robert E., *The Mexican Revolution, 1914-1915*, University of Indiana Press, Bloomington, IN, 1960. Also Friedrich Katz, Alan Knight, Charles Cumberland all analyzed the convention and underlying causes of the Villa-Carranza split. For the purpose of this paper, the fact of the split is more important than the underlying causes.

135   *The New York Times*, October 12, 1914, "American troops fire on Mexicans."

136   Ibid.

137   *The New York Times*, October 27, 1914, "Truce holds at border."

138   NA RG 65 FBI Case Files, M1085, Roll 854, file 232, Agent Breniman to Department, November 15, 1914.

139   Scott, *Some Memories of a Soldier*, p. 508.

140   *The New York Times*, December 10, 1914, "Artillery at Naco to await Orders."

141   *The New York Times*, December 8, 1914, "Naco Baffles Government."

142   *The New York Times*, December 11, 1914, "Gen. Bliss under fire."

143   Ibid.

144   United States War Department, *Annual Reports 1915*, Government Printing Office, Washington D.C., 1916, p. 151. Also *The New York Times*, December 16, 1914, "3,000 New Troops ordered to Naco to aid Gen. Bliss."

145   *The New York Times*, December 17, 1914, "Ultimatum sent to Naco Chiefs."

146   Scott, *Some Memories of a Soldier*, p. 508.

147   Papers of Hugh Lenox Scott, Library of Congress, Washington, D.C., Box 15, General Correspondence, Scott to Bliss, December 20, 1914.

148   Ibid., Hopkins to Scott, December 22, 1914; *El Paso Herald*, December 16, 1914, "Sommerfeld to Return."

149   *The New York Times*, December 20, 1914, "Bliss has Plan for Border Peace."

150 United States War Department, *Annual Reports 1915*, p. 151.

151 Papers of Hugh Lenox Scott, Library of Congress, Washington, D.C., Box 15, General Correspondence, Hopkins to Scott, December 22, 1914.

152 Ibid., Hopkins to Scott, December 21, 1914.

153 Hugh Lenox Scott, *Some Memories of a Soldier*, p. 502.

154 Papers of Hugh Lenox Scott, Library of Congress, Washington, D.C., Box 15, General Correspondence, Hopkins to Scott, December 22, 1914.

155 Ibid.

156 Ibid., F. Viscanino to Scott, December 21, 1914.

157 Ibid., Hopkins to Scott, December 22, 1914.

158 Ibid., Scott to Garrison, December 23, 1914.

159 Ibid., Scott to Garrison, December 24, 1914.

160 Mumme, "The Battle of Naco," p. 182.

161 Papers of Hugh Lenox Scott, Library of Congress, Washington, D.C., Box 15, General Correspondence, Scott to Secwar, December 24, 1914.

162 Ibid., Scott to Secwar, December 25, 1914.

163 *The El Paso Herald*, December 26, 1914, "Maytorena asks Instructions."

164 Papers of Hugh Lenox Scott, Library of Congress, Washington, D.C., Box 15, General Correspondence, Scott to Secwar, December 26, 1914.

165 *The El Paso Herald*, December 26, 1914, "Maytorena asks Instructions."

166 *The New York Times*, November 25, 1914, "Zapata Hordes in Mexico City." Throughout the revolution, the fear of Indian warriors from Morelos ransacking the capital was represented in numerous reports and caricatures in the foreign press of Mexico City.

167 *The Boston Evening Transcript*, January 15, 1915, "Protest to Carranza."

168 Teitelbaum, *Woodrow Wilson and the Mexican Revolution*, p. 220. He refers to H. C. Cummins. H. Cunard Cummins had been the consul at Torreón and moved to the embassy in Mexico City in the summer of 1914.

169 See for example Silvestre Terrazas Papers, University of California at Berkeley,

Bancroft Library, M-B-18 Part 1, box 40, "Lista de los enemigos del pueblo," undated.

170   *The New York Times*, December 29, 1914, "Iturbide a Fugitive."

171   *The El Paso Herald*, December 26, 1914, "Iturbide still in Mexico City."

172   *The El Paso Herald*, December 26, 1914, "Says U.S. Consul Accepted Bribe."

173   As quoted in Teitelbaum, *Woodrow Wilson and the Mexican Revolution*, p. 220.

174   Teitelbaum, *Woodrow Wilson and the Mexican Revolution*, p. 221.

175   Ibid., p. 223.

176   *The Boston Evening Transcript*, December 28, 1914, "Canova bars out Mexicans."

177   Silvestre Terrazas Papers, University of California at Berkley, Bancroft Library, M-B-18, Part 1, Box 40, Silvestre Terrazas to Leon Canova, December 25, 1914.

178   *The Boston Evening Transcript*, January 15, 1915, "Protest to Carranza."

179   Ibid.

180   McLynn, Frank, *Villa and Zapata: A History of the Mexican Revolution*, Basic Books, New York, NY, 2000, p. 229. Also Teitelbaum, *Woodrow Wilson and the Mexican Revolution*, pp. 162-163. While many rumors circulated about Carothers, it seems more likely that he disagreed with Secretary Bryan on policy issues. It is significant to note that General Scott specifically asked Carothers to stay with Villa in the negotiation surrounding the siege of Naco. Scott had serious and well-documented disagreements with Bryan.

181   Papers of Hugh Lenox Scott, Library of Congress, Washington, D.C., Box 15, General Correspondence, Breckenridge to Scott, December 27, 1914.

182   Ibid.

183   Ibid., John A. Harper to Carothers, January 3, 1915.

184   Ibid., Scott to Secwar, January 1, 1915.

185   Scott, *Some Memories of a Soldier*, p. 512.

186   Ibid.

187   Papers of Hugh Lenox Scott, Library of Congress, Washington, D.C., Box 15, General Correspondence, Scott to Secwar, January 1, 1915.

188   Ibid., Sommerfeld to Villa, December 31, 1914, translated from Spanish by the author.

189   Ibid., Villa to Sommerfeld, December 31, 1914.

190   Ibid., Scott to Secretary of War, January 1, 1915.

191   United States Senate, *Investigation of Mexican Affairs*, Government Printing Office, Washington D.C., 1919, p. 823.

192   Papers of Hugh Lenox Scott, Library of Congress, Washington, D.C., Box 15, General Correspondence, Breckenridge to Scott, January 2, 1915.

193   Ibid., Scott to Sommerfeld, January 2, 1915.

194   *The New York Times*, January 9, 1914, "Villa and Scott meet in El Paso."

195   Ibid.

196   Papers of Hugh Lenox Scott, Library of Congress, Washington, D.C., Box 15, General Correspondence, Garrison to Scott, January 6, 1915.

197   Scott, *Some Memories of a Soldier*, p. 510.

198   Photo courtesy El Paso Public Library, Aultman Collection.

199   *The New York Sun*, January 10, 1915, "Scott and Villa Fix up a Neutral Border Zone."

200   *The New York Times*, December 4, 1914, "Villa leads March to National Palace."

201   Scott, *Some Memories of a Soldier*, p. 502.

202   Papers of Hugh Lenox Scott, Library of Congress, Washington, D.C., Box 15, General Correspondence, Sommerfeld to Scott, December 23, 1915.

203   See von Feilitzsch, *In Plain Sight*, Chapter 21.

204   Ibid.

205   Eckardt to Bethmann Hollweg, October 12, 1915, as quoted in Katz, Friedrich, *The Secret War in Mexico: Europe, the United States, and the Mexican Revolution*, The University of Chicago Press, Chicago, IL, 1981, p. 389.

206   *The World's Work*, Volume 36, May to October 1918, Doubleday, Page and Company, New York, NY, 1918, "German Intrigue in Mexico," by George MacAdam, pp. 495-500.

207   NA RG 242, Captured German Documents, T141, Roll 20, von Eckardt to Foreign Office, July 30, 1915.

208   As quoted in Doerries, Reinhard R., *Imperial Challenge: Ambassador Count Bernstorff and German-American Relations, 1908-1917*, University of North Carolina Press, Chapel Hill, NC, 1989, p.167.

209   As quoted in Katz, *The Secret War in Mexico*, p. 343.

210   NA RG 242, T141, Captured German Documents, Roll 19, von Papen to General Staff, March 17, 1915.

211   Ibid.

212   NA RG 59 Department of State, Passport #4875, issued in Berlin, February 6, 1915. Also NA RG 59 Department of State, Passport #3138, issued in Berne, February 20, 1915. Passports, at the time, were issued for a specific travel location. Meloy's travel plans obviously changed abruptly on February 6, 1915, because he went to the American Embassy and asked for an emergency paper to travel to Switzerland. Another emergency passport issued on February 20, 1915, allowed Meloy to visit more European countries. It mentioned that the "merchant" desired "to return to the U.S. via France, England, or Italy or Holland." The American consul in Berne hand wrote on the document, "good for six weeks." He left from Liverpool, Great Britain on March 17 and arrived back in New York on the 28th of the month.

213   NA RG 59 Department of State, file 341.112 M49/17, Walter Hines Page to Robert Lansing, September 10, 1915. No documentation of a direct link exist but the timing of Meloy's first trip coincided with the foundation of the "Mexican Peace Assembly," a group of influential Mexican exiles who were publicly appealing to all warring factions in Mexico to end the civil war. Meloy's plan of forming a coalition that could force an end to the strife seemed to be a logical extension of the "Peace Assembly." See Meyer, Michael C., *Huerta: A Political Portrait*, University of Nebraska Press, Lincoln, NE, 1972, p. 219.

214   NA RG 59 Department of State, file 341.112 M49/40 Statement of Juan Petit Hampson, August 21, 1915.

215   NA RG 59 Department of State, file 341.112 M49/17 Walter Hines Page to Robert Lansing, September 10, 1915, Statement of Andrew D. Meloy.

216   Ibid. He owned stock in the Mexico North Western and Mexico Western Railways.

217   Ibid.

218   See for example NA RG 85 Records of the Immigration and Naturalization Service, T715, Roll 2263, entry for arrivals from Havana, February 21, 1914.

219   *The New York Times*, September 8, 1915, "Lansing's Mexico Service."

220   NA RG 59 Department of State, file 341.112 M49/17 Walter Hines Page to Robert Lansing, September 10, 1915, Statement of Andrew D. Meloy.

221   Ibid.

222   Ibid.

223   NA RG 65 FBI Case Files, M1085, Roll 866, File 232-1266, Statement of John Roberts.

224   Ibid.

225   NA RG 65 FBI Case Files, M1085, Roll 856, File 232-101, President Wilson to all chiefs of factions in Mexico. Also, *The New York Times*, June 4, 1915, "Wilson will set limit for Mexico."

226   Katz, *The Life and Times of Pancho Villa*, p. 529. Also Lansing, Robert, *War Memoirs of Robert Lansing, Secretary of State*, The Bobbs-Merrill Company, New York, NY, 1935, p. 308.

227   Katz, *Life and Times of Pancho Villa*, pp. 506-507.

228   NA RG 59 Department of State, file 341.112 M49, Statement of Andrew D. Meloy, London, August 23, 1915.

229   Ibid.

230   NA RG 59 Department of State, file 812.00/15286½, Woodrow Wilson to Robert Lansing, June 18, 1915.

231   *The New York Times*, August 4, 1915, "Says Germany Used Huerta Against Us."

232   NA RG 59 Department of State, file 341.112 M49, Statement of Andrew D. Meloy, London, August 23, 1915.

233   NA RG 59 Department of State, file 341.112 M49/17, Counselor Warren to Leon Canova, September 15, 1915.

234   NA RG 65 Albert Papers, Box 13, Boy-Ed to Albert, July 21, 1915.

235   NA RG 59 Department of State, file 341.112 M49/17, Walter Hines Page to Robert Lansing, September 10, 1915.

236   NA RG 165 Military Intelligence Division, file 9140-878/129, Memorandum, March 19, 1918.

237   NA RG 59 Department of State, File 341.112 M49/17, Walter Hines Page to Robert Lansing, September 10, 1915.

238   *The New York Times*, April 11, 1915, "Villa Men Want Huerta Barred." Also *The New York Tribune*, April 1, 1915, "Huerta on Way for New Revolt."

239   *The New York Tribune*, April 13, 1915, "Exiled Dictator Silent on Mexican Affairs."

240   *The New York Times* and other papers reported when Huerta left Spain. See *The New York Times*, April 1, 1915, "Gen. Huerta on Ship Bound to West Indies."

241   Ibid., May 6, 1915, "Huerta Will Make Future Home Here."

242   *New York Tribune*, May 6, 1915, "Huerta for Long Island."

243   Library of Congress, Photographs and Prints Division, LC-USZ62-97991, copyright expired.

244   *The New York Times*, May 6, 1915, "Huerta Will Make Future Home Here."

245   NA RG 59 Department of State, file 351.112M49/46, Assistant Attorney General Warren to Secretary of State Lansing, September 15, 1915. Reference is made to a letter Rintelen wrote to Charles Douglas, in which he claims he "has been in Orozco's confidence."

246   NA RG 65 FBI Case Files, M1085, Roll 864, Cantrell to Chief, September 30, 1915.

247   Ibid.

248   Ann Lozano, "Seminary of St. Philip for Mexican students." Handbook of Texas Online (http://www.tshaonline.org/handbook/online/articles/iws01), accessed October 25, 2013. Published by the Texas State Historical Association.

249   See von Feilitzsch, *In Plain Sight*, chapter 13, "The Sommerfeld Organization."

250   NA RG 65, FBI Case Files, M1085, Roll 859, File 232-162, Beckham to Chief, May 6, 1915. Sommerfeld still controlled his former employees Powell Roberts, Hector Ramos, Sam Dreben, and Emil Holmdahl who all were providing information on the conspirators to the American government.

251   NA RG 65, FBI Case Files, M1085, Roll 859, File 232-162, Beckham to Chief, May 3, 1915.

252   See von Feilitzsch, *In Plain Sight*, chapter 13. Also Meyer, *Mexican Rebel*, p. 82.

253   NA RG 65 Roll 859 file 232-162, Beckham to Chief, April 24, 1915, re. Científico Movement.

254   NA RG 65 FBI Case Files, M1049, Roll 859, file 232-162, Beckham to Chief, May 12, 1915.

255   NA RG 65 FBI Case Files, M1049, Roll 858, file 232-162, Stone to Chief, August 14, 1915.

256   For example NA RG 65 FBI Case Files, M1049, Roll 859, file 232-164, Hopkins to Bielaski, July 13, 1915.

257   *The New York Times*, May 3, 1915, "Gen. Huerta's Aid to Open Bank Here."

258   NA RG 65 FBI Case Files, M1085, Roll 859, File 232-162, Sec. War to Attorney General, May 6, 1915.

259   NA RG 165 Military Intelligence Division, File 5761-1091/6, Sommerfeld to Garrison, April 23, 1915.

260   NA RG 85 Immigration and Naturalization, T715, Roll 2417.

261   *The New York Times*, June 24, 1915, "Villa Agent at Capital."

262   Harris, Charles H., III and Sadler, Louis R., *The Secret War in El Paso: Mexican Revolutionary Intrigue, 1906-1920*, University of New Mexico Press, Albuquerque, NM, 2009, p. 197.

263   Ibid.

264   See for example NA RG 65, FBI Case Files, M1085, BI reports dated May 2, 1915, May 6, 1915, May 27, 1915, June 7, 1915. Also NA RG 59 Department of State, File 812.113/3674, Cobb to Secretary of State, June 4, 1915, "Statement of arms and ammunition exported from El Paso, April 12 to June 4, 1915 … Villa has consumed half of above."

265   Boy-Ed, Karl, *Verschwoerer?* Verlag August Scherl GmbH, Berlin, Germany, 1920, p. 83.

266   Ibid.

267   *The Washington Times*, May 2, 1915, "Masons Expel Huerta, Felix Díaz, and Others."

268   Ibid.

269   NA RG 59 State Department, File 341.112M49/40, Page to Lansing, April 3, 1916.

270   NA RG 65 FBI Case Files, M1049, Roll 859, file 232, BI reports from May 20 to May 24.

271   NA RG 65 FBI Case Files, M1049, Roll 859, file 232-162, Cantrell to Chief, July 3, 1915.

272   NA RG 59 Department of State, File 812.113/3644, 3645, 3646, 3647.

273   Ibid.

274   NA RG 65 FBI Case Files, M1049, Roll 859, file 232-162, Agent Beckham to BI Chief, May 12, 1915.

275   Michael C. Meyer, "The Mexican-German Conspiracy of 1915," *The Americas*, Volume XXIII, July, 1966, No. 1, p. 86. Also Chalkley, John F., *Zach Lamar Cobb: El Paso Collector of Customs and Intelligence During the Mexican Revolution, 1913-1918*, Southwestern Studies, No. 103, University of Texas Press, El Paso, TX, 1998, p. 30.

276   Ibid., p. 31.

277   *The New York Tribune*, June 27, 1915, "New Huerta Plot Afoot on Border."

278   For a more detailed discussion, see Meyer, *Huerta*, pp. 226-227.

279   Harris and Sadler, *The Secret War in El Paso*, pp. 203-209.

280   Ibid., p. 510.

281   Ibid., p. 509.

282   Ibid., p. 510.

283   NA RG 65 FBI Case Files, M1085, Roll 858, File 232-162, Agent Benham to Department, November 6, 1915.

284   See Jones and Hollister, Landau, Tuchman, Katz, Meyer, Harris and Sadler.

285   *The New York Times*, August 4, 1915, "Says Germany Used Huerta Against Us."

286   Ibid.

287   Tuchman, Barbara, *The Zimmermann Telegram*, Macmillan Company, New York, NY, 1958, p. 76.

288   Rintelen's supposed trip to Spain before he came to the United States is also not factual. Rintelen was in Belgium before he came to the U.S. There are no reports that he went to Spain in 1915 nor that he had any meetings with Huerta in Europe. See Bundesarchiv für Militärgeschichte, RM 3, 7934, War financing.

289   NA RG 59 State Department, File 341.112M49/40, Page to Lansing, April 3, 1916.

290   Ibid., File 341.112M49/15.

291   NA RG 65 FBI Case Files, M1085, file 8000-174, Testimony of George Plochmann, undated (October 1915).

292   *The Washington Times*, July 2, 1915, "Consignment of Arms Intended for Batavia are Confiscated in Brooklyn." Also *The New York Sun*, July 2, 1915, "Shipment of Arms Reported Seized."

293   NA RG 65 FBI Case Files, M1085, Roll 855, File 232-37, W. Stokes Kirk to Howard P. Wright, January 6, 1917.

294   NA RG 131 Alien Property Custodian, Entry 199, Box 38, File 902, Winchester Repeating Arms Co.

295   NA RG 76 Mixed Claims Commission, Box 13, Memorandum, August 3, 1938. "July 16, 1915, Rintelen paid Meloy $10,000 through Stallforth."

296   NA RG 65 FBI Case Files, M1049, Roll 859, file 232-162, Agent Pinckney to BI Chief, July 7, 1915, list of Huerta recruits with sums paid to each of them.

297   Ibid., Agent Barnes to BI Chief, August 14, 1915.

298   Ibid., Agent Cantrell to BI Chief, July 3, 1915

299   As quoted in Katz, *The Secret War in Mexico*, p. 248.

300   NA RG 65 FBI Case Files, M1049, Roll 859, file 232-162, Statement of José Vasconcelos, June 30, 1915.

301   Ibid., Agent Cantrell to BI Chief, July 3, 1915.

302   Katz, *Life and Times of Pancho Villa*, p. 506.

303   *The New York Times*, September 8, 1915, "Lansing's Mexico Service." The article quotes a piece in *El Mexicano* alleging Lansing's legal services for Huerta.

304   See for example NA RG 60 Department of Justice, File 9-16-12-5305, Sommerfeld to Boy-Ed, November 11, 1914; Boy-Ed to Count Bernstorff, December 18, 1914; Sommerfeld to Boy-Ed, April 28, 1915; Sommerfeld to Boy-Ed, May 4, 1915.

305   NA RG 242 Captured German Documents, Roll 377, document 735, Bernhard Dernburg to Admiral Henning von Holtzendorff, May 10, 1915.

306   The response from Foreign Secretary von Jagow is referred to in Katz, *Secret War in Mexico*, p. 334.

307   NA RG 65 FBI Case Files, M1049, File 8000-174, William Offley to Chief Bielaski, June 28, 1915.

308   Willis tried everything in his power to get Sommerfeld released in 1918, such as getting General Hugh Lenox Scott to write a letter on his friend's behalf, as well as writing himself to the Justice Department.

309   Ibid.

310   *The New York Sun*, May 26, 1915, "Even British Ships Broke Own Blockade."

311   *The New York Times*, May 3, 1917, "Rintelen's Agent Warned Tumulty."

312   Ibid.

313   NA RG 65 FBI Case Files, M1085, File 8000-174, William Offley to Chief Bielaski, September 29, 1915.

314   Ibid.

315   Rintelen von Kleist, Franz, *The Dark Invader: Wartime Reminiscences of a German Naval Intelligence Officer*, with an introduction by Reinhard R. Doerries, Frank Cass Publishers, London, 1997, p. xxii.

316   NA RG 65 FBI Case Files, M1085, File 8000-3089, Captured document from Frederico Stallforth's office, report entry for August 13, 1915.

317   NA RG 59 Department of State, File 341.112, M49/35, Count Bernstorff to Robert Lansing, December 15, 1915. Also Ibid., 341.112M49/60, Robert Lansing to Woodrow Wilson, May 23, 1918.

318   *The Federal Reporter*, Volume 274, West Publishing Company, St. Paul, Minnesota, 1921, p. 172. Also National Archives, Southeast Region, Index to Atlanta Federal Penitentiary, Inmate Case Files, 1902-1921, File 5780, "Conspiracy and Delivery of Bomb Onboard Ship."

319   Captain von Rintelen, *The Dark Invader: War Reminiscences of a German Naval Intelligence Officer*, Lovat Dickson Limited, London, 1933.

320   Captain von Rintelen, *The Return of the Dark Invader*, Peter Davis, London, 1935.

321   See for example *The Milwaukee Journal*, November 5, 1943, "A True Story of First World War Spies That Outdoes Most Imaginative Fiction." Also *Delaware County Daily Times*, July 30. 1966, "50 Years Ago U.S. Felt Part of War." "In January 1940, von Rintelen declared he conceived the idea of the Black Tom explosion and while he was not in the United States at the time, he was certain it was carried out by his aides. 'I wanted to destroy the source of supply, but I issued orders that it be done without killing anyone,' Von Rintelen said. 'My idea was that I could get the watchmen drunk and the rest would be easy.'" See also NA RG 65 FBI Case Files, M1085, File 8000-174, Statement of J.C. Hammond, July 16, 1915.

322   See for example NA RG 65 FBI Case Files, M1085, File 8000-174, Agent Garbering to Chief Bielaski, September 27, 1916.

323   Ibid., Statement of J.C. Hammond, July 16, 1915. Also Ibid., Offley to Chief, October 15, 1915.

324   Ibid, Statement of Paul Hilken.

325   Bundesarchiv für Militärgeschichte, Freiburg, RM 3, File 7934, Rintelen to von Tirpitz, November 9, 1914.

326   NA RG 65 FBI Case Files, M1085, File 8000-174, Statement of J. C. Hammond, July 16, 1915.

327   NA RG 87 U.S. Secret Service, A1, entry 65, "Synopsis of Franz von Rintelen mission."

328   NA RG 65 FBI Case Files, M1085, File 8000-174, Statement of George Plochmann, undated (October 1915).

329   NA RG 65 Albert Papers, Box 23, diary entry for April 10, 1915.

330   NA RG 65 FBI Case Files, M1085, File 8000-174, L. M. Cantrell to Chief Bielaski, July 20, 1915.

331   U.S. Senate, *Investigation of Mexican Affairs*, Government Printing Office, Washington D.C., 1920, page 3339.

332   NA RG 242 Captured German Documents, T141, Roll 19, von Papen to War Department, March 7, 1915.

333   NA RG 242 Captured German Documents, T141, Roll 19, Count Bernstorff to von Bethmann Hollweg, February 16, 1915.

334   Ibid.

335   Ibid., Roll 20, von Eckardt to von Bethmann Hollweg, July 30, 1915, von Eckardt mentions that he reported from Mexico City on February 14.

336   Ibid.

337   Ibid., Roll 19, von Papen to Stellvertreter Generalstab der Armee, Abt. IIb, Nr. Pol. 1142, March 17, 1915.

338   Ibid., Roll 377, Document 735, Dernburg to Admiral Henning von Holtzendorff, Mai 10, 1915.

339   Ibid.

340   As quoted in Katz, *Secret War in Mexico*, p. 334.

341   BAMG, Freiburg, RM 2, file 2000.

342   Bauer, Hermann, *Als Führer der U-Boote im Weltkriege: Der Eintritt der U-Boot-Waffe in die Seekriegsführung*, Koehler und Amelang, Leipzig, 1941, p. 244.

343   Ibid., p. 300 and p. 315.

344   Ibid., p. 331.

345   NA RG 65 Albert Papers, Box 9, Diary of Karl Alexander Fuehr, entry for June 11 and June 12, 1915. Dernburg and his wife left on June 12, 1915 on the SS *Bergensfjord* of the Norwegian America Line to Bergen, Norway after a large reception in the German Club in New York the evening before.

346   NA RG 65 FBI Case Files M1085, File 8000-3089, captured report from the offices of Stallforth in 1917, entry for August 13, 1915.

347   See von Feilitzsch, *In Plain Sight*, pp. 124-127.

348   Ibid., p. 140.

349   Ibid., pp. 147-148.

350   Ibid., pp. 138-139.

351   Ibid. pp. 170-191.

352   See Michael C. Meyer, *Mexican Rebel: Pascual Orozco and the Mexican Revolution, 1910 - 1915*, University of Nebraska Press, Lincoln, NE, 1967, p. 82. Meyer confirms that Orozco largely lost because of shortages of arms and supplies, which the Sommerfeld organization had choked off. For more details, see von Feilitzsch, *In Plain Sight*, chapter 13.

353   NA RG 131 Alien Property Custodian, Entry 199, Box 28, File 654, Statement of Frederick A. Borgemeister. The bonds had been issued by the German government, not by the Reichsbank. They were, therefore, not treasury bonds, but unsecured German government bonds with a 5% interest valid for 9 months.

354   Ibid.

355   Unites States Senate, *Brewing and Liquor Interests and German Propaganda*, Subcommittee of the Committee of the Judiciary, Volume 2, Government Printing Office, Washington D.C., 1919, p. 2166.

356   NA RG 165 Military Intelligence Division, file 9140-1754, document 33.

357   Ibid., document 34.

358   NA RG 65 Albert Papers, Box 24, Amsinck and Company ledger.

359   Ibid., Box 34.

360   U.S. Senate, *Brewing and Liquor Interests and German Propaganda*, p. 2168.

361   NA RG 65 Albert Papers, Box 27, Albert to Merchant's Loan and Trust Company and Box 34, Cashier of St. Louis Union Bank to Albert, May 6, 1915. Albert deposited $100,000 with the Mississippi Valley Trust Company on April 1. He also deposited $150,000 at the Merchant's Loan and Trust Company in Chicago on April 5, unknown amounts with the Continental and Commercial Bank of Chicago, and the Wisconsin National Bank around the same time. He withdrew $50,000 from the Mississippi Valley Trust Company on April 12. He moved the other $50,000 to another bank, the St. Louis Union Bank, on April 29. From there and the Merchant's Loan and Trust bank in Chicago he withdrew $30,000 each in the first week of May and transferred the money to the Equitable Trust Company in New York. Albert also transferred 15,000 to the Equitable Trust from Milwaukee and Cleveland respectively. $40,000 transferred from the Continental and Commercial Bank in Chicago on May 28. Another $15,000 and $20,000 were transferred from Mississippi Valley Trust but without a record of destination.

362   NA RG 65 Albert Papers, Box 27 and 34, accounts of St. Louis Union Bank, Accounts of Mississippi Valley Trust Company, and Merchant's Loan and Trust Company as compared with Sommerfeld transactions on the Mississippi Valley Trust Company in U.S. Senate, Brewing and Liquor Interests and German Propaganda, p. 2168.

363   NA RG 65 Albert papers, Box 3, Folder 16. The account is marked K.M. account, short for *Kriegsministerium*.

364   See for example Lázaro De La Garza Collection, Benson Library, University of Texas at Austin, Box 9, Folder K, Carranza to De La Garza, September 26, 1917 returning ownership of De La Garza's house.

365   Katz, *Life and Times of Pancho Villa*, p. 487.

366   Lázaro De La Garza Collection, Benson Library, University of Texas at Austin, Box 2, Folder A, July, 1915.

367   Ibid., Box 1, Folder K, De La Garza to Villa, April 10, 1915.

368   Ibid., Box 9, Folder K, Entry July 7, 1915, "Sommerfeld telegrafía así: Tuve que parar desde hace tres días remesas de fábrica St. Louis y qui [sic] está también remesa de Winchester que no puedo pagar..." Also Ibid., Folder A, De La Garza's accounts show payments to Peters Cartridge Company in the end of April of $27,500 on a

contract for 500,000 7 mm cartridges for $55/thousand.

369   NA RG 65 FBI Case Files, M1085, Roll 857, file 232-134, Agent Phillips to Chief, February 14, 1915.

370   Ibid.

371   Ibid., File 8000-3089, Statement concerning several miscellaneous facts and persons, undated, (1918).

372   Stallforth Papers, Private collection, Guestbook entry July 25, 1915.

373   Ibid.

374   Lázaro De La Garza Collection, Benson Library, University of Texas at Austin, Box 5, Folder I, Check from De La Garza to Esteva Ruiz & Co., for $28,500, dated May 3, 1915.

375   NA RG 65 FBI Case Files, M1085, Roll 862, File 232-311, Franklin W. Olin to Felix A. Sommerfeld, February 19, 1915.

376   Lázaro De La Garza Collection, Benson Library, University of Texas at Austin, Box 9, Folder A, División Del Norte en cuenta con L. de la Garza, January 10 to October 11, 1915.

377   Ibid., Box 5, Folder E, Peters Cartridge Co. to De La Garza June 17, 1915. The documented Esteva order of 500,000 cartridges and 500 rifles seems to have been the same low price: Rifles cost around $20 to $25 a piece, leaving the 500 cases of cartridges to cost $35/case. Clearly, this was the price only Sommerfeld received at the time.

378   United States Senate, *Brewing and Liquor Interests and German Propaganda*, Subcommittee of the Committee of the Judiciary, Volume 2, Government Printing Office, Washington D.C., 1919, p. 2168.

379   Lázaro De La Garza Collection, Benson Library, University of Texas at Austin, Box 7, Folder C, Sommerfeld to F. W. Olin, May 17, 1915.

380   Ibid., Box 9, Folder A, División Del Norte en cuenta con L. de la Garza, January 10 to October 11, 1915.

381   Ibid., Box 2 Folder B, Cuenta de Cartuchos, 1915. The accounts contain two entries, $52,000 transferred to De La Garza on September 24, 1915 and $17, 431.47 transferred on October 27, both from James Manoil aka Carl Heynen.

382   Ibid., Box 5, Folder I, Check to the credit of Peters Cartridge Company, May 26, 1915.

383   Western Cartridge in fact bought Winchester in 1931.

384   Twenty-seven million times a difference of $15 per thousand equals $405,000, $8.5 million in today's value.

385   NA RG 65 Albert Papers, Box 5, Memorandum of Carl Heynen, September 30, 1915.

386   Lázaro De La Garza Collection, Benson Library, University of Texas at Austin, Box 1, Folder K, De La Garza to Villa quoting Sommerfeld, May 27, 1915.

387   NA RG 65 FBI Case Files, M1085, File 232-311, Shipping manifest of Western Cartridge Company for 1915.

388   Ibid.

389   NA RG 65 Albert Papers, Box 45, Credit memo dated June 18, 1915.

390   NA RG 65 FBI Case Files, M1085, File 232-311, Shipping manifest of Western Cartridge Company for 1915.

391   NA RG 65 Albert Papers, Box 45, Credit memo dated June 18, 1915.

392   Lázaro De La Garza Collection, Benson Library, University of Texas at Austin, Box 5, Folder E, Western Cartridge Company to De La Garza, September 16, 1915.

393   Ibid., Folder A, De La Garza to Emilio Madero, August 27, 1915.

394   Ibid., Box 2, Folder B, for founding of his own company, Memo dated July 1915 (no specific day). For offer to Carranza, ibid., De La Garza to José Farías, August 18, 1915.

395   Ibid., Box 5, Folder A, De La Garza to Emilio Madero, August 27, 1915.

396   NA RG 165 Military Intelligence Division, File 10541-272-16. Also *New York City Directory*, 1916, p. 2135.

397   NA RG 165 Military Intelligence Division, File 10541-272-17.

398   NA RG 85 Immigration and Naturalization, M237, T715, Roll 2392.

399   NA RG 165 Military Intelligence Division, File 10541-272-31, George P. Kennedy to Colonel Ralph H. Van Deman, May 20, 1918.

400   Lázaro De La Garza Collection, Benson Library, University of Texas at Austin, Box 5, Folder E, De La Garza to Western Cartridge Company, September 16, 1915.

401   NA RG 65 Albert Papers, Box 45, Credit memo dated August 18, 1915.

402   NA RG 60 Department of Justice, File 9-16-12-5305, Statement of Felix A. Sommerfeld, June 21, 1918.

403   NA RG 65 Albert Papers, Box 45, Credit memo dated August 18, 1915.

404   NA RG 65 FBI Case Files, M1085, File 232-37, Agent Webster to Chief Bielaski, September 17, 1915.

405   Ibid, September 18, 1915.

406   Lázaro De La Garza Collection, Benson Library, University of Texas at Austin, Box 5, Folder H, First National Bank of Los Angeles to Guaranty Trust Company, October 13, 1915.

407   Ibid., Box 2, Folder G, S. C. De La Garza to Lázaro De La Garza, September 7, 1915.

408   Ibid., Box 2, Folder G, S. C. De La Garza to Lázaro De La Garza, October 4, 1915.

409   *The New York Sun*, September 25, 1915, "Gen. Angeles and 15 Chiefs Desert Villa."

410   Lázaro De La Garza Collection, Benson Library, University of Texas at Austin, Box 5, Folder B, Standard Stoker Company to De La Garza, October 14, 1915.

411   Carranza eventually released De La Garza's property. See Lázaro De La Garza Collection, Benson Library, University of Texas at Austin, Box 9, Folder K, Venustiano Carranza to Lázaro De La Garza, September 26, 1917.

412   Lázaro De La Garza Collection, Benson Library, University of Texas at Austin, Box 9, Folder H. Clipping of article in L.A. Times, December 7, 1918. De La Garza's mansion allegedly cost over $100,000 ($2 million in today's value)

413   *The Los Angeles Evening Herald*, June 17, 1916, "$75,000 Suit over Cartridge Contract."

414   Lázaro De La Garza Collection, Benson Library, University of Texas at Austin, Box 9, Folder K, newspaper clipping, February 15, 1920.

415   Ibid., Box 9, Folder K. Leon Canova to Lázaro De La Garza, February 21, 1917.

416   Ibid., newspaper clipping, February 15, 1920.

417   Ibid., Box 7, Folder F, Permission to carry a concealed firearm, Mexico City, September 12, 1933.

418   For example: Lázaro De La Garza Collection, Benson Library, University of Texas

at Austin, Box 9, Folder C, newspaper clipping headed, "El Hombre que Robó a Pancho Villa $10.000,000.00 de dólares."

419   According to the Garza family of Torreón, Lázaro De La Garza moved back to Mexico in the early 1930s after his daughter had graduated from UCLA.

420   NA RG 165 Military Intelligence Division, File 10541-272-17, May 7, 1918.

421   James Manoil is well known as a business partner in the Manoil Manufacturing Company for making diecast figures and toy soldiers. Jack died on September 1, 1955.

422   The price difference between the $35 from the factory and $48.50 to the French amounted to roughly $75,000. De La Garza also received approximately $36,000 in commissions on the shipments to Carranza.

423   NA RG 59 Department of State, file 812.00/15412 ½, Woodrow Wilson to Robert Lansing, July 8, 1915.

424   Hans Tauscher sent one shipment of weapons to Guatemala in the summer of 1915. It is not documented but possible that this shipment supported Díaz's military venture. There are no other indications that Díaz had any interaction with German officials in the summer of 1915.

425   NA RG 59 Department of State, file 812.00/1585 ½, Wilson to Lansing, June 17, 1915.

426   Scott, *Some Memories of a Soldier*, p. 497.

427   Wilson kept mentioning the possibility of recognizing Carranza. See NA RG 59 Department of State, file 812.00, Memos Woodrow Wilson to W. J. Bryan and R. Lansing between June 2 and October 9, 1915.

428   Lansing Papers Volume 2, Wilson to Lansing June 18, 1915, p. 536

429   *The New York Times*, July 31, 1915, "Mexico's Nine Heads in Two Years."

430   NA RG 59 Department of State, file 812.00/15411 ½, Woodrow Wilson to Robert Lansing, July 7, 1915.

431   NA RG 60 Department of Justice, file 9-16-12-5305, Statement of Felix A. Sommerfeld, June 24, 1918.

432   Katz, *Life and Times of Pancho Villa*, p. 508.

433   Ibid., p. 509.

434   Scott, *Some Memories of a Soldier*, pp. 504-505.

435   Ibid., p. 505.

436   Ibid., p. 506.

437   NA RG 59 Department of State, file 812.00/15410 ½ a, Lansing to Wilson, July 5, 1915.

438   Ibid., August 6, 1915.

439   *The New York Times*, August 2, 1915, "Wilson Peace Plan Ready for Mexico."

440   *The New York Times*, August 8, 1915, "Vasquez Tagle, Mexico's Hope."

441   Ibid.

442   NA RG 59 Department of State, file 812.00/15753 ½, Wilson to Lansing, August 11, 1915.

443   See a discussion of Wilson's thought process in Link, Arthur S., Wilson: The Struggle for Neutrality, 1914-1915, Princeton University Press, Princeton, NJ, 1960, p. 491.

444   NA RG 59 Department of State, file 812.00/15412 ½, Wilson to Lansing, July 8, 1915.

445   Ibid.

446   Scott, *Some Memories of a Soldier*, p. 507.

447   NA RG 65 FBI Case Files, M1085, Roll 858, File 232-162, Agent Benham to Department, November 6, 1915.

448   Ibid., Hopkins to E. Vásquez Gómez, June 7, 1915.

449   The rebellion started in Ciudad Juarez and turned into the "Orozco Uprising" which almost caused the collapse of the Madero Administration and devastated Northern Mexico in heavy fighting that lasted until the fall of 1912.

450   Scott, *Some Memories of a Soldier*, pp. 513-514.

451   Cronlund Anderson, Mark, *Pancho Villa's Revolution by Headlines*, University of Oklahoma Press, Norman, OK, 2000, p. 42.

452   *The New York Times*, August 2, 1915, "Villa Expels Americans."

453   As quoted in Link, *Wilson: The Struggle for Neutrality*, p. 478.

454   Ibid.

455   The New York Times, August 30, 1915, "Scott Back with Mexico Report."

456   Scott, Some Memories of a Soldier, pp. 514-515.

457   NA RG 59 Department of State, file 812.00/15751 ½, Wilson to Lansing, August 7, 1915.

458   Lázaro De La Garza Collection, Benson Library, University of Texas at Austin, Box 2, Folder A, Farias to De La Garza, August 19, 1915.

459   The New York Times, August 30, 1915, "Zapata and Aids Accept Peace Plan." Also Link, Wilson: The Struggle for Neutrality, p. 630.

460   Lawrence supported Sommerfeld's release form detention in 1919. In a long and fascinating journalistic career Lawrence became the editor-in-chief of US News and World Report.

461   Link, Wilson: The Struggle for Neutrality, pp. 631-632.

462   The New York Times, September 1, 1915, "Carranza Refuses Any Outside Help."

463   The Century Magazine, September 1915, pp. 737-744, "The Inevitable Trend in Mexico." Lawrence became the founder and editor of U.S. News and World Report. He had spent years at the Mexican border while the Revolution raged. He was personally acquainted with Sommerfeld and actively tried to get him released from internment in 1919.

464   For example The New York Times, July 30, 1915, "Warn Mexicans to Let Food In."

465   For the complete plan and a thorough analysis see Harris, Charles H., III and Sadler, Louis R., The Plan de San Diego: Tejano Rebellion, Mexican Intrigues, University of Nebraska Press, Lincoln, NE, 2013. Also by the same authors, The Texas Rangers and the Mexican Revolution: The Bloodiest Decade, 1910-1920, University of New Mexico Press, Albuquerque, NM, 2004, pp. 210-211. Harris and Sadler make the point that so far no one has been able to prove whether or not the document indeed was drafted in San Diego, TX.

466   Harris and Sadler, The Plan de San Diego: Tejano Rebellion, Mexican Intrigues, pp. 1-4.

467   For an exhaustive and minutely researched account of the details and progression of violence as a result of the Plan see Harris and Sadler, The Plan de San Diego: Tejano Rebellion, Mexican Intrigues.

468   Historian Trinidad Gonzales traced a second separatist movement that succeeded the Plan de San Diego, called the revolución de Texas. This effort of Mexican-American minorities along the Mexican border to start a separatist movement turns

out to be part of the conspiracy of the *Plan de San Diego*.

469   As quoted in Katz, *The Life and Times of Pancho Villa*, p. 529. Also Haley, Edward P., *Revolution and Intervention: The Diplomacy of Taft and Wilson with Mexico, 1910-1917*, The MIT Press, Cambridge, MA, 1970, p. 184; and Tuchman, *The Zimmermann Telegram*, p. 86.

470   *Army History Journal*, Washington, D.C. No. 89 (Fall 2013), "Chasing Ghosts in Mexico," by Thomas Boghardt, pp. 10-11.

471   NA RG 65 Albert Papers, Box 26. On April 20, 1916, Albert received $1 million from Frederico Stallforth, "as a re-payment of the $1 Million given to Stallforth on April 5th." On April 24, 1916, Albert's "Reichsbank" (German Central Bank) account shows a debit of $94,921.87 for "Stallforth and Co., Inc. marked "M 500,000 [German Marks] were bought with the exchange rate of 75 15/16... " Two days later, $93,906.25 transferred to Stallforth, marked "M 500,000 for the exchange rate of 75 1/8..." Although Leon seemed to have seen earlier transactions by the German government, the transactions in April 1916 indicate that the German government indeed engaged in "heavy sales of German marks" in the spring of 1916.

472   Krumm-Heller, Arnold, *Für Freiheit und Recht: Meine Erlebnisse aus dem mexikanischen Bürgerkriege*, Otto Thiele Verlag, Halle, Germany, 1916, p. i.

473   *The El Paso Herald*, June 22, 1915, "Madero's Physician to Lecture on Revolution."

474   NA RG 242 Captured German Documents, T141, Roll 20, von Eckardt to von Bethmann Hollweg, May 5, 1916.

475   Cronland Anderson, *Pancho Villa's Revolution by the Headlines*, p. 105.

476   NA RG 242 Captured German Documents, T141, Roll 20, von Eckardt to von Bethmann Hollweg, May 5, 1916.

477   Ibid., p. 155.

478   NA RG 65 FBI Case Files, M1085, Roll 861, File 232-258, Carothers to Lansing, March 25, 1917.

479   NA RG 165 Military Intelligence Division, File 7140-5773/18, Assistant Chief, MID to Director, MID, March 24, 1920.

480   Scott to Garfield, September 10, 1915, as quoted in Link, *Wilson: The Struggle for Neutrality*, p. 633.

481   *The New York Times*, September 16, 1915, "Moves to Prevent Reprisals by Villa."

482   De Léon, Arnoldo, ed., *War Along the Border*, "The Mexican Revolution, Revolución de Texas and Matanza de 1915" by Trinidad Gonzales, Texas A&M, College

Station, Texas, 2012, p. 261.

483   The New York Times, September 6, 1915, "Kill Two Mexicans Across Rio Grande."

484   Harris and Sadler, The Texas Rangers and the Mexican Revolution, p. 296.

485   Ibid., p. 290.

486   Ibid., p. 297. Historian Gonzales disagrees that Carranza was the definite backer but agrees that "certainly Carranza wanted to end the attacks to facilitate official recognition." He argues without much detail that Carranza simply did not have the resources to do so until October.

487   For a detailed analysis refer to Harris and Sadler, The Plan de San Diego. Carranza wanted U.S. forces to leave Mexico. Instead, the Pershing Expedition garrisoned in Northern Chihuahua until troops finally pulled out in the beginning of 1917.

488   Katz, Life and Times of Pancho Villa, p. 519.

489   Ibid.

490   The New York Sun, September 25, 1915, "Gen. Angeles and 15 Chiefs Desert Villa."

491   The New York Times, October 6, 1915, "Lansing Hears Villa Side."

492   Ibid., October 9, 1915, "Villa sees Anarchy if Carranza Rules."

493   Ibid.

494   Link, Wilson: The Struggle for Neutrality, p. 639.

495   Ibid., p. 643.

496   Scott, Some Memories of a Soldier, p. 517.

497   De La Pedraja Tomán, René, Wars of Latin America, 1899-1941, McFarland and Company Inc., Jefferson, NC, 2006, p. 252.

498   Scott, Some Memories of a Soldier, p. 517.

499   Clendenen, The United States and Villa, pp. 203-205. It seems unlikely that, as Clendenen claimed, Wilson simply wanted to preserve the liberalism of the revolution and was influenced, in part, by the AFL endorsement of Carranza while becoming convinced by the anti-Villa propaganda portraying him as a tool of big business.

500   NA RG 165 Military Intelligence Division, File 5761-1091, Sommerfeld to Garrison, September 7, 1915.

501   Ibid.

502   Ibid., see for example Sommerfeld to Garrison, September 3, 1914, August 26, 1914, September 27, 1914. Also Garrison to Bryan, undated note (March 5, 1915).

503   Ibid., Sommerfeld to Garrison, April 23, 1915.

504   University of California, Los Angeles, Papers of Carey McWilliams, Box 1, Hugh Lenox Scott to Felix Sommerfeld, September 9, 1914. "The Secretary [Lane] would like you to have confidential inquiry made to trace Mr. Bierce. Anything you can do in this direction will be greatly appreciated by him and by the Secretary of War [Garrison]."

505   NA RG 65 FBI Case Files, M1085, Roll 856, File 232-101, Agent Pinckney to Department, November 2, 1915.

506   Ibid.

507   NA RG 59, Department of State, File 812.113, 3719.

508   The Federal Reporter, Volume 235, October - November 1916, West Publishing Company, St. Paul, MN, 1917, p. 611.

509   NA RG 60 Department of Justice, File 9-16-12-5305, Statement of F. A. Sommerfeld, June 22, 1918.

510   Cole, Carl H., "Douglas under Fire: An Account of Villa's Battle for Agua Prieta," www.cochisecountyhistory.org, viewed January 2014.

511   Clendenen, The United States and Villa, p. 209.

512   Ibid.

513   The New York Times, November 3, 1915, "Funston Asks Right to Cross Border."

514   As quoted in Katz, Life and Times of Pancho Villa, p. 526.

515   NA RG 165 Military Intelligence Division, File 5761-1091, Villa to Sommerfeld, September 27, 1914.

516   The Breckenridge News (Cloverport, KY), October 27, 1915, "Carranza Troops on American Soil."

517   El Paso Herald, October 30, 1915, "Without Food and in Poor Shape."

518   Cole, "Douglas under Fire.".

519   Ibid.

520   *El Paso Herald*, November 4, 1915, "Funston Tells of Seeing Villa."

521   *The Day Book*, November 2, 1915, "Nine American Wounded in Mexican Mix."

522   *El Paso Herald*, November 4, 1915, "Funston Tells of Seeing Villa."

523   *The New York Times*, November 3, 1915, "Funston Asks Right to Cross Border."

524   NA RG 65 FBI Case Files, M1085, Roll 856, File 232-101, Agent Pinckney to Department, November 2, 1915.

525   NA RG 59, Department of State, File 812.113, 3748.

526   *El Paso Herald*, November 3, 1915, "Silver Pay for Villa Soldiers."

527   Clendenen, *The United States and Villa*, p. 216.

528   Katz, *Life and Times of Pancho Villa*, p. 527.

529   Clendenen, *The United States and Pancho Villa*, p. 216.

530   Katz, *Life and Times of Pancho Villa*, p. 527.

531   Ibid., p. 528.

532   Katz, "Pancho Villa and the Attack on Columbus, New Mexico," *The American Historical Review*, Vol. 83, No. 1 (Feb., 1978), p. 110.

533   Katz, *Life and Times of Pancho Villa*, p. 529.

534   Ibid., p. 505.

535   Ibid., 508.

536   Katz, Friedrich, "Pancho Villa and the Attack on Columbus, New Mexico," *The American Historical Review*, Vol. 83, No. 1 (Feb., 1978), p. 127. Katz identified Keedy as a German agent but related him to Kurt Jahnke. The German Naval Intelligence was still headed by Karl Boy-Ed in the fall of 1915 (until his expulsion in December). Sommerfeld headed the Mexican missions for Boy-Ed and maintained control of the intervention mission into 1916.

537   As quoted in Katz, "Pancho Villa and the Attack on Columbus, New Mexico,", p. 114.

538   Ibid., p. 530.

539   *The New York Times*, October 31, 1915, "New Railways Boards." Also *The El Paso*

Herald, November 3, 1915, "Directors are Elected for National Railways."

540   See von Feilitzsch, *In Plain Sight*, p. 367.

541   Katz, "Pancho Villa and the Attack on Columbus, New Mexico," p. 117. Katz cautioned that Carranza would have released confiscated properties in any case. This is highly doubtful given the development of the new constitution for Mexico at the same time that set foreign property confiscation into law. In any case, the fact that Carranza moved on this issue exactly at the time Villa alleged the agreement to have been consummated is enough evidence to suppose a link.

542   *The New York Times*, July 30, 1916, "Currency Reform on Trial in Mexico."

543   *The El Paso Herald*, November 3, 1915, "Denies that U.S. Imposed Any Condition on Carranza."

544   NA RG 165 Military Intelligence Division, File 5761-1091/14, Sommerfeld to Garrison, November 12, 1915.

545   *The New York American*, November 12, 1915, "Whiskers Tie Mexico's Fate, Writes Villa."

546   NA RG 165 Military Intelligence Division, File 5761-1091/14, Sommerfeld to Garrison, November 12, 1915.

547   *The New York Times*, November 22, 1915, "Villa is Routed by Gen. Dieguez."

548   Ibid., November 20, 1915, "Mexicans in Battle for Sonora Cities."

549   Ibid., November 25, 1915, "Close Border at Nogales."

550   Ibid., November 27, 1915, "American Soldier Killed by Mexicans."

551   Ibid, November 27, 1915, "More Troops to the Scene."

552   Katz, *Life and Times of Pancho Villa*, pp. 532-533.

553   Ibid.

554   *The New York Tribune*, September 21, 1915, "U.S. Watching for Villa Move."

555   Ibid., p. 534.

556   *The New York Times*, December 14, 1915, "Villa Wreaks Spite on American Property."

557   NA RG 65 FBI Case Files, M1085, Roll 858, File 232-162, Agent Benham to Department, November 6, 1915.

558   *The New York Times*, December 23, 1915, "Defeat Big Villa Force."

559   Katz, *Life and Times of Pancho Villa*, p. 487.

560   Library of Congress, Papers of Hugh Lenox Scott, Box 16, General Correspondence, Sommerfeld to Scott, December 23, 1915.

561   Scott, *Some Memories of a Soldier*, p. 517.

562   McLynn, *Villa and Zapata*, p. 320.

563   *The New York Times*, January 13, 1916, "Swears Slayers are Villa Chiefs."

564   Ibid.

565   *The El Paso Herald*, January 17, 1916, "Jose Rodriguez Not Executed – Americans from South Report."

566   Ibid.

567   Ibid., January 13, 1916, "Díaz Lombardi [sic] Arrested Here."

568   Ibid., January 17, 1916, "Díaz Lombardo will not discuss American Massacre."

569   Ibid., January 14, 1916, "Crowd Starts Riot on Broadway."

570   See Ibid., January 17, 1916, "Nothing Done." Also NA RG 242 Captured German Documents, T141, Roll 20, Count Bernstorff to Foreign Office, January 13, 1916. Also Link, Arthur S., *Wilson: Confusion and Crises, 1915-1916*, Princeton University Press, Princeton, NJ, 1964, p. 201.

571   NA RG 242 Captured German Documents, T141, Roll 20, Count Bernstorff to Foreign Office, January 13, 1916.

572   As quoted in Link, *Wilson: Confusion and Crises, 1915-1916*, p. 46.

573   NA RG 242 Captured German Documents, T141, Roll 20, Count Bernstorff to Foreign Office, January 13, 1916.

574   *El Paso Herald*, January 14, 1916, "Army to Patrol Railway Lines."

575   *The New York Sun*, January 14, 1916, "Two More Americans are Slain by Mexican Bandits."

576   *The New York Times*, January 20, 1916, "Fight American Troopers."

577   *The New York Sun*, January 14, 1916, "Mining Men in Peril."

578   *The New York Evening World*, January 21, 1916, "Shooting Had Been Ordered at Once, After Capture, For Massacre."

579   Ibid.

580   See for example *The New York Times*, January 21, 1916, "Villa Not Yet Taken Prisoner."

581   *The El Paso Herald*, March 10, 1916, "Villa Invitation to Zapata to Join Attack on U.S. Found in Bandit's Papers." The date of the letter is in dispute since several versions have turned up over time. It is generally accepted that Villa's invitation had been drafted before the attack on Santa Ysabel in January, 1916. Villa asked Zapata around January 6 to join him in an attack on the United States six months later.

582   Ibid., May 27, 1916, "Villa Lives and Will Again Rule Vows Lopez Defiant to Death."

583   The handwritten distribution list includes several others that the author could not identify.

584   NA RG 242 Captured German Documents, T141, Roll 20, von Eckardt to von Bethmann Hollweg, September 25, 1915.

585   See Katz, Friedrich, "Pancho Villa and the Attack on Columbus, New Mexico," *The American Historical Review*, Vol. 83, No. 1 (Feb., 1978), pp. 101-130, as the prime scholarly work on this theory.

586   Tuchman, *The Zimmermann Telegram*, p. 90.

587   NA RG 65 FBI Case Files, M1085, Roll 860, File 232-237.

588   NA RG 85 Immigration and Naturalization, T715, Roll 2445, Arrival of Gonzalo Enrile in New York, December 19, 1915.

589   *The Oasis*, August 6, 1910, "An Unwarranted Insult to the Mexican Consul at Clifton."

590   *The Arizona Republican*, February 24, 1912, "Washington Gets Startling News."

591   *The Copper Era and Morenci Leader*, March 8, 1912, "Enrile Arrested in Juarez." Also *The Weekly Journal-Miner*, May 15, 1912, "Money Man Assaulted." Also *The Tacoma Times*, June 4, 1912, "Enrile – Man of Mystery and Cash in Revolt."

592   *The Copper Era and Morenci Leader*, March 8, 1912, "Enrile Arrested in Juarez." Also, U.S. Senate, *Revolutions in Mexico*, p. 634, Enrique Llorente issued a warrant for the arrest of Gonzalo C. Enrile, June 11, 1912.

593   NA RG 85 Immigration and Naturalization, T715, Roll 2017, Enrile arrival in New York on February 21, 1913.

594   *The Evening Independent*, October 16, 1913, "Foreign Envoys Ask Protection."

595   Harris and Sadler, *The Secret War in El Paso*, p. 250.

596   NA RG 65 FBI Case Files, M1085, Roll 860, File 232-237, William Offley to Department, March 1, 1916.

597   Ibid., Agent Breniman to Department, April 30, 1916.

598   Ibid., Roll, 856, File 232-101, Agent Blanford to Department, March 22, 1916.

599   Ibid.

600   Ibid.

601   Ibid., Agent [illegible] to Chief Bielaski, April 12, 1916.

602   NA RG 65, Albert Papers, Box 24, Albert Diaries, entry for March 12, 1916.

603   Description of Stahl in NA RG 65 FBI Case Files, M1085, Roll 862, File 232-402, Agent Scully to Department, April 29, 1916. The other "Stahl" in the realms of the Secret War Council was Gustav Stahl, a minor German operative who had lied under oath about the supposed armament of the *Lusitania*. He had been convicted meanwhile and was serving an eighteen-month prison term in Atlanta (*Washington Post*, December 18, 1915, "3 Held in Bomb Plot.").

604   NA RG 65 Albert Papers, Box 45, von Papen accounts, 1914 to 1917. Also ibid., Box 24, General Ledger.

605   Ibid., Box 26, Memorandum, December 28, 1916.

606   Ibid.

607   NA RG 65 FBI Case Files, M1085, Roll 862, File 232-402, Agent Kump to Department, February 24, 1916.

608   Ibid.

609   NA RG 65 Albert Papers, Box 33, Tauscher to von Igel, May 18, 1916. Also ibid., Tauscher to Stahl, March 23, 1916.

610   Ibid., Tauscher to Stahl, May 5, 1916.

611   NA RG 65 FBI Case Files, M1085, Roll 862, File 232-402, Agent Scully to Department, April 29, 1916.

612   Ibid.

613   Ibid.

614   Ibid.

615   NA RG 65 Albert Papers, Box 33, Box 24, G. Amsinck and Co. accounts 1916.

616   NA RG 65 FBI Case Files, M1085, Roll 862, File 232-311, Agent J. B. Rogers to Department, Interview with George R. Head, May 8, 1916.

617   NA RG 65 Albert Papers, Box 21, Debit Memo, January 1, 1916.

618   Ibid., Box 26, Memorandum, dated April 4, 1916.

619   *The Argus* (Melbourne, Australia), November 13, 1915, "*S.S. Zealandia* Case."

620   Link, *Woodrow Wilson and the Progressive Era, 1910-1917,* p. 135.

621   NA RG 65 FBI Case Files, M1085, Roll 861, File 232-237, Agent Pendleton to Department, May 2, 1916.

622   Ibid., Roll 860, File 232-237, Special Agent Cantrell to Department, March 4, 1916.

623   Ibid.

624   Ibid., Roll 857, File 232-101, Carothers to Lansing, March 3, 1916.

625   NA RG 242 Captured German documents, T141, Roll 20, Prince Ratibor to Auswärtiges Amt, August 16, 1916.

626   See for example Katz, *The Secret War in Mexico* and Boghardt, Thomas, *The Zimmermann Telegram: Intelligence, Diplomacy, and America's Entry into World War I,* Naval Institute Press, Annapolis, MD, 2012.

627   NA RG 242 Captured German Documents, T141, Roll 20, Count Bernstorff to von Papen, July 2, 1915.

628   *The El Paso Herald,* March 8, 1916, "Villa Captures Palomas Cowboys Including an American Foreman."

629   *The El Paso Herald,* March 9, 1916, "Five Troops chase Villa in Mexico."

630   NA RG 65 FBI Case Files, M1085, Roll 851, file 232-101, Carothers to Lansing, March 3, 1916.

631   Chalkley, John F., *Zach Lamar Cobb: El Paso Collector of Customs and Intelligence*

During the Mexican Revolution, 1913-1918, Texas Western Press, El Paso, TX, 1998, p. 64.

632   Ibid.

633   Library of Congress, Prints and Photographs Division, LC-USZ62-564.

634   NA RG 65 FBI Case Files, M1085, Roll 861, File 232-269, Agent Underhill to Department, April 20 and 22, 1916.

635   Ibid.

636   Ibid.

637   Sommerfeld supplied AP News with up to date reports on the Mexican Revolution between 1908 and 1911. He handled press access to President Madero after that, which brought him into close contact with journalists such as David Lawrence. As Villa's representatives in the U.S. from 1914 on, he largely managed Villa's publicity, as such also maintaining a large network of contacts.

638   Sommerfeld owed Warren $3,800 in 1918 when the former was arrested. Therefore, the BI examined Warren and Sommerfeld's relationship closely. Warren only gave evasive testimony. Warren again turned up in Sommerfeld's files as someone who had offered him a job in the film industry when Sommerfeld was released from internment in 1919.

639   NA RG 60 Department of Justice, File 9-16-12-5304.

640   Katz, *Life and Times of Pancho Villa*, p. 564. Also, Chalkley, *Zach Lamar Cobb*, pp. 64-66.

641   Sandos, James A., "German Involvement in Northern Mexico, 1915-1916: A New Look at the Columbus Raid," *The Hispanic American Historical Review*, Vol. 50, No. 1 (Feb., 1970), p. 77. Sandos' assessment of the Villista troop strength is the best researched estimate.

642   Ibid., p. 566. Ravel had gone to El Paso to see a dentist.

643   *The El Paso Herald*, March 27, 1916, "No Insurance for Columbus."

644   Katz, *Life and Times of Pancho Villa*, p. 564.

645   *The El Paso Herald*, March 9, 1916, "23 Villa Men Fall in Fight."

646   Ibid., March 10, 1916, "American Troops Kill over 75, Have close Call from Capture."

647   Scott, *Some Memoirs of a Soldier*, p. 519.

648   *The El Paso Herald*, March 9, 1916, "Five Troops Chase Villa in Mexico." Also Ibid., March 10, "Revised Casualty List."

649   Library of Congress, Prints and Photographs Division, Washington, D.C., LC-USZ62-92487.

650   See articles in the *El Paso Herald* and *The El Paso Times*.

651   Scott, *Some Memoirs of a Soldier*, p. 520.

652   For more detail see articles and books by Friedrich Katz, Michael Meyer, James Sandos, E. Bruce White, Charles H. Harris III, Tom Mahoney, Francis J. Munch, Clarence Clendenen, Alejandro Quesada, and Frank Tomkins.

653   Scott, *Some Memoirs of a Soldier*, p. 518.

654   See Sandos, "German Involvement in Northern Mexico, 1915-1916: A New Look at the Columbus Raid." Rauschbaum is not mentioned in any German document listing German agents active in Mexico or the United States. While he very well could have been an agent, his ability to provide material support for Villa is questionable. Sommerfeld was in a much more favorable position to affect military and financial support for Villa.

655   NA RG 65 FBI Case Files, M1085, Roll 856, File 232-101, J. W. Allen to Colonel M. M. Parker.

656   Ibid., Agent Beckham to Department, March 17, 1916.

657   Ibid.

658   Ibid., Roll 862, file 232-311, BI Chief Bielaski to William Offley.

659   Ibid., William Offley to BI Chief Bielaski, May 5, 1916.

660   Library of Congress, Papers of Hugh Lenox Scott, Box 21, Sommerfeld to Scott, March 10, 1916.

661   NA RG 65 FBI Case Files, M1085, Roll 860, File 232-237, George Lillard to Chief, February 28, 1916.

662   Ibid., Roll 862, File 232-311, Agent Berliner to Department.

663   Ibid., Roll 856, File 232-101, Agent Blanford to Department.

664   Ibid.

665   See for example Ibid., File 232-101, Agent Blanford to Department, May 8, 1916. Also Ibid., William Offley to Department, April 12, 1916.

666   See for example Meyer, Michael C., "Villa, Sommerfeld, Columbus y los Alemanes, Historia Mexicana, Vol. 28, No. 4, El Colegio de Mexico, 1979. Also Katz, Friedrich, "Pancho Villa and the Attack on Columbus, New Mexico," *The American Historical Review,* Vol. 83, No. 1 (Feb., 1978), pp. 101-130.

667   Colonel Tompkins, Frank, *Chasing Villa: The Last Campaign of the United States Cavalry,* Penguin Books, Harrisburg, PA, 1939.

668   NA RG 242 Captured German documents, T141, Roll 20, Kriminalschutzmann Schmidt to Police headquarters Berlin, June 17, 1916.

669   Ibid., Enrile to unknown (likely Count Montgelas who conducted the meetings), unknown date, secret.

670   Ibid.

671   Ibid., Enrile to Foreign Office, Confidential Memorandum, June 15, 1916.

672   Katz, "Pancho Villa and the Attack on Columbus, New Mexico," pp. 101-130.

673   See for example the raid on Glenn Springs, Texas in May, 1916.

674   NA RG 65 Albert Papers, Box 23, von Papen to Albert, March 9, 1916.

675   NA RG 65 Albert Papers, Box 31.

676   Ibid.

677   NA RG 242 Captured German Documents, T141, Roll 20, Count Bernstorff to von Bethmann Hollweg, March 20, 1916.

678   NA RG 165 Military Intelligence Division, File 9140-1754, Memorandum in Regard to Felix Summerfelt [sic], June 27, 1918. The MID thought that the wedding was in 1915. Marriage records show that the couple married on February 12, 1916.

679   Link, *Wilson: Confusion and Crises, 1915-1916,* p. 207.

680   Ibid. The same sentiment is given in Haley, *Revolution and Intervention,* p. 190.

681   See Braddy, Haldeen, "Pancho Villa at Columbus: The Raid of 1916," *Southwestern Studies,* Vol. 3, No. 1, (Spring 1965), Monograph No. 9; Meyer, Michael C., "Villa, Sommerfeld, Columbus Y Los Alemanes," *Sobretiro de Historia Mexicana,* Vol. XXVIII, No. 4, El Colegio de Mexico, 1979; Clendenen, Clarence, *The United States and Pancho Villa: A Study in Unconventional Diplomacy,* Cornell University Press, Ithaca, NY 1961; Sandos, James A., "German Involvement in Northern Mexico, 1915-1916: A New Look at the Columbus Raid," *The Hispanic American Historical Review,* Vol. 50, No. 1 (Feb., 1970), pp. 70-88; Katz, Friedrich, "Pancho Villa and the Attack on Columbus, New

Mexico," *The American Historical Review*, Vol. 83, No. 1 (Feb. 1978), pp. 101-130; White, E. Bruce, "The Muddied Waters of Columbus, New Mexico," *The Americas*, Vol. 32, No. 1 (Jul., 1975), pp. 72-98.

682   Sandos, "German Involvement in Northern Mexico, 1915-1916: A New Look at the Columbus Raid," pp. 70-88.

683   Katz, "Pancho Villa and the Attack on Columbus, New Mexico," pp. 101-130. To be discussed in greater detail later in the chapter.

684   As quoted from Tumulty in Link, *Wilson: Confusion and Crises, 1915 – 1916*, p. 214.

685   NA RG 242 Captured German Documents, T141, Roll 20, Montgelas to unknown recipients, March 17, 1916, top secret.

686   Link, *Wilson: Confusion and Crises, 1915-1916*, p. 210.

687   As quoted in Haley, *Revolution and Intervention*, p. 191.

688   Carranza to Lansing, March 11, 1916, Department of State, Foreign Relations, 1916, as quoted in "A strategic examination of the Punitive Expedition into Mexico, 1916-1917," by Cyrulik, John M., Major U.S. Army, Master Thesis in Military History, Fort Leavenworth, Kansas, 2003, p. 23.

689   Haley, *Diplomacy and Intervention*, p. 190.

690   See for example *El Paso Herald*, March 14, 1916, "El Paso is well protected by troops."

691   Lansing to Carranza, March 13, 1916, Department of State, Foreign Relations, 1916, as quoted in Cyrulik, "A strategic examination of the Punitive Expedition into Mexico, 1916-1917," p. 48.

692   Welsome, Eileen, *The General and the Jaguar: Pershing's Hunt for Pancho Villa*, University of Nebraska Press, Lincoln, NE, 2006, p. 173.

693   Carranza appointed both cabinet members on March 14, 1916. See *El Paso Herald*, March 14, 1916, "General Obregon Appointed Mexico Minister of War."

694   Haley, *Diplomacy and Intervention*, pp. 194-195.

695   Link, *Wilson: Confusion and Crises, 1915-1916*, pp. 217-218.

696   Scott, *Some Memories of a Soldier*, p. 521.

697   Welsome, *The General and the Jaguar*, pp. 164-168. The following biography of Pershing has been summarized from Welsome's excellent work on the Punitive Expedition.

698   McLynn, *Villa and Zapata*, p. 325.

699   NA RG 242 Captured German Documents, T141, Roll 20, von Eckardt to von Bethmann Hollweg, May 5, 1916. Von Eckardt announced the dispatch of Krumm-Heller to the Mexican embassy in Berlin. As part of his introduction of Krumm-Heller he wrote, "Since he has the full confidence of Carranza, he could also make valuable contributions for the German legation here."

700   Ibid., Count Bernstorff to von Bethmann Hollweg, March 14, March 20, March 29.

701   Harris and Sadler, *The Plan de San Diego*, p. 124.

702   NA RG 242 Captured German Documents, T141, Roll 20, Count Bernstorff to von Bethmann Hollweg, March 14, 1916.

703   Ibid., Count Bernstorff to von Bethmann Hollweg, March 29, 1916.

704   Ibid.

705   Ibid., Count Bernstorff to von Bethmann Hollweg, March 20, 1916.

706   Ibid.

707   Ibid.

708   Ibid., Freyer to Chief of the Navy, March 20, 1916.

709   Ibid.

710   Ibid., Montgelas to unknown recipients, March 17, 1916, top secret.

711   McLynn, *Villa and Zapata*, p. 325.

712   For more information on Dreben, Holmdahl, and other soldiers-of-fortune see von Feilitzsch, *In Plain Sight*.

713   NA RG 65 FBI Case Files, M1084, Roll 861, File 232-258, Chief Bielaski to U.S. Attorney in Houston, TX, June 21, 1916.

714   Ibid., Roll 862, File 232-311, Agent Harry Berliner to Chief Bielaski, May 30, 1916.

715   Ibid., Agent Pinckney to Department, April 28, 1916. "Sommerfeld is a purchasing agent for the Villa faction… His local associate [El Paso] is now in Mexico with Gen. Pershing as a scout." Also Ibid., Chief Bielaski to Brigadier General Henry P. McCain, May 8, 1916, "One Sam Dreben, who has been an active Villa agent in close touch with Felix A. Sommerfeld, is reported to have offered his services as scout in Mexico to

General Funston... his close association and activities for Villa would seem to warrant close watching... " Documenting Dreben's continued employment by Sommerfeld, see ibid., Agent Stone to Department, October 27, 1916, quoting a letter Felix Sommerfeld wrote to his uncle Ed Rosenbaum on September 14, 1916, "I am writing Mr. Dreben, who will give you the $300..."

716   Leibson, Art, *Sam Dreben, the Fighting Jew*, Westernlore Press, Tucson, AZ, 1996, pp. 110-111.

717   NA RG 65 FBI Case Files, M1085, Roll 866, File 232-1168, Memorandum for the Pardon Attorney, March 22, 1917. Also Library of Congress, Papers of Hugh Lenox Scott, Box 15, General Correspondence, Sommerfeld to Scott, July 10, 1914. See also von Feilitzsch, *In Plain Sight*, pp. 280-301.

718   Welsome, *The General and the Jaguar*, p. 170.

719   Chalkley, *Zach Lamar Cobb*, p. 71.

720   Katz, *Life and Times of Pancho Villa*, p. 571.

721   Ibid., p. 572.

722   Welsome, *The General and the Jaguar*, p. 174.

723   Ibid., p. 177.

724   Katz, *Life and Times of Pancho Villa*, p. 561.

725   For more information on the history of Namiquipa and other military colonies under Spanish colonial rule see Katz, *Life and Times of Pancho Villa*, pp. 13-18.

726   *The Ogden Standard*, March 31, 1916, "Villa Murders More Americans"

727   Welsome, *The General and the Jaguar*, p. 189.

728   Ibid., p. 192. General Pershing claimed 60 Villistas killed. See *The Bisbee Daily Review*, April 2, 1916, "Bandit's Loss at the Guerrero Battle Said About Sixty by Many."

729   Ibid.

730   Ibid.

731   Welsome, *The General and the Jaguar*, p. 193.

732   As quoted in Eisenhower, John S. D., *Intervention! The United States and the Mexican Revolution, 1913-1917*, W.W. Norton and Company Inc., New York, 1993, p. 261.

733   Welsome, *The General and the Jaguar*, p. 212.

734   Katz, *Life and Times of Pancho Villa*, p. 573.

735   Library of Congress, Prints and Photographs Division, LC-USZ62-132203.

736   Courtesy Creative Commons, author $1LENCE D0o6ooD.

737   Library of Congress, Prints and Photographs Division, LC-USZ62-563.

738   Ibid., LC-USZ62-89204.

739   Ibid., LC-USZ62-77977.

740   Ibid., LC-USZ62-89208.

741   Ibid., LC-USZ62-89224.

742   Ibid., LC-USZ62-89218.

743   Ibid., LC-USZ62-88742.

744   The old silver mining town had been the capital of what once was the Mexican frontier, the "Wild North of Mexico." Parral had seen tremendous growth in the 1880s. Foreign investors, mostly American, British, Spanish and French, financed mining development, street construction, bridges, the regional power plant, and electrification projects. The largest trading company and bank in the city was Stallforth Y Hermanos with financial connections to powerful German banking houses, the Deutsch-Südamerikanische Bank, subsidiary of the Dresdner Bank and the up-and-coming competition to Bleichröder und Sohn. Frederico Stallforth's uncle Friedrich had invested heavily into the social development of his community and was known as a great philanthropist. The official government website for Parral describes the Stallforth heritage:

"Don Frederick arrived in Hidalgo del Parral in 1862, close to 28 years old and moved to Wiesbaden, Germany, in 1881. During his short stay of 19 years he worked wonders, creating major industries and thus brought jobs to the regional economy: The Power Parral Mines procuring agency concentrated mineral ore from all the regional mines; the Power Plant which generated enough power for its [Parral's] industries; he donated electric light poles for the downtown; the Factory of Stoves and Heaters Parral; the Factory of Crucibles and Refractory Brick; the Maison Stallforth industrial supply and hardware store; he donated the Botica Charity; the Industrial School for Girls; the school La Esperanza; The Mercado Hidalgo; Guanajuato Bridge; the statue of Don Miguel Hidalgo, the bust of José María Morelos, etc., etc."

La Escuela Frederico Stallforth, donated by Frederico Senior in 1885 still exists today and proudly acknowledges the name of its founder as "el benefactor, quien donó el terreno donde se construyó el edificio." When hunger struck the population of Parral in 1877 as a result of a horrifically bad harvest, Don Frederico bought "large quantities of corn in Durango and afterwards sold it at cost to the entire needy population of the region... " One of the most prestigious buildings in downtown is the Casa Stallforth, today a hotel. Don Frederico financed the construction of this luxurious palace in 1908. Its baroque façade is decorated with Nordic mythological beings. The Casa Stallforth housed the renowned bank Stallforth Y Hermanos until the business finally folded in the 1920s.

It would be unfair to leave out the efforts of other Parral families in the development of the city. There was the Griensen family, Austrian immigrants who also made a fortune in the mining business, the Urquidi family who later intermarried with the Stallforths, and members of the Terrazas family whose patriarch Luis was governor of Chihuahua off and on between 1860 and 1904. The large German and Austrian immigrant community was highly recognized and appreciated in the community.

745 Welcome, *The General and the Jaguar*, p. 214.

746 http://tramoyam.blogspot.com/2008/04/elisa-griensen-zambrano-aniversario-de.html

747 Unknown military photographer - U.S. War Department, public domain.

748 Ibid., p. 215.

749 Cyrulik, "A strategic examination of the Punitive Expedition into Mexico, 1916-1917," pp. 44-45.

750 Welcome, *The General and the Jaguar*, p. 218.

751 As quoted in ibid., p. 219.

752 Pershing, John J., *My Life Before the World War, 1860-1917*, University Press of Kentucky, Lexington, KY, 2013, p. 351.

753 Scott, *Some Memories of a Soldier*, p. 525.

754 *The El Paso Herald*, May 12, 1916, "No Clash, Asserts Amador." Also Haley, *Revolution and Intervention*, p. 205.

755 Scott, *Some Memories of a Soldier*, p. 528.

756 Cyrulik, "A strategic examination of the Punitive Expedition into Mexico, 1916-1917," p. 53-54.

757 Stout, *Border Conflict*, p. 59.

758 Candelilla is a wax plant that grew abundantly around Glenn Springs. The factory employed forty to sixty workers and was founded in 1914.

759 *The El Paso Herald*, May 8, 1916, "Raid Started on U.S. Side?"

760   Stout, Joseph A. Jr., *Border Conflict: Villistas, Carranzistas and the Punitive Expedition, 1915-1920*, Texas Christian University Press, Fort Worth, TX, 1999, p. 77.

761   *The El Paso Herald*, May 9, 1916, "Eight Citizens Escape Bandits."

762   *The Bisbee Daily Review*, May 14, 1916, "U.S. Troops Overtake Five Hundred Raiders and Prepare for Battle."

763   Pershing to Funston, April 18, 1916, as quoted in Welsome, *The General and the Jaguar*, p. 222.

764   Scott, *Some Memories of a Soldier*, pp. 522-523.

765   Stout, *Border Conflict*, pp. 58-59.

766   Katz, *Life and Times of Pancho Villa*, p. 575.

767   Holmdahl Papers, University of California at Berkley, Bancroft Library, C-B 921, Box 1.

768   Holmdahl Papers, Bancroft Library, University of California at Berkley, C-B-921, Box 1, M. C. Schallenberger to Quartermaster at Columbus, NM, July 24, 1916, "Guide E. L. Holmdahl has been discharged and will leave for the border on the first transportation." His biographer Douglas Meed suggests that Holmdahl accepted an offer to assassinate Villa and was discharged for that purpose. It is more likely that Pershing suspected Holmdahl's disloyalty since he had been working for Sommerfeld, Villa, and more recently, Carranza.

769   NA RG 65 FBI Case Files, M1085, Roll 866, file 232, Memorandum for the Pardon Attorney, March 22, 1917.

770   *The New York Times*, June 6, 1916, "Pablo Lopez is Shot."

771   *The El Paso Herald*, May 27, 1916, "Villa Lives And Will Again Rule, Vows Lopez, Defiant to Death."

772   *The New York Times*, May 31, 1916, "Cache of Arms is Found By Americans."

773   Quintana, Alejandro, *Pancho Villa: A Biography*, ABC-CLIO, Santa Barbara, CA, 2012, p. 159.

774   Link, *Wilson: Confusion and Crises, 1915-1916*, p. 296.

775   Ibid.

776   Harris and Sadler, *The Plan de San Diego*.

777   Katz, *The Secret War in Mexico*, p. 341.

778   NA RG 242 Captured German Documents, T141, Roll 20, von Eckardt to von Jagow, April 5, 1916.

779   NA RG 65 Albert Papers, Box 45, credit memo signed by Carl Heynen, May 19, 1916.

780   Harris and Sadler, *The Plan de San Diego*, pp. 122-139.

781   De La Garza Papers, Box 5, Folder E, Western Cartridge to James Manoil, October 22, 1916; The letter is evidence of an on-going relationship between Western Cartridge Company and James Manoil after the recognition of Carranza.

782   Ibid., Western Cartridge to De La Garza, May 19, 1916.

783   Ibid., Franklin Olin to De La Garza, October 13, 1915.

784   Ibid., Box 2, Folder A, Gerard and Smyth to De La Garza, December 2, 1916

785   Ibid., Box 5, Folder E, Western Cartridge to De La Garza, May 19, 1916. The letter states that Serbian inspectors stopped deliveries on April 12th.

786   Ibid., Folder F, J. P. Morgan and Co. to De La Garza, May 16, 1916.

787   See von Feilitzsch, *In Plain Sight*, Chapter 20, "The Arms of the SS *Ypiranga*."

788   NA RG 65 FBI Case Files, M1085, Roll 861, file 232-281, William Offley to Department, April 1, 1916.

789   Ibid., Chief Bielaski to L. Garbarino, May 16, 1916.

790   Ibid., file 232-257, Agent Schmid to A. Bruce Bielaski, April 1, 1916.

791   Ibid., Roll 862, file 232-313, Agent Webb to Department, April 25, 1916.

792   Ibid., file 232-402, Agent Scully to Department, April 29, 1916.

793   Ibid., file 232-311, Agent Chalmers to Department, March 16, 1916.

794   De La Garza Papers, Box 5 Folder E, Western Cartridge Company to De La Garza, May 6, 1916.

795   NA RG 65 FBI Case Files, M1085, Roll 862, File 232-311, R. B. Spencer to Department, April 13, 1916.

796   Ibid.

797   Ibid.

798   NA RG 59 Department of State, M1490, Roll 562, Passport Applications, A. J. Norcom, August 1, 1918.

799   Harris and Sadler, *The Secret War in El Paso*, p. 262.

800   See von Feilitzsch, *In Plain Sight*, Chapter 13, "The Sommerfeld Organization."

801   NA RG 65 FBI Case Files, M1085, Roll 857, File 232-101, E. B. Stone to Department, June 19, 1916. Stone identified Hector Ramos and Henry Kramp as working for Villa. Both had worked in the secret service organization Sommerfeld built and ran from 1912-1914 as regional secret service leaders under whom dozens of agents worked.

802   Ibid., Roll 862, File 232-311, R. B. Spencer to Department, April 13, 1916.

803   Ibid., Roll 854, File 232, Office of Naval Intelligence Washington to BI Chief Bielaski, June 26, 1916.

804   Ibid., Roll 855, File 232-26, Informant Ibs to Department, January 13, 1917.

805   Ibid., Roll 854, File 232, Office of Naval Intelligence Washington to BI Chief Bielaski, June 26, 1916.

806   Ibid., Agent George Storak to Department, July 16, 1916.

807   NA RG 65 Albert Papers, Box 33, Tauscher accounting 1915, mentions pistol purchases on August 23 to F. S. Elias and on September 11 to Dr. Alfredo Caturegli. Elias would later become the Mexican Secretary of Agriculture.

808   NA RG 65 FBI Case Files, M1085, Roll 854, File 232-26, Agent Storak to Department, July 15, 1916.

809   Ibid.

810   Ibid., Juan T. Burns Account and Alfredo Caturegli Account, July 20, 1916.

811   NA RG 65 Albert Papers, Box 24 and 26, Account Ledgers and trial balance sheets 1916, Box 24.

812   Ibid., Box 26.

813   Ibid., Box 24.

814   Ibid., Box 26.

815   Ibid., Box 24. Investigators later tried to determine who "ST" might have been. Strauss is listed in another transaction on the same ledger as "Dr. J. Str." Which leaves ST as the designation for Stallforth.

816   For more details about the internal discussions in Germany and the U.S. concerning the note, see Link, *Wilson: Confusion and Crises, 1915-1916*, pp. 256-279.

817   As quoted in Katz, *The Secret War in Mexico*, p. 338.

818   NA RG 242 Captured German Documents, T141, Roll 20, Minister to Argentina Lucius to Auswärtiges Amt, June 29, 1916, copy of Count Bernstorff's telegram dated June 24.

819   Harris and Sadler, *The Plan de San Diego*, p. 138.

820   Ibid., p. 136.

821   As quoted in ibid., p. 132.

822   Ibid., p. 133.

823   Ibid., p. 135.

824   Ibid.

825   As quoted in ibid., p. 136.

826   NA RG 65 FBI Case files, M1085, Roll 861, File 232-258, report of George R. Head, May 13, 1916. Head went to Tampico in the middle of March and saw Luis de la Rosa in the rank of colonel working for Carrancista general Emiliano Naffarete.

827   Harris and Sadler, *The Plan de San Diego*, p. 136.

828   Haley, *Revolution and Intervention*, pp. 211-212.

829   Harris and Sadler, *The Plan de San Diego*, p. 141.

830   Ibid., p. 142.

831   Ibid., pp. 154-155.

832   Haley, *Revolution and Intervention*, p. 212.

833   Historians Harris and Sadler only recently discovered the personal papers of Augustín Garza which proved him to be the leader of the *Plan de San Diego* conspiracy.

834   Harris and Sadler, *The Plan de San Diego*, p. 168.

835   Ibid.

836   Ibid.

837   Ibid.

838   U.S. Senate, *Investigation of Mexican Affairs*, Volume 1, 1919, pp. 1247-1248.

839   Ibid., p. 1248.

840   Harris and Sadler, *The Plan de San Diego*, p. 178.

841   Ibid., p. 166.

842   Ibid., p. 183.

843   Pershing, *My Life Before the World War*, p. 356.

844   Harris and Sadler, *The Plan de San Diego*, p. 185.

845   Ibid., p. 185.

846   Haley, *Revolution and Intervention*, p. 213.

847   Cyrulik, "A strategic examination of the Punitive Expedition into Mexico, 1916-1917," p. 59.

848   Scott, *Some Memories of a Soldier*, p. 524.

849   Major General Winfield Scott took Mexico City in the Mexican-American War of 1846 to 1848.

850   Cyrulik, "A strategic examination of the Punitive Expedition into Mexico, 1916-1917," p. 58-59.

851   Ibid., p. 59.

852   Ibid.

853   Pershing, *My Life Before the World War*, p. 358.

854   Welsome, *The General and the Jaguar*, p. 272.

855   Pershing, *My Life Before the World War*, p. 358.

856   The arguments for Pershing trying to precipitate war are that he was extremely frustrated with his mission and the attitude of the Carranza government. He had asked to be allowed to occupy Chihuahua which had been denied. However, Pershing also was a model soldier and as such would not have acted against specific orders not to cause a clash. If, indeed, he sent the troops to cause a problem, it is very likely that military superiors such as Scott and Funston unofficially supported the challenge to

Carranza in order to move President Wilson to accept an intervention strategy.

857   The Mexican casualties have not been made public and are estimates, See Welsome, *The General and the Jaguar*, p. 283.

858   Haley, *Revolution and Intervention*, p. 215.

859   Welsome, *The General and the Jaguar*, p. 287.

860   As quoted in Katz, *Life and Times of Pancho Villa*, p. 605.

861   Harris, Charles H., III and Sadler, Louis R., *The Border and the Revolution: Clandestine Activities of the Mexican Revolution: 1910-1920*, High Lonesome Books, Silver City, NM, 1988, p. 15.

862   Ibid., pp. 17-22.

863   See for example *The Toledo Blade*, March 24, 1988, "Professors Say U.S. Tried to Poison Pancho Villa." Also *The Ellensburg Daily Record*, March 28, 1988, "U.S. Plotted to kill Pancho Villa."

864   Scott, *Some Memories of a Soldier*, p. 520.

865   Ibid., p. 521.

866   Ibid., pp. 520-521.

BIBLIOGRAPHY
SECONDARY LITERATURE

Ackermann, Carl W., *Mexico's Dilemma*, George H. Doran Company, New York, 1918.

Albertini, Luigi, *The Origins of the War of 1914*, vols. 1-3, Enigma Books, New York, 2005.

Baecker, Thomas, *Die deutsche Mexikopolitik 1913/14*, Colloquium Verlag, Berlin 1971.

Bailey, Thomas A., Ryan, Paul B., *The Lusitania Disaster: The Real Answers behind the World's most controversial Sea Tragedy*, The Free Press, New York, NY, 1975.

Baker, Ray Stannard, *Woodrow Wilson, Life and Letters*, seven volumes, Doubleday, Doran and Company, New York, 1938.

Bernstein, Herman, *Celebrities of our time: Interviews*, Joseph Lawren, New York, 1924.

Bihl, Wolf Dieter, ed., *Deutsche Quellen zur Geschichte des Ersten Weltkrieges*, Wissenschaftliche Buchgesellschaft, Darmstadt, 1991.

Bisher, Jamie, *World War I Intelligence in Latin America*, unpublished manuscript, 2008.

Boghardt, Thomas, *The Zimmermann Telegram: Intelligence, Diplomacy, and America's Entry into World War I*, Naval Institute Press, Annapolis, MD, 2012.

Bonsor, N. R. P., *North Atlantic Seaway: An Illustrated History of the Passenger Services Linking the Old World with the New*, four volumes, Brookside Publications, Wheat Ridge, Colorado, 1978.

Calvert, Peter, *The Mexican Revolution 1910-1914: The Diplomacy of Anglo-American Conflict*, Cambridge University Press, New York, 1968.

Carlisle, Rodney P., *World War I*, Facts on File Inc., New York, 2007.

Carosso, Vincent P., Carosso, Rose C., *The Morgans: Private International Bankers, 1854-1913*, Harvard Studies in Business History, Harvard University Press, Cambridge, MA, 1987.

Cartarius, Ulrich ed., *Deutschland im Ersten Weltkrieg: Texte und Dokumente*, DTV, München, 1982.

Cecil, Lamar, *Albert Ballin: Wirtschaft und Politik im Deutschen Kaiserreich*, Hoffmann und Campe, Hamburg, 1969.

Chalkley, John F., *Zach Lamar Cobb: El Paso Collector of Customs and Intelligence During the Mexican Revolution, 1913-1918*, Southwestern Studies, No. 103, University of Texas Press, El Paso, TX, 1998.

Colby, Frank Moore, Williams, Talcott, eds., *The New International Encyclopedia*, Volume 24, Dodd, Mead, and Company, New York, 1918.

Collier, Peter and Horowitz, David, *The Rockefellers, An American Dynasty*, Summit Books, New York, NY, 1989.

Cooper, John Milton Jr., *Woodrow Wilson: A Biography*, Alfred A. Knopf, New York, 2009.

Clendenen, Clarence, *The United States and Pancho Villa: A study in unconventional diplomacy*, Cornell University Press, Ithaca, NY, 1961.

Cronlund Anderson, Mark, *Pancho Villa's Revolution by Headlines*, University of Oklahoma Press, Norman, OK, 2000.

Cumberland, Charles C., *Mexican Revolution: The Constitutionalist Years*, University of Texas Press, Austin, TX, 1974.

Daniels, Josephus, *The Life of Woodrow Wilson*, John C. Winston Company, Chicago, Philadelphia, 1924.

De Bekker, Leander Jan, *The Plot Against Mexico*, Alfred A. Knopf Publishers, New York, NY, 1919.

De La Pedraja Tomán, René, *Wars of Latin America, 1899-1941*, McFarland and Company Inc., Jefferson, NC, 2006.

De Léon, Arnoldo, ed., *War Along the Border*, Texas A&M, College Station, Texas, 2012.

Dehn, Paul, Dernburg, Bernhard, Hale, William Bayard, Hall, Thomas C. and various editors, *The Truth About Germany: Facts about the War*, The Trow Press, New York, NY, 1914.

Doenecke, Justus D., *Nothing Less Than War: A New History of America's Entry into World War I*, The University Press of Kentucky, Lexington, KY, 2011.

Doerries, Reinhard R., *Imperial Challenge: Ambassador Count Bernstorff and German-American Relations, 1908-1917*, University of North Carolina Press, Chapel Hill, NC, 1989.

Doerries, Reinhard R., editor, *Diplomaten und Agenten: Nachrichtendienste in der Geschichte der deutsch-amerikanischen Beziehungen*, Universitätsverlag C. Winter, Heidelberg, Germany, 2001.

Doerries, Reinhard R., *Prelude to the Easter Rising: Sir Roger Casement in Imperial Germany*, Frank Cass Publishers, Portland, OR, 2000.

Hamilton, Douglas T., *Shrapnel Shell Manufacture*, The New Industrial Press, New York, NY, 1915.

Ecke, Heinz, *Four Spies Speak*, John Hamilton Limited, London, Great Britain, 1933.

Eisenhower, John S. D., *Intervention! The United States and the Mexican Revolution, 1913-1917*, W.W. Norton and Company Inc., New York, 1993.

Fabela, Isidro, *Historia diplomática de la Revolución Mexicana*, vol I. (1912-1917), México Ciudad, Fondo de Cultura Económica, 1958.

Feldman, Gerald D., *Army, Industry, and Labor in Germany, 1914-1918*, Berg Publishers Inc., Providence, RI, 1992.

Fischer, Fritz, *Griff nach der Weltmacht: Die Kriegszielpolitik des kaiserlichen Deutschland 1914/18*, Droste Verlag, Düsseldorf, 1961.

David French, *British Economic and Strategic Planning 1905 to 1915*, Routledge Library Editions, Abingdon, Great Britain, 2006.

Fuehr, Alexander, *The Neutrality of Belgium: A Study of the Belgian Case under its Aspects in Political History and International Law*, Funk and Wagnalls Company, New York, 1915.

Gabrielan, Randall, *Rumson: Shaping a Superlative Suburb*, Arcadia Publishing, Charleston, SC, 2003.

Geiss, Immanuel, Ed., *July 1914: The Outbreak of the First World War: Selected Documents*, Charles Scribner's and Sons, New York, 1967.

Geissler, Erhard, *Biologische Waffen – Nicht in Hitlers Arsenalen: Biologische and Toxin-Kampfmittel von 1915 bis 1945*, LIT Verlag, Münster, Germany, 1999.

Gerhardt, Johannes, *Albert Ballin*, Hamburg University Press, Hamburg, 2010.

Hadley, Michael L., Sarty, Roger Flynn, *Tin-Pots and Pirate Ships: Canadian Naval Forces and German Sea Raiders 1880 – 1918*, McGill-Queens University Press, 1991.

Hale, William Bayard, *Germany's Just Cause*, The Fatherland Press, 1914.

Hale, William Bayard, *The Case Against Armed Merchantmen*, timely reprints from the New York Press, "The Real Issue in Washington," pp. 6-9, unknown publisher, undated (1915).

Haley, Edward P., *Revolution and Intervention: The Diplomacy of Taft and Wilson with Mexico, 1910-1917*, The MIT Press, Cambridge, MA, 1970.

Hamilton, Douglas T., *Shrapnel Shell Manufacture*, The New Industrial Press, New York, NY, 1915.

Hardach, Gerd, *The First World War, 1914-1918*, University of California Press, Berkeley and Los Angeles, 1977.

Harris, Charles H., III and Sadler, Louis R., *The Secret War in El Paso: Mexican Revolutionary Intrigue, 1906-1920*, University of New Mexico Press, Albuquerque, NM, 2009.

Harris, Charles H., III and Sadler, Louis R., *The Texas Rangers and the Mexican Revolution: The Bloodiest Decade, 1910-1920*, University of New Mexico Press, Albuquerque, NM, 2004.

Harris, Charles H., III and Sadler, Louis R., *The Plan de San Diego: Tejano Rebellion, Mexican Intrigues*, University of Nebraska Press, Lincoln, NE, 2013.

Harris, Charles H., III and Sadler, Louis R., *The Border and the Revolution: Clandestine Activities of the Mexican Revolution: 1910-1920*, High Lonesome Books, Silver City, NM, 1988.

Hau, George William, *War Echoes or Germany and Austria in the Crisis*, Morton M. Malone, Chicago, 1915.

Hirst, David Wayne, *German Propaganda in the United States, 1914-1917*, Northwestern University PhD. Dissertation, Evanston, IL, 1962.

Hopkins, J. Castell, editor, *The Canadian annual review of public affairs, 1915*, The Annual Review Publishing Company, Toronto, 1916.

Huertner, Johannes, editor, *Paul von Hintze: Marineoffizier, Diplomat, Staatssekretär, Dokumente einer Karriere zwischen Militär und Politik, 1903-1918*, Harald Boldt Verlag, München, Germany, 1998.

Huldermann, Bernhard, *Albert Ballin*, Cassell and Company Ltd., New York, NY, 1922.

Jeffreys, Diarmuid, *Aspirin: The Remarkable Story of a Wonder Drug*, Bloomsbury Publishing, New York, NY, 2005.

Jeffreys-Jones, Rhodri, *Cloak and Dollar: A History of American Secret Intelligence*, Yale University Press, New Haven, CT, 2002.

Jensen, Joan M., *The Price of Vigilance*, Rand McNally and Company, Chicago, IL, New York, NY, 1968.

Jones, John Price, *The German Spy in America: The Secret Plotting of German Spies in the United States and the Inside Story of the Sinking of the Lusitania*, Hutchinson and Co., London, Great Britain, 1917.

Jones, John Price, Hollister, Paul Merrick, *The German Secret Service in America, 1914-1918*, Small, Maynard and Company, Boston, MA 1918.

Katz, Friedrich, *The Secret War in Mexico: Europe, the United States, and the Mexican Revolution*, The University of Chicago Press, Chicago, IL, 1981.

Katz, Friedrich, *The Life and Times of Pancho Villa*, Stanford University Press, Stanford, CA, 1998.

Keegan, John, *The First World War*, Alfred A. Knopf, Inc., New York, NY 1999.

Kelly, Patrick J., *Tirpitz and the Imperial German Navy*, Indiana University Press, Bloomington, IN, 2011.

Kessler, Graf Harry, *Walther Rathenau: His Life and Work*, Harcourt, Brace and Company, New York, NY, 1930.

Knight, Alan, *The Mexican Revolution: Volume 2: Counter-revolution and Reconstruction*, Cambridge University Press, Cambridge, MA, 1986.

Koenig, Louis W., *Bryan: A Political Biography of William Jennings Bryan*, G.P. Putnam's Sons, New York, NY, 1971.

Koenig, Robert L., *The Fourth Horseman: One Man's Mission to Wage the Great War in America*, Public Affairs, New York, NY, 2006.

Koerver, Joachim, ed., *German Submarine Warfare 1914-1918 in the Eyes of British Intelligence: Selected Sources from the British National Archives, Kew*, Schaltungsdienst Lange, Berlin, Germany, 2010.

Landau, Henry, *The Enemy Within: The Inside Story of German Sabotage in America*, G.P. Putnam's Sons, New York, NY, 1937.

Leibson, Art, *Sam Dreben, the Fighting Jew*, Westernlore Press, Tucson, AZ, 1996.

Lemke, William, *Crimes Against Mexico*, Great West Publishing Company, Minneapolis, MN, 1915.

Lill, Thomas Russell, *National Debt of Mexico: History and Present Status*, Searle, Nicholson and Lill C.P.A.'s, New York, NY, 1919.

Link, Arthur S., editor, *Woodrow Wilson and a revolutionary world, 1913-1921*, New York, NY, 1982.

Link, Arthur S., *Wilson and the Progressive Era 1910 to 1917*, Harper and Brothers, New York, NY, 1954.

Link, Arthur S., *Wilson: The Struggle for Neutrality, 1914-1915*, Princeton University Press, Princeton, NJ, 1960.

Link, Arthur S., *Wilson: Confusion and Crises, 1915-1916*, Princeton University Press, Princeton, NJ, 1964.

Link, Arthur S., *The Papers of Woodrow Wilson*, vols. 23-26, Princeton University Press, Princeton, NJ, 1966.

Löwer, Thomas, *American Jews in World War I - German Propaganda Courting the American Jewry*, München, GRIN Publishing GmbH, 2004.

Love, Alaina and Marc Cugnon, *The Purpose Linked Organization: How passionate leaders inspire winning teams and great results*, McGraw Hill, New York, NY, 2009.

Ludwig, Emil, *Wilhelm Hohenzollern: The Last of the Kaisers*, G. P. Putnam's Sons, New York, 1927.

Luebke, Frederick C., *Bonds of Loyalty: German-Americans and World War I*, Northern Illinois University Press, DeKalb, IL, 1974.

Jennifer Luff, *Commonsense Anticommunism: Labor and Civil Liberties between the World Wars*, University of North Carolina Press, Raleigh, NC, 2012.

Machado, Manuel A. Jr., *Centaur of the North: Francisco Villa, the Mexican Revolution, and Northern Mexico*, Eakin Press, Austin, TX, 1988.

Mauch, Christoff, *The Shadow War Against Hitler: The Covert Operations of America's Wartime Secret Intelligence Service*, Columbia University Press, New York, NY, 1999.

McKenna, Marthe, *My Master Spy: A Narrative of the Secret Service*, Jarrolds Publishers Ltd., London, Great Britain, 1936.

McLynn, Frank, *Villa and Zapata: A History of the Mexican Revolution*, Basic Books, New York, NY, 2000.

McMaster, John Bach, *The United States in the World War*, D. Appleton and Company, New York, NY, 1918.

Meed, Douglas V., *Soldier of Fortune*, Halcyon Press, Ltd., Houston, TX, 2003.

Meyer, Michael C., *Huerta: A Political Portrait*, University of Nebraska Press, Lincoln, NE, 1972.

Millman, Chad, *The Detonators: The Secret Plot to Destroy America and an Epic Hunt for Justice*, Little, Brown and Company, New York, 2006.

Muensterberg, Hugo, *The War and America*, D. Appleton and Co., New York, NY, 1914.

Nasaw, David, *The Chief: The Life of William Randolph Hearst*, Houghton Mifflin Company, New York, NY, 2000.

Newman, Bernard, *Secrets of German Espionage*, The Right Book Club, London, Great Britain, 1940.

Peterson, Horace Cornelius, *Propaganda for War: The Campaign against American Neutrality, 1914-1917*, University of Oklahoma Press, Norman, OK, 1939.

Preston, Diana, *Lusitania: An Epic Tragedy*, Walker and Company, New York, NY, 2002.

Quintana, Alejandro, *Pancho Villa: A Biography*, ABC-CLIO, Santa Barbara, CA, 2012.

Quirk, Robert E. *The Mexican Revolution, 1914-1915: The Convention of Aguascalientes*, University of Indiana Press, Bloomington, IN, 1960.

Raat, W. Dirk and Beezley, William H., editors, *Twentieth Century Mexico*, University of Nebraska Press, Lincoln, NE, 1986.

Rafalko, Frank J., Ed., *A Counterintelligence Reader*, volume I, Chapter 3 "Post Civil War to World War I," www.fas.org/irp/ops/ci/docs/ci1, viewed 9-22-2011.

Reiling, Johannes, *Deutschland: Safe for Democracy?* Franz Steiner Verlag, Stuttgart, Germany, 1997.

Ritter, Gerhard, *Der Schlieffenplan: Kritik eines Mythos*, Verlag R. Oldenbourg, München, Germany, 1956.

Ritter, Gerhard, *Staatskunst und Kriegshandwerk*, Verlag R. Oldenbourg, München, Germany, 1954.

Roessler, Eberhard, *Die Unterseeboote der Kaiserlichen Marine*, Bernard und Graefe Verlag, Bonn, Germany, 1997.

Scheina, Robert L., *Villa, Soldier of the Mexican Revolution*, Potomac Books, Washington D.C., 2004.

Schieffel, Werner, *Bernhard Dernburg 1865 - 1937: Kolonialpolitiker und Bankier im wilhelminischen Deutschland*, Atlantis Verlag, Zürich, Switzerland, 1974.

Schroeder, Joachim, *Die U-Boote des Kaisers: Die Geschichte des deutschen U-Boot-Krieges gegen Grossbritannien im Ersten Weltkrieg*, Bernard und Gräfe, Lauf a. d. Pegnitz, 2003.

Scott, James Brown, editor, *The Declaration of London: A Collection of Official Papers and Documents relating to the International Naval Conference held in London December, 1908 to February, 1909*, Oxford University Press, New York, NY, 1919.

Shrapnel and other War Material: A Reprint of Important Articles Presented in the American Machinist from January to June 1915, McGraw-Hill Book Company, New York, NY, 1915.

Skaggs, William H., *German Conspiracies in America*, T. Fisher Unwin Ltd., London, Great Britain, 1916 (estimated).

Small, Michael, *The Forgotten Peace: Mediation at Niagara Falls, 1914*, University of Ottawa Press, Canada, 2009.

Smith, Arthur D. Howden, *Mr. House of Texas*, Funk and Wagnalls Company, New York, NY, 1940.

Smith, Arthur D. Howden, *The Real Mr. House*, George H. Doran Company, New York, NY, 1918.

Smith, Leonard V., Audoin-Rousseau, Stephanie, Becker, Annette, *France and the Great War, 1914-1918*, Cambridge University Press, Cambridge, Great Britain, 2003.

Sperry, Earl Evelyn, Willis Mason West, *German Plots and Intrigues in the United Stated during the Period of our Neutrality*, Committee on Public Information, Washington D.C., July 1918.

Starke, Holger, *Vom Brauereihandwerk zur Brauindustrie, Die Geschichte der Bierbrauerei in Dresden und Sachsen, 1800-1914*, Böhlan Verlag, Köln, Germany, 2005.

Stout, Joseph A. Jr., *Border Conflict: Villistas, Carranzistas and the Punitive Expedition, 1915-1920*, Texas Christian University Press, Fort Worth, TX, 1999.

Strother, French, *Fighting Germany's Spies*, Doubleday Page and Company, Garden City, NY, 1918.

Stubmann, Peter Franz, *Ballin: Leben und Werk eines deutschen Reeders*, Hermann Klemm AG., Berlin, Germany, 1926.

Synon, Mary, *McAdoo: The Man and his Times, A Panorama in Democracy*, The Bobbs-Merrill Company, Indianapolis, IN, 1924.

Teitelbaum, Louis M., *Woodrow Wilson and the Mexican Revolution, 1913-1916*, Exposition Press, New York, NY, 1967.

Thomas, William H. Jr., *Unsafe for Democracy: World War I and the U.S. Justice Department's Covert Campaign to Suppress Dissent*, The University of Wisconsin Press, Madison, WI, 2008.

Tuchman, Barbara, *The Zimmermann Telegram*, Macmillan Company, New York, NY, 1958.

Turner, John Kenneth, *Hands off Mexico*, Rand School of Social Science, New York, NY, 1920.

Volkman, Ernest, *Espionage: The Greatest Spy Operations of the 20th Century*, John Wiley and Sons Inc., New York, NY, 1995.

Volkman, Ernest and Baggett, Blaine, *Secret Intelligence: The Inside Story of America's Espionage Empire*, Doubleday, New York, NY, 1989.

Von Mach, Edmund, *What Germany Wants*, Little, Brown and Company, Boston, MA, 1914.

Welsome, Eileen, *The General and the Jaguar: Pershing's Hunt for Pancho Villa,* University of Nebraska Press, Lincoln, NE 2006.

West, Nigel, *Historical Dictionary of Sexspionage*, Scarecrow Press Inc., Plymouth, Great Britain, 2009.

Wile, Frederic William, *Men around the Kaiser: The Makers of Modern Germany*, The MacLean Publishing Company, Toronto, Canada, 1913.

Wilkins, Mira, *The History of Foreign Investment in the United States, 1914-1945,* Harvard University Press, Cambridge, MA, 2004.

Witcover Jules, *Sabotage at Black Tom*, Algonquin Books of Chapel Hill, Chapel Hill, NC, 1989.

Wittke, Carl, *The German-Language Press in America*, University of Kentucky Press, Louisville, KY, 1957.

Womack, John, Jr., *Zapata and the Mexican Revolution*, Alfred A. Knopf Inc., New York, NY, 1968.

Young, William, *German Diplomatic Relations, 1871-1945*, iUniverse, Inc.,

New York, NY, 2006.

Zuber, Terence, *Inventing the Schlieffen Plan: German War Planning 1871-1914*, Oxford University Press, New York, NY, 2002.

NEWSPAPERS, BULLETINS, DIRECTORIES, AND MAGAZINES

The Americas, Vol. 30, No. 1 (Jul., 1973), "The Arms of the Ypiranga: The German Side," by Thomas Baecker, pp. 1-17.

The Americas, Vol. 32, No. 1 (Jul., 1975), "The Muddied Waters of Columbus, New Mexico," by E. Bruce While and Francisco Villa.

The Americas, Vol. 39, No. 1 (July, 1982), "The Underside of the Mexican Revolution: El Paso, 1912," by Charles H. Harris, III and Louis R. Sadler.

The American Historical Review, Vol. 83, No. 1 (Feb., 1978), "Pancho Villa and the Attack on Columbus, New Mexico," by Friedrich Katz.

American Machinist, Volume 29, 1906.

Arizona and the West, Volume 21, No. 2 (Summer, 1979), pp. 157-186, "The Battle of Naco, Factionalism and Conflict in Sonora: 1914-1915," by Stephen P. Mumme.

The Arizona Republican, 1912.

Army History Journal, Washington, D.C. No. 89 (Fall 2013), "Chasing Ghosts in Mexico," by Thomas Boghardt.

The Bankers Magazine, Volume 77 (July to December 1908), Bankers Publishing Company, New York, NY, 1908.

Centre for Constitutional Studies, University of Alberta, "German Internment During the First and Second World Wars," by

Alexandra Bailey, http://www.law.ualberta.ca/centres/ccs/issues/germaninternment.php, viewed 12-2011.

www.ColorantsHistory.Org, "Spies and Dies," by Robert J. Baptista, updated March 4, 2010.

The Day Book, Chicago, IL, 1914.

The El Paso Herald, El Paso, TX, 1910-1920.

The Federal Reporter, Volume 235, October - November 1916, West Publishing Company, St. Paul, MN, 1917.

Film History, Volume 4, No. 2 (1990), pp. 123-129, "Shooting the Great War: Albert Dawson and the American Correspondent Film Company,1914-1918," by Ron van Dopperen.

German Studies Review, Volume 8, German Studies Association, "The Hindu Conspiracy in California, 1913-1918," by Karl Hoover, pp. 245-261.

Harpers Magazine, September, October, November 1917, "Diplomatic Days in Mexico, First, Second, Third Papers," by Edith O'Shaughnessy.

Harper's Magazine, November 1942, "The wind that swept Mexico: Part I, II, and III, by Anita Brenner.

History Review, December 2002: "The unpredictable dynamo: Germany's Economy, 1870-1918," by F.G. Stapleton.

Huachuca Illustrated, Volume 1, 1993, by James P. Finley, Fort Huachuca, AZ.

Journal of Intelligence History, Volume 4, Number 1, Summer 2004, Reinhard R. Doerries.

Journal of Latin American Studies, Vol. 35, No. 1 (Feb. 2003), "Railroad, Oil and Other Foreign Interests in the Mexican Revolution, 1911 to 1914," by John Skirius, Cambridge University Press.

Journal of Military and Strategic Studies, Fall 2005, Vol. 8, Issue 1, "Karl Respa and German Espionage in Canada during World War One," by Grant W. Grams.

The Journal of Interdisciplinary History, Vol. 2, No. 1, Summer, 1971, "George Sylvester Viereck: The Psychology of a German-American Militant" by Phyllis Keller.

Law Notes, Volume 7, April 1903 to March 1904, Edward Thompson Company, Northport, Long Island, NY, 1904.

Lewiston Evening Journal, 1915.

The Massey-Gilbert Blue Book of Mexico for 1903: A Directory in English of the City of Mexico, The Massey-Qilbert Company, Sucs., Mexico D.F., Mexico, 1903.

Metal Industry Magazine, Volume 13, January to December 1915, The Metal Industry Publishing Company, New York, NY, 1916.

The Mexican Yearbook 1912, McCorqudale and Company Limited, London, Great Britain, 1912.

Mexican Studies, Vol. 17, No.1 (Winter, 2001), "Exiliados de la Revolucion mexicana: El caso de los villistas (1915-1921)," by Victoria Lerner.

The Nation, volume 109, July 1, 1919 to December 31, 1919, The Nation Press, NY 1919.

The Northern Mariner/Le marin du nord, XVII, No. 3 (July, 2007), "The Attacks on U.S. Shipping that Precipitated American Entry into World War I," by Rodney Carlisle, pp. 41-66.

Oakland Tribune, Oakland, CA, April 18th, 1915.

The Pacific Historical Review, Vol. 17, No. 3, "The Hindu Conspiracy, 1914-1917," by Giles Brown, pp. 299-310.

The Pacific Historical Review, volume 40, "The Hindu Conspiracy in Anglo-American Relations during World War I," by Don Dignan, pp. 57-76.

Sabazius, "The Invisible Basilica: Dr. Arnoldo Krumm-Heller (1876 -1949 e.v.)," Ordo Templi Orientis, United States, 1997.

Southwestern Studies, Monograph number 47, "Luther T. Ellsworth: U.S. Consul on the Border During the Mexican Revolution," by Dorothy Pierson Kerig, Texas Western Press, El Paso, TX 1975.

The Historian, Volume 59, Issue 1, pages 89–112, "K. A. Jahnke and the German Sabotage Campaign in the United States and Mexico, 1914-1918," by Richard B. Spence, September 1996.

The Boston Evening Transcript, Boston, MA, 1915-1916.

The Day, New London, CT, 1914-1916.

The El Paso Herald, El Paso, TX, 1908-1920.

The Evening Herald, Albuquerque, NM, 1914-1916

The Fatherland, Volumes I and II, The Fatherland Cooperation, New York, NY, 1914 to 1917.

The Financier, Volume 114, New York, August 1, 1919.

The Fort Wayne News, Fort Wayne, TX, 1914 to 1918.

The Milwaukee Journal, Milwaukee, WI, 1942.

The Metal Industry, Vol. 13, January to December 1915, The Metal Industry Publishing Company, New York, NY, 1916.

The Morning Call, "Forging America: The Story of Bethlehem Steel," November 1, 2010.

The New York Sun, New York, NY, 1914-1917.

The New York Times, New York, NY, Archives 1896-1942.

The New York Times Current History: The European War, Volume 1, The New York Times Company, New York, NY, 1915.

The New York Tribune, New York, NY, 1910-1918.

The Ogden Standard, March 31, 1916.

The Times-Picayune, New Orleans, LA, July 1 to July 6, 1914.

The San Francisco Call and Post, San Francisco, CA, 1908-1917.

St. John Daily Sun, St. John, Newfoundland, Canada, 1899.

"The United Kingdom during World War I: Business as usual?" June 2003, by Stephen Broadberry and Peter Howlett, www2.warwick.ac.uk/fac/soc/economics /staff/.../wp/wwipap4.pdf, viewed 12-2012.

The Washington Post, Washington, D.C., 1911-1922.

The Washington Herald, Washington, D.C., 1910-1922

The Washington Times, Washington D.C., 1910-1914

The Weekly Journal-Miner, May 15, 1912.

The World's Work, Volume 28, May to October 1914, Doubleday, Page and Co., New York, NY, 1914.

The World's Work, Volume 30, May to October 1918, Doubleday, Page and Co., New York, NY, 1915.

The World's Work, Volume 36, May to October 1918, Doubleday, Page and Co., New York, NY, 1918.

www.rootsweb.ancestry.com/~ww1can/cef14_15.htm, "A Brief History of the Canadian Expeditionary Force," by Brian Lee Massey, 1997 – 2007.

www.HistoryLink.org, "U.S. Customs at Grays Harbor seizes the schooner Annie Larsen loaded with arms and ammunition on June 29, 1915," by David Wilma, May 18, 2006.

University of Calgary, "The Peopling of Canada: 1891-1921," The Applied Research Group, 1997.

The Trow: Copartnership and Corporation Directory of the Boroughs of Manhattan and the Bronx, Association of American Directory Publishers, New York, NY, March 1908.

The New York Times Current History: The European War, Volume 17, October, November, December 1918, New York Times Company, New York, NY, 1919

ORIGINAL, ARCHIVAL, AND GOVERNMENT SOURCES

National Intelligence Center, *American Revolution to World War II*, Chapter 3, Central Intelligence Reader, www.fas.org.

Department of Commerce, Bureau of Foreign and Domestic Commerce, Miscellaneous Series, No. 57, *German Foreign Trade Organization*, Government Printing Office, 1917.

Ministry of National Defense, Commonwealth of Canada, *The Official History of the Canadian Army: The Canadian Expeditionary Force, 1914-1919*, by Colonel G. W. L. Nicholson, C.D., Army Historical Section, Roger Duhamel, F.R.S.C. Queen's Printer and Controller of Stationary, Ottawa, 1962.

Holmdahl Papers, University of California at Berkley, Bancroft Library, C-B-921.

German Diplomatic Papers, University of California at Berkley, Bancroft Library, M-B 12.

Horne, Charles F., editor, *Source Records of the Great War*, Volumes I to VII, National Alumni, New York, 1923.

Koerver, Joachim, ed., *German Submarine Warfare 1914-1918 in the Eyes of British Intelligence: Selected Sources from the British National Archives, Kew*, Schaltungsdienst Lange, Berlin, Germany, 2010.

Silvestre Terrazas Papers, University of California at Berkley, Bancroft Library, M-B-18.

Carey McWilliams Papers, University of California at Los Angeles, 277.

Lázaro De La Garza Collection, University of Texas, Benson Library, Austin, TX.

Papers of Hugh Lenox Scott, Library of Congress, Washington, D.C.

Library and Archives Canada, Department of Militia and Defence, Record Group 13.

The National Archives of the UK, Board of Trade, Commercial and Statistical Department and successors, Inwards Passenger Lists, Kew, Surrey, England, BT26.

National Archives, Washington DC

Record Group 36	Records of the U.S. Customs Service, Vessels arriving in New York 1820-1897 and 1897-1957
Record Group 38	Office of Naval Intelligence 1913 to 1924
Record Group 45	Naval Records Collection, Caribbean File 1911 to 1927
Record Group 59	Department of State 1908 to 1927, specifically Papers of Robert Lansing, Volume I and II, Papers relating to the foreign relations of the United States 1914, 1915, 1916 (Latin America), File 812.00 (Mexico).
Record Group 60	Records of the Dept of Justice, Straight Numerical File, 157013, Boxes 1230 to 1236; Specifically file 9-16-12-5305, Statement of F. A. Sommerfeld, June 21 to June 24, 1918.
Record Group 65	Bureau of Investigations Case Files 1908-1922, Bureau of Investigations Miscellaneous Case Files 1908-1922, Papers of Dr. Heinrich F. Albert, Numbered Correspondence 1914 to 1917,

	Old German Files, Old Mexican Files.
Record Group 76	Mixed Claims Commission, 1922 to 1941.
Record Group 80	General Records of the Navy 1916 to 1926.
Record Group 85	Records of the Immigration and Naturalization Service.
Record Group 87	Records of the U.S. Secret Service, Daily Reports 1875 to 1936.
Record Group 131	Records of the Alien Property Custodian, Records seized by the APC.
Record Group 165	Records of the War Department, MID Specifically file 9140-1754 (Felix A. Sommerfeld), file 9140-878 (Frederico Stallforth), file 9140-646 (Franz Rintelen).
Record Group 242	German Captured Documents, Foreign Office, Mexiko Band 1 bis 10, "Old German Files."
Record Group 395	Records of the Army Overseas Operations, Mexican Punitive Expedition.

United States Senate, *Investigation of Mexican Affairs, Hearing before a Subcommittee of the Committee of Foreign Relations*, Government Printing Office, Washington, DC, 1920.

Unites States Senate, *Brewing and Liquor Interests and German Propaganda, Subcommittee of the Committee of the Judiciary*, Volume 2, Government Printing Office, Washington D.C., 1919.

United States Senate, *Revolutions in Mexico, Hearing before a Subcommittee of the Committee of Foreign Relations*, Government Printing Office, Washington, DC, 1912.

United Nations, Reports of International Arbitral Awards: Lehigh Valley Railroad Company, Agency of Canadian Car and Foundry Company, Limited, and Various Underwriters (United States) v. Germany (Sabotage Cases), June 15, 1939, Volume VIII, pp. 225-460, New York, NY, 2006.

YIVO Institute for Jewish Research, New York, Record Group 713, Papers of Herman Bernstein (1876-1935).

Die Österreichisch-Ungarischen Dokumente zum Kriegsausbruch, hrsg. vom Staatsamt für Äußeres in Wien, National-Verlag, Berlin, 1923.

G.P. Gooch, D.Litt, and Harold Temperley, editors, *British Documents on the Origins of the War, 1898-1914, Vol. XI: The Outbreak of War: Foreign Office Documents*, June 28th-August 4th, 1914, His Majesty's Stationery Office, 1926.

Staatsarchiv Hamburg, Hamburger Passagierlisten, 1850-1934.

Auswaertiges Amt, Politisches Archiv Berlin, Mexiko volumes I to X.

Staatsarchiv Berlin, Deutsche Dienststelle (WASt), Deutsche Verlustlisten 1914 bis 1917, Berlin, Deutschland.

Marine Crew Chronik MIM620/CREW, Marineschule Mürwik, Flensburg, Deutschland.

Marineschule Mürwik, Verlustlisten 1914-1915, MIM381, KAI17 040 (Band 3).

Bundesarchiv fuer Militärgeschichte, Freiburg; Record Groups RM 2, RM 3, RM 5.

Rangliste der Koeniglich Preussischen Armee und des XIII (Koeniglich Wuertembergschen) Armeekorps fuer 1907, Ernst Siegfried Mittler und Sohn, Berlin, Germany, 1907.

Rangliste der Deutschen Marine fuer das Jahr 1914, Ernst Siegfried Mittler und Sohn, Berlin, Germany, 1914.

Stallforth Papers, Private Collection by Mary Prevo.

United Nations, *Reports of International Arbitral Awards*, "S. S. 'Edna.' *Disposal of pecuniary claims arising out of the recent war (1914-1918)*,

United States, Great Britain, Volume III, December, 1934, pp. 1585-1606.

United States Census, *Cotton Production and Distribution*, Government Printing Office, Washington D.C., 1915.

United States Department of Agriculture, *Monthly Crop Reporter, May 10, 1915*, Government Printing Office, Washington, D.C.,1915.

United States Department of Commerce, *Commerce Reports, Part 3, July, August, September, 1918*, Government Printing Office, Washington, D.C., 1918.

The United States Senate, *Hearing before a Subcommittee of the Committee on Foreign Relations, Revolutions in Mexico*, Government Printing Office, Washington D. C., 1913.

United States Senate, Committee of the Judiciary, *Alleged Dye Monopoly*, Senate Resolution 77, Government Printing Office, Washington D.C.,1922.

United States War Department, *Annual Reports 1915*, Government Printing Office, Washington D.C.

The Southern Division of the United States District Court for the Northern District of California, First Division, United States of America vs. Franz Bopp, et al., April 23, 1918.

Immigrant Ancestors: A List of 2,500 Immigrants to America before 1750, Frederick Virkus, editor; Genealogical Publishing Co., Baltimore, Maryland, 1964.

Scott, James Brown, editor, *Diplomatic Correspondence Between the United States and Germany, August 1, 1914 - April 6, 1917*, Oxford University Press, New York, NY, 1918.

Secretaría de Comunicaciones y Obras Públicas, Estadística de ferrocarriles de jurisdicción federal año de 1918. México, Talleres Gráficos de la Nación, 1924.

AUTOBIOGRAPHICAL WORKS

Albert, Heinrich F., *Aufzeichnungen*, Büxenstein, Germany, 1956.

Dr. Atl, *The Mexican Revolution and the Nationalization of the Land: The Foreign Interests and Reaction*, Whitehall Building, Room 334, New York, NY, 1915.

Bauer, Hermann, *Als Fuehrer der U-Boote im Weltkriege: Der Eintritt der U-Boot-Waffe in die Seekriegsfuehrung*, Koehler und Amelang, Leipzig, 1941.

Boy-Ed, Karl, *Verschwoerer?* Verlag August Scherl GmbH, Berlin, Germany,1920.

Charles, Heinrich, *The Electro-Individualistic Manifesto: The Anti-Thesis of the Communistic Manifesto by Karl Marx and Friedrich Engels, and the Synthesis of Social-Individualism*, published by the author, New York, NY, 1913.

Churchill, Winston S., *The World Crisis, 1911 to 1918*, Odhams Press Limited, London, Great Britain, 1939.

Count von Bernstorff, Johann Heinrich, *My Three Years in America*, Skeffington and Son, London, Great Britain, unknown date (approximately 1940).

Count von Bernstorff, Johann Heinrich, *Memoirs of Count Bernstorff*, Random House, New York, NY, 1936.

Delbrück, Hans, *Delbrück's Modern Military History*, translated by Arden Bucholz, University of Nebraska Press, Lincoln, NE, 1997.

Dernburg, Bernhard, *Search-Lights on the War*, The Fatherland Corporation, New York, NY, 1915.

The Truth about Germany: Facts about the War, unknown authors, unknown publisher (likely the "Fatherland" press, unknown place (likely New York), September 20, 1914.

Garibaldi, Guiseppe, *A Toast To Rebellion*, The Bobbs-Merrill Company, New York, NY, 1935.

Gerard, James W., *My first eighty three years in America: Memoirs of James W. Gerard*, Doubleday and Company, Inc, Garden City, NY, 1951.

Gerard, James W., *Face to Face with Kaiserism*, George H. Doran Company, New York, NY, 1918.

Guzmán, Martin Luis, *Memoirs of Pancho Villa*, translated by Virginia H. Taylor, University of Texas Press, Austin, TX, 1975.

Hale, William Bayard, *The Story of a Style*, B. W. Huebsch, New York, NY, 1920.

Krumm-Heller, Arnold, *Für Freiheit und Recht: Meine Erlebnisse aus dem mexikanischen Bürgerkriege*, Otto Thiele Verlag, Halle, Germany, 1916.

Lansing, Robert, *War Memoirs of Robert Lansing, Secretary of State*, The Bobbs-Merrill Company, New York, NY, 1935.

McClure, Samuel S., *My Autobiography*, Frederick A. Stokes Company, New York, NY, 1914.

Mencken, H. L., *My Life as Author and Editor*, Alfred A. Knopf Inc., New York, 1993.

Nicolai, Walter, *The German Secret Service, translated with an additional chapter by George Renwick*, Stanley Paul and Co., London, Great Britain, 1924.

Pershing, John J., *My Life Before the World War, 1860-1917*, University Press of Kentucky, Lexington, KY, 2013.

Rintelen von Kleist, Franz, *The Dark Invader: Wartime Reminiscences of a German Naval Intelligence Officer*, Lovat Dickson Limited, London, Great Britain, 1933.

Rintelen von Kleist, Franz, *The Return of the Dark Invader*, Peter Davies Limited, London, Great Britain, 1935.

Rintelen von Kleist, Franz, *The Dark Invader: Wartime Reminiscences of a German Naval Intelligence Officer*, with an introduction by Reinhard R. Doerries, Frank Cass Publishers, London, 1997.

Rumely, Edward A., *The Gravest 366 Days, Editorials Reprinted from the Evening Mail of New York City*, The New York Evening Mail, New York, NY, 1916.

Scheer, Reinhard, *Germany's High Sea Fleet in the World War*, Cassell and Company, London, Great Britain, 1920.

Scott, Hugh Lenox, *Some Memories of a Soldier*, The Century Company, New York, NY, 1928.

Steffens, Lincoln, *The Autobiography of Lincoln Steffens*, Harcourt, Brace and Company, New York, NY, 1931.

Colonel Tompkins, Frank, *Chasing Villa: The Last Campaign of the United States Cavalry*, Penguin Books, Harrisburg, PA, 1939.

Tunney, Thomas J., *Throttled: The Detection of the German and Anarchist Bomb Plotters in the United States*, Small Maynard and Company, Boston, MA, 1919.

Viereck, George Sylvester, *Spreading Germs of Hate*, Duckworth, London, Great Britain, 1931.

Von Bethmann Hollweg, *Reflections on the World War*, Part 1, Thornton Butterworth, Ltd., 62 St. Martin's Lane, London, Great Britain, 1920.

Von der Goltz, Horst, *My Adventures as a German Secret Agent*, Robert M. McBride and Company, New York, NY, 1917.

Von der Goltz, Horst, *Sworn Statement*, Presented to both Houses of Parliament by Command of His Majesty, April 1916.

Von Papen, Franz, *Memoirs*, Translated into English by Brian Connell, E. P. Dutton and Company, Inc., New York, NY, 1953.

Von Schlieffen, Count Alfred, *Cannae*, The Command and General Staff School Press, Fort Leavenworth, KS, 1931.

Von Tirpitz, Alfred, *Erinnerungen*, K. F. Koehler Verlag, Berlin, Germany, 1927.

Voska, Emanuel Victor and Irwin, Will, *Spy and Counter-Spy*, George G. Harrap and Co Ltd., London, 1941.

Wilson, Woodrow and Hale, William Bayard, *The New Freedom*, Doubleday, Page and Co., New York, NY, 1913.

Wilson, Henry Lane, *Diplomatic Episodes in Mexico, Belgium and Chile*, Kinnikat Press, Port Washington, NY, 1971, reprint of original 1927.

Wilson, Henry Lane, "Errors with Reference to Mexico and Events that have occurred there," *International Relations of the United States: The Annals*, Vol. LIV, July 1914.

INDEX

with Obregón 38, 40; relations with Sherburne Hopkins 76; release of Douglas and Holmdahl 20-21; representation through Sommerfeld 57-59; rise against Huerta 6; secret U.S.- Carranza agreement 170-171, 173-174; Sommerfeld-Dernburg proposal 90, 95, 99, 102; Sonora campaign 145, 149, 159-160; stolen money 119-121; supply organization of 22; tries to execute Obregón 44-45; visit in El Paso 40-41

Villa, Hipólito, 105, 177

Villa Secret Service, 61, 80-81, 84

Villareal, Pedro, 239

Villavicencio, Francisco R., 232

W

Wachendorf, Franz, xv-xviii, 27-29, 92

Walker, Herold, 192

Walker Brothers, 51

Wall Street, xv, 2, 6, 138, 155, 170-171, 174, 201; Wolf of, see Lamar, David

Waldorf Astoria, Hotel, 172

Warburg, Max, 93, 170

War College Division, U.S., 242

War Intelligence Agency, German, see *Kriegsnachrichtendienst*

Warren, Francis E., 200

Warren, Fred B., 180

Watson, Charles, R., 166, 205

West Point, U.S. Military Academy at, 200

Western Cartridge Company, xi; dealings with De La Garza 110-111, 118; dealings with Hans Tauscher 88, 232, 235; dealings with Sommerfeld 84, 113-114; founder Olin 23, 25; German paid hydraulic presses 112; German purchases from 103, 115-118, 231; quality problems with 112; sales to Carranza 135, 229; sales to French government 122, 230; share in U.S. market 24

Wilhelm II of Prussia, xiii, xix, 1, 30, 93, 101, 170

Williams, Alexander, 86, 132

Williams. Summer, 208

Willis, William, 90

Wilson, Henry Lane, 167

Wilson, T. Woodrow, viii-ix, xii-xiii; activates militias 222, 241; administration of xv, 18; appoints Paul Fuller 127-128; brokers talks between revolutionaries 38, 43; cabinet of 12; conservatives against 167; dealings with John Lind 6; democrats for 168; diplomatic relations with Germany 100, 138; fight against Huerta 73; Huerta-Orozco-Mondragón plot 78; issues ultimatum to Mexican factions 75, 101, 126-127, 137; Naco affair 55-56, 68; Niagara conference 14; occupation of Veracruz 69; Pan-American conference 130, 136, 145; papers of xx; Punitive Expedition 193, 198, 225; recognition of Carranza 76, 123, 131, 143, 147-148, 163, 185; reins in Lansing 130; relations with Carranza 198, 201, 219-220, 244; relations with Villa 48, 63-64, 146, 157, 162, 169, 171, 178, 180, 182; relationship with Hugh L. Scott xix, 65, 85, 112, 125, 246; Rintelen mission 90-91, 93; secret agreement with Carranza155, 189; Sommerfeld relations with 15, 19, 125, 128; stands up to military advisers 245; suspects Germany behind Mexican unrest 195, 247; talks with Ángeles 86, 132-133; tries to pacify border 102

Winchester Repeating Arms Company, xi, 24-25, 51, 84, 109, 111-112

Wolf of Wall Street, see Lamar, David

Works, John D., 167, 193

World Fair Exhibition, see Panama-Pacific International Exposition

38927338R00226

Made in the USA
Charleston, SC
23 February 2015